MW00979403

CORPORATE CRIME & FINANCIAL FRAUD

Legal and Financial Implications of Corporate Misconduct

MIRIAM F. WEISMANN

Cover design by ABA Publishing/Sonya Taylor.

Printed in the United States of America

16 15 14 13 12 5 4 3 2 1

Library of Congress Cataloging-in-Publication Data

Weismann, Miriam F.
Corporate crime and financial fraud : legal and financial implications of corporate misconduct / By Miriam F. Weismann.
p. cm.
Includes bibliographical references and index.
ISBN 978-1-61438-506-6 (print : alk. paper)
1. Corporations—Corrupt practices—United States. 2. Corporate governance—Law and legislation—United States. 3. Commercial crimes—United States. 4. White collar crimes—United States. I. Title.

KF9351.W45 2012
364.16'80973—dc23

2012012701

This book is dedicated to my children, Aaron and Rachel, and the rest of the new generation of lawyers they will join.

Did you ever expect a corporation to have a conscience, when it has no soul to be damned, and no body to be kicked?

—Lord Chancellor Edward Thurlow, British jurist (1731–1806).

I see in the near future a crisis approaching that unnerves me and causes me to tremble for the safety of my country. . . . Corporations have been enthroned and an era of corruption in high places will follow, and the money power of the country will endeavor to prolong its reign by working upon the prejudices of the people until all wealth is aggregated in a few hands and the Republic is destroyed.

—Letter from President Abraham Lincoln to Col. William F. Elkins (Nov. 21, 1864), in Archer H. Shaw, The Lincoln Encyclopedia *(1950).*

The sale [of Wachovia to Citigroup] would further concentrate Americans' bank deposits in the hands of just three banks: Bank of America, JPMorgan Chase and Citigroup. Together, those three would be so large that they would dominate the industry, with unrivaled power to set prices for their loans and services.

—"Citigroup Buys Bank Operations of Wachovia," New York Times, *September 29, 2008*

The stimulus package the U.S. Congress is completing would raise the government's commitment to solving the financial crisis to $9.7 trillion, enough to pay off more than 90 percent of the nation's home mortgages.

—"U.S. Taxpayers Risk $9.7 Trillion on Bailout Programs," Bloomberg News, *February 9, 2009*

CONTENTS

Dedication iii

Quotations v

Preface xiii

Acknowledgments xv

About the Author xvii

Introduction xix

CHAPTER 1 Exposing the Corporate Criminal: An Exercise in Corporate Transparency 1

I. Understanding the Reasons Why: It Matters to the Jury 1

II. Rational-Choice Theory: The Behavior of Corporate Criminals 6

III. Shifting Behavior by Punishment: Understanding the Federal Sentencing Guidelines Policy 8

CHAPTER 2 The Facts Behind the Fiction: Theories of Corporate Criminal Liability 11

I. Respondeat Superior 12

A. Imputing Acts of the Agent: Strict Liability in Criminal Law 12

B. Collective Knowledge Doctrine 13

C. Collective Entity Doctrine 15

II. The Corporate Fiduciary: Circumstantial Evidence of Guilt 16

III. Business Judgment Rule: Not a Defense 17

IV. Chinese Walls 18

CHAPTER 3 Crime and Punishment: Statutory Tools 21

I. Fraud 21

II. Specific Crimes 24

A. General Principles: ***Mens Rea*** and ***Actus Reus*** ***24***

B. Conspiracy: 18 U.S.C. § 371 26

C. Mail and Wire Fraud 30

D. Bank Fraud 33

E. Bribery and Illegal Gratuities 34

F. Program Fraud 35

G. Money Laundering 36

H. Securities Fraud 38

I. Corporate Tax Fraud 41

J. "Process Crimes" 42

CHAPTER 4 Constitutional Perspectives: Few Rights and Even Fewer Privileges 45

I. The Fifth Amendment 46

A. Defining "Organization" 46

B. "John Doe" Act of Production Immunity 47

C. Foregone Conclusion Doctrine 47

D. Other Exceptions 48

II. The Fourth Amendment 48

A. The Warrant Requirement: Regulatory and Administrative Search Exception 49

B. Overly Broad Document Subpoenas 50

C. No Zone of Privacy 52

III. The Sixth Amendment 52

A. The Right to Counsel 52

B. The Right to Appointed Counsel 54

C. The Right to Confrontation 54

D. Other Sixth Amendment Rights 55

IV. Privileges 55

A. Attorney-Client Privilege 55

B. Work Product Privilege 60

C. Internal Corporate Investigations and Privilege Protection 61

D. Rule 502(FRE) Limitations on Waiver of Privilege 62

CHAPTER 5 Affirmative Defenses: Denying Liability and Deflecting Blame 65

I. The Good Faith Defense 65

A. Negating the Mens Rea 65

B. Reliance on Third-Party Professionals 66

II. Can a Corporation or Other Business Organization Withdraw from a Conspiracy or Otherwise Avoid Successor Conspiratorial Liability? 67

A. Defense of Withdrawal 67

B. Defense of No Successor Liability 69

III. Unauthorized Acts of Agents 69

IV. Defense Theory Instructions 70

V. Use of Subpoenas Prior to Trial 71

CHAPTER 6 Structuring Corporate Plea and Settlement Agreements: An Exercise in Damage Control 73

I. Making Choices Pretrial 73

II. Types of Pretrial Agreements 75

III. Federal Plea Agreements: An Analysis of the Department of Justice Guidelines 77

A. The Desirability of Entering into a Plea Agreement from the Government's Perspective 78

B. DOJ Guidelines as Limitations 78

C. DOJ Guidelines as Negotiating Opportunities 81

D. Corporate Compliance Programs 83

E. Make Sure It's a Done Deal 85

IV. Other Plea Options: Informal Resolution Through Nonprosecution Agreements and Deferred Prosecution Agreements 85

A. Resolution Without Formal Conviction 85

B. Recent Statistics: Increased Use of Informal Dispositions 87

C. Corporate Monitors 88

V. DOJ Parallel Proceedings Policy: Resolving Civil Liability 89

A. Evidentiary Pitfalls: Civil Case Admissions 91

CHAPTER 7 Tax Consequences and Planning Opportunities: Crime Doesn't Pay but It May Be Tax-Deductible 93

I. Legal Fees and Costs Paid to Defend the Corporation 94

II. Legal Fees and Costs Paid to Defend a Corporate Employee 95

III. Fines and Penalties 96

IV. Restitution 97

V. Tax Consequences to Fraud Victims 99

VI. Treasury Department Regulations Governing Practice Before the Internal Revenue Service 101

CHAPTER 8 Accounting "Hocus-Pocus": Earnings Management 103

I. Hocus-Pocus: Five Accounting Tricks of Earnings Management 104

A. Large-Charge Restructuring 105

B. Creative Acquisition Accounting 106

C. Cookie Jar Reserves 107

D. Materiality 107

E. Revenue Recognition 109

II. Warning Signs of Earnings Management: Spotting Accounting Frauds 109

III. Criminal Prosecutions: The Case of Bristol-Myers Squibb 111

CHAPTER 9 The Foreign Corrupt Practices Act: Bribery as a Global Market Entry Strategy 113

I. Understanding the Act 114

A. The "Watergate" Connection: The Enactment of the FCPA 114

B. Legislative Provisions and Limitations of Enforcement 116

II. Antibribery Provisions 118

III. Recordkeeping Provisions 122

IV. Enforcement Statistics: 1978–2011 123

A. The Prosecutive Policy of Nonenforcement: 1978-2006 123

B. The "Cost of Doing Business" Enforcement Strategy: 2006-2011 128

V. DOJ Investigations, Opinion Procedure, and Prosecutive Policy 131

A. Red Flags 131

B. Department of Justice Guidance: Opinion Procedure 132

C. Prosecutive Policy 135

VI. Tax Deductibility of "Grease Payments" 136

CHAPTER 10 Statutory Reforms Post-Enron: The New Corporate Governance Model 139

I. The Failure of Credible Oversight 139

II. Post-Enron Sarbanes-Oxley Reforms 143

A. Changes to Audit Standards 143

B. SOX Changes to Lawyers' Ethics: In-House and Outside Counsel Rules 145

III. Wall Street Reform and Consumer Protection Act of 2010 150

A. New Criminal Offense Conduct 151

B. Whistleblower Protections 151

IV. Expansion of the False Claims Act: Fraud Enforcement and Recovery Act of 2009 153

V. Proposed Legislation 155

A. Public Corruption Prosecution Improvements Act of 2011 155

VI. Conclusion 156

Appendix A: New Criminal Offenses Promulgated by the Wall Street Reform and Consumer Protection Act of 2010 159

Appendix B: Excerpts From USAM Chapter 9-27.000 Principles of Federal Prosecution 163

Appendix C: USAM Chapter 9-28.000 Principles of Federal Prosecution of Business Organizations 201

Appendix D: Morford Memo 225

Appendix E: Foreign Corrupt Practices Act—Case Statistics (1978–2011) 235

Appendix F: FCPA Enforcement Statistics (1998-2010) 315

Table of Authorities 335

Index 359

PREFACE

The first edition of this book's publication coincided with a massive global financial crisis dubbed the worst recession since World War II. The culprit was and, in the continuing current financial crisis, remains unbridled corporate power that has overtaken judgment, trust, and self-restraint—all cornerstones of a normally functioning capital marketplace. Cult personalities and mystical investment "quant" models in the financial world have subsumed rational business judgment and replaced the logical functioning of companies under traditional finance risk and reward principles incident to economic growth.

I was reading Alan Greenspan's recent book, The Age of Turbulence: Adventures in a New World, thinking what a smart guy he was until he got to the part about derivatives. He wrote about the tiny Wall Street brain trust that claimed to know how derivatives "really worked" as if they were geniuses as opposed to the greedy cabal of opportunists exposed during the unprecedented global collapse of the marketplace. In short, we trusted corporations to do the right thing because of a system of checks and balances defined by the legal relationship of fiduciary duty owed to shareholders by boards of directors and corporate management. The duties of care and loyalty were supposed to protect investor interests as part of corporate governance guided by these fiduciary responsibilities. Unfortunately, corporate governance was replaced by personality. Ken Lay, Bernie Ebbers, and most recently, Bernard Madoff, have undermined corporate functionality through fraud. Perceived as the "smartest guys in the room," not even the SEC could be counted on to look past the persona.

How did they get away with it for so long? The answer is inescapable: it takes a community of participation to operate so openly and notoriously. The proverbial "watchdogs," including banks, appraisers, financial advisors, accountants, lawyers, and even regulators, either participated in the scheme or closed their eyes to known risks.

The consequences to the corporation include legal action and financial ruin. Indicting a corporation has been described by some as corporate capital punishment. The company, even if it chooses to fight, even if it is ultimately the winner, dies. Sound familiar? We only need to remember the case of Arthur Andersen to know that this is true.

Corporations are separate, distinct legal beings from the people who run them. These fictional beings, created at birth by the law, do possess a financial soul. That "soul" may cease to exist as a consequence of even the threat of corporate prosecution for white-collar crime. This book addresses not just the financial and legal consequences of prosecution but also places into a broader perspective for the practitioner and observer what the motivations are, how the financial schemes look, what the law prohibits, and how to engage in effective damage control in an effort to resuscitate the dying patient.

It's not just a "how to" book, it's also a "what not to do" book. As Mark Twain once said so eloquently: "What we need now is not more rules, what we need is sanity."

My hope for the coming decade is not just recovery, but a sane one. The second edition updates changes in the law after 2009 to include the Supreme Court's post-Enron changes to the "honest-services" fraud theory of prosecution under Title 18 U.S.C. §1346; the increased use of parallel proceedings through the expansion of the False Claims Act by the Fraud Enforcement and Recovery Act of 2009; the Dodd-Frank Wall Street Reform and Consumer Protection Act of 2010, including the enhanced whistleblower protections; updated Foreign Corrupt Practices Act enforcement statistics through 2011; major revisions to the Department of Justice policies on criminal discovery and more.

Boston, 2012

ACKNOWLEDGMENTS

A special thanks to my editor, Sarah Forbes Orwig, for her interest and continuing support for this project. Much appreciation to Dean and Professor Morris McInnes and my department chair, Professor Anthony Eonas, for their friendship and encouragement, and many thanks for the assistance of some very talented graduate students at Suffolk University: Erin Secord and Chih-Wei Liu. Also thanks to CAB.

For the second edition, special thanks to Aaron F. Weismann, Esq. and Christine Brooks, graduate student at Suffolk University, for their excellent research and editorial assistance.

ABOUT THE AUTHOR

Miriam F. Weismann, JD, LLM (taxation)
Professor of Business and Law
Director, Center for Global Business Ethics and Law
Sawyer Business School, Suffolk University, Boston, MA.

Miriam Weismann teaches in the JD/MBA graduate program at Suffolk University and in the undergraduate business school. Her areas of specialization include white-collar crime and financial fraud, international law, taxation, and legal ethics. Her publications include scholarly books, articles, and chapter publications in the fields of global and domestic corporate governance and white-collar crime.

Miriam started in private practice in 1978 and shortly thereafter founded a law firm specializing in white-collar criminal defense work and corporate law. She later merged her practice into the national law firm of Keck, Mahin & Cate, where she became a capital partner. There, she handled white-collar criminal defense work and major securities and tax-related litigation. She also argued a case before the U.S. Supreme Court.

In 1991, she joined the U.S. Attorney's Office in Brooklyn, New York, as an assistant federal prosecutor, assigned to the Business and Securities Fraud division. She later served as Supervisory Assistant Special Counsel in the Office of Special Counsel John C. Danforth in the Waco, Texas, investigation. In 2003, she was appointed by President Bush to serve as the U.S. Attorney for the Southern District of Illinois. Her major case prosecutions include the Ford/Firestone investigation and the prosecution of Sears Roebuck& Co. and Exide Technologies in connection with the Die-Hard battery. She also prosecuted organized crime and public corruption cases. While serving as a federal prosecutor, she received the Director's Award for excellence in the prosecution of a major public corruption case from then Attorney General Janet Reno and numerous case prosecution awards from the FBI, IRS, DEA, and Postal Inspection Service.

Before joining Suffolk, she taught as an adjunct professor at Northwestern University School of Law in Chicago and Washington University School of Law in St. Louis. She was an associate professor of law at the Southern New England School of Law.

Miriam is a member of the state bar of Illinois, the U.S. Supreme Court, and the U.S. Tax Court. She received her law degrees from Kent College of Law and DePaul College of Law and her BA from the University of Arizona. She has recently published her second book with the American Bar Association, Parallel Proceedings: Navigating Multiple Case Litigation (First Chair Press, 2011).

INTRODUCTION

The New Age of Corporate Crime

Whatever happened to the good old days . . . when the typical scenario of corporate crime involved slush funds, fraudulent billing schemes, and tax cheats? Corporate misconduct was hidden from accountants, corporate general counsel, and outside counsel. It was an inside job. But the world has changed. The third-party corporate "watchdogs," including accountants, banks, investment advisors, and attorneys, who were supposed to "bark" when clients crossed the line between legal and illegal conduct, have now become part of the problem and, often, integral players in the scheme. Violations by and within an organization are facilitated by other business organizations in the same network.

In plain terms, viewing corporate white-collar crime as discreet and relatively straightforward financial transactions has changed. The nature of corporate crime has morphed into a new paradigm of accounting frauds and investment schemes facilitated by the speed of technology and the genius and expertise of business professionals whose compensation is tied to short-term performance. When the company fails to perform, the new whiz kid professionals make it perform by engaging in new and complicated forms of accounting, such as earnings management and balance-sheet accounting. They find new financial packages and products to facilitate deception. Former Federal Reserve Board Chairman Alan Greenspan, before the fatal descent of the subprime mortgage market, commented on the positive contribution made by derivatives in the financial market, noting also that only a very few on

Wall Street knew how they worked.[1] Now, in the aftermath of the derivatives crash, we have relearned the sage investment advice repeated by Investment Management Association chairman Robert Jenkins: if you don't understand it, don't invest in it.

During the Enron hearings, the Senate observed that the corporate "watchdogs" entrusted with the responsibility of protecting the public failed to "bark." Law firms, accounting firms, auditors, investment advisors, banks, and even the regulators failed to protect the public from runaway organizational corporate behavior that injected chaos into America's capital markets.

How did this happen? Greed, sometimes referred to as "lure" in the behavioral finance literature, is the motivator. For example, the business of accounting has dramatically changed. Arthur Andersen used to be touted as the "Marines of the auditing field." Everything was by the book and subject to tough scrutiny. Andersen and the other big firms discovered that they could make more money, substantially more money, by also providing consulting services to corporate clients interested in public offerings or creating new financial products. As the consulting side of the firm became far more profitable than the audit side of the practice, auditors were "ordered" to take "less aggressive" positions about company books and records so as not to jeopardize the lucrative consulting relationship with the same client. Thus began the massive conflict-of-interest situation that led to the corporate debacles of Enron, WorldCom, Refco, Tyco, and a laundry list of others.

Thinking that we had patched things up with the passage of the Sarbanes-Oxley Act, we found that the worst was yet to come. We are only beginning to unravel the major financial debacles of the century, including the failures of Bear Stearns and Lehman Brothers, not to mention the billions of federal dollars to bail out Fannie Mae, Freddie Mac, AIG, and others.

What does this mean for the practitioner? Whether prosecuting or defending, understanding organizational crime has become more difficult because of the increased multi-organizational character of corporate crime. Investigations conducted by various special court-appointed examiners revealed that no single organizational group could have succeeded in the crime without the involvement or imprimatur of a cadre of other organizational professionals working with the client corporation to assure performance goals at whatever cost. Corporations found that it was easier to just pay enormous professional fees and elicit help in facilitating the scheme than to engage in conduct to hide the behavior. Lure wins out as a market strategy once again. Because most corporate crime involves multiple organizational

---

1. Alan Greenspan, Chairman, Fed. Reserve Bd., Banking Evolution, Remarks at the 36th Annual Conference on Bank Structure and Competition of the Federal Reserve Bank of Chicago (Chicago, May 4, 2000), http://www.federalreserve.gov/BOARDDOCS/SPEECHES/2000/20000504.htm.

defendants, as well as multiple individual defendants, the legal rules of the game have become more complicated in the context of prosecuting or defending a case.

This book provides a needed reexamination of how traditional legal rules and their application have changed as the nature of corporate crime has changed in the last decade. Therefore, the focus here is primarily on organizational and corporate crime. The issues regarding individuals, except as they affect the organizational issues, are not addressed by this book. While individual criminality is assuredly a feature of business fraud, the higher-impact crimes have become organizational in nature.

Any effort to effectively prosecute or defend organizational crime requires more than a mechanical application of legal concepts. It is also helpful to contextualize the crime in the business environment in which it originates. In the end, a deeper understanding of business motivations better explains the underlying theories of prosecution and the reasons for engaging in criminal conduct in the first instance. These issues, often more business-oriented than legal, manage to seep into the trial as juries try to understand in practical, nonlegal terms "Why did they do it?" "Who got hurt?" and "Who is ultimately responsible?"

This said, it is axiomatic that violations are committed by neither individuals nor organizations acting separate and apart from each other. Indeed, the success of organizational behavior frequently involves the use by individuals of coercive organizational power created by a network of organizations. Individuals harness that coercive organizational power to achieve unlawful objectives by using the organization's position of power, influence, or trust to facilitate the crime.

In other words, without the strength of the organization(s), the individual would be unlikely to achieve the desired result. This book describes those phenomena not only in the context of traditional legal principles governing prosecution and defense of white-collar crime but also by providing insight into some of the nuts and bolts of the financial and accounting schemes utilized to achieve unlawful results and the business motivations fueling entity criminal behavior.

The first chapter addresses corporate culture and motive. True, the government is not required to prove motive as one of the essential elements of the crime. But anyone who has tried jury cases knows one important truth: Juries want to know why. Why did the company do what it is accused of doing? Without proof of a corrupt culture or sufficient lure to commit the crime, juries might not believe the government's case.

Proving greed and motive becomes as important to jurors as the facts. Nowhere was this more apparent than in the conviction of Arthur Andersen. Subsequent juror interviews illuminate the point. The first-day results of the initial juror poll showed that four thought the firm was innocent, four thought it guilty, and four were undecided. Much of the evidence, including the tale of pervasive document shredding, failed to impress the jury much at all. After months of hearing evidence, it boiled down to a single document and the efforts of one employee, a lawyer with Enron, to revise a single memorandum sent to Andersen. That act signaled to the jury that something was wrong with the way Andersen was doing business.

Oscar Criner, the jury foreman, commented after the trial: "I think the problem is much more than the Andersen case itself. I think there are questions about American business that have to be addressed here, and the direction that business has been going."[2] The importance of corporate culture and organizational behavior exhibited by employees is the first step in engaging in a meaningful thought process about how a jury might perceive the evidence.

We will also introduce the regulatory environment in which publicly traded corporations operate and the concepts of transparency and self-regulation. Both are the ideal for achieving a fair and ethical corporate culture. The discussion will then focus on the departure from the ideal state of business grace to the factual paradigms that characterize the new wave of corporate crime. Finally, we will look briefly at the enactments of the Sarbanes-Oxley Act (SOX), the Wall Street Reform and Consumer Protection Act of 2010 (Reform Act), and the new congressional vision for corporate governance in the 21st century. The specific auditing and legal ethics provisions enacted by SOX and the Reform Act are addressed in detail in Chapter 10. The newly added criminal provisions are covered in Chapters 3 and 10.

In Chapter 2, the historical development of the legal theory of entity liability is explained in the context of several legal principles including *respondeat superior*, the collective entity doctrine, Chinese Walls, fiduciary duty, business judgment rule, conflicts of interest, and others. While a corporation may be a "legal fiction" at law, its legal exposure is elevated to that of a natural person faced with the challenge of strict legal liability imposed as a result of the acts of its agents. When prosecuted, the severity of financial consequences has been likened to "entity capital punishment."

Chapter 3 examines the statutory tools most frequently employed to prosecute organizational crimes. The federal arsenal includes conspiracy, mail fraud, wire fraud, obstruction of justice, perjury, changes introduced with the passage of SOX, Reform Act, and others. The chapter will also review differing *mens rea* requirements, overlapping application of the statutes, jury instructions, and recent developments in the case law.

Corporations do not share the full panoply of constitutional rights and privileges accorded individuals. Chapter 4 explores the application of the Fourth, Fifth, and Sixth Amendments to corporations and other business organizations; the application of the work product privilege and its relation to internal corporate audits; the application of the attorney-client privilege to corporate upper and middle management; the role of corporate counsel;[3] the Department of Justice

2. Jonathan Glater, *Enron's Many Strands: The Deliberations; Jurors Tell of Emotional Days in a Small Room*, N.Y. Times, June 17, 2002, at http://www.nytimes.com/2002/06/17/business/17JURY.html.

3. *See* Chapter 10 for an in-depth discussion of the application of SOX to in-house general counsel.

(DOJ) rules governing discoverability of internal corporate investigations by the government;[4] joint defense agreements; and conflicts in multiple representation.

Chapter 5 examines corporate affirmative defenses and the art of denying benefit and deflecting blame. The chapter considers the circumstances under which it makes sense for the corporation to defend itself and, parenthetically, its shareholders against the unauthorized acts of corporate management; the "good faith" defense; extricating a corporation from the conspiracy; defense-tendered jury instructions; and the early return of trial subpoenas. Finally, the chapter discusses the legal significance, in terms of defense strategy, of the Supreme Court decision in the Arthur Andersen case.

Assuming a deal has been struck and a trial avoided, Chapter 6 addresses structuring corporate plea agreements, nonprosecution agreements, and other means for accomplishing damage control for the company. Current DOJ guidelines for plea agreements, corporate compliance plans, and corporate monitors are included in the discussion. The recent changes in the Corporate Charging Guidelines are also highlighted.

Chapter 7 examines the tax consequences and planning opportunities attendant to the payments of fines and restitutions. Crime may not pay, but some portion may be tax-deductible for the organization.

So, exactly how do they do it? What are the accounting tricks employed by business organizations to "cook the books" and commit financial fraud? Surprisingly, the various forms of "earnings management" are not very complex, and understanding them can provide a window into better understanding the conduct being charged. Some form or combination of these various techniques of earnings management were used by Enron, WorldCom, Refco, and others in facilitating the accounting schemes used to commit crimes under the aegis of the powerful organizational shell. Chapter 8 provides a fairly basic explanation of these accounting techniques in an effort to explain the underlying financial aspects typical of these schemes.

Chapter 9 looks at organizational crime from a global perspective. Very few companies, even "mom and pop" operations, operate purely domestically. The trend toward increased globalization of business is inevitable. This chapter closely examines the Foreign Corrupt Practices Act (FCPA), the global antibribery initiative passed by Congress to prevent the use of bribery as a global market entry strategy. The enforcement statistics from 1978, when the statute was first enacted, through 2011 are compiled in Appendix E. It is perhaps the most current and complete data compilation in the field, providing the practitioner with critical case information that cannot be accessed from any single data source.

4. As a practice note, in July 2008, Attorney General Michael Mukasey stated in a hearing before Congress that the 2006 rules may be revised. That statement was followed by the Filip Memo, issued by DOJ in August 2008, discussed in Chapters 4 and 6.

Finally, Chapter 10 concludes by examining the "New Era of Corporate Governance." This is a post-Enron examination of new legislation with a focus on increased regulation in the field. The enactment of the Fraud Enforcement and Recovery Act of 2009 expands the application of the False Claims Act, providing the DOJ with more ammunition to punish corporate wrongdoers. Thus, the risk of defending the criminal case is now compounded by the expanded use of parallel civil fraud proceedings. The Dodd-Frank Wall Street Reform and Consumer Protection Act of 2010, including the enhanced whistleblower protections, is also explored.

One caveat. There is a great temptation to pontificate about the failure of the moral compass of corporate America at this point. True, that is not the role of the practitioner whose job it is to engage in zealous representation within the boundaries of the law. But Abraham Lincoln's observations remain prescient:

> I see in the near future a crisis approaching that unnerves me and causes me to tremble for the safety of my country. . . . Corporations have been enthroned and an era of corruption in high places will follow, and the money power of the country will endeavor to prolong its reign by working upon the prejudices of the people until all wealth is aggregated in a few hands and the Republic is destroyed.[5]

A jury may be having the same thought.

5. Letter from President Abraham Lincoln to Col. William F. Elkins (Nov. 21, 1864), *in* Archer H. Shaw, The Lincoln Encyclopedia (1950).

CHAPTER 1

EXPOSING THE CORPORATE CRIMINAL
AN EXERCISE IN CORPORATE TRANSPARENCY

I. Understanding the Reasons Why: It Matters to the Jury

The apparent ease by which corporations manage to engage in undetected criminality is a function of the regulatory framework of government-sanctioned self-regulation. After corporations emerged in the 20th century as the dominant form of economic organization, the debate about how to regulate closely followed. The creation of the Securities and Exchange Commission (SEC) in 1934, in response to the uncontrolled corporate debacles of the 1920s, provided not only a regulatory organization to supervise the conduct of issuers, but a policy organization as well. One of the most significant policies promulgated by the SEC and Congress is the belief that corporations are best regulated through the model of self-regulation and minimal regulatory interference.

Simply, self-regulation is the manner in which all firms self-police their own activities to ensure that they are meeting all fiduciary and other duties to their clients. In fact, the old "shingle theory" was based on the principle that if you hold yourself out to the public as offering to do business, you are implicitly representing that you will do so in a fair and honest manner. As such, self-regulation became the cornerstone of most businesses, including the securities industry, beginning in the early part of the 20th century.[1]

As then SEC Chairman, and later Supreme Court Justice, William O. Douglas observed, "self-discipline is always more welcome than discipline imposed from above." He summarized the benefits of self-regulation in an address before the Bond Club of Hartford in 1938 as follows: "From the broad public viewpoint, such regulation can be far more effective [than direct regulation] . . . self-regulation . . . can be persuasive and subtle in its conditioning influence over business practices and business morality. By and large, government can operate satisfactorily only by proscription. That leaves untouched large areas of conduct and activity; some of it susceptible of government regulation but in fact too minute for satisfactory control, some of it lying beyond the periphery of the law in the realm of ethics and morality. Into these large areas, self-government and self-government alone, can effectively reach. For these reasons, self-regulation is by far the preferable course from all viewpoints."[2]

Corporate regulation is, therefore, dependent for the most part on self-restraint and ethical corporate governance within the regulatory environment mandated by Congress. The role of regulators and law enforcement is proscriptive in nature as opposed to proactive. This means that the government is not in a meaningful position to prevent misconduct. Instead, its role is largely reactive, punishing and/or prosecuting once the misconduct is uncovered. Often, the conduct is so severe that it requires Congress to respond with legislation, such as the Sarbanes-Oxley Act of 2002 (SOX),[3] in an effort to restore customer confidence in the marketplace and attract investors back into the market economy. With the recent collapse of the

1. Prior to congressional passage of the securities laws, firms organized to create another layer of organization—stock exchanges. By 1934, each of the stock exchanges had a constitution and bylaws that prescribed collective rules for the admission, discipline, and expulsion of stock exchange members. These rules were regarded as a contract between the organization and the member. For example, the New York Stock Exchange implemented a system of self-regulation through a governance committee that appointed other committees to carry out the business of regulating the activities of its members. The exchanges are now referred to as SROs, or self-regulatory organizations. The Securities Exchange Act of 1934 also codified the existing self-regulatory system for broker-dealers. The SROs retained primary authority to regulate their members, but the SEC was given the power to suspend or revoke an exchange's registration if the exchange failed to enforce compliance by its members with the Exchange Act.

2. Joel Seligman, *Cautious Evolution or Perennial Irresolution: Self-Regulation and Market Structure During the First 70 Years of the Securities and Exchange Commission*, 59 Bus. Law. 1347, 1361–1362 (2004) (quoting Supreme Court Justice William O. Douglas, Address at Bond Club of Hartford (1938)).

3. Pub. L. No. 107-204, 116 Stat. 745 (2002).

unregulated derivatives and hedge fund markets, the heady exuberance of the SOX initiatives quickly evaporated, leaving consumer suspicion of the markets at an all-time high. Congress went back to the drawing board.

In enacting the Wall Street Reform and Consumer Protection Act of 2010 (Reform Act),[4] Congress recognized that the existing regulatory oversight structure narrowly focused regulators on individual institutions and markets, which allowed supervisory gaps to grow and regulatory inconsistencies to emerge—in turn, allowing arbitrage and weakened standards. No single entity had responsibility for monitoring and addressing risks to financial stability posed by different types of financial firms operating in and across multiple markets. As a result, important parts of the system were left unregulated.

As Federal Reserve Board Chairman Ben Bernanke explained,[5] the purpose of the newly created Financial Stability Oversight Committee (FSOC), a central feature of the new Reform Act, is to provide a forum for agencies with differing responsibilities and perspectives to share information and approaches, and facilitate identification and mitigation of emerging threats to financial stability. [6] It is intended "that the lines of accountability for systemic oversight be clearly drawn, [but that] the council should not be directly involved in rule-writing and supervision. Rather, those functions should remain with the relevant supervisors, with the council in a coordinating role." In short, the current system of regulatory oversight will remain relatively intact, operating in tandem with the self-regulatory model in the private sector.

The current benchmark for self-regulated corporate behavior is "corporate transparency." Alan Greenspan, former chairman of the Federal Reserve Board, explains the meaning and importance of corporate transparency: "Transparency implies that [disclosure of] information allows an understanding of a firm's exposures and risks without distortion. The goal of improved transparency thus represents a higher bar than the goal of improved disclosures. Transparency challenges market participants not only to provide information but also to place that information in a context that makes it meaningful. Transparency challenges market participants to present information in ways that accurately reflect risks."[7] Disclosure and transparency are clearly not one and the same thing.

---

4. Dodd-Frank Wall Street Reform and Consumer Protection Act, Pub. L. No. 111-203 (July 21, 2010), *available at* http://www.gpo.gov/fdsys/pkg/PLAW-111publ203/contentdetail.html.

5. Remarks of Chairman Ben Bernanke on the Squam Lake Report: Fixing the Financial System (2010) at http://www.federalreserve.gov/newsevents/speech/bernanke20100616a.htm.

6. Reform Act, 2010, Title I, Subtitle B, Section 1107.

7. Alan Greenspan, Chairman, Fed. Reserve Bd., Corporate Governance, Remarks at the 2003 Conference on Bank Structure and Competition (May 8, 2003), http://www.federalreserve.gov/boarddocs/speeches/2003/20030508/default.htm.

With the standard of self-regulation combined with the goal of full, fair, and meaningful disclosure as the preferred model for corporate governance, the obvious problem is that not all companies manage to follow the principles of corporate self-restraint. One major lesson from Enron, WorldCom, HealthSouth, and Refco, to name only a few, has been that tying executive compensation to measures of performance breeds conflict of interest and fraud. The mantra becomes growth at any cost and a "wink and a nod" with respect to corporate compliance programs that mandate self-restraint. Contemporary corporate culture, built on the foundation of cult personalities displacing the checks and balances of internal corporate management, explains in large measure the psychology that propels otherwise highly educated, law-abiding citizens into the mire of corporate crime. The timing of economic downturns and unrealistic earnings goals explain the motivation to cheat.

When asked what conditions brought us to this point of corporate failure, William McDonough, then chairman of the Public Company Accounting Oversight Board (PCAOB), accurately summed up the crisis:

> They could be summed up as mass confusion. We saw confusion about the role of the CEO. We saw the advent of the CEO superstar and an explosion in compensation that made those superstar CEOs actually believe that they were worth more than 400 times the pay of their average workers, an increase in the multiple by 10 times in 20 years—thoroughly unjustified, economically and morally. We saw confusion about the importance of earnings reports. When the private sector pinned its success to a report and not to actual earnings, the end was in sight. It became fashionable for public companies to encourage allegedly independent investment analysts to reach a consensus on the company's quarterly and annual earnings, a consensus that was closely guided by the financial management of the company. Then the market decided that the genius CEO was truly a genius if the company met or beat the estimate by a penny, but was a failure or a fool if the estimate was missed by a penny. Now anybody with a memory knows that there is a business cycle, a product cycle and the law of gravity. However, if quarter after quarter you have to match or beat the last quarter's results to stay in favor, there is an immense incentive to cook the books.
>
> And the books got cooked by company managements, all too often with the collaboration or collusion of bankers, investment bankers, lawyers, and, yes, even accountants, irrespective of the true cost to the nation, not to mention to the participants themselves. It was a sickness, a kind of moral blindness and lack of courage to do what is right, that threatened to strike at the very soul of our national confidence.
>
> The shock wave started with Enron, then rolled through Adelphia, WorldCom, HealthSouth and others. The American people looked at the wreckage of our vaunted private sector, and they got angry. The people got angry with the CEOs, with the boards, with the accounting profession and even with those of us in the regulatory sector. In a democracy, when people get angry, they will insist on

change. Congress and the President responded, and the result was the Sarbanes-Oxley Act of 2002.[8]

These explanations of management psychology and stakeholder motivations are key theories exploited in the courtroom. The government has no obligation to prove either, but juries want to know "why." Evidence regarding the corporate culture, the personalities of key management officials, and the failure of the fiduciaries to follow internal guidelines become the framework in which proof of the charges contained in the indictment is presented to the jury. Concealment, false statements, misleading financial statements, document shredding, and other forms of obstruction are typical indicia of a scheme and artifice to defraud—not to mention the use of e-mail, which has become the most powerful evidence in some cases.[9]

Contemporary corporate crime adds a new dimension: the use of business networks to facilitate complicated financial crimes. Simply put, corporations get away with it when banks, financial analysts, underwriters, accounting firms, and law firms look the other way in order to collect enormous fees with respect to the prohibited transactions. This is another variant of the conflict of interest problem created by exorbitant fees paid for services rendered to the company. Arthur Andersen had no intention of giving up $52 million a year in fees to give Enron an answer it did not want to hear. Similarly, the current subprime mortgage crisis generated handsome fees paid to Wall Street firms like Bear Stearns, now defunct as a result, and banks like Washington Mutual (WaMu), also now defunct with the distinction of being the largest banking failure in U.S. history.[10]

The financial firms and banks, along with the analysts, were willing to close their eyes to "no-doc" portfolios—packages of loans sold in the secondary mortgage market without basic documentation establishing mortgage value and risk.[11] Open

8. Quoted in *The Editor Interviews William J. McDonough, Chairman, Public Company Accounting Oversight Board*, Metro. Corp. Couns., Sept. 2004, at 46, *available at* http://www.metrocorpcounsel.com/current .php?artType=view&EntryNo=1655.

9. For a description of the evidentiary use at trial of e-mail to establish fraud indicia and criminal intent, *see United States v. Arthur Andersen, LLP*, 374 F.3d 281 (5th Cir. 2004), *rev'd on other grounds*, 544 U.S. 696 (2005), where Enron's corporate counsel, Nancy Temple, suggested a deletion in a critical e-mail. One juror, Wanda McKay, said in an interview after the trial that it was not the document shredding that proved to be decisive but the evidence about Temple's efforts to revise a single e-mail memorandum. Jonathan Glater, *Enron's Many Strands: The Deliberations; Jurors Tell of Emotional Days in a Small Room*, N.Y. Times, June 17, 2002. *But see New York v. Microsoft*, 2002 WL 649951 (D.D.C. 2002) where the court excluded e-mail evidence on the grounds that there was insufficient foundation to establish that an e-mail satisfied the business-record exception under Federal Rules of Evidence 803(6).

10. WaMu lost $16.7 billion in deposits as of September 15, 2008, according to the Office of Thrift Supervision. John Letzing, *WaMu Seized, Sold to J.P. Morgan Chase,* Mkt. Watch, Wall St. J Digital Network, Sept. 26, 2008, http://www.marketwatch.com.

11. For an excellent and short explanation of how subprime mortgages caused the current financial disaster, see A.W. Bodine & C.J. Nagel, *Quants Gone Wild: The Subprime Crisis,* 24/7 WallSt.com, Mar. 27, 2008, http://www.247wallst.com/2008/03/quants-gone-wil.html.

and notorious financial behavior cannot generally succeed unless otherwise highly respected financial institutions and consultants are in on the caper. Thus, the issue of "who knew what and when" becomes another salient question in the prosecution and defense of entity-defendants that act only through their agents. Who was acting and with what authority?

As the Senate Enron hearings showed, there is usually enough blame to spread around. Yet, the more recent trend appears to be prosecutive restraint. For example, the Department of Justice (DOJ) has shown little interest, since the demise of Arthur Andersen, in prosecuting culpable banking institutions that also serve as the backbone of the financial industry. With indictment and conviction seen as a form of entity "capital punishment," the use of alternative prosecutive choices such as deferred prosecution agreements, corporate monitors, fines, restitution, and the like are on the rise. These alternatives are discussed in detail in Chapter 6.

II. Rational-Choice Theory: The Behavior of Corporate Criminals

Financial behavioralist literature explains that the central reason organizational actors engage in corporate crime is a simple one—they *choose* to do so. Crime-as-choice, also referred to as rational-choice theory, is not new.[12] Philosophers advanced the theory about two centuries ago. Over time, it has been adapted to the business context through the identification of the cost/benefit analysis as the primary paradigm of business judgment in reaching the choice to engage in otherwise unlawful behavior.

Why cost/benefit analysis? Profit maximization in capitalist society is the key organizational goal. One of the critical variables in calculating profitability is determining the time span over which profitability and return on investment can be expected by investors.[13] Logically, it follows that increased pressure to produce the best financial results over the shortest period of time becomes management's overarching business strategy. Corporate culture develops in a way designed to maximize profitability. Perhaps this strategy explains one of the primary characteristics of white collar crime: the steadfast denial of guilt, or, put another way, "This is just how business is done."

The cost/benefit analysis in its simplest form evaluates the benefit of the potential financial gain, achieved through unlawful means, against the risk or likelihood of getting caught and the expected consequences. Particularly in times of economic growth, when regulatory oversight is eased almost to the point of becoming noncredible oversight and the certainty of punishment is uncertain, rule-breaking becomes

12. Neal Shover & Andy Hochstetler, Choosing White-Collar Crime (2006).

13. Frank Pearce, *Crime and Capitalist Business Corporations*, in Crimes of Privilege: Readings in White-Collar Crime 35 (Neal Shover & John Paul Wright, eds., Oxford Univ. Press 2001).

more common. For example, after Enron and WorldCom, and the fleeting comfort provided investors by the passage of SOX, the Federal Reserve Board moved toward policies of loose money fostered by low interest rates to reinvigorate the markets. As a consequence, since 2002, banks, mortgage companies, institutional investors, and largely unregulated hedge funds were willing to take higher risks to manufacture higher investor returns. With the lure of higher spreads on subprime loans, investment banks sank billions into acquiring these mortgages.

When balanced against the new DOJ policy shift toward deferred prosecutions or even nonprosecution agreements after the postprosecution demise of Arthur Andersen (see Chapter 6), the organizational choice to engage in unlawful behavior, where increased personal compensation within the organization is tied to earnings performance, is a "no-brainer." Not to mention the fact that nobody was telling on anybody else in the organizational network of financial institutions, lawyers, accountants, and analysts.

In the same way, the timing of economic downturns provides motivation to cheat. Here, the lure is the need to continue growth at any cost. Unrealistic earnings expectations by shareholders and Wall Street analysts pressure organizations to engage in conduct aimed at satisfying investors.

In the absence of credible oversight, financial lure easily becomes criminal opportunity.[14] Lure has been likened to an unattended purse in a busy marketplace. It turns heads and makes one wonder if it can be taken without notice. It is a combination of opportunity and the absence of oversight. The strength of desire or predisposition to grab the proverbial purse is a function of the "G" word: greed. In the old days, when reputation and institutional longevity were prized business commodities, self-restraint and self-governance did shape organizational ethical preferences. Indeed, many theorists still suggest that reputational cost can shift ethical preferences.[15] In all fairness, the literature probably needs some time to catch up to the new business realities brought about by the demise in 2008 of such long-standing and reputable companies as Bear Stearns, Lehman Brothers, and Washington Mutual. The bailouts of Merrill Lynch, Fannie Mae, Freddie Mac, and AIG also undermine the real value of reputational cost as a determining factor in the cost/benefit analysis. Arthur Andersen, once viewed as the "Marines" of the accounting world, puts the analytical icing on the cake.

Rational-choice theory is not a mental exercise confined to academicians trying to discover how many angels can dance on the head of a pin. Understanding this theory is crucial for determining motive or defending against charges of willful

---

14. Shover & Hochstetler, *supra* note 12, at 107.

15. *Id.* at 169. Adam Smith, sometimes thought of as the "father" of capitalism, said: "The real and effectual discipline which is exercised over a workman is . . . that of his customers. It is the fear of losing their employment which restrains his frauds and corrects his negligence." The Wealth of Nations 113 (Hayes Barton Press ed. 1956) (1776).

and unlawful organizational behavior. We are still at the point of talking about the motives and imbedded characteristics of any particular corporate culture. Juries want to know the reason that organizational actors engage in unlawful conduct. As the Enron juror interviews disclosed, at the close of the first round of deliberations only four members committed to a guilty verdict. That suggests the government was not very convincing in its case about the reasons for claiming a crime had been committed. The ultimate decision to convict, according to the interviewed jurors, had much to do with the jury instructions they received from the judge. (Parenthetically, the case was later reversed based on those faulty jury instructions.) Oversimplification of the process is always a danger, but there can be no question that any effective prosecution or defense must answer the most important question: Why did they do it?

III. Shifting Behavior by Punishment: Understanding the Federal Sentencing Guidelines Policy

The organizational federal sentencing guidelines, like the rest of the guidelines, are discretionary and not mandatory. The trend toward deflating the legal force of the guidelines and increasing judicial discretion in sentencing is underscored in the decisions *Gall v. United States*, 552 U.S. 38 (2007), and *Kimbrough v. United States*, 552 U.S. 85 (2007). The standard of review is abuse of discretion after the court takes into consideration, among other factors, the policies of the Federal Sentencing Commission in drafting the guidelines. That leaves open the very important question about the nature of the other information that judges tend to consider in adjudicating corporate sentences.

The current organizational sentencing guidelines focus on two factors: the seriousness of the offense and the organization's "culpability" factor. Culpability generally will be determined by the steps taken by the organization prior to the offense to prevent and detect criminal conduct, the level and extent of involvement in or tolerance of the offense by certain personnel, and the organization's action after an offense has been committed.[16] In a sense, the court considers, in punishing the company, whether the decision to engage in unlawful conduct was primarily an organizational choice prompted by management or the misfortune of failing to supervise a rogue employee. Choice dominates the sentencing landscape.

In any event, certainty of punishment, the key to reducing unlawful behavior in a rational-choice scheme, may be questionable under the current sentencing rules. For example, if the court finds that an organization will be unable to pay its restitution order, "no fine should be imposed."[17] Additionally, where the minimum guideline

16. U.S. Sentencing Guidelines Manual ch. 8, introductory cmt.
17. *Id.* § 8C2.2.

fine calculation is greater than the statutory maximum fine, the statutory fine controls, regardless of actual culpability.[18] The Offense Level Fine Table in the sentencing guidelines is hardly enforceable if the guideline calculation is inconsistent with the authorized statutory fines. This may explain in some measure the government policy in favor of resolving organizational disputes by plea agreement or deferred prosecution agreements. It also explains the willingness of organizations to seek informal resolution where possible. In the end, the real damage in the form of economic harm to the organization may be more closely aligned with the decision to prosecute by formal indictment as opposed to the judicial imposition of a fine or restitution after the case has been resolved through negotiated resolution. This is discussed in detail in Chapter 6.

In an effort to strengthen the impact of the guidelines, Congress enacted Sarbanes-Oxley in part to increase certain institutional penalties and required corporations to adopt a code of ethics, dubbed by the DOJ a "Corporate Compliance Plan," or explain publicly why they do not have one.[19] The absence of such a code or plan at the time of sentencing can be treated as an aggravating sentencing factor by the court. The New York Stock Exchange further requires listed companies to promptly publish a code of ethics and disclose any waiver of the code by officers or directors[20] in an apparent attempt to diminish the influence of cult-type management personalities who circumvent corporate ethics policies with impunity.

However, despite these efforts at shifting corporate behavior by law or even through punishment, the SEC is perhaps more realistic in its assessment that firms must create an internal "culture of compliance." "If you've been listening, you know it's not enough to have policies. It's not enough to have procedures. It's not enough to have good intentions. All of these can help. But to be successful, compliance must be an embedded part of [the] firm's culture."[21] In short, the company must create a culture that makes the choice to behave in accordance with the law. Again, that is certainly the philosophy adopted by the Sentencing Commission in drafting policy. In the commentary to the Chapter 8 revisions sent to Congress on May 1, 2004, the Commission stated: "[T]he promotion of desired organizational culture [is] indicated by the fulfillment of seven minimum requirements, which are the hallmarks of an effective program that encourages compliance with the law and ethical conduct."[22]

Revised Chapter 8 Guidelines were approved by the Federal Sentencing Commission in April 2010 and took effect November 1, 2010. The revised guidelines

---

18. *Id.* § 8C3.1(b).

19. Sarbanes-Oxley Act § 406(a).

20. N.Y. Stock Exch., Listed Company Manual § 303A.10 (2008).

21. Lori Richards, Dir., Office of Compliance Inspections and Examinations, U.S. Sec. & Exchange Comm'n, The Culture of Compliance, Address at the Spring Compliance Conference of National Regulatory Services (Apr. 23, 2003), http:// www.sec.gov/news/speech/spch042303lar.htm.

22. U.S. Sentencing Comm'n, Amendments to Sentencing Guidelines 74, 86 (2004).

expressly strengthen Guideline No. 7 regarding the appropriate response by an organization when criminal conduct or misconduct is detected. Guideline No. 7 now states that organizations should "remedy the harm resulting from the criminal conduct," including providing restitution to identifiable victims, self-reporting, and cooperation with authorities. The guidelines also now explicitly state that the organization should act to prevent further similar criminal conduct by assessing and making modifications to its compliance and ethics program to "ensure the program is effective," including the "use of an outside professional adviser to ensure adequate assessment and implementation of modifications."

Another change is that an organization can now gain credit in the culpability scoring process, even if a high-level executive is involved in the offense, if the organization meets four factors:

- The person or persons with operational responsibility for the compliance and ethics program have "direct reporting obligations to the governing authority or an appropriate sub-group," such as an audit committee;
- The compliance program must have detected the offense before anyone outside the organization or "before such discovery was reasonably likely;"
- The company "promptly reported the offense to appropriate governmental authorities;" and
- No one "with operational responsibility for the ethics and compliance program participated in, condoned, or was willfully ignorant to the offense."

The guidelines also describe the individuals deemed to have operational responsibility for the compliance program as having "express authority to communicate personally to the governing authority, or appropriate subgroup thereof, (a) promptly on any matter involving criminal conduct or potential criminal conduct; and (b) no less than annually on the implementation and effectiveness of the compliance and ethics program."

It is apparent that when answering the motive question, behavior and corporate culture ultimately play major roles in establishing guilt and, later, punishment. Because self-regulation is the prevailing business model for evaluating the true measure of internal corporate governance, the burden rests heavily on the organization to justify its choices. Case strategy, whether at the preindictment investigatory phase, at trial, or at sentencing, depends to some degree upon the portrayal of the organization as either a law-abiding citizen or a mastermind at the cost/benefit equation.

Chapter 2

THE FACTS BEHIND THE FICTION

THEORIES OF CORPORATE CRIMINAL LIABILITY

It was the sociologist Edwin Sutherland who first coined the term "white-collar" crime, in a 1939 address to the American Sociological Association. It was a new idea in American jurisprudence. This is not surprising given the legal development of entity liability in this country. Prior to the American industrial revolution in the early 20th century, the notion of entity criminal liability was unknown at common law. Corporate charters were granted as a privilege from the sovereign and limited to a particular financial transaction. The corporation was an extension or arm of the state.

With the onset of the industrial revolution, the entire notion of corporate identity changed from a government entity subject to external control to a private form of business operation with internal management. This dramatic change in entity formation and operation was at first not addressed by Congress because it was not a "federal" phenomenon as such; the corporation was an entity licensed by the state and under its jurisdiction.

The development of a body of law explaining organizational liability came from the Supreme Court and it remains the law today. As the impact of corporate conduct on interstate commerce increased, Congress stepped in to legislate. White-collar crime is for the most part a creature of federal statute and prosecuted at the federal level. Licensure remains within the purview of state control, but criminal conduct is almost exclusively regulated by federal law.

I. Respondeat Superior

A. Imputing Acts of the Agent: Strict Liability in Criminal Law

In *Trustees of Dartmouth College v. Woodward*, 17 U.S. 518 (1918), the original founders of the college had obtained a charter from the Crown to operate prior to the American Revolution and independence. However, the state of New Hampshire, postrevolution, sought to pass a law abrogating the college's rights under the charter. The U.S. Supreme Court rejected New Hampshire's attempt to do so, holding that the creation of a corporation, even by royal charter, was a contract within the constitutional provision of Article 1, Section 10, prohibiting states from passing laws impairing contractual obligations. But the full significance of the case was the opportunity for the Court to delineate the contours of a separate corporate existence under the law. The legal fiction was now here to stay. Thus, the Court observed that "a corporation is an artificial being, invisible, intangible, and existing only in contemplation of the law." *Id.* at 636. A corporation therefore has no power except what is given by its incorporating act, either expressly or as incidental to its existence. As such, a corporation may sue and be sued and may enter into contracts.

In 1886, an Ohio citizen sued the Lake Shore & Michigan Southern Railway Co., an Illinois corporation, in federal district court, to recover damages in tort for the wrongful acts of its servants. On review, the Supreme Court held that it was well-established that, in actions for tort, the corporation may be held liable for damages for the acts of its agents within the scope of the agent's employment. *Lake Shore & Mich. S. Ry. Co. v. Prentice*, 147 U.S. 101 (1893). Citing state law precedent, the Court likewise observed that a corporation is "doubtless liable" for any tort committed by an agent in the course of his employment, even if the act is done wantonly, recklessly, or against the express orders of the principal. A corporation may be held liable for a libel, or a malicious prosecution, by its agent within the scope of his employment, and the malice necessary to prove to support either action, "if proved in the agent, may be imputed to the corporation." *Id.* at 110.

Of course, imputing the acts of the agent to the principal within the scope of his employment, under the venerable doctrine of *respondeat superior*, was merely a restatement of the common law: "Let the master answer."[1] Acts done by the agents of a corporation, in the course of its business and of their employment, are imputed to

1. Black's Law Dictionary 1179 (5th ed. 1979).

the corporation. Thus, the corporation is responsible in the same manner and to the same extent as an individual is responsible under similar circumstances.

It was not until 1909 that the Supreme Court decided that a corporation could be held criminally responsible for an act done while an authorized agent is exercising authority conferred by the corporation. In *New York Central & Hudson River Railroad Co. v. United States*, 212 U.S. 481 (1909), a case involving kickbacks in the form of rebates paid by the company to the shipper in violation of the Elkins Act, the Court extended the civil tort concept of *respondeat superior* to criminal corporate liability: "If the act was . . . done [by a corporate employee] it will be imputed to the corporation. . . . There is no distinction any longer in essence between the civil and criminal liability of corporations, based upon the element of intent or wrongful purpose."

The Court rejected the policy argument that shareholders who did not authorize these acts would be unintended victims of the corporate prosecution. The Court could no longer "shut its eyes" to the fact that most business was being conducted through corporations and that "interstate commerce is almost entirely in their hands." To give corporations immunity from corporate prosecution would take away "the only effective means" of controlling corporate abuses. A corollary to this view is that criminal liability will heighten supervision of employee conduct.

One significant expansion of the doctrine is that even where the agent's acts are actually or potentially detrimental to the corporation, the agent's conduct may still be imputed to the corporation for purposes of imposing criminal liability if the agent's acts are motivated, at least in part, to benefit the principal. *United States v. Sun-Diamond Growers of Cal.*, 138 F.3d 961 (DC Cir. 1998) (citing the leading case, *United States v. Automated Med. Labs., Inc.*, 770 F.2d 399, 406–07 (4th Cir. 1985)), *aff'd*, 526 U.S. 398 (1999); *accord United States v. Singh*, 518 F. 3d 236 (4th Cir. 2008).

Likewise, imputation of criminal liability may apply even where the acts are expressly forbidden by the principal. *United States v. Potter*, 463 F.3d 9, 25–26 (1st Cir. 2006); *United States v. Hilton Hotels Corp.*, 467 F.2d 1000 (9th Cir. 1972); *accord Halliburton Co. v. Dow Chem. Co.*, 514 F.2d 377 (10th Cir. 1975).

B. Collective Knowledge Doctrine

A corporation's vicarious liability also extends beyond simple vicarious liability for the criminal acts of a single employee. The courts have formulated a theory of collective liability to permit conviction of the corporation where no single employee could be found to have violated the law. This is known as the collective knowledge doctrine. In *United States v. Bank of New England, N.A.*, 821 F.2d 844 (1st Cir. 1987), the rule was stated: "A corporation cannot plead innocence by asserting that the information obtained by several employees was not acquired by any one individual who then would have comprehended its full import. Rather the corporation is considered to have acquired the collective knowledge of its employees and is held responsible for their failure to act accordingly." *See also United States v. Arthur Andersen, LLP.*, 374 F.3d 281 (5th Cir. 2004), *rev'd on other grounds*, 544 U.S. 696 (2005). (The court concluded that direct evidence of pervasive knowledge of the same facts by numerous Andersen employees made it unnecessary to resolve whether the collective knowledge doctrine should be applied to impute knowledge to the entity).

The collective knowledge doctrine has been held to apply even where specific intent is imputed. *United States v. Phillip Morris USA, Inc.*, 449 F. Supp. 2d 1, 893–98 (D.D.C. 2006) (the opinion is reported in six parts, each with its own Westlaw number, due to length; citations here are to part 5, 2006 WL 2380650). The opinion is a little hazy in terms of the test to be applied. First, noting the circuit court's rejection of the requirement that a corporate state of mind can be established only by looking at each corporate agent at the time he acted, the opinion concedes that the courts have not clearly articulated "exactly what degree of proof is required." *Id.* at 896. Adopting the public policy arguments made in the *Bank of New England* decision, the court concluded that it is "both appropriate and equitable to conclude that a company's fraudulent intent may be inferred from all of the circumstantial evidence including the company's collective knowledge." *Id.* at 896–97.

More recently, the court explained the doctrine in the context of a civil suit filed under the False Claims Act (FCA). In *United States v. Science Applications International Corp. (SAIC)*, 555 F. Supp. 2d 40 (D.D.C. 2008), the court observed that the FCA requires a "knowing" submission of a material false claim for payment to the government. Relying on the *Phillip Morris* decision and *United States ex. rel. Harrison v. Westinghouse Savannah River Co.*, 352 F.3d 908 (4th Cir. 2003), the court concluded that the "at least one" rule applied to establish liability. The knowledge of at least one employee raised a genuine dispute of fact regarding whether a corporation's certifications were knowingly false. In fact, a corporation could be held liable even if the certifying employee was unaware of the wrongful conduct of another employee. *Sci. Applications*, 555 F. Supp. 2d at 56.

The jury instruction upheld in *Westinghouse,* another FCA case, is highly instructive:

> [I]n order to find that [Westinghouse] took any action knowingly, you must find that at least one individual employee had all of the relevant factual information to satisfy that standard as to the fact or action at issue. In this particular case, that means that you would need to find that at least one individual employee of [Westinghouse] knew that GPC [General Physics Corporation] was submitting a bid on the subcontract, and knew of facts which would have required disclosure of an organizational conflict of interest by GPC. You do not need to consider whether this individual knew that a certification would be required or what information the GPC was actually disclosing on it.

Westinghouse, 352 F.3d at 918.

The *Westinghouse* court rejected the "single actor" standard requiring the same employee to know both the wrongful conduct and the certification requirement. The court concluded that acceptance of the rule would create an anomalous precedent. In the future, corporations could merely segregate certifying officers who did nothing more than sign government contracts and thereby immunize the company against liability.

C. Collective Entity Doctrine

The collective entity doctrine was a legal corollary to the inapplicability of the Fifth Amendment to business organizations other than sole proprietorships. After a long hiatus, the doctrine was revitalized by the Supreme Court in its decision in *Braswell v. United States*, 487 U.S. 99 (1988). Rejecting the prior rationale for the development of the doctrine, the Court applied a new rationale—the "agency rationale"—to the attempt by a corporate records custodian to assert a Fifth Amendment privilege in response to a subpoena requesting company documents. The Court held that a corporate record custodian's act of production "is not deemed a personal act" because unlike a sole proprietor, the corporate actor "holds . . . documents in a representative capacity rather than a personal capacity." The logic of the decision is coextensive with the law on corporate privilege in that "[a] claim of Fifth Amendment privilege asserted by the agent would be tantamount to a claim of privilege by the corporation—which of course possesses no such privilege." *Id.* at 110.

However, with the proliferation of new forms of business entities since *Braswell* was decided in 1988, some have argued that the doctrine's agency rationale has not withstood the test of time. For example, single-member LLCs (limited liability companies) differ in many important ways from the corporate operating structure like the one in *Braswell.* In many states, LLCs are permitted to operate less formally, without adherence to the same corporate formalities that even closely held corporations must follow. In many states they are not required to have officers, and management rights can be vested in individual LLC members.

Not surprisingly, LLCs have waged a frontal legal attack against the *Braswell* rationale, arguing that they do not conduct themselves as agents of a separate corporate collective entity. In other words, the agency rationale of *Braswell* does not fit either the legal or operational reality. Of course, the inapplicability of the Fifth Amendment to partnerships, *United States v. Fisher*, 425 U.S. 391 (1976), established long before *Braswell,* would seem to deflate the argument in the context of the noncorporate form. Nonetheless, the argument was recently tried in a proceeding by a sole-member LLC to quash a grand jury subpoena calling for the production of business records in the case *United States v. Feng Juan Lu*, 248 Fed. Appx. 806 (9th Cir. 2007). There, the court rejected the claim that the sole member was not acting in a representative capacity of a collective entity because state law required the

LLC to maintain a state-registered agent. That fact alone was enough to establish agency.

In short, the vitality of the legal characteristics of the principal-agent relationship in business organizations, other than sole proprietorships, remains fixed in the law, defining both rights and liabilities. The issue of corporate privilege is revisited in Chapter 4 at length. The purpose of mentioning the collective entity doctrine here is to complete the big-picture understanding about the principal-agent legal relationship and the expanse of its application.

II. The Corporate Fiduciary: Circumstantial Evidence of Guilt

Here is one place where the corporation, while treated as a legal person for some purposes, does not share the attributes of a human being, not even through agency principles. Fiduciary responsibility is owed to the owner of the corporation—the shareholder—and that responsibility is placed squarely upon the shoulders of the board of directors and managers. So, why talk about fiduciary duty in the context of a criminal case and potential corporate exposure? The breach of a fiduciary duty can be used as circumstantial evidence establishing guilt of corporate officials acting on behalf of the company in at least two ways. Breaking a rule and knowingly engaging in bad conduct can be used as circumstantial evidence to establish consciousness of guilt of the company, its directors, and management. *See Galaxy Computer Servs., Inc. v. Baker*, 325 B.R. 544 (E.D. Va. 2005). Breach of fiduciary duty has also served as a prosecutive theory supporting a finding of guilt under the mail fraud statute, 18 U.S.C. § 1341, both pre- and post-*McNally*.[2] *United States v. Johns*, 742 F. Supp. 196 (E.D. Pa. 1990), *aff'd*, 972 F.2d 1333 (3d Cir. 1991).

The seminal case summarizing this duty is *Aronson v. Lewis*, 473 A.2d 805 (Del. 1984). Simply put, directors of a solvent company owe fiduciary duties of care and loyalty to the shareholders with respect to decisions made on behalf of the corporation. The duties of care and loyalty are separate and have different legal attributes.

Pursuant to the duty of care, directors and managers are required to exercise the degree of care that an ordinarily prudent person would exercise under like circumstances. They have the obligation to make all reasonable efforts to be fully informed prior to making a business decision and may not engage in acts of gross negligence

2. McNally v. United States, 483 U.S. 350 (1987). In the now famous footnote 10 of his dissent in *McNally*, Justice Stevens observed: "When a person is being paid a salary for his loyal services, any breach of that loyalty would appear to carry with it some loss of money to the employer—who is not getting what he paid for. Additionally, '[i]f an agent receives anything as a result of his violation of his duty of loyalty to the principal, he is subject to a liability to deliver it, its value, or its proceeds, to the principal.' Restatement (Second) of Agency § 403 (1958)." *Id.* at 377.

when acting on behalf of the corporation. The duty of care can be violated by nonfeasance (failing to act) or misfeasance (committing bad acts). The decisions of directors who are also corporate officers are subject to a higher level of scrutiny than those of outside directors because inside directors have superior knowledge of the day-to-day affairs of the corporation.

As the Sarbanes-Oxley Act has made clear, a director may no longer serve as a mere figurehead. Ignorance of the company's affairs is not a defense. Thus, the directors must hold, attend, and participate in regular meetings. Prior to voting, directors should obtain all reasonably available materials germane to the decision-making process. The law focuses almost exclusively on how the decision was made as opposed to the correctness of the final judgment as evidenced by the application of the business judgment rule in this context, discussed in the next section. Courts have no interest in second-guessing business decisions of directors and management.

The duty of loyalty addresses conflicts of interests. Here, second-guessing is the name of the game. Directors and managers must avoid any conflict of interest that would affect their ability to make decisions that are in the best interest of the company. The best interests of the company require the exercise of judgment without regard to outside or personal interests. Directors and managers cannot engage in conduct that would injure the corporation or deprive it of profit or advantage. Examples of typical violations include fraud, bad faith, self-dealing without full disclosure and approval, and favoring one group of shareholders over another.

Not every form of self-dealing is prohibited. Generally, a self-dealing transaction, otherwise viewed as a conflict of interest, can be legally acceptable if, after all material facts of the transaction and the director's interest are disclosed, the transaction is then approved by a majority vote of the disinterested directors. Otherwise, transactions that benefit an interested director create a rebuttable inference that the director acted adversely to the corporation. The director must rebut by demonstrating that the actions not disclosed or approved were fair and in the corporation's best interests. To avoid even the appearance of impropriety, the best practice is full and fair disclosure, and the interested member should abstain from voting.

Usurping corporate opportunities is one of the more serious and most frequently litigated areas under breach of the duty of loyalty. In short, corporate opportunities belong to the corporation, and a director cannot commandeer a corporate opportunity to the director's own use or benefit. Of course, once the corporation rejects the opportunity, after having all information fully and fairly presented, the director can pursue the opportunity in safety after notifying the company.

III. Business Judgment Rule: Not a Defense

The business judgment rule is one applied in the courtroom in determining whether a lawsuit, usually filed as derivative action by shareholders, should proceed against the directors and/or management. While it applies in cases alleging breach of the duty of care, it has no application to suits alleging breach of the duty of loyalty or conflict of interest.

The business judgment rule is not a legal standard of conduct or a prescribed duty of care. Rather, it is a "rebuttable presumption" applied by the court in assessing the merits of a motion to dismiss an action. It is a rebuttable presumption that directors acted properly. Directors can assert protection under this rule if they have acted within the scope of their authority, in good faith, with reasonable care, and for a rational business purpose. In other words, they should not be subject to suit for an honest mistake in judgment, even where there are negative consequences to the corporation. Otherwise, a judge would become a super-director, second-guessing business judgments of corporate executives and directors involving business transactions that the judge may not understand or know little or nothing about.

The bottom line is that generally, directors are found to have breached their duty of care only if they act in a grossly negligent manner, exhibiting reckless indifference or deliberate disregard for the interests of the shareholders. Any actions outside the bounds of reason will suffice to impose liability.

Note that the shareholders of a solvent company can file a derivative action on behalf of the corporation, seeking redress for an alleged breach of fiduciary duty. However, in the event of corporate insolvency, it is the creditors who have standing to assert the action and seek redress for harm to the company. To meet the burden to plead insolvency, the creditor must show either: (1) a deficiency of assets below liabilities with no reasonable prospect that the business can be successfully continued or (2) an inability to meet maturing obligations as they fall due in the ordinary course of business. *Prod. Res. Group, L.L.C. v. NCT Group, Inc.*, 863 A.2d 772, 782 (Del. Ch. 2004).

IV. Chinese Walls

"Chinese Walls," or information barriers, do not provide an absolute defense to legal misconduct nor to defendants who engage in financial misconduct. Frequently, a Chinese Wall turns out to have been no "Great Wall" at all, "but more like a wall in a stage set, designed for show." *United States v. Helmsley*, 726 F. Supp. 929, 937 (S.D.N.Y. 1989). It is, as its name implies, a partition of sorts, which is recognized in varying degrees by the courts as a means to prevent some actual or potential form of taint.

The government frequently invokes the use of a Chinese Wall in *Kastigar* hearings,[3] in suppression hearings dealing with computer and/or electronic data

3. Kastigar v. United States, 406 U.S. 441 (1972), held that a grant of immunity prohibits the use in a subsequent prosecution of compelled incriminating evidence of the "fruits directly attributable thereto." The doctrine has been extended to nonevidentiary as well as evidentiary use. The burden, and it is a heavy one, is on the government to show that its evidence emanates from an independent source—hence the need for a Chinese Wall where evidence derives from immunized disclosures.

seizures,[4] and in other such evidence-gathering techniques where prosecutors handling the case must be careful to avoid any taint to the case by reviewing or utilizing immunized or other privacy-protected information. Government taint teams are frequently used to accomplish the goal of avoiding contamination of case prosecutors or evidence in a case. *See, e.g., United States v. Poindexter*, 698 F. Supp. 300 (D.D.C. 1998).

In a business context, there is no definitive case law finding that the use of a Chinese Wall constitutes a legal defense to charges of corporate liability. Regulators are more willing to accept its use. For example, the Securities and Exchange Commission (SEC) adopted rule 14e-3,[5] relating to securities firms engaged in a nonpublic tender offer where an employee executes a trade for a firm in the takeover target's securities. The firm is absolved if effective screening procedures were in place, that is, if the employee making the investment decision was "screened off" or partitioned from the persons with knowledge of the tender offer. The SEC indicated that Chinese Walls were an appropriate device under the rule to satisfy the screening requirement.[6]

The problem with Chinese Walls in business is that there are no guarantees against failure.[7] Nowhere is that more apparent than in the conclusions of the Senate investigation report of the Enron collapse.[8] For that reason, Sarbanes-Oxley has written Chinese Walls into law. Title V of Sarbanes-Oxley amends the Securities and Exchange Act of 1934 by inserting new Section 15D, entitled "Securities Analysts and Research Reports"[9] in an effort to:

> establish structural and institutional safeguards within registered brokers or dealers to assure that securities analysts are separated by appropriate informational professional partitions within the firm from the review, pressure, or oversight of those whose involvement in investment banking activities might potentially bias their judgment or supervision.

The bottom line is that a Chinese Wall may provide a mitigating factor to be considered by a court or a jury in assessing knowledge and/or blame. However, for highly

4. For a complete discussion of Department of Justice procedures, see Searching and Seizing Computers and Obtaining Electronic Evidence in Criminal Investigations (Computer Crime & Intellectual Prop. Section, Criminal Div., U.S.D.O.J., July 2002), http://www.usdoj.gov/criminal/cybercrime/s&smanual2002.htm.

5. 17 C.F.R. § 240.14e-3 (1988).

6. SEC Release No. 17,120, [1980 Transfer Binder] Fed. Sec. L. Rep. (CCH) ¶ 82,046 at 83,461 (Sept. 4, 1980).

7. Lynn Turner, former Chief Auditor of the SEC, Address at the International Monetary Fund Seminar on Current Developments in Monetary and Financial Law (June 4, 2004), http://www.imf.org/external/np/leg/sem/2004/cdmfl/eng/turner.pdf.

8. For a more complete discussion, see Miriam Miquelon-Weismann, *Selling Out Corporate Reform: Eliminating the "Disinterested Person" Requirement for Investment Bankers Advising Chapter 11 Debtors*, 2 N.Y.U.J.L. & Bus. 731, 749–53 (2006).

9. 15 U.S.C. § 78o-6(a)(3).

regulated businesses, the Chinese Wall may already be required by law and would provide indicia of wrongdoing where a breach of the legally mandated partition evidences a breach of fiduciary duty.

Chapter 3

CRIME AND PUNISHMENT STATUTORY TOOLS

"White-collar criminality in business is expressed most frequently in the form of misrepresentation in financial statements of corporations, manipulation in the stock exchange, commercial bribery, bribery of public officials directly or indirectly in order to secure favorable contracts and legislation, misrepresentation in advertising and salesmanship, embezzlement and misapplication of funds, short weights and measures and misgrading of commodities, tax frauds, misapplication of funds in receiverships and bankruptcies. These are what Al Capone called 'the legitimate rackets.'"[1]

I. Fraud

Corporate crime is primarily financial crime. This chapter describes the most common forms of financial fraud in terms of various statutory criminal offenses, including: mail fraud and wire fraud, the proverbial scheme and artifice to deprive the victim of money or property using the mails or the wires; bank fraud, which is closely

1. Edwin H. Sutherland, *White-Collar Criminality, in* Crimes of Privilege: Readings in White-Collar Crime 4, 6 (Neal Shover & John Paul Wright, eds., Oxford Univ. Press 2001).

related to mail and wire fraud; money laundering, hiding the source or nature of cash generated in violation of some other provision of federal law; bribery of public officials; program fraud by theft; tax fraud, including illegal slush funds or false reporting; securities fraud and the application of Rule 10(b)(5); "process crimes" including obstruction, perjury, and false statements; and conspiracy. The discussion is aimed at identifying the most common forms of corporate and organizational misconduct as opposed to the nuanced aspects of any particular statute.

In terms of corporate prosecutions, these crimes are typified by discreet financial transactions or a pattern of transactions. The crimes are usually engineered by management and/or employees of the corporation. They are often not complex and do not involve much technical knowledge of finance or accounting. Most prosecutors and practitioners understand the targeted transactions in fairly short order. Often, the most complicating factor is the paper. Usually there is lots of it, and the crimes are pieced together by federal agents experienced in such matters from the Federal Bureau of Investigation (FBI), the Internal Revenue Service (IRS), the Postal Inspection Service, and other federal agencies. Because these cases are labor intensive, prosecutors routinely seek to simplify the charges, opting to prosecute the easiest case under the most straightforward statute. However, after 9/11, most of the available case agents were reassigned to antiterrorism task forces reducing the number of white collar criminal prosecutions. Despite Department of Justice (DOJ) attempts to put a positive spin on the statistics in its *2008 Corporate Fraud Task Force: Report to the President,*[2] an enforcement study covering the period 2002–2008, shows that from 2000 to 2007, prosecutions of frauds against financial institutions dropped 48 percent, insurance fraud cases dropped 75 percent, and securities fraud cases dropped 17 percent.[3] In the 2007 budget cycle, the FBI obtained money to fund the hiring of a single agent for criminal investigations.

The Transactional Records Access Clearinghouse (TRAC),[4] which compiles its statistics through Freedom of Information Act requests to the DOJ, provides further insight into national profile and enforcement trends on a monthly and annual basis. The fiscal year 2008 report of FBI convictions, including statistics through June 2008, shows that monthly convictions for current FY 2008 were down 1.3 percent from the same periods the year before, and down 9.8 percent from five years before.[5] According to the data for the month of June 2008, the government reported 943 con-

2. Available at http://www.usdoj.gov/dag/cftf/corporate-fraud2008.pdf.

3. Eric Lichtblau, David Johnston, & Ron Nixon, *F.B.I. Struggles to Handle Wave of Financial Fraud Cases,* N.Y. Times, Oct. 19, 2008.

4. Based at Syracuse University, TRAC gathers, researches, and distributes information about staffing, spending, and enforcement activities of the federal government. http://trac.syr.edu/.

5. Transactional Access Clearinghouse, Convictions for June 2008, http://trac.syr.edu/tracreports/bulletins/ jfbi/monthlyjun08/gui/ (Oct. 2008).

victions for cases referred by the FBI. Of the 934 convictions reported, only 2 percent accounted for "Fraud—Other Business" crimes.

The statistics remain much the same for FY 2011. The latest available data from the Justice Department shows that during the first nine months of FY 2011, the government reported 8,421 new convictions for cases referred by the FBI. If this activity continues at the same pace, the annual total of convictions is expected to increase 0.1 percent for FY 2011. However, compared to five years ago, the estimate of FY 2011 convictions is down 7.8 percent. Convictions over FY 2011 are lower than they were 10 years ago.

Overall, the data shows that FBI related convictions are down 17.3 percent from the level reported in 2001. Cases were classified by prosecutors into more specific types. The single largest number of convictions of FBI cases through June 2011 was for "Narcotics/Drugs," accounting for 24.1 percent of convictions. The second largest category was "White Collar Crime," accounting for 20.8 percent of total convictions. Within the "other" category, which includes a diverse group of programs, the largest specific program prosecutions include: "Weapons," 4.8 percent, "Official Corruption," 2.6 percent, and "Organized Crime," 2.5 percent.[6]

What about the IRS and white collar crime? The FY 2007 audit rate for the nation's largest corporations "plunged to its lowest level in the last 20 years, less than half what it was in FY 1988," according to TRAC figures.[7] The IRS has apparently changed its strategy to increase audits for smaller corporations with assets of $50 million or less because they take less time and cost less. The results of this strategy are dubious. The TRAC report reveals that in FY 2007, for each revenue-agent hour spent auditing the smallest corporations, the IRS gained $682 in additional tax revenues; midsized corporations produced only $474 in recommended additional taxes. However, for corporations with over $250 million in assets, the agents recommended additional taxes of $7,498 per revenue-agent hour. The internal IRS data further concludes that about one-third of all revenue-agent time spent auditing smaller and midsized corporations resulted in absolutely no changes in recommended taxes that were owed. These are termed "nonproductive" audits by the IRS.

According to the April 12, 2010 TRAC report, as of FY 2009, the audit activity of large corporations continued in a steady decline despite the growing federal deficit. Specifically, IRS audits of large corporations fell from 4,693 in FY 2005 to only 3,675 in FY 2009. Audit rates fell even faster.[8]

6. Transactional Access Clearinghouse, Convictions for June 2011, http://tracfed.syr.edu/results/9x704e87441419.html (Sept. 2011).

7. Transactional Access Clearinghouse, Audits of Largest Corporations Slide to All Time Low, http://trac.syr.edu/tracirs/newfindings/current/ (Oct. 2008).

8. Transactional Access Clearinghouse, Convictions for June 2011, http://trac.syr.edu/tracirs/newfindings/v15/ (Oct. 2011).

While the level of IRS convictions increased in 2008 by 19.3 percent from five years ago in FY 2003, the largest number of prosecutions, 45 percent, is for tax fraud. The second largest category is 20.7 percent for the Drugs Organized Crime Task Force. In business-related prosecutions, the category "Fraud—Other" accounts for 4.5 percent; "Fraud—Unspecified," 4.5 percent; "Money Laundering," 4.5 percent; and "Fraud—Health Care," 2.7 percent.

The statistics do not show whether the convictions for such crimes as fraud, money laundering, and health care fraud are being double-counted by law enforcement agencies such as the FBI, the Drug Enforcement Agency, or the Postal Inspection Service. Such double-counting, where two or more federal agencies report the same conviction as part of their annual prosecution statistics, is a common practice when more than one agency has a case agent assigned to a particular criminal case. Granted, statistics can be slippery; however, where audits of large corporations have diminished and about one-third of small to midsized company audits are nonproductive, it may be reasonable to infer that IRS statistics do not reflect a significant increase in the prosecution of white-collar crime.

II. Specific Crimes

A. General Principles: *Mens Rea* and *Actus Reus*

White collar offenses, like other criminal offenses, require a *mens rea, actus reus,* and causation. These elements are defined by the particular statutory provision proscribing the crime. In *Liparota v. United States*, 471 U.S. 419, 424 (1985) the Supreme Court stated: "The definition of the elements of a criminal offense is entrusted to the legislature, particularly in the case of federal crimes, which are solely creatures of statute." And in a later case, "[W]e have long recognized that determining the mental state required for the commission of a federal crime requires 'construction of the statute and . . . inference of the intent of Congress.'" *Staples v. United States*, 511 U.S. 600, 605 (1994).

The most direct approach to understanding the meaning of the *mens rea* and *actus reus* elements is to examine the jury instructions in the federal jurisdiction where the case is being prosecuted. It is not unusual for the same concepts to have different meanings, sometimes to the point of conflicting meanings, in application. Generally, however, the terms have agreed upon meanings as a result of Supreme Court cases resolving various legal disputes.

With the exception of public welfare statutes that impose strict liability and negate the *mens rea* requirement altogether, all federal statutes contain a defined *mens rea* requirement. Public welfare offenses that negate the *mens rea* requirement are statutes that regulate potentially harmful or injurious items. The courts have upheld these statutes, despite the common law construct requiring both a guilty mind and a bad act in order to impose criminal liability, on the reasoning that as long as the defendant knows that he is dealing with a dangerous device of a character that places him "in responsible relation to a public danger," he must "ascertain at his peril whether [his conduct] comes within the inhibition of the statute." *Id.* at 607.

Most federal statutes, however, require that the defendant act "willfully" in the performance of the bad act. Sometimes the language states that the defendant must "willfully and knowingly" engage in the conduct. We consider "willfully" first. The Supreme Court observes that "willfully" is "a word of many meanings" whose construction often depends on the context in which it appears. *Bryan v. United States*, 524 U.S. 184, 191 (1998). In general, a willful act is one undertaken with a bad purpose. In other words, the government must prove that the defendant acted with knowledge that his conduct was unlawful. *Ratzlaf v. United States*, 510 U.S. 135, 137 (1994). The Supreme Court construction is incorporated in the federal pattern jury instructions as follows: "Willfully means to act with knowledge that one's conduct is unlawful and with the intent to do something the law forbids, that is to say with the bad purpose to disobey or disregard the law."[9]

As for the term "knowingly," the Supreme Court remarks that unless the text of the statute dictates a different result, "knowingly" merely requires "proof of knowledge of the facts that constitute the offense." *Bryan*, 524 U.S. at 193. Thus, the knowledge requisite to a knowing violation of the statute is factual knowledge as distinguished from knowledge of the law, based on the maxim that ignorance of the law is no excuse or defense to a crime. Although these two terms have been subject to different legal interpretation by the courts, it is not unusual for the terms "willfully" and "knowingly" to be used almost interchangeably in statutes and jury instructions.

One area that is an exception to these general rules is dealing with tax offenses. In *Cheek v. United States*, 498 U.S. 192 (1991), the Court distinguished this class of cases as one where Congress does require a specific intent to violate the law as an element of the offense. The theory underlying *Cheek* is that tax laws are more difficult to comprehend than other federal statutes and so require knowledge of the law that is intended to be broken.

Interestingly, the federal criminal code does not distinguish between specific intent and general intent crimes. The Supreme Court has likewise criticized the distinction in numerous cases. *See, e.g., Liparota v. United States*, 471 U.S. 419, 433 n.16 (1985); *United States v. Bailey*, 444 U.S. 394, 403–06 (1980). Jury instruction committees have sought to abandon the distinction as well.[10] As a practical matter, the

---

9. L. Sand, J. Seiffert, W. Loughlin, & S. Reiss, Modern Federal Jury Instructions ¶3A.01, at 3A-18 (1997).

10. "Each of the jury instruction committees of the circuit courts of appeal have followed suit and discouraged the use of jury instructions on specific intent." Kevin F. O'Malley et al., Federal Jury Practice and Instructions §17.03 (5th ed. 2000).

distinction nonetheless continues to exist at trial. It may best be explained in general terms: "a 'specific intent' offense is one in which the definition of the crime: (1) includes an intent to do some future act, or achieve some future consequence (i.e., a special motive for the conduct), *beyond the conduct or result that constitutes the actus reus of the offense;* or (2) provides that the actor must be aware of the statutory attendant circumstance. An offense that does not contain either of these offenses is termed 'general intent.'"[11] As a helpful rule of thumb, statutory language that includes doing some act using the terminology "with the intent to" achieve some goal or purpose is typically a specific intent statute.

Why does this make a difference? If the crime is a general intent crime, only reasonable mistakes of fact or law provide a defense; by contrast, even unreasonable mistakes may be introduced to defend against a prosecution for a specific intent crime. Of particular importance to business organizations at trial are the good faith defense and the reasonable reliance on counsel defense, both of which can be asserted only to defend against a specific intent crime.[12]

The *actus reus*—the bad act or the failure to act where there is a duty—is discussed next with an examination of the types of offense conduct statutorily proscribed under the federal system. These offenses include conspiracy, mail and wire fraud, bank fraud, bribery and illegal gratuities, program fraud, money laundering, securities fraud, corporate tax fraud, perjury, and so-called process crimes such as perjury and obstruction of justice.

B. Conspiracy: 18 U.S.C. § 371

Judge Learned Hand aptly described conspiracy as "that darling of the modern prosecutor's nursery." *Harrison v. United States*, 7 F.2d 259, 263 (2d Cir 1925). What makes it such a darling is the evidentiary and procedural benefits attendant to its use. As a threshold matter, conspiracy is an inchoate offense, an unlawful agreement between two or more persons to commit an unlawful objective and an overt act in furtherance of the agreement. Because the agreement is the gravamen of the offense, the unlawful objective need not be accomplished before the crime can be charged. In fact, the coconspirators can fail in the attempt to commit the unlawful objective. Even the impossibility of success is no defense. *United States v. Jimenez Recio*, 537 U.S. 270, 275 (2003).

However, assuming the coconspirators are successful in achieving the commission of the unlawful objective, the conspiracy charge does not merge with the completion of the unlawful, substantive criminal offense. Both are separate crimes and carry separate punishments.

---

11. Josh Dressler, Understanding Criminal Law 102 (Matthew Bender & Co. 1995).
12. United States v. Stevens, 771 F.Supp.2d 556 (D.Md. 2011).

While not the only federal conspiracy statute—there are other special conspiracy statutes for narcotics, racketeering, and securities fraud, to name a few—18 U.S.C. § 371, Conspiracy to Defraud the United States, is the main one and perhaps the easiest to plead and prove. Section 371 requires proof of three elements: (1) an agreement to achieve an unlawful objective or objectives; (2) knowing and voluntary participation; and (3) the commission of an overt act in furtherance of the conspiracy.

The agreement must be between two or more persons. A corporation is a person under the statute. While all of the coconspirators must agree on the essential nature of the plan, it is not necessary to prove that all coconspirators had knowledge of all of the details of the agreement or even know of the existence or identity of all other coconspirators.

Under the Pinkerton doctrine, *Pinkerton v. United States*, 328 U.S. 640, 646–47 (1946), every coconspirator is liable for the foreseeable acts of coconspirators performed in furtherance of the conspiracy even where the identity of the coconspirator performing the act is unknown to every coconspirator and/or not all conspirators even had knowledge of the act or agreed to the performance of the act. A party must only have knowledge of the conspiracy and agree to participate. The existence of the conspiracy is a question for determination by the court under the preponderance of evidence standard. The statements of the coconspirators may be used as evidence to establish proof of the existence of the conspiracy.[13]

There are two types of unlawful objectives prohibited under § 371: (1) an agreement to commit any offense against the United States, such as any offense arising under Titles 8, 18, 21, 26, 31, and others; or (2) an agreement to defraud the United States or one of its agencies, often referred to as an agreement to impair, impede, and obstruct an agency from engaging in or performing its lawful functions. *Hammerschmidt v. United States*, 265 U.S. 182 (1924); *United States v. Arch Trading Co.*, 987 F.2d 1087 (4th Cir. 1992). The agreement may have as its objective the intent to commit an unlawful act or a lawful act by unlawful means. The indictment can identify multiple objectives but the prosecution need not prove all of the objectives, nor is a defendant typically entitled to a special verdict form identifying which objective was proved beyond a reasonable doubt to the jury.

An overt act can be a lawful act or an unlawful act. It must simply be one performed in furtherance of the unlawful agreement. The conspiracy arises with the formation of the agreement and is completed with the commission of the overt act. Thus, a coconspirator can withdraw only in the time between the agreement and the commission of the overt act.[14] Once the overt act is completed, with or without the knowledge and/or agreement of all coconspirators, there can be no further withdrawal;

---

13. Bourjaily v. United States, 483 U.S. 171 (1987).

14. The affirmative defense of abandonment from the conspiracy, which does not negate liability for the conspiracy but merely for future substantive crimes, is discussed in Chapter 5.

each coconspirator is guilty of the conspiracy and, under *Pinkerton*, guilty of any foreseeable crimes committed in furtherance of the conspiracy. It does not matter if one defendant is the leader and another is a bit player in the overall scheme. Each coconspirator is equally responsible for the offense.

From an evidentiary standpoint, conspiracy is very difficult to defend against because of the breadth of relevant evidence and the exception to the hearsay rules. As a procedural matter, all coconspirators can be joined and tried together regardless of relative culpability. Severance is not an option.[15] Evidence relative to one coconspirator is, therefore, admissible against all members. Without a conspiracy charge, defendants might be otherwise entitled to separate trials where relevant evidence would be limited to the participation of a single defendant. Damage control in the form of cautionary instructions to the jury is about as much as can be hoped for, and then only in a limited number of instances.

Additionally, hearsay statements of a coconspirator of a party, regardless of whether the declarant is formally charged, made during the course and in furtherance of the conspiracy are admissible as one of the hearsay exceptions.[16] This provision offers the prosecution the ability to throw in the proverbial "kitchen sink" when introducing evidence at trial. Here, conspiracy trumps the *Bruton* rule.[17] The *Bruton* rule protects the right to confront witnesses against the defendant thus preventing the admission of an unavailable codefendant's inculpatory statements or confessions implicating the defendant. However, the charge of conspiracy allows into evidence the statements of an indicted or unindicted, available or unavailable, coconspirator which implicates or incriminates the defendant without the right to confront the coconspirator. So, for example, an uncharged coconspirator cooperates with the police and incriminates the defendant but now asserts the Fifth Amendment and refuses to testify at the defendant's trial. The police officer may still testify at trial to the statement made by the unavailable coconspirator incriminating the defendant despite the defendant's inability to cross-examine the coconspirator about the statement.

Another evidentiary pitfall is the admissibility of the guilty pleas and allocution statements of coconspirators made prior to trial. Under Federal Rule of Evidence 803(3)(b), the statement may be admissible as a statement against penal interest where the coconspirator is now "unavailable" based upon the assertion of the Fifth Amendment privilege at the time of a subsequent trial. The courts have likewise held that the Confrontation Clause is not violated by the admission of such evidence. *See, e.g., United States v. Aguilar*, 295 F.3d 1018 (8th Cir. 2002); *United States v. Centracchio*, 265 F.3d 518 (7th Cir. 2001); *United States v. Gallego*, 191 F.3d 156 (2d Cir. 1999).

---

15. United States v. Novaton, 271 F.3d 968 (11th Cir. 2001); United States v. Triumph Capital Group, Inc., 260 F.Supp.2d 432 (D.C. Conn. 2002).

16. Fed. R. Evid. 801(d)(2)(E).

17. *Bruton v. United States*, 391 U.S. 123 (1968),

There is also a procedural advantage to the prosecution in terms of venue. The case can be prosecuted in the place where the conspiracy was formed or where any overt act took place. The prosecutor may pick and choose among the overt act or acts charged in the indictment.

1. *Intracorporate Conspiracy*

A seminal case in the field of corporate conspiracy law is *United States v. Stevens*, 909 F.2d 431 (11th Cir. 1990). There, the court held that in a criminal conspiracy case, a sole stockholder who completely controls a corporation and is the sole actor in the performance of corporate activities cannot be guilty of a criminal conspiracy with that corporation in the absence of another human actor. In other words, the court found that the "plurality" requirement of two or more persons had not been met.

The court distinguished the case from the factual situation where a corporation is charged with conspiring with its officers or employees. In its earlier opinion, *United States v. Hartley*, 678 F.2d 961, 972 (11th Cir. 1982), the court rejected the "single entity theory" that all agents of the corporation engaging in corporate conduct form a single, collective legal person; that is, the corporation and the acts of each agent shall constitute the acts of the corporation.

As the *Stevens* court observed, *Hartley* established two important principles in the area of intracorporate conspiracy. First, a group of people cannot defeat conspiratorial liability simply because they are acting on behalf of the same corporation. Second, the case reaffirms the imputation of criminal liability to the corporation based on the rule of *respondeat superior.*[18]

2. *Intercorporate Conspiracy*

Two corporations can form a conspiracy where two separate individuals are associated with each. However, where a single agent is acting for each corporation, the plurality requirement is not satisfied. *United States v. Santa Rita Shore Co.*, 16 N.M. 3, 113 P. 620 (N.M. 1911).

3. *Impact of the Acquittal of Individual Coconspirators*

In *United States v. Hughes Aircraft Co.*, 20 F.3d 974 (9th Cir. 1994), the company and one of its employees were charged with one count of conspiracy to defraud and two substantive counts of making false statements. The individual employee was acquitted on all counts; the company was convicted on the conspiracy charge but acquitted on the false statement counts. Hughes argued on appeal that its conspiracy conviction should be reversed because the same jury had acquitted the "indispensible

18. In a similar case, *Copperweld Corp. v. Independence Tube Corp.*, 467 U.S. 752, 768 (1984), the Supreme Court ruled that a parent corporation and its wholly owned subsidiary were incapable of conspiring with each other for purposes of Section 1 of the Sherman Antitrust Act, finding the conduct to be "wholly unilateral."

coconspirator" upon whose acts the corporate liability necessarily rested. Rejecting the company's argument on appeal, the court applied conventional conspiracy principles for the proposition that "the conviction of one coconspirator is valid even when all the other coconspirators are acquitted." *Id.* at 978.

C. Mail and Wire Fraud

After the collapse of Enron, the Sarbanes-Oxley Act of 2002 (SOX) quadrupled the maximum statutory sentences for mail and wire fraud, from five years to 20 years. Yet the net effect of post-Enron reform is dubious. First, between 2001 and 2006, the percentage of federal offenders charged with fraud as the primary offense fell from 11.4 percent to 9.7 percent. The increase in sentences for economic crimes amounted to less than one month in comparison with sentences pre-Enron.[19] Arguably, the potential for increased sentences does add real incentive to plea bargain cases. (This is addressed in detail in Chapter 6.) That, perhaps, is the hook for evaluating the effectiveness of post-Enron reforms in terms of corporate prosecutions.

Changes to the mail fraud statute in 2002 by SOX and in 2008[20] have increased financial penalties to $1 million if the violation occurs in relation to a major disaster or emergency declared by the President or affects a financial institution.[21] Because each mailing constitutes a separate and distinct crime and may be charged and sentenced as separate crimes subject to separate penalties, a fine could be crippling to a company engaged in such misconduct. The same statutory penalty language is included in the wire fraud statute.

Specifically, the mail fraud statute, 18 U.S.C. § 1341, prohibits any scheme or artifice to defraud another of money or property by fraudulent means and the use of a mailing, either through the postal service or by private carrier, in order to execute the scheme. The "scheme to defraud" element is as broad as the criminal's imagination. It is not limited by the common law definition of fraud. Conduct characterized by the deprivation of something of value by "trick, deceit, chicane, or overreaching" is encompassed within the terms of the statute. *Hammerschmidt v. United States*, 265 U.S. 182 (1924).

The scheme to defraud requires that defendant act with the intent to defraud. The intent to deceive does not always coincide with the intent to defraud requirement. For example, in *United States v. Regent Office Supply Co.*, 421 F.2d 1174 (2d Cir. 1970), the company used false pretenses to obtain access to customers but later delivered goods of the price and quality represented during the sales pitch. The Second Circuit concluded that where false pretenses are "not directed to the quality, ade-

---

19. Lucian Dervan, *Plea Bargaining's Survival: Financial Crimes Plea Bargaining, a Continued Triumph in a Post-Enron World*, 60 OKLA. L. REV. 451 (2007).

20. Pub. L. No. 110-179, § 4, 121 Stat. 2557 (Jan. 7, 2008).

21. The increased penalty provisions apply to the wire fraud § 1343 and bank fraud § 1344 provisions as well.

quacy or price of goods to be sold, or otherwise to the nature of the bargain," they do not support a finding of a scheme to defraud. *Id.* at 1183.

Although actual harm is not required for conviction, the government must still demonstrate that "some actual harm or injury was contemplated by the schemer." *Id.* at 1180. As a practical matter, prosecutors typically do not prosecute technical violations of the statute without the ability to demonstrate material harm to the victim. Jurors tend to view technical violations as a "so what?" or "no harm, no foul" exercise.

Finally, materiality is an essential element of mail, wire, and bank fraud. The Supreme Court observed that "the common law could not have conceived of 'fraud' without proof of materiality." *Neder v. United States*, 527 U.S. 1, 22 (1999).

The wire fraud statute, 18 U.S.C. § 1343, mirrors the mail fraud statute with the exception that the wires must be used in *interstate* or foreign commerce to effectuate the scheme. There is no requirement that the defendant must know or foresee that the transmission is going interstate. *United States v. Bryant*, 766 F. 2d 370 (8th Cir. 1985). A simple long-distance phone call will suffice. Notably, the case law precedent developed under the mail fraud statute and the wire fraud statute generally applies to interpreting both statutes.

A third related provision to the mail and wire fraud statutes is 18 U.S.C. § 1346, which provides a statutory definition for one type of scheme or artifice to defraud known as the "deprivation of honest services" offense. The reason that Congress had to single out this specific type of fraud resulted from the Supreme Court decision in *McNally v. United States*, 483 U.S. 350 (1987), which held that absent a statutory provision to the contrary, it was unconstitutional to charge a scheme or artifice to defraud that resulted in a mere deprivation to the company of an employee's honest and faithful services through a fraudulent course of self-dealing. An actual deprivation of money or property was required. In other words, deprivation of intangible rights, as opposed to the deprivation of tangible rights, was insufficient to charge a scheme or artifice to defraud the principal company under either statute.

In response, Congress passed Title 18 U.S.C. § 1346 to add the intangible rights theory of "honest-services fraud" to the definition of proscribed conduct. Section 1346 provides in pertinent part: "For purposes of [Title 18 that prohibits mail fraud § 1341, and wire fraud § 1343], the term 'scheme or artifice to defraud' includes a scheme or artifice to deprive another of the intangible right of honest services."

However, the Supreme Court once again narrowed the application of § 1346 honest-services fraud prosecutions to only bribery and/or kickback schemes arising under the mail fraud and wire fraud statutes. *Skilling v. United States*, 130 S. Ct. 1568 (2010). Defendant Jeffrey Skilling, the mastermind of the Enron collapse, was indicted with two other Enron executives and charged with multiple counts of securities fraud, wire fraud, making false representations to Enron's auditors, and insider trading.

Count 1 of the indictment charged Skilling with, among other things, conspiracy to commit honest services fraud under § 1346. The theory of the indictment was that

Skilling "placed his interests in conflict with that of the [Enron] shareholders, when, for his own financial benefit, he engaged in an undisclosed scheme to artificially inflate the stock's price by deceiving the shareholders and others about the company's true financial condition." However, Skilling was not charged with soliciting or accepting any bribes or kickbacks in connection with the scheme. The Supreme Court, in reversing that count of conviction, held that conflict of interest cases are not qualified schemes under the honest services doctrine. Prosecution under the statute is thus limited to schemes involving bribery and/or kickbacks.

In practice, § 1346 may protect a corporation from the imputation of criminal liability for the criminal acts of its agents, under the theory of *respondeat superior*, when victimized by an agent acting for the agent's own benefit to the detriment of the company. The company is, thus, deprived of the agent's honest and faithful services. But the use of the statute to cut off agent imputation under the theory of *respondeat superior* has been narrowly circumscribed by the courts.

The ground rules were well-established in the seminal case *United States v. Sun-Diamond Growers of California*, 138 F. 3d 961, *aff'd on other grounds*, 526 U.S. 398 (1999). Sun-Diamond was a large agricultural cooperative owned by individual member cooperatives. Among other responsibilities, Sun-Diamond acted as a lobbyist on behalf of the cooperatives in Washington, D.C., in an effort to seek favorable agricultural policies. Then Secretary of Agriculture Mike Espy recruited Sun-Diamond to assist in retiring the political debt incurred by Espy's brother in a failed political campaign. Unfortunately, the law prohibited both corporate contributions for congressional campaigns and disguised contributions. To circumvent this, the company's vice president of corporate affairs and Espy came up with a scheme in which the company persuaded individual employees to make contributions, for which the employees received reimbursement using corporate funds. Sun-Diamond was later convicted of, among other crimes, wire fraud.

On appeal Sun-Diamond claimed that the scheme was designed to defraud Sun-Diamond and not to benefit the company and, therefore, it was a victim, deprived of the honest services of its employee, and not a perpetrator of the scheme. The court rejected the argument for several reasons: (1) the corporate agent need not be acting solely, or even predominantly, with the intent to benefit the corporate principal; and (2) the corporation need not actually receive the corporate benefit. The Supreme Court upheld the conviction on the theory that while the scheme came at a cost to Sun-Diamond, there was still the promise of a benefit in obtaining favorable regulatory treatment in the future.

One of the Enron cases led to a reaffirmation of the same principles but with the anomalous result of reversing the individual defendants' convictions. In *United States v. Brown*, 459 F.3d 509, 522, *cert. denied*, 127 S. Ct. 2249 (2007), the famous "Enron barge case," the court held that where there is *no* evidence that the agent was acting contrary to the principal's interest, there may be no breach of duty and, thus, no deprivation of honest services. Here, the government charged the defendants with a mail fraud scheme based on a sham transaction designed to help Enron meet its earnings projections. "This case, in which Enron employees breached a fiduciary duty in pursuit of what they understood to be a corporate goal, presents a situation in which the dishonest conduct is disassociated from bribery or self-dealing and … concomitant to the employer's immediate interest."

D. Bank Fraud

The scheme to defraud as used under the bank fraud statute, 18 U.S.C. § 1344, mirrors the use of the terminology in the mail and wire fraud statutes. The bank fraud statute is broad and includes any scheme to defraud a federally insured financial institution. *United States v. Jimenez*, 513 F.3d 62 (3d Cir. 2008). Where the victim is not a bank and the fraud does not threaten the financial integrity of a federally insured institution, the statute does not apply. *United States v. Blackmon*, 839 F.2d 900 (2d Cir. 1988).

Bank fraud requires only that the defendant put the bank at the risk of loss, not that the bank actually suffer a loss. It is not a defense to the charge that a depositor colluded with a bank officer to commit bank fraud. It is the financial institution itself—not its officers or agents—that is the victim of the fraud protected under § 1344. *United States v. Waldroop*, 431 F.3d 736, 742 (10th Cir. 2005); *United States v. Saks*, 964 F.2d 1514 (5th Cir. 1992). Thus, even if a bank officer knew of the true nature of the fraudulent transactions, the banking institution could nonetheless be defrauded. *United States v. Rackley*, 986 F.2d 1357 (10th Cir.), *cert. denied*, 510 U.S. 860 (1993).

Likewise, repayment may not absolve the defendant of liability. A jury instruction that "[a]ctual repayment to the bank may negate an intent to defraud the bank only if coupled with other evidence that likewise negates an intent to defraud," was upheld on the basis that it appropriately focuses the jury's attention on the defendant's intent at the time of the charged conduct. *Jimenez*, 513 F.3d at 75 (citing *United States v. Abboud*, 438 F.3d 554, 594 (6th Cir.), *cert. denied*, 127 S. Ct. 446 (2006)).

For an instructive discussion of the most common types of fraudulent schemes engaged in by corporate commercial enterprises to defraud banks, see *United States v. RW Professional Leasing Services Corp.*, 452 F. Supp. 2d 159 (E.D.N.Y. 2006). The opinion provides a useful factual description of the multiple schemes engaged in by the corporate defendant. For example, one common scheme included disguising unsecured loans as loans secured by the sale and leaseback of new equipment. This was accomplished by submitting phony invoices to the bank purporting to show the borrower's purchase of new equipment from the company that could be used as collateral to secure the loans under the lease agreements. In fact, the purchased equipment was not new and the sale and leaseback agreements were phony and prepared without the knowledge or consent of the borrower.

As corporations such as Enron and WorldCom experienced corporate failures, chief corporate executives defended based on the consent and approval of their actions by the board of directors. In one case, the chief executive officers of a bank disclosed their actions to the bank's directors and obtained director approval. The Ninth Circuit in an unpublished decision, *United States v. Whitmore*, 35 Fed. Appx. 307 (9th Cir.), *cert. denied*, 123 U.S. 659 (2002), rejected the defense, citing well-established precedent that the "board's knowledge, ratification and consent are not per se defenses to the charge of [bank fraud] … [r]eview by the board is a particularly dubious basis for exculpating the [defendant where] the evidence showed that [the defendant] was the moving force behind the board of directors." *United States v. Unruh*, 855 F.2d 1363, 1368 (9th Cir.) *cert. den.*, 488 U.S. 974 (1989).

E. Bribery and Illegal Gratuities

Prosecutors have a wide statutory arsenal to prosecute official corruption. Corruption is frequently charged under one of three statutes that have some overlap: Bribery of Public Officials and Witnesses, 18 U.S.C. § 201; the Hobbs Act, 18 U.S.C. § 1951; and the Travel Act, 18 U.S.C. § 1952. The most frequently used statute is § 201. This statute focuses on prohibiting conduct seeking preferential treatment from public officials and prohibiting public officials from using their office for private gain. Bribery under § 201(b) requires proof that something of value was given, offered, or promised to a federal public official corruptly to influence an official act. The crime requires a "quid pro quo," a payment in exchange for influence. The value of that influence is determined subjectively by the importance attached by the defendant. Bribery is always forward-looking, a thing of value being given in exchange for being influenced.

Illegal gratuities are punished under § 201(c). The gratuity statute does not require a quid pro quo. Unlike bribery, "it may constitute merely a reward for some future act that the public official will take, or for a past act he has already taken." *United States v. Sun-Diamond Growers of Cal.*, 526 U.S. 398, 405 (1999). The payment can be a mere "thank you" for a past act or to create a pool of "good will" for the future; there is no requirement that the public official be influenced in any way.

Perhaps one of the more colorful cases under the statute involved the guilty plea in 2005 of Congressman Randy "Duke" Cunningham. Cunningham was a member of the powerful House Appropriations Committee from 1998 to 2005. He used that position to solicit bribes from defense contractors in exchange for the award of lucrative defense contracts. Cunningham delivered a "bribe menu," written on congressional stationary, to the president of MZM, Inc., which delineated what each million dollars in contracts would require in terms of bribe payments. As the quid pro quo, in exchange for approximately $160 million in Pentagon contracts, MZM gave Cunningham more than $1 million in payments and gifts, including money to pay off his mortgage, free travel on a charter jet, a Rolls-Royce, antique furnishings, and the cost of his daughter's birthday party.

However, not every act of a public official constitutes an "official act" sufficient to create liability under the statute. In *United States v. Muntain*, 610 F.2d 964, 967-8 (D.C.Cir. 1979), the court found that the defendant Muntain, an Assistant to the Secretary for Labor Relations at the Department of Housing and Urban Development (HUD), had not accepted illegal gratuities for an official act when he was compensated by private persons for selling private auto insurance schemes to labor unions with whose leaders he also dealt on official HUD business.

The court rejected the government's argument that official acts "encompass any acts within the range of an official's public duties," which the government argued included Muntain's meetings with labor union officials. As the promotion of group auto insurance was not a matter that "could be brought before Muntain—or, for that matter, anyone else at HUD—in an official capacity," there was no danger that the gratuities received could have induced Muntain "to act improperly in deciding a HUD-related matter." Accord; *United States v. Valdes,* 437 F.3d 1276 (D.C.Cir. 2006).

However, the courts have applied the brakes to FBI seizures in congressional investigations. Congressman William Jefferson was charged with, among other crimes, soliciting bribes from companies seeking to benefit from his African connections in the telecommunications business. To prove his involvement with these companies, the FBI obtained search warrants to search his congressional office. In *United States v. Rayburn House Office Building*, 497 F.3d 654 (2d Cir.), *cert. denied*, 128 S. Ct. 1738 (2008), the court held that under the Speech and Debate Clause, the FBI is barred from searching a location containing legislative materials without the member's consent.[22] This limitation increases the pressure to search the premises and records of the companies doing business with corrupt politicians.

Apparently, Congress is concerned that the current legislative tools are not adequate. A new public corruption bill, the Public Corruption Prosecution Improvements Act of 2011, is currently pending approval. This recent legislative development, which also significantly affects mail and wire fraud, bribery, and illegal gratuities statutes, is discussed in greater detail in Chapter 10.

F. Program Fraud

The federal bribery statute, 18 U.S.C. § 666, prohibits defrauding organizations that "receive, in any one year period, benefits in excess of $10,000 under a federal program." § 666(b). Section 666 has become a very effective tool in prosecuting health care fraud. Because of the complexity of the criminal statutes under the Medicare and Medicaid statutes, § 666 offers a more direct route to conviction for prosecutors.

---

22. *See* David F. DuMouchel, George B. Donnini & Joseph E. Richotte, *Call the Question: Is Capitol Hill A Warrant-Free Zone Post*-Rayburn?, *in* WHITE COLLAR CRIME 2008, at G-1 (ABA Criminal Justice Section & the Ctr. for Cont. Legal Ed. 2008).

That route was further facilitated by the Supreme Court's decision in *Fisher v. United States*, 529 U.S. 667 (2000), finding that the statute applied to the role and regulated status of hospitals as health care providers and beneficiaries under the Medicare program within the meaning of the statute. The decision is immensely significant in expanding the potential criminal exposure of companies doing business with hospitals. A lesser charge of fraud or commercial bribery may be elevated to the more serious offense of federal program fraud even though the hospital is not a federal agency but merely a recipient of federal funds.

The decision has also become the eye of the storm in the new debate over whether the receipt of federal funding should legally result in the "federalization" of fraudulent criminal behavior. Corporate defendants argue that the prosecution is pushing the envelope in charging cases under this section. For a more detailed understanding of the debate, see Justice Thomas's dissent in the *Fisher* decision, *id.* at 682.

For a discussion of civil fraud causes of action and penalties under the False Claims Act and the Fraud Enforcement and Recovery Act, refer to Chapter 10.

G. Money Laundering

Sections 1956 and 1957 of Title 18, the money laundering statutes, target financial transactions involving the proceeds of unlawful activities. The statutes also cover currency-reporting violations involving proceeds of unlawful activity "knowing that the transaction is designed in whole or in part . . . to avoid a transaction reporting requirement under State or Federal law."[23] More specifically, § 1957(a) prohibits knowingly engaging or attempting to engage in monetary transactions involving "criminally derived property that is of a value greater than ten thousand dollars and is derived from specified unlawful activity [SUA]."

Section 1956 (a)(1) prohibits domestic money laundering. Section 1956(a)(2) prohibits international money laundering, and § 1956(a)(3) is designed for government sting operations using government property represented to be proceeds of a SUA.

The most common prosecution is under § 1956(a)(1), and the essential elements include (1) the defendant took part in the financial transaction; (2) the defendant knew that the property involved in the transaction involved the proceeds of an illegal activity; (3) the property involved was in fact the proceeds of a SUA; and (4) the defendant knew that the transaction was designed in whole or in part to conceal or disguise the nature, source, location, ownership, or control of the illegal proceeds.

A "specified unlawful activity" or SUA is defined as part of a list of offenses in § 1961(1) "racketeering activity" and certain Title 31 offenses. The list is broad, including everything from murder, kidnapping, and drug transactions to mail fraud and computer fraud. The same SUA definition is included in § 1957. However, the crime of money laundering must be a crime distinct from the SUA by which the money is

23. 18 U.S.C. § 1956(a)(1)(B).

obtained. The money laundering statute is not merely an additional criminal penalty for the same conduct. It is a separate prohibition of processing the fruits of the crime or a completed phase of an ongoing offense. *United States v. Abuhouran*, 162 F.3d 230 (3d Cir. 1998). This is known as the doctrine of merger under the money laundering statute, that is, the question whether the money laundering statute is being used to criminalize the very same conduct as the predicate unlawful activity.

In *United States v. Santos*, 553 U.S. 507 (2008), the Supreme Court, in a 5-4 decision, interpreted the meaning of the word "proceeds." To avoid mere criminalization of the underlying SUA, the Court held that "proceeds" under § 1956 includes only the profits, not the "total amount brought in" or gross receipts, from the SUA to "ensure that the severe money laundering penalties will be imposed only for the removal of profits from criminal activity, which permit the leveraging of one criminal activity to the next." Subsequently, Congress passed the Fraud Enforcement and Recovery Act of 2009 (FERA), rejecting the Court's decision and defining "proceeds" to now include the gross receipts of an unlawful activity, not just the profits garnered from such activity.[24]

In another decision aimed at clarifying statutory ambiguity, *Cuellar v. United States*, 553 U.S. 550 (2008), the Court addressed the complex *mens rea* requirement under § 1956. The case involved an attempt to transport illicit funds across an international border. In order to understand the potential significance of this decision, it is important to understand the dramatic increase of the incidences of money laundering in the global context.

According to the interagency *Money Laundering Threat Assessment Report* issued in 2005,[25] the use of international trade by corporations and organizations to disguise the transfer of funds has burgeoned. These new trade-based money laundering schemes are difficult to monitor because of technological advances. For example, "stored value cards," like prepaid cash or phone service cards, provide an easy means to store and access cash value without the use of an identifiable bank account. Card management firms use "pooled accounts" opened in the name of a company or organization without verification of cardholder identity.

These cases have now become even more difficult to prosecute in light of the Court's interpretation of the *mens rea* requirement under the statute in *Cuellar*. There, a jury convicted the defendant of attempting to transport illicit funds across the border, knowing that the transportation was "designed ... to conceal or disguise the nature, the location, the source, the ownership, or the control of the proceeds of [SUA]" under § 1956(a)(1)(B)(i).

---

24. According to Section 1956 (c)(9), the term "proceeds" means any property derived from or obtained or retained, directly or indirectly, through some form of unlawful activity, including the gross receipts of such activity.

25. Available at http://www.ustreas.gov/press/releases/reports/js3077_01112005_MLTA.pdf.

The Court reversed the conviction, finding that evidentiary proof of "design" requires that the defendant knows that the *purpose* of transporting the funds is to conceal or disguise the attributes of the funds described in the statute (nature, location, source, etc.). It is not enough that the secretive aspects of the transportation were employed to *facilitate* the transportation; the evidence must show that secrecy was the *purpose* of the transportation. In other words, moving "dirty money" across international borders in a secretive manner is not enough. The defendant must be moving the money with the intent of concealing source, location, ownership, or control of the funds.

H. Securities Fraud

There is an overlap between civil and criminal law in the area of securities fraud, subjecting a violator to civil and criminal penalties for the same conduct. Although there is an array of federal statutes to prosecute securities fraud, most prosecutions are brought under the Securities Act of 1933 and the Securities and Exchange Act of 1934.[26] Prosecutions for securities fraud have concentrated on violations of Section 17(a) under the 1933 Act and Sections 10(b) and 10(b)(5) under the 1934 Act. In recent years, the focus has been primarily on abuses occasioned by insider trading.

Insider trading generally refers to the purchase, sale, or transfer of securities using material, nonpublic information in breach of fiduciary duty or a similar duty of trust and confidence. While not specifically defined by any statute, there are two types of inside information that may serve as the basis for an insider trading prosecution.

One type is information that generally concerns the internal business affairs of the company whose stock is being traded, such as unreleased facts about earnings, dividends (e.g., *Dirks v. United States*, 463 U.S. 646 (1983) (liability of the "tippee")), or other factors affecting the stock value. Such was the stock trading scandal of ImClone and Martha Stewart, involving the knowledge that the Food and Drug Administration was unlikely to approve a new drug developed by the company. The other kind of inside information is "market" information, which relates to the existence of the market potential for the sale of company securities rather than to the intrinsic value of the securities themselves (e.g., *Chiarella v. United States*, 445 U.S. 222 (1980) (breach of corporate fiduciary duties by insiders)).

The seminal corporate insider trading case is *Securities and Exchange Commission v. Texas Gulf Sulphur Co.*, 401 F.2d 833 (2d Cir. 1968). That case reiterated that companies are required to behave according to certain fairness principles intrinsic in the capital market system. There is "an expectation of the securities marketplace that investors trading on impersonal exchanges have relatively equal access to material

---

26. For a discussion of the recent changes to the SEC Manual regarding disposition by plea agreement or other negotiating opportunities involving securities prosecutions, see Chapter 6.

information." The progeny of cases following *Texas Gulf Sulphur* address who is an insider, when it is necessary to disclose otherwise nonpublic information, and whether the failure to disclose was material. Materiality of information is a critical component.

Examples of individual insiders include officers, directors, and controlling shareholders. Historically, the direct consequences of criminal prosecution for securities fraud usually affect the accused individuals as opposed to the company. However, it is important to emphasize that the collateral consequences of prosecution, including the economic impact on corporate stock following the initiation of an investigation and following a conviction, may be substantial to the corporation. Depending on the facts and circumstances, the corporation may truly be characterized as a victim, giving rise to a cause of action against the offending officers, directors, employees, and other third parties.

The Dodd-Frank Wall Street Reform and Consumer Protection Act of 2010 (Reform Act) has expanded the definition of insider trading. Compared to the existing insider trading federal code provision, 7 U.S.C. § 13(e), the prohibitions of Section 746 under the Reform Act are broader and vaguer. The existing provision sets forth two types of insider trading. The first, 7 U.S.C. § 13(e)(1), is limited to those who are insiders and who "willfully and knowingly" trade upon or disclose "any material nonpublic information obtained through special access related to the performance of such duties." The second, 7 U.S.C. § 13(e)(2), applies to "any person" but is limited to "willfully and knowingly" trading upon the basis of any "material nonpublic information that such person knows was obtained in violation of paragraph (1) from [an insider]."

Section 746 broadens the criminal insider trading prohibition already in the U.S. Code. First, it expands the application of the insider trading prohibition to any employees or agents of the federal government and any individual who uses information imparted by such employees or agents. Second, it broadens the definition of insider information to include "information that may affect or tend to affect the price of any commodity in interstate commerce, or for future delivery, or any swap, and which information has not been disseminated by the department or agency of the Federal Government holding or creating the information in a manner which makes it generally available to the trading public. . ." Third, it creates a "Theft of Nonpublic Information" offense, which makes it criminal to "steal, convert, or misappropriate" nonpublic information "where such person knows, or acts in reckless disregard of the fact, that such information" is nonpublic. This offense will also be enforced under 7 U.S.C. § 13(a)(5).

The issue of insider trading has received considerable attention in the courts over the last 30 years, *see, e.g.*, *Chiarella v. United States*, 445 U.S. 222 (1980) (breach of corporate fiduciary duties by insiders); *Dirks v. United States*, 463 U.S. 646 (1983) (liability of the "tippee"); *United States v. O'Hagan*, 521 U.S. 642 (1997) (the use of confidential information as a breach of fiduciary duty); and, more recently, *SEC v. Zandford*, 535 U.S. 813 (2002) (involving misappropriation of client property). The prosecutive trend, seen by many as singularly unfair, is not to charge the insider trading offense but instead to prosecute the attempt to lie and cover it up. These crimes have been labeled "process crimes" and are discussed later in this chapter. The homemaker turned billionaire mogul, Martha Stewart, is the most recent example. The insider information she received one day before it was released publicly saved her approximately $51,000 in trading losses. Never actually charged with a securities offense, because few prosecutors would ever waste office resources in an effort to prosecute this kind of insider trading case, she was sentenced on charges of obstruction of justice and lying to investigators. The punishment included five months in jail, five months on home detention, and a fine. However, the out-of-court, or collateral, consequences to Stewart and her publicly traded company involved the loss of millions of dollars. Many believe that the resulting punishment in the marketplace in response to a criminal indictment, particularly where a civil resolution of the securities issue was considered more appropriate, simply was too onerous and did not fit the crime.

To further fortify the antifraud provisions, the Reform Act expanded the application of Section 10(b) and Rule 10b-5 to include extraterritorial misconduct. In 2010, the Supreme Court ruled in *Morrison v. National Bank Ltd.*, 130 S. Ct. 2869 (2010), that Section 10(b) and Rule 10b-5 applied "only in connection with a purchase or sale of a security listed on an American stock exchange, and the purchase or sale of any other security in the United States." In response to the court's decision, Congress added to the Reform Act Section 929O(b) which applies the antifraud provisions extraterritorially to: "(1) conduct within the United States that constitutes significant steps in furtherance of the violation, even if the securities transaction occurs outside the United States and involves only foreign investors; or (2) conduct occurring outside the United States that has a foreseeable substantial effect within the United States."

The Reform Act also expands the civil enforcement penalties under the securities laws for retaliation against whistleblowers passed as part of SOX, 18 U.S.C. § 1514A.[27] The new whistleblower provisions of the Act are addressed in greater detail in Chapter 10.

SOX also added a new section to the prosecutive arsenal in the specific area of securities fraud, 18 U.S.C. § 1348. This statute, in conformity with existing criminal statutes under the 1933 and 1934 securities acts, criminalizes a scheme or artifice to defraud anyone "in connection with any security" or a scheme to obtain by false or fraudulent pretenses "any money or property in connection with the purchase or sale of any security." In the past, most cases were simply charged under the mail and wire fraud statutes for obvious reasons of simplicity in prosecution. Section 1348, styled in the same statutory language as the mail and wire fraud statutes, is intended to offer the same ease of prosecution when compared with the more complex securities statutes.

Additionally, the Fraud Enforcement and Recovery Act of 2009 (FERA) amends the definition of securities fraud under 18 U.S.C. § 1348 to include fraud related to

27. Section 806 of the Sarbanes Oxley Act.

commodities futures and options in addition to the existing category of registered securities under the Securities Exchange Act of 1934.

There are few reported cases under §1348 and none relating to organizational conduct. In *United States v. Motz*, 652 F. Supp. 284 (E.D.N.Y. 2009) the corporate broker–dealer was defunct by the time of the indictment. In *United States v. Mahaffy*, 499 F. Supp. 2d 291 (E.D.N.Y. 2007), the defendants were all acquitted under the §1348 charge. In another, the court dismissed the counts. Finally, in a third case, *United States v. Vought*, 2006 WL 1662882 (D. Conn. 2006), the court, in an unpublished opinion, noted the close similarity between §1348 and the bank fraud statute under §1344 in seeking guidance in construing the elements of proof. The case, however, failed to resolve the question of whether the government was required to prove under §1348 that the scheme actually subjected a person to a risk of loss. In short, the extent to which newly enacted §1348 will be utilized as the favored prosecutive tool in securities cases remains relatively untested.

Finally, it is significant that SOX imposes obligations on the chief executive officer and the chief financial officer to certify that the financial reports of the issuer report fairly, in all material respects, the financial condition and results of operations of the issuer under the recently enacted § 1350. The penalties are stiff. A knowing violation carries a maximum incarceratory penalty of 10 years and a $1 million fine and a willful violation carries a 20-year maximum penalty and a $5 million fine.

I. Corporate Tax Fraud

Section 9-28.400 of the U.S. Attorneys Manual (USAM), entitled "Principles of Federal Prosecution of Business Organizations," issued by the Department of Justice in 2008,[28] provides: "[The] Tax Division has a strong preference for prosecuting responsible individuals, rather than entities, for corporate tax offenses." There are many reasons for that policy decision. The most obvious, illustrated by the statistics at the beginning of this chapter, are the facts that IRS audits of big companies are practically nonexistent and almost one-third of the audits of small to midsized companies are deemed nonproductive. In short, there are not enough resources to take on criminal tax prosecutions of companies.

Second, it is easier to target and convict an individual. Third, most prosecutors avoid tax statutes either because of general unfamiliarity or because the "methods of proof" that must be employed to establish criminal liability are somewhat complicated and jurors tend to get lost in the jury instructions. Prosecutors generally take the path of least resistance to conviction, meaning that the most frequently used statutes in the prosecutive arsenal will be employed.

28. Appendix C. USAM at http://www.justice.gov/opa/documents/corp-charging-guidelines.pdf. The prior memoranda, which are superseded by these provisions of the USAM, were issued by Deputy U.S. Attorneys General Mark Filip (August 2008), Paul J. McNulty (December 2006), Larry Thompson (January 2003), and Eric Holder (June 1999).

Tax offenses are located in Title 26 of the U.S. Code. Prosecutors must seek special permission from the Tax Division at the DOJ to initiate a separate "tax grand jury" to initiate a tax prosecution. Additionally, once a defendant is indicted for a tax offense, the U.S. Attorney's Office must seek permission to dispose of a tax count by plea agreement or by dismissal. The somewhat bureaucratic inflexibility is yet another reason that prosecutors tend to shy away from charging tax offenses.

On the other hand, tax offenses can be a very useful trial strategy when added as a count to the indictment. The practice is informally referred to as "stacking" counts. If a prosecutor is concerned about the strength of the evidence on certain counts, a tax count can be used to convince the jury that if the defendant lied about its taxes, it probably has lied or is lying about everything else.

One interesting case in this area deals with the liability of corporate tax preparation firms and the misconduct of tax accountants seeking to provide illegal tax benefits to clients in an effort to retain business. In *United States v. Shortt Accountancy Corp.*, 785 F.2d 1448 (9th Cir. 1986), the accounting corporation was convicted under 26 U.S.C. § 7206(1), which penalizes subscribing to a false and fraudulent tax return. In *Shortt,* the accounting corporation, through its chief operating officer, fraudulently structured certain investments to appear as if they were made before certain changes in the law, resulting in undeserved tax benefits for its clients. The corporation claimed that it could not be prosecuted under § 7206(1) because the clients were apparently unaware that they had subscribed to a false return.

In rejecting the argument, the court concluded that § 7206(1) was in the nature of a perjury statute, and therefore anyone who makes a false return could be prosecuted under this section. To hold otherwise would permit the accountant to escape liability "by arranging for an innocent employee to complete the proscribed act of subscribing a false return."

J. "Process Crimes"

Process crimes include perjury (18 U.S.C. §§ 1621 and 1623) and obstruction of justice (18 U.S.C. §§ 1501 *et seq.*). Newly enacted § 1519 was the congressional SOX response to the Arthur Andersen shredding episode in the Enron investigation. This obstruction statute is aimed directly at organizational attempts to destroy, alter, or falsify records and other evidence or otherwise cover up in an attempt to impair or impede an investigation. Section 1520 is another SOX follow-up aimed directly at auditors and organizations, requiring the maintenance of audit records in conformity with the requirements of the securities acts for a period of five years. Unlawful destruction of such records now is a criminal offense.

In terms of organizational or corporate prosecution, there is not much to report under the perjury statutes and that will not be a focus of this discussion. However, several important cases in the organizational context have been recently prosecuted under § 1519. In *United States v. Ionia Management S.A.*, 526 F. Supp. 2d 319, 323

(D. Conn. 2007), the court rejected the argument that the actions of its employee to obstruct a federal investigation could not be imputed to the employer-company. The court reaffirmed the principle that an agent need not have conferred any actual benefit to the employer; it is sufficient if there was an intent, at least in part, to benefit the employer. The following jury instruction was incorporated into the trial instructions:

> If you find that the agent was acting within the scope of the employment, the fact that the agent's act was illegal, contrary to his employer's instructions, or against the corporation's policies will not relieve the corporation of responsibility for it. However, you may consider the fact that the agent disobeyed or violated company policy in determining whether the agent intended to benefit the corporation, or was acting within his authority.[29]

A critical aspect of this decision distinguishes § 1519 from other obstruction statutes such as § 1505 and § 1512. The court observed that § 1519, referred to euphemistically as the "antishredding" provision, is meant to apply broadly to any acts to destroy or fabricate physical evidence so long as they are done with an "intent to obstruct" an investigation. However, unlike the other obstruction statutes, the terminology does not require the defendant to be aware of a federal proceeding, or even that a proceeding is actually pending. The decision signals a clear departure from the *Aguilar* nexus requirement between the act of obstruction and knowledge of the existence of a pending federal proceeding. To satisfy that requirement, the defendant's conduct must "have a relationship in time, causation, or logic with the judicial proceedings." In other words, "the endeavor must have the natural and probable effect of interfering with the due administration of justice." *United States v. Aguilar*, 515 U.S. 593 (1995).

The case law as applied to § 1512 and its various subsections is inconsistent. For example, the accounting firm Arthur Andersen was charged with obstruction under § 1512(b)(2), which required proof of the *Aguilar* nexus. However, some courts have been unwilling to extend the nexus requirement applicable to that section to other subsections within the same statutory provision, such as § 1512(b)(3). *See United States v. Rhonda*, 455 F.3d 1273 (11th Cir. 2006).

Section 1512(c) was added to the statute as part of the SOX revisions. Conviction under § 1512(c)(1) requires proof that evidence is destroyed "with the intent to impair the object's integrity or availability for use in an official proceeding." Interpreting this provision in *Arthur Andersen v. United States,* 544 U.S. 696, 707-08 (2005), which involved document shredding, the Supreme Court concluded that it is "one thing to say that a proceeding 'need not be pending or about to be instituted at the time of the offense,' and quite another to say a proceeding need not even be foreseen."

---

29. Leonard B. Sand, et al., Modern Federal Jury Instructions—Criminal ¶ 2.01, Instr. 2-7 (2007).

This language requiring the element of foreseeability appears to be a departure from the stricter *Aguilar* standard. However, in *United States v. Reich*, 479 F.3d 179 (2d Cir. 2007), involving a prosecution under 18 U.S.C. § 1512(c)(2) which subjects to criminal liability one who corruptly obstructs, influences, or impedes any official proceeding or attempts to do so, the court held that the *Aguilar* nexus test does apply to the application of this subsection.

Chapter **4**

CONSTITUTIONAL PERSPECTIVES
FEW RIGHTS AND EVEN FEWER PRIVILEGES

This chapter addresses the status of corporations and other business organizations under the Fourth, Fifth, and Sixth Amendments to the U.S. Constitution. Here, the legal definition of a corporation as a "person" shrinks back into its more fictional existence; meaning that business organizations may share equally with individual persons in terms of exposure to criminal liability but they do not share equally in the same constitutional protections.

The Supreme Court's decision in *Hale v. Henkel*, 201 U.S. 43 (1906), established both the logic and the basic ground rules for the development of corporate and organizational constitutional rights and it remains the law today. There, the Court held that a corporation could assert the constitutional protections of the Fourth Amendment to prevent the government from engaging in unreasonable searches and seizures of its records but that it could not assert the protections of the Fifth Amendment and refuse compelled production of the same records. No, to a Fifth Amendment privilege against compulsory self-incrimination and yes, to a Fourth Amendment privilege against unreasonable searches and seizures.

Arguably, the case makes some sense in economic terms. A corporate assertion of the privilege against self-incrimination could have the impact of frustrating the government's need to prosecute corporate unlawful economic activity. However, because the Fourth Amendment is aimed at unreasonable government intrusions, allowing a corporation a Fourth Amendment privilege would not necessarily insulate the company from prosecution. In any case, in those instances where the Fourth Amendment has provided too much protection, the courts have created exceptions, such as the administrative search doctrine and others, to dilute the scope of protection.

I. The Fifth Amendment

Corporations have no Fifth Amendment privilege against compulsory self-incrimination. But incorporation is not the only form of business organization. No matter; other forms of business organizations have no such constitutional protection either. In *United States v. White*, 322 U.S. 694, 700–01 (1944), the Supreme Court upheld a records subpoena demanding the production of union records. The Court held that "the power to compel the production of the records of any organization, whether it be incorporated or not, arises out of the inherent and necessary power of the federal and state governments to enforce their laws." Bottom line: The Fifth Amendment's protection applies only to natural individuals acting in their own private capacity and in some cases as a sole proprietor, but not to an organization.

A. Defining "Organization"

The Court did provide a definition for the term "organization": "The test . . . is whether one can fairly say under all circumstances that a particular type of organization has a character so impersonal in the scope of its membership and activities that it cannot be said to embody or represent the purely private or personal interests of its constituents, but rather to embody their common or group interests only." Bottom line: If the organization satisfies this definition, organizational records must be produced even if they are personally incriminating to the membership.

The definition of organization has been used liberally in barring the assertion of the privilege against self-incrimination by other noncorporate forms of business organizations. In *Bellis v. United States*, 417 U.S. 85, 92–93 (1974), the Court upheld a subpoena issued to a three-person law firm. The Court concluded that "groups" cannot assert the privilege if they are "relatively well organized and structured, and not merely a loose, informal association of individuals. It must maintain a distinct set of organizational records, and recognize rights in its members of control and access to them." Bottom line: Size does not matter. If it looks like a duck and quacks like a duck. . . .

B. "John Doe" Act of Production Immunity

Based on the decision in *Fisher v. United States*, 425 U.S. 391 (1976), even in the case of a sole proprietorship, the contents of voluntarily prepared documents are not protected. However, in the case of a sole proprietor or other records custodian, an assertion of privilege might be permissible where the act of production may incriminate the sole proprietor or individual custodian. This is known as the Act of Production Doctrine. Under this doctrine, the Court recognized that compliance with a subpoena has communicative aspects of its own—acknowledgement of the existence of the documents; acknowledgement of possession and control; and potential authentication by identification. But in each case, the court remains obliged to determine whether that communication is both "testimonial" and "incriminating."

In *United States v. Doe*, 465 U.S. 605 (1984), involving a grand jury subpoena, the court found that the act of producing the records, in itself, would involve testimonial incrimination. The Court noted that immunizing the act of production could solve the problem. As a result, the government has fashioned an informal type of letter immunity referred to as "John Doe Immunity." A custodian will receive an informal letter from the government "immunizing" the act of production to facilitate production without a court battle. Notably, the immunity applies only to the act of production, not to the contents of the documents produced.

C. Foregone Conclusion Doctrine

The Court was quick to carve out an exception to the doctrine by creating the "foregone conclusion" standard. Where the existence and location of the documents are a "foregone conclusion" and the act of production adds little or nothing to the sum total of the government's information that the custodian has the records, "no constitutional rights are touched." Bottom line: The act of production doctrine does not apply where (1) the existence, possession, and authentication of the records are a foregone conclusion; or (2) the act of production, although testimonial in nature, does not present a realistic potential for incrimination.

Subsequently, in *Braswell v. United States*, 487 U.S. 99 (1988), involving a subpoena for records of a closely held corporation, the Court held that the records had to be produced. However, again recognizing that the act of production might tend to incriminate the individual custodian, the Court prohibited the government from making any evidentiary use of the individual custodian's act on behalf of the corporation against that individual in a subsequent prosecution. Bottom line: The government is entitled to the records but cannot introduce evidence related to the act of production against the individual custodian in a subsequent prosecution of that individual.

In conclusion, corporations and other business organizations do not possess a Fifth Amendment privilege against compulsory self-incrimination. A sole proprietor or other records custodian may assert the privilege where the act of production would tend to incriminate that individual in a subsequent prosecution.

The application of the *Fisher* foregone conclusion doctrine was rejected in *United States v. Hubbell*, 530 U.S. 27 (2000), where the government had issued a subpoena requesting 11 categories of business records that ultimately generated the production of over 13,000 pages of documents. The Court reasoned that given the breadth of the 11 categories, the nature of the demanded business information, and the number of records, the foregone conclusion doctrine did not apply to negate the protection under the act of production doctrine. Bottom line: Certain accounting and financial records, such as tax returns and accountant's workpapers, will probably fit under the foregone conclusion doctrine, whereas general demands for business records dealing with business operations and transactions, unless required by law to be kept, will not.

D. Other Exceptions

In *Shapiro v. United States*, 335 U.S. 1 (1948), the Supreme Court held that the Fifth Amendment provides no protection where individuals engage in a regulated business and are required to make and keep records available for inspection by public officials. This is known as the required records exception.

Transferring documents to an independent professional to avoid the reach of a subpoena also does not work. *Couch v. United States*, 409 U.S. 322 (1973). In *Couch*, the taxpayer delivered the records to her accountants to prepare her tax returns and the IRS subsequently issued a subpoena for the records to her accountants. In *Fisher*, the IRS directed a summons to a lawyer in possession of the records from a client seeking legal advice. In both cases, the clients asserted the protection of the privilege and in both cases, the Supreme Court rejected the argument because the persons compelled to produce the documents were not the clients but the professionals in possession of the documents.

What about the other rights under the Fifth Amendment? The Supreme Court has assumed, without actually deciding, that the Double Jeopardy Clause does apply to corporations. The Indictment Clause's applicability to corporations has yet to be decided by the Supreme Court. However, the two lower court decisions on the issue concluded that a corporation does not have to be charged by indictment and that the Fifth Amendment does not apply. *United States v. Yellow Freight Sys., Inc.*, 637 F.2d 1248 (9th Cir.), *cert. denied*, 454 U.S. 815 (1981); *United States v. Armored Transp., Inc.*, 629 F.2d 1313 (9th Cir.), *cert. denied*, 450 U.S. 965 (1981). *In dicta, United States v. Fitapelli*, 786 F.2d 1461 (11th Cir. 1986).

II. The Fourth Amendment

Corporations have Fourth Amendment protection against unreasonable searches and seizures. However, the Supreme Court has made it clear that corporate rights are not coextensive with individual rights under the Fourth Amendment. In *United States v. Morton Salt*, 338 U.S. 632, 652 (1950), the Court stated: "[C]orporations can claim no equality with individuals in the enjoyment of a right to privacy."

Here, we consider two aspects of Fourth Amendment protection: the warrant requirement to search commercial premises and the legitimacy of government-issued subpoenas for the production of corporate books and records, most commonly in connection with a grand jury proceeding. In terms of criminal investigations, the government has two choices for collecting evidence from a commercial entity: It can do so through the execution of a search warrant at the commercial premises, usually done to avoid destruction of records and/or other incriminating evidence, or by grand jury subpoena, where production is typically voluminous and the element of surprise is not an issue.

A. The Warrant Requirement: Regulatory and Administrative Search Exception

In *See v. City of Seattle*, 387 U.S. 541 (1967), the Court held that the warrant requirement of the Fourth Amendment applied to government searches of business property. That declaration, however, was followed by a series of cases creating exceptions to the warrant requirement in the business context.

The Court reiterated that the Fourth Amendment applies to regulatory searches of business premises in *Camara v. Municipal Court*, 387 U.S. 523 (1967). However, unlike a search conducted as part of a criminal investigation, regulatory searches require a different and lesser standard of probable cause. Instead, *Camara* formulates a balancing test to determine whether a particular inspection is reasonable, that is, weighing the "need to search against the invasion which the search entails . . . in meeting the reasonable goals of code enforcement." *Id.* at 535. Probable cause may still be found to exist without a "particularized showing" of reason to believe that an instrumentality of a crime or other evidence is at the place to be searched. As long as the agency follows an administrative scheme that provides search criteria to protect against arbitrariness in selection and procedure for the search, the Fourth Amendment is satisfied. This legal precedent has firmly survived the test of time. *See, e.g.*, *Nasca v. Town of Brookhaven*, 2008 WL 4426906 (E.D.N.Y. 2008).

In some instances, the courts have exempted regulatory searches from the warrant requirement altogether. For example, a warrant may be required for routine fire department and Occupational Safety and Health Administration (OSHA) inspections (*Marshall v. Barlow*, 436 U.S. 307 (1978)), but not for inspections of liquor licensees (*Colonnade Catering Corp. v. United States*, 397 U.S. 72 (1970)), licensed firearms dealers (*United States v. Biswell*, 406 U.S. 311 (1972)), and mining operations (*Donovan v. Dewey*, 452 U.S. 594 (1981)). The logic behind the warrant exception was stated in *Donovan*: "[I]t is the pervasiveness and regularity of federal regulation that ultimately determines whether a warrant is necessary to render an inspection program reasonable under the Fourth Amendment."

Finally, in *New York v. Berger*, 482 U.S. 691 (1987), the Court upheld the warrantless search of an automobile junkyard's books and records because the operation was deemed a "pervasively regulated business." *Id.* at 704–05. The Court mandated three criteria for a statutory scheme permitting warrantless inspections of commercial property to pass constitutional muster: (1) there is a substantial governmental interest; (2) warrantless entry is required to avoid alerting business owners or managers; and (3) the inspection program is reasonable as to time, place, and scope.

Note that the failure of a regulatory agency to follow its own internal rules in obtaining evidence may also be excused as a basis for suppressing evidence. In *United States v. Caceres*, 440 U.S. 741, 742 (1979),[1] the Supreme Court explained that "a court has a duty to enforce an agency regulation [only] when compliance with the regulation is mandated by the Constitution or federal law."

B. Overly Broad Document Subpoenas

Starting with the decision in *Haas v. Henkel*, 216 U.S. 462 (1910), the Court recognized that "an order for the production of books and papers" could constitute an unreasonable search and seizure. The key issue noted by the Court was whether the subpoena *duces tecum* was "far too sweeping in its terms to be regarded as reasonable." However, there was no requirement of probable cause in connection with the issuance of a subpoena.

Later, in *Silverthorne Lumber Co. v. United States*, 251 U.S. 385 (1920), the government unlawfully searched a corporation's offices and was ordered by the court to return the seized documents. Thereafter, the government issued a subpoena for the same records, and the Supreme Court sternly rejected the government's argument that the subpoena was lawful. It held that the "rights of a corporation against unlawful search and seizure are to be protected even if the same result might have been achieved in a lawful way." A string of similar cases followed. *Accord, Fed. Trade Comm'n v. Am. Tobacco Co.*, 264 U.S. 298 (1924); *Go-Bart Importing Co. v. United States*, 282 U.S. 344 (1931). These cases were not predicated on a constitutional overbreadth analysis because government misconduct was so blatant that the Court didn't waste much time talking about the law. However, as regulatory subpoena power expanded, the Supreme Court readjusted its approach and began to shrink the constitutional parameters of protection.

In *Oklahoma Press Publishing Co. v. Walling*, 327 U.S. 186 (1946), the Supreme Court rejected a Fourth Amendment claim of overbreadth in connection with a subpoena *duces tecum* issued under the Federal Labor Standards Act for the production of

1. In *Caceres*, a taxpayer's conversations with the IRS were recorded without Department of Justice approval in violation of internal IRS regulation.

records from newspaper publishers to determine compliance with the Act. The Court concluded that when an order for production of documents was judicially authorized, the only issue was "reasonableness" of the subpoena. That standard is codified in Rule 17(c) of the Federal Rules of Criminal Procedure, which applies to the issuance of both trial and grand jury subpoenas in a criminal investigation.

1. *Rule 17(c)*

Rule 17(c) permits a subpoena to be quashed only "on motion" and if "compliance would be unreasonable." The Supreme Court observed that this standard is not self-explanatory and that what is reasonable depends on the context. *United States v. R. Enters., Inc.*, 498 U.S. 292 (1991).

2. *Trial Subpoenas*

As a general rule with respect to any trial subpoena, "[a] subpoena for documents may be quashed [under Rule 17(c)] if their production would be 'unreasonable or oppressive,' but not otherwise." *United States v. Nixon*, 418 U.S. 683 (1974).[2] Relevance is not determinative but certainly may be raised at the time admission is sought at trial.

3. *Grand Jury Subpoenas*

The *Nixon* standard does not apply to grand jury subpoenas and so the Court held in *United States v. R. Enterprises, Inc.*, 498 U.S. 292, 299 (1991). There, the Court decided the standards to apply when a party seeks to avoid compliance with a subpoena *duces tecum* issued in connection with a grand jury investigation. Grand juries are not licensed to engage in fishing expeditions, nor may they select targets of investigation out of malice or out of an intent to harass. However, the grand jury "'can investigate merely on the suspicion that the law is being violated, or even just because it wants assurance that it is not.'" *Id.* at 297 (quoting *United States v. Morton Salt Co.*, 338 U.S. 632, 642–43 (1950)). "[T]he law presumes, absent a strong showing to the contrary, that a grand jury acts within the legitimate scope of its authority. Consequently, a grand jury subpoena issued through normal channels is presumed to be reasonable, and the burden of showing unreasonableness must be on the recipient who seeks to avoid compliance." *Id.* at 300.

A challenge based on relevance "must be denied unless the district court determines that there is no reasonable possibility that the category of materials the Government seeks will produce information relevant to the general subject of the grand jury's investigation." *Id.* at 301. The Court concludes that it is basically impossible for a party to make that showing because the challenging party may not be privy to the secret deliberations of the grand jury and a grand jury is entitled to determine for itself whether a crime has been committed. Thus, a Fourth Amendment challenge

2. The topic of discovery for the defense is addressed in Chapter 5.

to a grand jury subpoena should be decided based upon reasonableness and over-breadth but not relevance. Several lower federal courts have attempted, with limited success (*see, e.g., United States v. Gurule*, 437 F.2d 239 (10th Cir. 1970)), to add to the reasonableness determination the issue of relevance to the investigation.

C. No Zone of Privacy

When considered against the backdrop of *Hale v. Henkel*, the Fourth Amendment decisions reflect the imperative that the need to permit effective enforcement of the criminal law against corporations outweighs the danger of the misuse of government power. In short, the Fourth Amendment does protect the corporation from the abuse of government power in evidence-gathering pursuits, but it does not create a zone of privacy that protects commercial enterprises from government scrutiny. In pervasively regulated industries, the protection of the Fourth Amendment is virtually absent.

III. The Sixth Amendment

A. The Right to Counsel

Most judicial decisions interpreting the right to counsel involve individual defendants, but the Sixth Amendment also affords corporations the right to counsel, and so the courts have held. *United States v. Rad-O-Lite of Philadelphia, Inc.*, 612 F.2d 740, 743 (3d Cir. 1979); *see also United States v. Unimex, Inc.*, 991 F.2d 546, 549 (9th Cir. 1993) (holding that "a corporation has a Sixth Amendment right to be represented by counsel" at trial); *United States v. Thevis*, 665 F.2d 616, 645 n.35 (5th Cir.) (accused corporation can avail itself of guarantees provided to "an 'accused'" by Sixth Amendment), *cert. denied*, 459 U.S. 825 (1982). However, once the corporation is indicted, it is not clear if law enforcement questioning of executive level corporate employees must terminate, as is constitutionally required with an individual defendant (*Massiah v. United States*, 377 U.S. 201 (1966)). Because a corporation "'is an artificial entity that can only act through agents,'" *Am. Airways Charters, Inc. v. Regan*, 746 F.2d 865, 873 n.14 (D.C. Cir. 1984), the prohibition against interrogation in the absence of counsel after the commencement of adversary judicial proceedings has created some confusion. The Department of Justice (DOJ) policy regarding this issue is also included in the following discussion.[3]

1. *Criminal Proceedings Involving Corporations*

Once the government files criminal charges against a corporation, the Sixth Amendment forecloses interrogation of the corporation outside the presence of corporate

3. Sixth Amendment Implications of Law Enforcement Contact with Corporate Executives, Memorandum for Merrick B. Garland, Principal Assoc. Deputy Attorney General (Apr. 15, 1994) [hereinafter Sixth Amendment Implications], http://www.usdoj.gov/olc/garland.htm.

counsel. *United States v. Kilpatrick*, 594 F. Supp. 1324, 1350 (D. Colo. 1984), *rev'd on other grounds*, 821 F.2d 1456 (10th Cir. 1987), *aff'd sub nom. Bank of Nova Scotia v. United States*, 487 U.S. 250 (1988).[4] The issue is whether interrogation of high-level corporate executives amounts to contact with the corporation itself.

DOJ acknowledges that it does for several reasons. First, corporate executives possess the power to invoke a corporation's right to counsel. *Potashnick v. Port City Constr. Co.*, 609 F.2d 1101, 1119 & n.12 (5th Cir.), *cert. denied*, 449 U.S. 820 (1980). Second, statements made by high-level corporate executives can be imputed to the corporation itself as admissions. *Miano v. AC & R Advertising, Inc.*, 148 F.R.D. 68, 76–77 (S.D.N.Y.) (Katz, Magistrate J.), *adopted*, 834 F. Supp. 632 (S.D.N.Y. 1993). Thus, a corporation can invoke constitutional rights and make binding inculpatory statements through its high-ranking executives, and interrogation of corporate executives is deemed to be interrogation of the corporation itself. According to DOJ policy,[5] when law enforcement officials question high-ranking corporate executives after the initiation of formal criminal proceedings, the Sixth Amendment dictates that, absent a valid waiver of the right to counsel, all statements made by corporate executives are inadmissible against the corporation at a criminal trial.[6]

2. Civil Penalty Actions Against Corporations

Courts traditionally have rejected assertions of the Sixth Amendment right to counsel in civil penalty proceedings on the assumption that the Sixth Amendment applies only after the filing of criminal charges. *See, e.g., Williams v. United States Dep't of Transp.*, 781 F.2d 1573, 1578 n.6 (11th Cir. 1986); *Collins v. Commodity Futures Trading Comm'n*, 737 F. Supp. 1467, 1482–83 (N.D. Ill. 1990). One commentator has suggested, however, that the Supreme Court's ruling in *United States v. Halper*, 490 U.S. 435 (1989), may have future implications on the application of the rule.[7]

---

4. Although the district court opinion in *Kilpatrick* provides the only direct affirmation of this proposition, Sixth Amendment precedent bolsters the conclusion reached in *Kilpatrick*. The Supreme Court has emphasized that the Sixth Amendment Counsel Clause "provides the right to counsel at postarraignment interrogations." Michigan v. Jackson, 475 U.S. 625, 629 (1986). Because the Sixth Amendment right to counsel applies to corporations as well as individuals, *Unimex*, 991 F.2d at 549; *Rad-O-Lite*, 612 F.2d at 743, corporations—like individuals—cannot be subjected to interrogation outside the presence of counsel after the initiation of criminal proceedings. *See* Maine v. Moulton, 474 U.S. 159, 170 (1985); *Ethical Restraints of the ABA Code of Professional Responsibility on Federal Criminal Investigations*, 4B Op. O.L.C. 576, 580 (1980) ("Once the right to counsel has attached, the government may not elicit incriminating statements from the [defendant] unless it has obtained a waiver of his Sixth Amendment right.").

5. *Id.*

6. DOJ warns, however, that if those executives have not been formally charged, the statement they make can be introduced in a subsequent criminal proceeding against them, citing Maine v. Moulton, 474 U.S. 159, 180 (1985).

7. Linda S. Eads, *Separating Crime from Punishment: The Constitutional Implications of United States v. Halper*, 68 Wash. U. L.Q. 929, 971–72 (1990).

B. The Right to Appointed Counsel

Neither the Constitution nor the Criminal Justice Act[8] provides corporations a right of court-appointed counsel. The Criminal Justice Act does provide for the appointment of counsel for an indigent "person," but it does not clarify whether a corporation is a "person" for purposes of appointment of counsel. The word "person" in a federal statute includes corporations "unless the context indicates otherwise."[9] Arguably, the statute providing for appointment of counsel does provide the appropriate context to "indicate otherwise" and satisfy the rule.

In any case, the statutory text includes a list of classes of persons eligible, with catch-all clauses for a financially eligible person who "is entitled to appointment of counsel under the sixth amendment to the constitution" or "faces loss of liberty."[10] Although there is not much authority on the point, the Criminal Justice Act does not expressly include corporations.

The few cases to have considered the issue conclude that corporations have a right to counsel, but no right to appointed counsel in the event of insolvency or other financial hardship. *United States v. Unimex*, 991 F.2d 546, 549–50 (11th Cir. 1993); *United States v. Hartsell*, 127 F.3d 343, 350 (4th Cir. 1997) ("We [find] no suggestion anywhere in 18 U.S.C. § 3006A that corporations are entitled to publicly appointed counsel."); *United States v. Rivera*, 912 F. Supp. 634, 638 (D.P.R. 1996) ("[We] find that neither under Puerto Rico Local Rule 402 . . . § 3006A, or the Sixth Amendment of the United States Constitution are corporate defendants, even if financially unable, entitled to the appointment of counsel" under the Criminal Justice Act.).

C. The Right to Confrontation

Another right guaranteed by the Sixth Amendment is the right to confront witnesses against the defendant. The right applies to corporations. In *United States v. Nippon Paper Industries Co., Ltd.*, 17 F. Supp. 2d 38 (D. Mass. 1998), a Japanese corporation was charged with a conspiracy to fix prices for the export of thermal fax paper to the United States. The government was unable to compel the attendance of a key witness from Japan. However, the witness had given a pretrial videotaped deposition that the government was seeking to introduce at the criminal trial. In denying the government's motion, the court relied on the corporation's right under the Sixth Amendment to confront witnesses against it. The court held that a foreign corporation being prosecuted in a U.S. court under U.S. law had the same rights as a domestic corporation under the Sixth Amendment.

That's not the real problem. The problem is an evidentiary one grounded in the doctrine of *respondeat superior.* Typically, the evidence introduced against the

8. 18 U.S.C. § 3006A(a).

9. 1 U.S.C. § 1.

10. 18 U.S.C. § 3006A(a)(1)(H), (I).

corporation to establish guilt is the product of out-of-court statements made by corporate agents and/or documents generated by the organization, all of which the law attributes to the corporation. Out-of-court statements made by employees are admissible against the corporation as admissions of a party-opponent,[11] and the testimony recounting employees' statements may come from third parties with whom they spoke, including government agents. The same employee who made the incriminating statements, which are imputed to the corporation, may now refuse to testify at the company's trial, asserting a Fifth Amendment privilege against self-incrimination. The admissions are still not hearsay, yet the corporation is now precluded from cross-examining the witness.

The courts have uniformly held that the corporation's right to confrontation does not trump a witness's privilege against self-incrimination and the evidence remains admissible at trial. *See United States v. Follin*, 979 F.2d 369, 374 (5th Cir. 1992); *United States v. King*, 134 F.3d 1173 (2d Cir. 1998). The bottom line is that the corporation will have little success in seeking to prevent admission of the most incriminating evidence against it based on the assertion of its constitutional right to confront witnesses.

D. Other Sixth Amendment Rights

Corporations have Double Jeopardy protection. *United States v. Martin Linen Supply Co.*, 430 U.S. 564 (1977). They also have a right to a jury trial. *United States v. Twentieth Century Fox Film Corp.*, 882 F.2d 656 (2d Cir. 1989); *United Mine Workers v. Bagwell*, 114 S. Ct. 2552 (1994) (establishing the right of organizations to a jury trial in criminal contempt proceedings).

IV. Privileges

The protections afforded by the attorney-client privilege and the work product privilege are critical in the defense of white-collar criminal proceedings, particularly where internal corporate investigations have been initiated by the target company.

A. Attorney-Client Privilege

1. Scope

The attorney-client privilege is an evidentiary privilege, recognized under Federal Rule of Evidence 501, that protects confidential communications between a client and an attorney where legal advice, as opposed to business advice,[12] is being sought by the client. As explained by the Supreme Court in the seminal case establishing the parameters of the attorney-client privilege for corporations, *Upjohn v. United States*,

11. Fed. R. Evid. 801(d)(2)(A).

12. The privilege does not apply when the attorney is being asked for business advice. United States v. Rowe, 96 F.3d 1294, 1297 (9th Cir. 1996).

449 U.S. 383 (1981), the privilege protects only the disclosure of communications; it does not protect disclosure of underlying facts by those who communicated with the attorney.

In formulating the contours of the privilege, the Supreme Court rejected the "control group" test as being too narrow and as frustrating the purpose of the privilege, which is to afford full and frank disclosure to the company's attorney. The restriction of the privilege to only those employees included in upper management or the control group ignores the fact that "it will frequently be employees beyond the control group ... who will possess the information needed by the corporation's lawyers. Middle-level—and indeed lower-level—employees can, by actions within the scope of their employment, embroil the corporation in serious legal difficulties, and it is only natural that these employees would have the relevant information needed by corporate counsel if he is adequately to advise the client with respect to such actual or potential difficulties." *Id.* at 391.

The Court refused to develop any hard and fast rules regarding who is covered by the privilege. The application is decided on a case-by-case basis, which does inject some uncertainty into the process.

The party invoking the privilege has the burden of proving that an attorney-client relationship existed and that the particular communications were confidential; meaning that the communication was made confidentially, outside the presence of any third parties, in the attorney's professional capacity for the purpose of securing legal advice or assistance. The key issue is whether the client reasonably understood that the consultation was confidential. *United States v. Schaltenbrand*, 930 F.2d 1554, 1562 (11th Cir.), *cert. denied*, 502 U.S. 1005 (1991). However, third parties *retained by the lawyer* to assist in providing legal services, such as an accountant, may be present during client communications and the privilege is still preserved. The workpapers of the attorney's agent are similarly covered by the protection of the privilege. *United States v. Kovel*, 296 F.2d 918 (2d Cir. 1961); *United States v. Ackert*, 169 F.3d 136 (2d Cir. 1999) (elaborating on the *Kovel* standard). Tax advice, however, does not qualify for protection. *United States v. Adlman*, 68 F.3d 1495, 1500 (2d Cir. 1995).

Communications between an organizational client and its outside counsel are "presumed" to be made for the purpose of obtaining legal advice. *United States v. Chen*, 99 F.3d 1495, 1501 (9th Cir. 1996). Because in-house counsel may operate in a purely or primarily business capacity in connection with corporate matters, the same presumption that applies to communications with outside counsel does not apply to inside counsel. *United States v. Chevron Corp.*, 1996 WL 264769 (N.D. Cal. 1996). In *United States v. ChevronTexaco Corp.*, 241 F. Supp.2d 1065, 1077 (N.D. Cal. 2002), the trial court held that materials transmitted between nonlawyer employees of the company that reflect matters about which the corporate client intends to seek legal advice are protected in the same way that an individual client's notes would be protected.

The privilege is the client's, not the attorney's, to assert and waive. However, if the client may invoke the privilege, then the client's attorney may also do so on the client's behalf. *See Fisher v. United States*, 425 U.S. 391, 402 n.8 (1976). Corporate officers do not have the authority to waive corporate privilege; it must be done by formal action approved by corporate management and is normally exercised by its officers and board of directors. *Commodity Futures Trading Comm'n v. Weintraub*, 471 U.S. 343, 348–49 (1985). As a practice note, counsel must carefully prepare organizational employees testifying before the grand jury or at trial to exercise great caution in answering questions where those answers might result in an unauthorized waiver of the corporate privilege that could subject the employee to liability. It is not the employee's privilege to waive.

When the control of a corporation passes to new management, the authority to assert and waive the corporation's attorney-client privilege passes as well. New managers put in place as part of a takeover, merger, or normal succession may also assert or waive. *Id.* at 349.

A subsidiary does not have an automatic right to assert the parent corporation's privilege, even where the parent is now defunct. *In re Grand Jury Subpoena No. 06-1*, 274 Fed. Appx. 306 (4th Cir. 2008). The court recognized that close corporate affiliation, including that shared by a parent and a subsidiary, suffices to render those entities "joint-clients" or "co-clients" such that they may assert joint privilege in communications with an attorney pertaining to matters of common interest. However, the scope of the joint-client or co-client privilege is circumscribed by the "limited congruence of the clients' interests" (citing *In re Teleglobe Commc'ns Corp.*, 493 F.3d 345, 362–63 (3d Cir. 2007)).

2. Bankruptcy Trustee Waiver

The Supreme Court also held in *Commodity Futures Trading Commission v. Weintraub*, 471 U.S. 343, 439–58 (1985), that the trustee of a corporation in bankruptcy has the power to waive the corporation's attorney-client privilege in bankruptcy with respect to prebankruptcy communications. The trustee plays the role "most closely analogous to that of solvent corporation's management." If the corporate debtor remains in possession and a trustee is not appointed, the debtor's directors assume the same fiduciary duties as those of a trustee.

As a practice note, it is apparent that where an insolvent corporation and/or its officers, directors, and employees are the targets or subjects of a criminal investigation, the decision to file for bankruptcy protection opens up the files of the company not only to the bankruptcy trustee but also to the government should the trustee determine that waiving the privilege is in the best interests of the creditors and shareholders to whom the trustee owes a fiduciary duty. Trustees frequently cooperate with the government, which increases the risk of civil and criminal liability for the company and prior management.

3. *Crime-Fraud Exception*

Client communications made for the purpose of furthering an ongoing or future crime are not protected by the privilege. The party asserting the exception, usually the government, has the burden of presenting a threshold "showing of a factual basis adequate to support a good faith belief by a reasonable person" that the hearing would reveal evidence of a crime or fraud. *United States v. Zolin*, 491 U.S. 554 (1989).

Once that threshold showing is made, a trial court can determine whether the crime-fraud exception applies in one of two ways. A judge can make an *in camera* inspection of the allegedly confidential documents to assist the court in determining if the crime-fraud exception should apply given the government's prima facie showing, rejecting the "independent evidence rule." Alternatively, the court can examine only the government's proof *ex parte* and *in camera* without examining the allegedly privileged documents, which would excuse the need to make a prima facie showing before the submission.

Communications between a corporation, through its agents, and corporate counsel that are made in furtherance of a crime or fraud are outside of the scope and protection of the privilege. *United States v. BDO Seidman, LLP*, 492 F.3d 806, 818 (7th Cir. 2007).

4. *Joint Defense Agreements*

The common interest doctrine, also referred to as the joint defense privilege, protects communications between parties who share a common interest in litigation. *In re Grand Jury Subpoena: Under Seal*, 415 F.3d 333, 341 (4th Cir. 2005). The purpose is to allow persons with a common interest to communicate with their respective attorneys and with each other to more effectively prosecute or defend their claims. *Id.* The common interest doctrine "presupposes the existence of an otherwise valid privilege," and, therefore, is an extension of the attorney-client privilege and the attorney work product doctrine. *Hunton & Williams, LLP, v. U.S. Dep't of Justice*, 2008 WL 906783 (E.D. Va. 2008) (citing *In re Grand Jury Subpoenas*, 902 F.2d 244, 249 (4th Cir. 1990)). The party asserting the privilege has the burden to show both that there was a common interest and that the parties intended to engage in a cooperative effort in obtaining legal advice.

Two points of caution. First, the privilege applies only when clients are represented by separate counsel. Second, the clients must share a common interest in the litigation. *In re Teleglobe Commc'ns Corp.*, 493 F.3d 345 (3d Cir. 2007). Given the sometimes indeterminate length of an investigation, it is unnecessary that there be actual litigation in progress. *United States v. Aramony*, 88 F.3d 1369 (4th Cir. 1996).

The more serious problem with entering into a joint defense agreement arises when a member abandons the agreement and decides to cooperate with the government. The courts have held that a defendant may cross-examine the cooperator using the cooperator's statements made to the defendant's attorney during the course of the joint defense agreement, on the theory that the cooperating defendant waived his right to the attorney-client privilege when he pled guilty. *United States v. Alameida*, 341 F.3d 1318, 1323 (11th Cir. 2003). However, in *United States v. Henke*, 222 F.3d 633 (9th Cir. 2000), the privilege was held to have created a "disqualifying" conflict of interest at trial when it prevented defense attorneys from adequately cross-examining the cooperating defendant at trial. The defendants' convictions were reversed.

The bottom line is that the joint defense privilege cannot be waived without the consent of all parties to the defense, except in the situation where one of the joint defendants becomes an adverse party in the litigation. *Matter of Grand Jury Subpoena*, 406 F. Supp. 381, 393–94 (S.D.N.Y. 1975).

As a practice pointer, a written agreement is not necessary, but it can be very helpful to the court in later determining whether a joint defense agreement exists *United States v. Dose*, 2005 WL 106493 (N.D. Iowa 2005), who is a party to the agreement, when it was entered into, and what the "common interest" was between the parties at the time of the communication. *See, e.g., Beneficial Franchise Co., Inc. v. Bank One, N.A.*, 205 F.R.D. 212 (N.D. Ill. 2001); *Block Drug Co., Inc. v. Sedona Labs., Inc.*, 2007 WL 1183828 (D. Del. 2007).

The DOJ has changed its position on joint defense agreements. In August 2008, in a statement issued by Deputy Attorney General Mark Filip ("Filip memo"),[13] the DOJ announced revisions to its Corporate Charging Guidelines.[14] Under the new policy, federal prosecutors may not consider whether the corporation has entered into a joint defense agreement in evaluating whether to give the corporation credit for cooperating.

5. *Conflict of Interest in Representation*

The Sixth Amendment right to have effective assistance of counsel encompasses the right to have counsel untainted by conflicts of interest. *Holloway v. Arkansas*, 435 U.S. 475 (1978). The rules of professional conduct allow an attorney to serve multiple clients on the same matter so long as all clients consent and there is no substantial risk of the lawyer being unable to fulfill the attorney's duties to them.[15]

There is a great temptation by corporate defense lawyers to take the position with the government that they represent all of the existing corporate employees and the corporation. However, in the event that a conflict between the employees and the corporation or between employees arises, counsel may find itself disqualified

---

13. Remarks Prepared for Delivery by Deputy Attorney Gen. Mark R. Filip at Press Conference Announcing Revisions to Corporate Charging Guidelines (Aug. 28, 2008), http://federalevidence.com/pdf/2008/FRE502/DOJFilip_Remarks_8-28-08.pdf.

14. U.S. Attorneys' Manual Tit. 9, Ch. 9-28.000 *et seq.*, Principles of Federal Prosecution of Business Organizations, http://www.usdoj.gov/opa/documents/corp-charging-guidelines.pdf and attached as Appendix C.

15. Restatement (Third) of the Law Governing Lawyers §§ 128–131.

from representing all parties and without any client. In *Wheat v. United States*, 486 U.S. 153, 159 (1988), the Supreme Court observed that joint representation of criminal defendants "engenders special dangers of which a court must be aware."

Client waivers do not automatically resolve the problem. In fact, Rule 44 of the Federal Rules of Criminal Procedure directs trial judges to conduct an investigation and personally advise each defendant of their right to effective assistance of counsel. If the court determines that a conflict exists, it must act to protect each defendant's constitutional rights. This means that a court can reject the waiver and assign separate counsel. Under *Wheat*, the court is given substantial latitude.

An attorney in a conflict of interest situation, such as where one of the multiple defendants decides to plead guilty or otherwise cooperate, must be disqualified from all representation where it creates an inability to adequately represent the interests of the remaining defendants. The better practice is to retain separate counsel for the corporation and each of its employees who may be the subject or target of an investigation. Defense counsel should refrain from advising corporate employees not to cooperate in the government's investigation to avoid a possible later accusation that the attorney engaged in obstructing justice. Employees may be advised, however, that they do not have a legal obligation to cooperate.

In a joint defense agreement situation where one defendant later cooperates and abandons the agreement, the remaining defense counsel are not automatically disqualified but the area is very uncertain in application. "The mere inability to utilize the privileged communications is not itself a manifestation of a conflict of interest, because no lawyer in the world could utilize those communications. Rather, the potential conflict of interest stems from the fact that [the defendant's] lawyer might be so tongue-tied (due to his fear of revealing the confidential communications made by [the cooperating defendant]) that his representation of [the defendant] suffers." *United States v. Alameida*, 341 F.3d 1318, 1323–24 (11th Cir. 2003). As noted above, in *United States v. Henke*, 222 F.3d 633 (9th Cir. 2000), the privilege was held to have created such a "disqualifying" conflict of interest at trial, resulting in the reversal of the defendants' convictions on appeal.

B. Work Product Privilege

At the core of the doctrine, the work product privilege shelters the mental processes of the attorney, providing an area of privilege within which the attorney can analyze and prepare the client's case. *United States v. Nobles*, 422 U.S. 225, 238 (1975). First formulated in the seminal case *Hickman v. Taylor*, 329 U.S. 495, 510–11 (1947), the doctrine was designed to create a "zone of privacy" in which an attorney is encouraged to write down litigation theories and strategies without fear that the opponent will capitalize on that attorney's work product. The work product doctrine is separate from the attorney-client privilege and broader in scope. *Nobles* at 238. As provided in Federal Rule of Criminal Procedure 26, the rule extends not only to work by the attorney but also to litigation preparation work by the party or its representatives.

The party asserting the protection of the work product doctrine bears the evidentiary burden to establish that the documents are prepared "in anticipation of litigation." *Resolution Trust Corp. v. Dabney*, 73 F.3d 262, 266 (10th Cir. 1995); Fed. R. Civ. P. 26. The opposing party can overcome the privilege if it can demonstrate that it has a "substantial need" for the documents and that it is unable to otherwise obtain the "substantial equivalent" of the withheld documents without "undue hardship."[16] Even in this circumstance, the court must protect against the disclosure of the mental impressions, conclusions, opinions, or legal theories of an attorney.[17]

A voluntary disclosure of materials to a third party may constitute waiver. Work product disclosed to a third party, not an adversary, and with a "common interest" is typically not a waiver because that third party also seeks to prevent disclosure to the adversary. Courts do not treat inadvertent disclosure, even to an adversary, as an automatic waiver.

C. Internal Corporate Investigations and Privilege Protection

Internal investigative reports are treated as work product. Even so, some aspects of the investigation will not be protected by the work product doctrine. For example, the identity of persons interviewed by counsel is not protected. Preexisting documents left in possession of counsel are not protected. The results of internal examinations may not be protected from disclosure to the government in a subsequent grand jury investigation.

The DOJ has recently changed its policy regarding the need for corporations to disclose the results of internal corporate investigations. This is discussed in greater detail in Chapter 6 but bears repeating here because of its critical importance to defense lawyers and companies engaged in internal investigations to pinpoint the source of criminal wrongdoing. The Filip Memo, issued on August 28, 2008,[18] provides that credit for cooperation will not depend on whether a corporation has waived attorney-client privilege or work product protections. Corporations that provide timely disclosure may receive due credit for cooperation; those who choose not to, receive no credit. Refusal by a corporation to cooperate is not treated as evidence of guilt.

---

16. Fed. R. Civ. P. 26 (b)(3).

17. *Id.*

18. Remarks Prepared for Delivery by Deputy Attorney Gen. Mark R. Filip at Press Conference Announcing Revisions to Corporate Charging Guidelines (Aug. 28, 2008), http://federalevidence.com/pdf/2008/FRE502/DOJFilip_Remarks_8-28-08.pdf.

D. Rule 502(FRE) Limitations on Waiver of Privilege

In 2008, Rule 502 was added to the Federal Rules of Evidence[19] to resolve court disputes involving waiver by disclosure of certain communications otherwise protected by the attorney-client or work product privileges. It does not apply to waiver under any other common law privilege and does not determine if either privilege applies in the first instance. Subsection (a) of the rule addresses scope of the waiver and subsection (b) addresses inadvertent disclosure. Under subsection (a), if privileged material is disclosed to the government, any waiver that occurs only extends to additional, undisclosed material if, in the case of an intentional waiver, the disclosed and undisclosed materials concern the same subject matter and "ought in fairness to be considered together." As the Advisory Notes to Rule 502(a) make clear, a finding of waiver in such circumstances should be "reserved for those unusual situations in which fairness requires a further disclosure of related, protected information, in order to prevent a selective and misleading presentation of evidence to the disadvantage of the adversary." [20] With respect to inadvertent disclosure, there is no waiver if the privilege holder took reasonable steps to prevent disclosure and also promptly took reasonable steps to rectify the waiver.[21]

Under subsection (d) of the rule, disclosure of materials in a litigation or other federal proceeding may be protected from waiver of attorney-client privilege or work

19. Rule 502(FRE): (a) Scope of waiver. When the disclosure is made in a Federal proceeding or to a Federal office or agency and waives the attorney-client privilege or work-product protection, the waiver extends to an undisclosed communication or information in a Federal or State proceeding only if: (1) the waiver is intentional; (2) the disclosed and undisclosed communications or information concern the same subject matter; and (3) they ought in fairness to be considered together. (b) Inadvertent disclosure. When made in a Federal proceeding or to a Federal office or agency, the disclosure does not operate as a waiver in a Federal or State proceeding if: (1) the disclosure is inadvertent; (2) the holder of the privilege or protection took reasonable steps to prevent disclosure; and (3) the holder promptly took reasonable steps to rectify the error, including (if applicable) following Federal Rule of Civil Procedure 26(b)(5)(B). Disclosure Made in a State Proceeding—When the disclosure is made in a State proceeding and is not the subject of a State-court order concerning waiver, the disclosure does not operate as a waiver in a Federal proceeding if the disclosure: (1) would not be a waiver under this rule if it had been made in a Federal proceeding; or (2) is not a waiver under the law of the State where the disclosure occurred. (d) Controlling Effect of a Court Order—A Federal court may order that the privilege or protection is not waived by disclosure connected with the litigation pending before the court—in which event the disclosure is also not a waiver in any other Federal or State proceeding. (e) Controlling Effect of a Party Agreement—An agreement on the effect of disclosure in a Federal proceeding is binding only on the parties to the agreement, unless it is incorporated into a court order. (f) Controlling Effect of This Rule—Notwithstanding Rules 101 and 1101, this rule applies to State proceedings and to Federal court-annexed and Federal court-mandated arbitration proceedings, in the circumstances set out in the rule. And notwithstanding Rule 501, this rule applies even if State law provides the rule of decision. (g) Definitions—In this rule: (1) "attorney-client privilege" means the protection that applicable law provides for confidential attorney-client communications; and (2) "work-product protection" means the protection that applicable law provides for tangible material (or its intangible equivalent) prepared in anticipation of litigation or for trial.

20. *See* United States v. Treacy, 2009 Wl 812033 (2009), not published in F.Supp.

21. Advisory Committee Notes, subdivision (b) (2007).

product protection by a court order. These are referred to as "confidentiality orders." The rule provides that when a confidentiality order governing the consequences of disclosure is entered in a federal proceeding, its terms are enforceable against non-parties in any federal or state proceeding. State confidentiality orders have been upheld in federal proceedings under the rules of comity pursuant to Title 28 U.S.C. § 1738.

Under subsection (e), the parties can still enter into an agreement to limit waiver through disclosure on their own but it is only binding on the parties to the agreement. It will not be binding on nonparties to the agreement unless it is made part of a court order under subsection (d).

Chapter 5

AFFIRMATIVE DEFENSES
DENYING LIABILITY AND DEFLECTING BLAME

I. The Good Faith Defense

The good faith defense arises in two ways at trial: to negate the *mens rea* requirement or to assert good faith reliance on the advice of an outside professional to negate criminal liability. Both are double-edged swords because the claim of good faith typically results in the automatic waiver of attorney-client privilege.

A. Negating the Mens Rea

In *United States v. Exxon Corp.*, 94 F.R.D. 246 (D.D.C. 1981), Exxon raised, as one of its defenses, the affirmative defense of good faith reliance on government regulations and communications with the Department of Energy to avoid liability for price overcharges on the sale of crude oil. The government argued that the defense put the "corporate state of mind at issue." The court found that Exxon had waived its attorney-client privilege and that its corporate files had to be released because they were "highly relevant" to the merits of its good faith compliance with government regulations. Exxon's internal statements "should also reveal whether Exxon honestly believed that it acted in good faith."

In another oft-cited decision, *Hearn v. Ray*, 68 F.R.D. 574, 581 n.5 (E.D. Wash. 1975), the court held that defendants impliedly waived the attorney-client privilege when they raised the affirmative defense of qualified immunity. The court explained that by asserting the defense, the defendants imposed on the plaintiff the burden of proving a *mens rea* of malice or disregard of settled, indisputable law. Since the legal advice that defendants may have received is relevant to the proof, the information was discoverable.

Both the *Exxon Corp.* and *Hearn* decisions were cited with approval in the leading case on the issue, *United States v. Bilzerian*, 926 F.2d 1285, 1292 (2d Cir. 1991). There, the court said that "a defendant may not use the privilege to prejudice his opponent's case or disclose some communications for self-serving purposes. . . . The privilege may be implicitly waived when defendant asserts a claim that in fairness requires examination of the protected communications."

When putting mental state at issue, the corporation's internal documentation and the advice that it received become "highly relevant" in evaluating the good faith defense. The defense may be seen as the "affirmative converse of the government's burden of proving . . . intent to commit a crime." *United States v. Cavin*, 39 F.3d 1299, 1310 (5th Cir. 1994).

However, the tide may be receding from *Hearn* and its progeny, at least in the Second Circuit. In the recent decision *In re County of Erie*, 2008 U.S. App. LEXIS 21496 (2d Cir. Oct. 14, 2008), the court rejected the *Hearn* test as overly broad and confined the application of the implied "at issue" waiver only to those instances where "a party must *rely* on privileged advice from his counsel to make his claim or defense." [Emphasis in the original]. *Id.* at 16.

B. Reliance on Third-Party Professionals

Another instance in which the attorney-client privilege can be impliedly waived is where a defendant asserts a defense that puts his attorney's advice at issue in the litigation. This is particularly dangerous for the corporation in matters testified to by management before the grand jury. In *In re Grand Jury Proceedings*, 219 F.3d 175, 181 (2d Cir. 2000), the court implied a waiver where the founder, chairman, and CEO of the target company made selective disclosure of counsel's advice in an "exculpatory manner." The witness had volunteered the information where the question did not call for it. As a result of the exculpatory manner in which the witness used expert advice, the privilege was "in fairness" deemed waived. The same testimony had the effect of waiving work product privilege with respect to the advice as well. The court examined the case law at length regarding the ability of a corporate agent to waive the privilege on behalf of the corporation. Even though the privilege belongs to the corporation and cannot be waived by the agent without its consent, implied waiver will be applied where fairness otherwise requires it. That issue must necessarily be decided on a case-by-case basis. *Id.*

II. Can a Corporation or Other Business Organization Withdraw from a Conspiracy or Otherwise Avoid Successor Conspiratorial Liability?

Why is this question so important? In almost every criminal case and in civil cases, such as antitrust litigation, the government and/or private plaintiff litigants charge conspiracy to avail the parties of the evidentiary benefits of the coconspirator exception to the hearsay rules.[1] Consequently, limiting organizational liability from the acts of coconspirators is not only essential at trial but may be a useful defense strategy where an internal investigation reveals liability and continuing exposure of the organization. The fact that an affirmative action is done by an organization to withdraw from criminal activity before discovery by authorities may also assist the organization in arguing that it should not be formally charged and is a proper candidate for informal prosecutive disposition, as discussed in more detail in Chapter 6.

A. Defense of Withdrawal

The gravamen of the conspiracy is the unlawful agreement to accomplish an unlawful objective and the commission of an overt act, lawful or unlawful in character, in furtherance of the conspiracy. At the federal level, any coconspirator can withdraw from the conspiracy before the commission of the overt act and avoid criminal liability.

However, once the conspiracy is formed, as a general rule, the defense of withdrawal from the conspiracy does not exonerate a defendant from the crime of conspiracy or other past unlawful conduct; it can only exonerate the defendant as to future conduct engaged in by defendant's coconspirators. *See Pinkerton v. United States*, 328 U.S. 640 (1946). In order to withdraw, a defendant must take affirmative action, either by reporting to authorities or by communicating the defendant's intentions to coconspirators; mere cessation of participation is not sufficient. *United States v. Gypsum Co.*, 438 U.S. 422, 464–65 (1978). The defendant's continued participation in a criminal activity that it claims to have disavowed negates the withdrawal defense. *United States v. Starrett*, 55 F.3d 1525, 1555 (11th Cir. 1995); *United States v. Swiss Family Farms Co., Inc.*, 912 F. Supp. 401 (C.D. Ill. 1995). Because the defense of withdrawal is an affirmative defense, the defendant has the burden to prove it by a preponderance of evidence. If a coconspirator establishes the defense of withdrawal, the statute of limitations will begin to run as to that defendant at the time of withdrawal; otherwise, the statute will not begin to run until the occurrence of the final act of the conspiracy. *United States v. Arias*, 431 F.3d 1327, 1340 (11th Cir. 2005).

In *United States v. Hughes*, 191 F.3d 1317 (10th Cir. 1999), an individual defendant was charged with conspiring with a business trust managed by the defendant, a

---

1. Fed. R. Evid. 801(d)(2)(E).

related partnership, and other individuals in a scheme involving the fraudulent use of performance bonds for a government contract. The defendant, in his capacity as trustee for ARCO Business Services, Ltd., issued a letter on partnership letterhead stating that ARCO "does not intend to seek or claim further benefit of any kind" and requests that the recipient "convey ARCO's current position . . . to all of the other concerned/involved parties."

The court held that the jury was correct in finding that the partnership/trust organization properly withdrew based on the affirmative act evidenced by the letter but that the guilty verdict as to the individual defendant trustee was not inconsistent because the trustee signed the letter in his capacity as trustee only and not in an individual capacity. The court also observed that the letter did not exonerate a related partnership, Arco Properties, because that partnership was likewise not expressly referred to in the letter. Evidence of withdrawal must be an affirmative act and must address each individual coconspirator. It is not enough for coconspirators to have overlapping or identical interests.

Several courts have crafted useful jury instructions. For example, in *United States v. Continental Group, Inc.*:

> An individual or corporation may withdraw or abandon a conspiracy by renunciation or by engaging in conduct which is inconsistent with the idea of continued participation in the alleged scheme. Mere cessation of activity in furtherance of the conspiracy is not sufficient to establish withdrawal. For a defendant to be deemed to have withdrawn there must be evidence showing withdrawal by some affirmative action. Such action must consist of a definite and decisive step of some kind which shows complete disassociation. For example, to disavow or defeat the purpose of conspiracy . . . would be the type of decisive act that a party could look to as being the basis for withdrawal. A defendant may also withdraw from a price fixing conspiracy by notifying his alleged coconspirators of his intent to withdraw. . . .

603 F.2d 444, 466 (3d Cir.), *cert. denied*, 444 U.S. 1032 (1979).

The courts have also held, for example, that evidence of the resumption of competitive behavior is sufficient to establish affirmative action to defeat or disavow the purpose of a bid-rigging conspiracy and establish the defense of withdrawal. *United States v. Nippon Paper Indus. Co., Ltd.*, 62 F. Supp. 2d 173 (D. Mass. 1999).

Another example of an affirmative act of withdrawal involved cigarette manufacturers charged with a RICO conspiracy arising out of a scheme to defraud consumers by misrepresenting the adverse health effects of cigarette smoking. The court found that evidence of a manufacturer "breaking ranks" with the tobacco industry, by cooperating with the state Attorney General and publicly announcing its withdrawal, established the defense. *United States v. Philip Morris USA, Inc.*, 449 F. Supp. 2d 1 (D.D.C. 2006).

B. Defense of No Successor Liability

In *In re Catfish Antitrust Litigation*, 908 F. Supp. 400 (N.D. Miss. 1995), the plaintiffs were food distributors purchasing catfish and catfish products from defendant companies. Plaintiffs filed a claim under Section 4 of the Clayton Act alleging that defendant companies engaged in a conspiracy to eliminate competition and fix prices in the catfish industry on a nationwide basis. The corporate defendants named in the suit included ConAgra, Delta Pride Catfish, and Hormel Foods. Hormel defended on the basis that while it had acquired a guilty subsidiary, it was not a member of the conspiracy based on successor liability as the new parent.

The courts have developed various tests for determining whether a purchasing company may be a "mere continuation" of the seller for purposes of imputing liability. In the instant case, the factors include (1) whether there is a basic continuity of the enterprise of the seller organization, including retention of key personnel, assets, and even the seller's name; (2) the seller ceased ordinary business operations, liquidated, and dissolved postacquisition; (3) the purchasing company assumed the liabilities and obligations of the seller only in the course of the normal business operations of the seller; and (4) the purchasing corporation held itself out to third parties as the effective continuation of the seller. If the purchaser is deemed to be a mere continuation of the seller under a theory of successor liability, whether a withdrawal from the conspiracy can be proved may depend on the actions of the seller. *Id.* at 415.

III. Unauthorized Acts of Agents

The decision in *United States v. Hilton Hotels Corp.*, 467 F.2d 1000, 1007 (9th Cir.), *cert. denied*, (1973), holding that a corporation is criminally liable for the acts of its agents in the scope of their employment, even though contrary to general corporate policy and express instructions to the agent, fairly limits the ability to defend the corporation based on the claims that the acts of the agent were unauthorized or in violation of express corporate policy to the contrary. It remains good law today and has been cited across the circuits with approval. The jury instructions upheld in the decision have also been frequently upheld by the courts.

Likewise in *United States v. Sun-Diamond Growers of California*, 138 F.3d 961, 971 (1998), the court reaffirmed the principle that where an agent's conduct is actually or potentially detrimental to the corporation, it may nonetheless be imputed to the corporation in criminal cases if the agent was motivated in part to benefit the company to "any appreciable extent" (citations omitted).

There is some authority for the proposition that the agent employee's position within the organization should not be ignored in determining scope of employment. The opinion does not elaborate. Presumably, a lower-level employee may be deemed to be a renegade employee as opposed to the case of a higher-level employee responsible for formulating company policy. *See, e.g.*, *City of Vernon v. S. Cal. Edison*, 955 F.2d 1361, 1370 (9th Cir. 1992).

Notably, in the U.S. Attorneys' Manual, *Principles of Federal Prosecution of Business Organizations: VII. Charging a Corporation: Corporate Compliance Programs*, Comment B cites *Hilton Hotels Corp.* for the proposition that "a corporate compliance plan, even one specifically prohibiting the very conduct in question, does not absolve the corporation from criminal liability under the doctrine of *respondeat superior*."[2]

In sum, the defense is difficult at best and will not likely shield a corporation from prosecution under the Department of Justice guidelines.

IV. Defense Theory Instructions

A defendant is entitled to a theory instruction at trial provided that (1) the instruction represents an accurate statement of the law; (2) the instruction reflects a theory that is supported by the evidence; (3) the instruction reflects a theory that is not already part of the charge; and (4) the failure to include the instruction would deny appellant a fair trial. *United States v. Useni*, 516 F.3d 634 (7th Cir. 2008). Defense argument is not the purpose of a theory instruction. *Id.*

Some examples where organizational convictions have been reversed based on the refusal to tender the defense requested instruction include *United States v. GAF Corp.*, 928 F.2d 1253 (2d Cir. 1991), and *Arthur Andersen LLP v. United States*, 544 U.S. 696 (2005).

Arthur Andersen LLP involved an obstruction of justice charge under 18 U.S.C. § 1512 and the meaning of "knowingly . . . and corruptly persuade" as used in that statute. The defendant vigorously disputed at trial how the jury would be instructed on the term "corruptly." The government insisted that the court remove the word "dishonestly" from the approved Fifth Circuit pattern instruction and won. The conviction was reversed because the instructions did not properly define the requisite criminal intent required by the statute. The instructions charged that defendants "knowingly . . . corruptly persuaded another person with intent to . . . cause that person to withhold documents from, or alter documents for use in, an official proceeding." *Id.* at 703 (*internal citations omitted*). The instruction erroneously allowed a conviction for an act of persuasion that also included innocent conduct if the defendants otherwise sincerely believed that the conduct was lawful. Additionally, the instructions incorrectly permitted the jury to believe that it did not have to find a nexus between the corrupt persuasion to destroy documents and the official proceeding.

2. Attached as Appendix C.

In terms of the legacy of *Arthur Andersen LLP*, the case does not open a major new avenue in terms of organizational defense strategy. To obviate the complexity of "corrupt" intent, the Sarbanes-Oxley Act of 2002 added two new provisions to the criminal code, 18 U.S.C. §§ 1519 and 1520. Both code sections address the destruction, alteration, or falsification of documents; in the case of § 1519, with the intent to impair, impede, or obstruct an investigation. Neither of these statutes incorporates a "corrupt" *mens rea* requirement similar to the § 1512 obstruction statute.

V. Use of Subpoenas Prior to Trial

Federal Rule of Criminal Procedure 17(c) governs the issuance of both trial and grand jury subpoenas in criminal cases. It is also the primary means by which the defense can obtain materials from persons not covered under *Brady*, Federal Rule of Criminal Procedure 16, or the Jencks Act requirements (18 U.S.C. §§ 3500, *et seq.*). Trial subpoenas are returnable on the day of trial unless a party moves for an early return date under Rule 17(c). In *United States v. Nixon*, 418 U.S. 683, 699–700 (1974), *superseded by statute on other grounds, Bourjaily v. United States,* 483 U.S. 171 (1987); *see also United States v. Cuthbertson,* 630 F.2d 139, 144 (3d Cir.1980), the Court considered the pretrial issuance of trial subpoenas and the basis for quashing them.

In order to require production before trial, the moving party must show (1) that the documents are evidentiary and relevant; (2) that they are not otherwise procurable reasonably in advance of trial by the exercise of due diligence; (3) that the party cannot properly prepare for trial without such production and that the failure to produce will result in a delay at trial; and (4) that the request is in good faith and not a "fishing expedition." In short, the moving party must clear three hurdles: "relevancy, admissibility, and specificity." Remember, the *Nixon* test does not apply to grand jury subpoenas.

Chapter 6

STRUCTURING CORPORATE PLEA AND SETTLEMENT AGREEMENTS
AN EXERCISE IN DAMAGE CONTROL

I. Making Choices Pretrial

Corporations do not go to jail. As explained in previous chapters, the law elevates corporate fictional "existence" to a chargeable "legal person," one without a physical body but not without an economic soul.[1] Indeed, corporate punishment, in the form of economic sanctions, strikes at the very soul of the corporation—its bottom line. Fines, penalties, restitution, and possible forfeiture may have the draconian effect of

1. Corporations, while artificial in nature, are "legal persons" capable of suing and being sued, and capable of committing crimes. See Chapter 2.

permanently injuring the continuing economic viability of the corporation, occasionally resulting in its permanent demise.

At the very least, monetary penalties can dramatically affect current and future profitability. Where the company is publicly traded, the economic consequences surely affect stock value and future offering potential in the marketplace. These are the more obvious economic consequences. The less obvious collateral consequences[2] may include the possible suspension or debarment of eligibility for government contracts, forfeiting licensure, and/or adverse tax treatment of various forms of economic penalties.

The decision to go to trial on criminal charges is the highest-risk strategy that can be pursued by a corporation in attempting to resolve liability issues. The failure of that strategy in terms of entity demise is best illustrated by the complete disappearance of the national accounting firm Arthur Andersen after a jury conviction in 2004.[3] The fact that the conviction was later overturned on appeal did nothing to rejuvenate the already disbanded organization. *See Arthur Andersen v. United States*, 544 U.S. 696 (2005) (conviction reversed based on faulty jury instructions that failed to convey the requisite consciousness of wrongdoing under the obstruction of justice statute, 18 U.S.C. § 1512).

Because of the high-risk potential of an unsuccessful bid at acquittal, pretrial resolution is the most common and pragmatic strategy. However, pretrial resolution is no economic panacea. While pretrial resolution lessens the risk of corporate demise, the inevitable economic sanctions included in the settlement may nonetheless damage the corporation. Of course, that is the government's point. Any settlement should punish the offender. Consequently, the corporation's goal is to engage in damage control. Control is the operative word.

Obviously, pretrial resolution offers some greater degree of control over the extent to which a corporation may suffer economic damage as opposed to leaving the ultimate disposition of liability in the province of the jury and the sentencing court. This chapter addresses the degree to which control can be exercised over the direct

---

2. U.S. Attorneys Manual (USAM), Principles of Federal Prosecution of Business Organizations Chapter 9-28.1000 (2008). (Attached in Appendix C.) The USAM addresses the impact of collateral consequences and allows prosecutors to consider the impact of these consequences in the course of arriving at a charging decision. USAM at http://www.justice.gov/opa/documents/corp-charging-guide lines.pdf. The prior memoranda, which are superseded by these provisions of the USAM, were issued by Deputy U.S. Attorneys General Mark Filip (August 2008), Paul J. McNulty (December 2006), Larry Thompson (January 2003), and Eric Holder (June 1999).

3. Arthur Andersen LLP served as Enron's auditor. Subsequent to the revelation of gross financial mismanagement and concealment of debt in Enron's form 8K Restatement filed with the Securities and Exchange Commission in November 2000, Arthur Andersen instructed its employees to destroy documents pursuant to its document retention policy in violation of federal law. For a more complete discussion of Andersen's role in the demise of Enron, see Staff of Senate Comm. on Governmental Affairs, 107th Cong., Financial Oversight of Enron: The SEC and Private-Sector Watchdogs (Comm. Print 2002), *available at* http://www.senate.gov~-gov_affairs/100702watchdogsreport.pdf.

and collateral consequences of economic punishment as part of negotiating a final settlement agreement. Chapter 7, which follows, offers possible tax-planning techniques that should be considered when negotiating and drafting pretrial agreements in an effort to ameliorate the consequences of economic sanctions.[4]

II. Types of Pretrial Agreements

Criminal charges can be resolved pretrial using three different alternatives: plea agreements, deferred prosecution agreements (DPAs), and nonprosecution agreements (NPAs). Historically, DPA and NPA opportunities were very limited. Not surprisingly, after the demise of several more notable publicly traded corporations following criminal conviction,[5] the Department of Justice (DOJ) reconsidered its previous intransigent position disfavoring nonprosecution and deferred prosecution agreements. In fact, in the four-year period 2002–2005, the DOJ entered into twice as many NPA and DPA agreements combined than it had during the previous 10-year period, 1992–2001.[6]

Despite this increase and ostensible change in policy, plea agreements accompanied by a guilty plea remain the most utilized tool pretrial in most areas of white-collar crime prosecutions, with some notable exceptions.[7] There are no definitive written guidelines for determining when DOJ will consent to something less than a plea agreement (i.e., an NPA or a DPA). Much depends on the facts that caused the government to conclude that criminal charges were appropriate in the first instance,[8] including the amount of loss to the victims, the type of fraud or other unlawful conduct, the pervasiveness of criminal conduct in management, the overall benefit of the unlawful conduct to the corporation, the existence of corporate compliance programs, the willingness of the corporation to cooperate in the continuing investigation, and other such factors. In short, as in most negotiations, the decisions are

---

4. Notably, there are specific rules regarding the imposition of restitution in lieu of fines and penalties. In the absence of careful drafting, a payment claimed to be made as restitution may lose its character, and thus, its deductibility.

5. The Enron bankruptcy was declared to be the largest bankruptcy in the nation's history. Subsequently, WorldCom superseded Enron as the largest bankruptcy. Simon Romero & Riva D. Atlas, *WorldCom's Collapse: The Overview; WorldCom Files for Bankruptcy; Largest U.S. Case*, N.Y. Times, July 22, 2002, at A-1.

6. *Crime Without Conviction: The Rise of Deferred and Non Prosecution Agreements*, Corp. Crime Rep. Dec. 28, 2005, http://www.corporatecrimereporter.com.

7. This is not the case in prosecutions under the Foreign Corrupt Practices Act where the majority of case dispositions are in the form of NPAs or DPAs. For a detailed discussion, see Chapter 9.

8. USAM § 9-27.220 (1997). Appendix B.

subjective and usually based on DOJ's assessment of the risk of litigation based on the strength of the government's evidence.[9]

In January 2010, the Securities and Exchange Commission (SEC) revitalized its own enforcement agenda using the same tools. The new initiative, codified in Section 6 of the SEC Enforcement Manual entitled "Fostering Cooperation,"[10] establishes incentives for individuals and companies to cooperate and assist with SEC investigations and enforcement actions, and provides new tools to help investigators develop first-hand evidence to build the strongest possible cases. To improve the quality, quantity, and timeliness of information and assistance it receives, the SEC approved the following measures:

- Cooperation Agreements—Formal written agreements in which the Enforcement Division agrees to recommend to the Commission that a cooperator receive credit for cooperating in investigations or related enforcement actions if the cooperator provides substantial assistance such as full and truthful information and testimony.
- Deferred Prosecution Agreements—Formal written agreements in which the Commission agrees to forego an enforcement action against a cooperator if the individual or company agrees, among other things, to cooperate fully and truthfully and to comply with express prohibitions and undertakings during a period of deferred prosecution.
- Nonprosecution Agreements—Formal written agreements, entered into under limited and appropriate circumstances, in which the Commission agrees not to pursue an enforcement action against a cooperator if the individual or company agrees, among other things, to cooperate fully and truthfully and comply with express undertakings.

Additionally, the SEC streamlined the process for submitting witness immunity requests to the Justice Department for witnesses who have the capacity to assist in its investigations and related enforcement actions.

Section 6 of the Enforcement Manual also delineates the way in which the SEC will evaluate whether, how much, and in what manner to credit cooperation by individuals to ensure that potential cooperation arrangements maximize the Commission's law enforcement interests. This pronouncement is similar to the "Seaboard Report" that was issued in 2001, which details the factors the SEC considers when

---

9. Miriam F. Miquelon-Weismann, *Dispositions in Criminal Prosecutions of Business Organizations*, 51(3) U.S. ATT'Y'S BULL.: CORP. FRAUD ISSUES 33, 34 (May 2003), *available at* http://www.usdoj.gov/usao/eousa/foia_reading_room/usab5103.pdf.

10. 17 CFR § 202.12 "Policy Statement of the Securities and Exchange Commission Concerning Cooperation by Individuals in its Investigations and Related Enforcement Actions" cited in full in Section 6 of the SEC Enforcement Manual at http://www.sec.gov/divisions/enforce/enforcementmanual.pdf.

evaluating cooperation by companies.[11] Consistent with that report, the SEC identifies four general considerations:

- The assistance provided by the cooperating individual;
- The importance of the underlying matter in which the individual cooperated;
- The societal interest in ensuring the individual is held accountable for his or her misconduct;
- The appropriateness of cooperation credit based on the risk profile of the cooperating individual.

III. Federal Plea Agreements: An Analysis of the Department of Justice Guidelines

The federal guidelines governing corporate plea agreements are included in the United States Attorneys' Manual (USAM), The Principles of Federal Prosecutions of Business Organizations, Chapter 9-28.000, *et. seq.*, in 2008.[12] The initial plea policy formulation began with then Deputy Attorney General Larry Thompson in 2003 with the issuance of the Thompson Memo.[13] Revisions to DOJ charging policy were made on December 12, 2006, when Deputy Attorney General Paul McNulty issued *Guidelines for Prosecuting Corporate Fraud* ("McNulty Memo").[14] These guidelines, in connection with credit for corporate cooperation, were revised and once again updated on August 28, 2008, with the issuance of the *Revisions to Corporate Charging Guidelines* ("Filip Memo").[15] This process of revisions to the policy culminated in the incorporation in final policy form into the USAM. Though the prosecution guidelines contain significant limitations, they also provide useful opportunities for negotiation. Again, much depends on the subjective strengths and weaknesses of the government's evidence. This point is illustrated in the following discussion with a view toward understanding the application of the USAM guidelines and maximizing their possible benefits to the corporation in resolving liability "by agreement."

11. The Seaboard Report appears in Exchange Act Release No. 44969, and is entitled, "Report of Investigation Pursuant to Section 21(a) of the Securities Exchange Act of 1934 and Commission Statement on the Relationship of Cooperation to Agency Enforcement Decisions."

12. Available at http://www.usdoj.gov/opa/documents/corp-charging-guidelines.pdf. and attached in Appendix C.

13. Thompson Memorandum—Principles of Federal Prosecution of Business Organizations (2003) at http://www.justice.gov/dag/cftf/corporate_guidelines.htm.

14. Guidelines for Prosecuting Corporate Fraud, Dep't of Justice Press Release (Dec. 14, 2006), http://www.usdoj.gov/opa/pr/2006/December/06_odag_828.html.

15. Remarks Prepared for Delivery by Deputy Attorney Gen. Mark R. Filip at Press Conference Announcing Revisions to Corporate Charging Guidelines (Aug. 28, 2008), http://www.justice.gov/archive/dag/speeches/2008/dag-speech-0805071.html.

A. The Desirability of Entering into a Plea Agreement from the Government's Perspective

The Principles of Federal Prosecution USAM Chapter 9-27.000 *et. seq.* address the DOJ guidelines for prosecutors to follow in exercising the discretion to prosecute cases. Those guidelines are attached in Appendix B. Pursuant to this section of the USAM, the government should weigh the following relevant factors in evaluating the desirability of entering into a plea arrangement:[16]

- The defendant's willingness to cooperate in the investigation or prosecution of others;
- The defendant's history with respect to criminal activity;
- The nature and seriousness of the offense or offenses charged;
- The defendant's remorse or contrition and his or her willingness to assume responsibility for his or her conduct;
- The desirability of prompt and certain disposition of the case;
- The likelihood of obtaining a conviction at trial;
- The probable effect on witnesses;
- The probable sentence or other consequences if the defendant is convicted;
- The public interest in having the case tried rather than disposed of by a guilty plea;
- The expense of trial and appeal;
- The need to avoid delay in the disposition of other pending cases; and
- The effect on the victim's right to restitution.

Perhaps the most significant part of this weighing process is the ultimate usefulness and overall credibility of the defendant at a subsequent trial. Also, the government must consider the possible effect that a plea arrangement will have on the trial of any remaining individual defendants. The more valuable the corporate cooperation, the more desirable the plea agreement.

B. DOJ Guidelines as Limitations

The USAM provision, *Plea Agreements with Corporations,* begins with a serious and significant limitation on the individual prosecutor's bargaining authority. The first "general principle" provides that in negotiating plea agreements with corporations, prosecutors should seek a plea to "the most serious, readily provable offense charged."

---

16. USAM § 9-27.420 (1997), Plea Agreements. Appendix B.

This is also referred to as the "top count" policy.[17] This means that the corporation should be required to plead guilty to the most serious provable offense charged or the top count charged in the indictment.

The theory behind applying the top count policy to corporate pleas is twofold. First, a corporation should be made to realize that pleading guilty to criminal charges constitutes "an admission of guilt and not merely a resolution of an inconvenient distraction from its business."[18] Second, prosecutors may enter into plea agreements with corporations for the same reasons and under the same constraints that apply to plea agreements with natural persons.[19] Thus, the top count policy as applied to natural persons is applied equally to the corporate entity.

As with natural persons, pleas must be structured so that the corporation may not later "proclaim lack of culpability or even complete innocence."[20] That also necessitates a statement in the plea agreement or other court record wherein there is a sufficient factual basis for the plea to prevent later corporate assertions of innocence.[21]

In addition, the guidelines require that the terms of the plea agreement include appropriate provisions to ensure "punishment, deterrence, rehabilitation, and compliance" with the plea agreement in the corporate context.[22] This means several things in the context of the specific terms of the plea agreement. First, the corporation must implement a useful and uniformly enforced corporate compliance program, as described in more detail later in this chapter. Second, punishment and deterrence in the corporate context are generally accomplished "by substantial fines, mandatory restitution, and institution of appropriate compliance measures, including, if necessary, continued judicial oversight or the use of special masters."[23]

In addition, where the corporation is a government contractor, permanent or temporary debarment may be appropriate. These collateral consequences are discussed in more detail below. However, the guidelines are clear that where the corporation is charged in connection with government contracting fraud, a prosecutor may not negotiate away an agency's right to debar or to delist the corporate defendant.[24]

---

17. USAM §§ 9-27.400–500 (1997), http://www.usdoj.gov/usao/eousa/foia_reading_room/usam/title9/27mcrm.htm#9-27.400. Appendix B.

18. Thompson Memo, *supra* note 13, at XII.B.

19. *Id.*

20. *See* USAM §§ 9-27.420(b)(4), 9-27.440, 9-27.500 (1997). Appendix B.

21. Thompson Memo, *supra* note 13.

22. *Id.* In making this determination, the attorney for the government considers such factors as the sentencing guideline range yielded by the charge, whether the penalty yielded by such sentencing range is proportional to the seriousness of the defendant's conduct, and whether the charge achieves such purposes of the criminal law as punishment, protection of the public, specific and general deterrence, and rehabilitation. Also referencing Memorandum from Eric Holder, Deputy Att'y Gen., U.S. Dep't of Justice, Federal Prosecution of Corporations (June 16, 1999). This is the predecessor to the Thompson memo.

23. *See* U.S. Sentencing Guidelines Manual §§ 8B1.1, 8C2.1 *et seq.* (2008).

24. Thompson Memo, *supra* note 13.

It must be underscored that only under "special circumstances," not described with any particularity in the guidelines, may a prosecutor agree to accept a corporate guilty plea in exchange for the nonprosecution or dismissal of charges against individual officers and employees.[25] Indeed, the express language of the comment to the guidelines provides that one factor that a prosecutor may consider in determining whether to enter into a plea agreement in the first instance is whether the corporation is seeking immunity for its employees and officers or whether the corporation is willing to cooperate in the investigation of culpable individuals. "Prosecutors should rarely negotiate away individual criminal liability in a corporate plea."[26]

Both the Filip Memo and the McNulty Memo make significant changes in the interpretation of "corporate cooperation" and abolish some of the restrictions contained in the Thompson Memo. Previously, the corporate cooperation provisions in the Thompson Memo required individual prosecutors to ensure that the cooperation is "complete and truthful" by demanding that the corporation waive attorney-client and work product protection, make employees and agents available for debriefing, disclose the results of its internal investigation, file appropriate certified financial statements, agree to governmental or third-party audits, and take whatever other steps are necessary to ensure that the full scope of the corporate wrongdoing is disclosed and that the responsible culprits are identified and, if appropriate, prosecuted.[27] These categories defining corporate cooperation were typically included as provisions in the plea agreement.[28]

The McNulty Memo, ostensibly in response to the raging battle over the waiver requirements,[29] required prosecutors to seek DOJ approval pursuant to a new set of requirements before the government could even request waivers of attorney-client privilege and work product protections from corporations in criminal investigations. The Filip Memo now expressly forbids prosecutors from making such requests for protected materials.

More significantly, the Filip Memo prohibits the government from treating the corporate refusal, either to waive attorney-client privilege and/or provide communications protected by the work product privilege, as a failure of cooperation. This

---

25. *Id.*

26. *Id.*

27. *Id.*

28. For example, paragraphs 11, 13, and 14 in the plea agreement entered into in February 2006 in the case *United States v. Allied Freight Forwarding Inc.*, which can be accessed at the DOJ website at http://www.justice.gov/atr/cases/f216300/216317.pdf.

29. *See* ABA Task Force on the Attorney-Client Privilege, Report to the ABA House of Dele-gates 13 (May 18, 2005), http://www.abanet.org/buslaw/attorneyclient/materials/hod/report.pdf; Nat'l Ass'n of Criminal Def. Lawyers, Survey: The Attorney-Client Privilege Is Under Attack (Apr. 2005), http://www.nacdl.org/public.nsf/0/d5a7720a477e251d8525700300674928/$FILE/AC_Survey.pdf; Ass'n of Corporate Counsel, Survey: Is the Attorney-Client Privilege Under Attack? (Apr. 2005), http://www.acc.com/Surveys/attyclient.pdf.

directly contradicts prior DOJ policy under the Thompson Memo. Specifically, if a corporation chooses not to provide attorney-client communications, prosecutors are directed not to consider that refusal against the corporation in their charging decisions. Now, prosecutors can no longer make the request.

The Filip Memo announces five new revisions relating to credit for corporate cooperation that have been incorporated into the USAM, Title 9, Chapter 9-28.000 *et seq.*:

1. Credit for cooperation will not depend on whether a corporation has waived attorney-client privilege or work product protection, or produced materials protected under either privilege;
2. With two recognized legal exceptions, prosecutors may no longer request disclosure of nonfactual attorney-client privilege and work product, such as legal advice;
3. Prosecutors may not consider whether a corporation has advanced attorneys' fees to officers, directors, or employees when evaluating cooperativeness;
4. Prosecutors may no longer consider if the corporation entered into a joint defense agreement in evaluating whether to give credit for cooperation; and
5. Prosecutors may not consider whether a corporation had disciplined or terminated employees for the purpose of evaluating cooperation.

The Filip Memo concludes that "Refusal by a corporation to cooperate, just like refusal of an individual to cooperate, is not evidence of guilt."

The concessions made in the Filip and McNulty Memos were still not enough assurances for Congress. In November 2007, the House passed H.R. 3013, the Attorney-Client Privilege Protection Act of 2007. However, as of 2011, the measure was still in the Senate awaiting further consideration.[30] The bill would make it unlawful for federal prosecutors and other law enforcement officials to demand that a company under investigation disclose confidential legal information, such as the results of an internal corporate investigation, or risk being indicted—a consequence viewed as corporate capital punishment. The bill does not prevent corporations from voluntarily disclosing the information to prosecutors.

C. DOJ Guidelines as Negotiating Opportunities

In the context of drafting plea agreements, there are five "hot button" issues for both sides during negotiations: identifying the charge; agreeing on economic sanctions; liability of individuals; cooperation; and the factual statement or basis for the plea made part of the record.

30. For updates, see H.R. 3013, http://www.govtrack.us/congress/bill.xpd?bill=h110-3013.

Where the corporation has not yet been indicted, the individual prosecutor has more flexibility in deciding the most readily provable count to which the corporation must plead. Each U.S. Attorney's office will decide for itself, based on its evaluation of the evidence, what makes sense. The government will inevitably consider the risk of litigation and the cost and time commitment to a prosecution. Smaller districts are more inclined to plead out cases where case agents are scarce and prosecutors who are trained in white-collar prosecutions may be in even greater demand. However, where the corporation has already been indicted, the prosecutor must demand a plea to the most serious count in the indictment or otherwise seek DOJ approval in order to bind the government to a plea to a lesser count.[31]

As explained in detail in the following chapter, economic sanctions in the form of fines and penalties are not tax-deductible. Generally, a corporation may deduct the amount of a restitution payment. The characterization of the payment in the settlement agreement is usually determinative both to the courts and to the Internal Revenue Service.[32] Careful attention must be paid to the rules and correct drafting is essential.

As the USAM indicates, corporations cannot pay large amounts of money to free culpable employees from prosecution. However, the extent of employee knowledge and culpability does make a difference. Also, the willingness of less culpable employees to cooperate may also contribute to a resolution of individual liability. As a practical matter, much will depend on the strength of the government's evidence and whether the testimony of a particular individual is considered necessary to prove its case. Consequently, individuals should be separately represented by counsel to avoid any conflict of interest.[33]

With the changes regarding the requirements for corporate cooperation, less is required to make a deal. The USAM now represents a significant departure from prior DOJ policy in this area. Nonetheless, obstructionist behavior will be viewed as antithetical to the negotiation process and may result in a failure to successfully negotiate an agreement.

Finally, the corporation will be required to provide a factual basis for the criminal charge. Unless there is a resolution of civil and/or administrative liability and/or other state criminal and civil exposure, every attempt should be made to limit the extent and nature of the corporation's admissions. The accompanying statement of fact is usually made part of the court record and is likewise available to private litigants, and thus useful in the pursuit of shareholder and creditor suits. As for entering

---

31. USAM § 9-27.400, cmt. B (1997). Appendix B.

32. See Chapter 7.

33. Representation pursuant to joint defense agreements can further complicate pretrial negotiations, particularly where a participant later decides to cooperate with the government. Care should be exercised in deciding whether to use joint defense agreements.

into a nolo contendere plea to avoid the admissions problem, one can always ask, but the standard justice policy is to refuse the request.

As a caveat, most courts will not accept a corporate plea agreement that is executed by counsel for the company. An authorized corporate officer, not the company attorney, must normally sign the plea agreement, which must be accompanied by a resolution of the board of directors granting that officer the power to enter into the agreement on behalf of the company.[34]

D. Corporate Compliance Programs

The USAM stresses that deterrence and rehabilitation are critical components in the negotiating process.[35] Deterrence takes two forms: the internal corporate message about the need to change whatever corporate culture fomented the violation and the external message sent to the rest of the industry that similarly situated companies engaging in similar behavior should beware.

Rehabilitation requires that the corporation undertake to be law-abiding in the future. The USAM recommends that, as a condition of probation, the corporation be required to implement a compliance program or to reform an existing one.[36]

Compliance programs are not intended to facilitate a slap on the corporate wrist. They are intended to be meaningful programs that change corrupt corporate practices and the culture that encourages profitability at any cost. According to the federal sentencing guidelines, the "general principle" governing rehabilitation is a compliance program designed to prevent and to detect misconduct and to ensure that corporate activities are conducted in accordance with all applicable criminal and civil laws, regulations, and rules. DOJ expressly encourages corporate self-policing, including voluntary disclosures to the government of any problems that a corporation discovers on its own. At the same time, the existence of a compliance program is not sufficient, in and of itself, to justify not charging a corporation for criminal conduct undertaken by its officers, directors, employees, or agents.

The guidelines recognize that the commission of corporate crimes in the face of a compliance program may suggest that the corporate management is not adequately enforcing its program. Indeed, corporations frequently use compliance programs as corporate window dressing to be set aside with a "nod and a wink" under the pressures of business exigencies.[37]

---

34. *See* U.S. Dep't of Justice, Antitrust Div., *Model Corporate Plea Agreement*, http://www.usdoj.gov/atr/public/guidelines/corp_plea_agree.htm.

35. USAM § 9-27.420 (1997). Appendix B.

36. USAM § 9-28.800(2008). Appendix C.

37. "Prosecutors should therefore attempt to determine whether a corporation's compliance program is merely a 'paper program' or whether it was designed and implemented in an effective manner." USAM § 9-28.800 (2008). Appendix C.

The DOJ has no formal guidelines for corporate compliance programs. The fundamental questions are: "Is the corporation's compliance program well-designed?" and "Does the corporation's compliance program work?" In answering these questions, DOJ considers the comprehensiveness of the compliance program; the extent and pervasiveness of the criminal conduct; the number and level of the corporate employees involved; the seriousness, duration, and frequency of the misconduct; and any remedial actions taken by the corporation, including restitution, disciplinary action, and revisions to corporate compliance programs.

The success of any preexisting program will most likely be judged by the promptness of any disclosure of wrongdoing to the government and whether the corporation has established corporate governance mechanisms that can effectively detect and prevent misconduct. In other words, did it work when it was supposed to prevent misconduct?

In addition, compliance programs should be designed to detect the particular types of misconduct most likely to occur in a particular corporation's line of business. Many corporations operate in complex regulatory environments outside the normal experience of criminal prosecutors. Consequently, the corporation has some flexibility in proposing an adequate and cost-efficient compliance program.

The Wall Street Reform and Consumer Protection Act has beefed up the requirements applicable to compliance plans. Specifically, on November 1, 2010, new changes to Chapter 8 of the Federal Sentencing Guidelines went into effect which now apply to corporate compliance programs. In summary, the new changes to the guidelines no longer focus primarily on the conduct of individual high-level managers. The amendments to the guidelines emphasize the effectiveness of the compliance program overall. Chapter 10 sets forth the amendments in detail but for convenience, the changes are summarized here.

Under the prior law, participation or willful ignorance of "high-level personnel" in the underlying offense functioned as a bar to any potential reduction for corporate good behavior. Now, if the company can show that it maintained an effective compliance program, it may nonetheless still qualify for leniency. The new guidelines make clear, however, that favorable treatment is only available to a company whose compliance program has certain characteristics, such as a direct "up-the-ladder" reporting mechanism from its chief compliance officer to the Board of Directors or Audit Committee, which is consistent with the changes mandated by the Sarbanes-Oxley Act (SOX).[38] The company also must have detected the violation before it is discovered by the government. Prompt self-reporting of the violation to the authorities is required in this instance.

---

38. See Chapter 10.

Previously, the guidelines generally required a company to "take reasonable steps to respond appropriately" after discovering wrongdoing. For the government to consider a compliance program effective, the new guidelines now specifically mandate that a company should take steps to remedy any harm that the wrongdoing may have caused, including restitution to identifiable victims where appropriate.

E. Make Sure It's a Done Deal

A plea agreement is binding only on the parties to the agreement. It is not a "universal settlement." The USAM is clear that the prosecutor has no authority to bargain away agency actions.[39] Likewise, a plea agreement does not resolve claims by the civil division of the DOJ. Those claims can be resolved as part of the same agreement; however, the civil division may require fines, penalties, restitution, and/or forfeiture in addition to any criminal sanctions. Agencies outside of the civil division that are empowered to bring administrative actions may still seek potential suspension or debarment from government contracts and programs. Again, potential exposure can be resolved in the plea agreement but only with the direct involvement of the affected agencies.

The USAM expressly provides that if the criminal behavior occurred in more than one federal jurisdiction, the plea agreement entered into in one federal district is not binding on another district without the express written approval and consent of the other affected district.[40] The prosecutor is responsible for obtaining a "global" consent from other affected districts, if consent is part of the negotiated deal. Once it is made part of the plea agreement, the mechanics are simple: the prosecutor typically sends an e-mail with the plea agreement to the other federal districts and requests consent. Unless there is a pending investigation in an affected district, the matter is usually resolved fairly expeditiously.

IV. Other Plea Options: Informal Resolution Through Nonprosecution Agreements and Deferred Prosecution Agreements

A. Resolution Without Formal Conviction

The use of DPAs and NPAs permit case resolution against a corporation without a formal conviction. DOJ defines a deferred prosecution agreement as one "typically predicated upon the filing of a formal charging document by the government and the agreement is filed with the appropriate court. In the non-prosecution context,

39. USAM § 9-27.420 (1997). Appendix B.
40. USAM § 9-27.641 (1997). Appendix B.

formal charges are not filed and the agreement is maintained by the parties rather than being filed with the court."[41]

NPAs are the exception and not the rule. Their primary purpose is to obtain necessary cooperation to investigate or prosecute a criminal case. The USAM requires the NPA to be precisely limited to its purpose. Specifically, in entering into a NPA, the government will attempt, if practicable, to explicitly limit the scope of its commitment to nonprosecution based directly or indirectly on the testimony or other information provided, or nonprosecution within the federal district with respect to a pending charge, or to a specific offense then known to have been committed by the person.[42]

The USAM describes three circumstances that should exist before government attorneys enter into NPAs in return for cooperation: the unavailability or ineffectiveness of other means of obtaining the desired cooperation; the apparent necessity of the cooperation to the public interest; and the approval of such a course of action by an appropriate supervisory official.[43]

In determining whether cooperation may be necessary to the public interest, the attorney for the government, and those whose approval is necessary, will weigh all relevant considerations, including the following:

- The importance of the investigation or prosecution to an effective program of law enforcement;
- The value of the person's cooperation to the investigation or prosecution; and
- The person's relative culpability in connection with the offense or offenses being investigated or prosecuted and his or her history with respect to criminal activity.[44]

As a general rule, corporations seldom obtain NPAs. The more likely option is a DPA. The USAM explicitly recognizes deferred prosecution as an alternative disposition in corporate criminal investigations.[45] In a typical deferred prosecution case, the government files with the court a criminal information charging the corpora-

41. Memorandum from Craig S. Morford, Acting Deputy Att'y Gen., U.S. Dep't of Justice, to Heads of Department Components and U.S. Attorneys, Selection and Use of Monitors in Deferred Prosecution Agreements and Non-Prosecution Agreements with Corporations (Morford Memo) (Mar. 7, 2008), http://www.usdoj.gov/dag/morford-useofmonitorsmemo-03072008.pdf and attached at Appendix D.

42. USAM § 9-27.630 (1997). Appendix B. *See also* § 9-27.650 describing the requirements of the written record that prosecutors must prepare reflecting the precise terms of the agreement as part of the case file. The government is likewise obligated to disclose the existence of the agreement, where appropriate pursuant to *Giglio v. United States*, 405 U.S. 150 (1972).

43. *Id.* at § 9-27.600.

44. *Id.* at § 9-27.620, Entering into Non-Prosecution Agreements in Return for Cooperation—Considerations to Be Weighed.

45. *Id.* at § 9-27.250.

tion, along with a DPA that contains an admission of wrongdoing by the corporation. The government agrees, pursuant to the express terms of the agreement, to "defer" prosecution of the case and to dismiss the charge if the corporation pays whatever economic sanctions are imposed and agrees to implement the appropriate corporate compliance programs or other reforms. There are numerous examples where DPAs have been approved by DOJ, including in the prosecutions of the accounting firm BDO Seidman,[46] Sears, Roebuck & Co.,[47] and the accounting firm KPMG.[48]

The best strategy for convincing the government to agree to a deferred prosecution agreement is the collateral consequences argument. While the USAM notes that the mere existence of collateral consequences is not a sufficient basis to automatically justify a DPA,[49] the idea that the actual punishment should be proportional to the crime is recognized by DOJ. Where a criminal prosecution may result in the complete decimation of the corporation and the extent of corporate participation and benefit to the shareholders is not widespread or is otherwise de minimis, a less aggressive approach to resolving the case is warranted. The goal is to achieve appropriate discipline that is not disproportionate in terms of the collateral consequences to the corporation, its shareholders, and employees that will inevitably follow a felony conviction.

The DPA is hardly a panacea. It provides some damage control, but the corporation is still required to pay appropriate fines, penalties, and restitution; acknowledge its own wrongdoing (which may affect parallel civil proceedings); and cooperate in the continuing investigation. Additionally, the corporation will still be required to implement an effective corporate compliance program. While burdensome, a DPA still avoids the draconian collateral consequences that accompany a felony conviction.

B. Recent Statistics: Increased Use of Informal Dispositions

The number of corporate pretrial dispositions increased from 20 in 2006 to 35 in 2007.[50] In 2008 and 2009, the numbers decreased slightly with a rise to 32 informal corporate pretrial dispositions in 2010.[51] The number of agreements requiring attorney-client and work product waivers has declined: in 2007, only three DPAs contained waivers and no NPAs contained waivers, resulting in nearly a 50 percent

46. Miquelon-Weismann, *supra* note 9.

47. *Id.*

48. KPMG Deferred Prosecution Agreement (Aug. 2005), http://www.usdoj.gov/usao/nys/press releases/August05/kpmgdpagmt.pdf.

49. USAM § 9-27.250. Appendix B.

50. Lawrence D. Finder & Ryan D. McConnell, Annual Corporate Pre-Trial Agreement Update—2007, 22nd National Institute on White Collar Crime (Mar. 2008), http://ssrn.com/abstract=1080263.

51. Gibson Dunn, 2010 Year-End Update on Corporate Deferred Prosecution and Non-Prosecution Agreements (January 2011) http://www.gibsondunn.com/publications/pages/2010Year-EndUpdate-CorporateDeferredProsecutionAndNon-ProsecutionAgreements.aspx.

decline in waivers in the period following Thompson Memo statistics (2003–2006).[52] However, in the area of prosecutions under the Foreign Corrupt Practices Act, the most common form of disposition involves the use of DPAs and NPAs. This is discussed in detail in Chapter 9.

C. Corporate Monitors

The use of corporate monitors does apply to plea agreements, which involve formal conviction of a corporation in a court proceeding. Corporate monitors are used where DPAs or NPAs are negotiated to resolve the criminal case. The good news is that the percentage of pretrial agreements mandating the use of corporate monitors has remained constant during the period from 2003 to 2007.[53] The bad news for corporate defendants is the foray by the government into the internal affairs of corporate defendants postprosecution through the use of court-appointed corporate monitors to ensure compliance with the conditions of sentencing. The fees and costs of the monitor are sometimes exorbitant and the burden is on the corporate defendant to pay the expense.

Not surprisingly, the practice has turned into a "political plum" for former DOJ employees. In a recent disclosure to Congress, the Justice Department identified 40 corporate monitors appointed since 2000 to follow up on the agreements, including former Attorney General John Ashcroft. This group was made up overwhelmingly of former government officials, at least 30 in all. They included 23 former prosecutors. Also not surprisingly, there are claims of abuses in the system. The practice drew media attention in 2008 after it was disclosed that Ashcroft had been selected by the U.S. Attorney for New Jersey, Christopher Christie, as a corporate monitor for a medical supply company. The job, assigned without competitive bidding, would pay Ashcroft's consulting firm up to $52 million. Ashcroft said at a contentious congressional hearing in March 2008 that there was nothing improper about the arrangement.[54]

In an effort to quell building unrest in Congress about the appointments, DOJ issued a formal memorandum setting forth formal procedures for the selection and use of corporate monitors. The memo, issued by Acting Deputy Attorney General Craig S. Morford on March 10, 2008, has come to be known as the "Morford Memo."[55] The Morford Memo requires the selection of monitors based on "merit" and identifies minimum selection requirements. Additionally, the monitor must be an independent third party, not an employee or agent of the corporation or the government.

---

52. For an analysis of the use of pretrial agreements during the Thompson Memo period (2003–2006), see Lawrence D. Finder & Ryan D. McConnell, *Devolution of Authority: The Department of Justice's Corporate Charging Policies*, 51 St. Louis U. L. J. 1 (2006).

53. Finder & McConnell, *supra* note 50.

54. Eric Lichtblau & Kitty Bennett, *30 Former Officials Became Corporate Monitors*, N.Y. Times, May 23, 2008, *available at* http://www.nytimes.com/2008/05/23/washington/23justice.html.

55. Morford Memo, *supra* note 41; USAM 9, Criminal Resource Manual (2008), at 163. Appendix D.

The monitor is primarily responsible for ensuring compliance with the agreement in an effort to prevent the risk of recurrence of the corporation's misconduct. While not a government agent, the corporate monitor may make periodic written reports to the government. Where the corporation chooses not to adopt the monitor's recommendations, such recalcitrance is to be reported to the government and used to evaluate corporate compliance with the agreement. The guidelines are fuzzy on the duration of the monitor's presence. It depends on the nature of the remedial measures included in the agreement. Finally, the agreement can, in the sole discretion of the government, be subject to early termination or extension based on the compliance of the corporation with the plan.

One odd caveat. The Morford Memo provides that the agreement should provide "that as to evidence of other such misconduct [undisclosed or new], the monitor will have the discretion to report the misconduct to the government or the corporation or both."[56] The commentary provides a list of "mitigating" factors that the monitor can consider in deciding whether to disclose evidence of misconduct to the government. In other words, the monitor may not be obligated to report all later discovered criminal conduct to the government. The agreement should address this ambiguity by providing guidelines to permit a corporate response, prior to report, in the event the monitor identifies claimed misconduct. By the way, the memo is conspicuously silent as to the applicability of any attorney-client privilege in the context of the principles. The privilege appears to have no application to the presence of the corporate monitor.

On March 11, 2008, the day after the Morford Memo was issued, the House Subcommittee on Commercial and Administrative Law held a hearing entitled "Deferred Prosecution: Should Corporate Settlement Agreements Be Without Guidelines?" Rep. John Conyers was unimpressed with the memo, stating that "this guidance still fails to ensure uniformity in the agreements themselves."[57] Bottom line: Get as much in writing in the agreement as possible to avoid the ambiguities inherent in the process of monitor selection and placement inside the corporation.

V. DOJ Parallel Proceedings Policy: Resolving Civil Liability

DOJ policy *requires* consideration of civil parallel proceedings in cases involving reports of fraud against the government.[58] Therefore, it is essential to resolve any

56. Morford Memo, *supra* note 41.

57. *See Deferred Prosecution: Should Corporate Settlement Agreements Be Without Guidelines?: Hearing Before the H. Subcomm. on Commercial and Admin. Law*, 110th Cong. (Mar. 11, 2008) (statement of Rep. Conyers).

58. For an in-depth analysis of the use of parallel proceedings, *see* Miriam F. Weismann, *Parallel Proceedings: Navigating Multiple Case Litigation*, American Bar Association, First Chair Press (2011).

potential civil exposure with the government in the plea agreement. Specifically, the USAM provides: "Every report of fraud or official corruption should be analyzed for its civil potential before the file is closed[59] . . . Cases pursued criminally must also be analyzed for civil potential. This analysis should be conducted at the earliest possible stage. Criminal dispositions by plea bargain should not waive or release the government's civil interests, except in return for adequate consideration, as measured by the Department's standards for civil settlements generally."[60]

There is an affirmative policy to initiate, where appropriate, criminal and civil parallel proceedings: "The [Commercial Litigation] Branch coordinates its cases with the appropriate United States Attorney to *ensure the pursuit of both civil and criminal redress*. Cases are similarly coordinated within the United States Attorneys' offices. This coordination may include the simultaneous initiation of civil and criminal proceedings in cases in which the monetary recovery to the government and the deterrent effect will be enhanced, giving due consideration to the risks to the criminal case and the availability of protective orders and stays. (Emphasis added.)[61] . . . Absent a specific, detailed statement that there is a strong likelihood that institution of a civil action would materially prejudice contemplated criminal prosecution of specific subjects, the decision to institute civil action is governed solely by the standards specified in 38 Op. Att'y Gen. 98 (1934). That is, the suit is instituted unless there is doubt as to collectibility or doubt as to the facts or law."[62]

The Commercial Litigation Branch and the U.S. Attorneys' offices are likewise accorded "significant latitude" in urging government agencies to withhold payment of claims presented by any subject "known to have engaged in fraudulent conduct."[63] In these cases, government "self-help" to withhold and terminate payments is viewed as a means to acquire leverage for the government in settling the dispute.[64] Additionally, plea agreements in criminal cases must be carefully scrutinized in many instances by the Attorney General before any U.S. Attorney's Office may enter into the agreement. Bottom line: Make sure to address civil exposure in the plea agreement!

---

59. USAM 9-42.010(A).

60. USAM 9-42.010(C).

61. USAM 9-42.010(D).

62. USAM 9-42.010(F).

63. USAM 9-42.010(H). Additionally, the government's common law right to withhold payment by setoff has been upheld by the U.S. Supreme Court. *United States v. Munsey Trust Co.*, 332 U.S. 234 (1947).

64. *Id.* The USAM provides: "Withholding is an important tool for effecting civil redress, and in recent years the government has successfully defended a number of cases in which client agencies have employed this self-help remedy. *See, e.g.,* Peterson v. Weinberger, 508 F.2d 45 (5th Cir. 1975); Brown v. United States, 524 F.2d 693 (Cl. Ct. 1975), as amended, (1976); Continental Management, Inc. v. United States, 527 F.2d 613 (Cl. Ct. 1975). [Italics in the original]. The negotiation of favorable settlements in unliquidated matters also may be enhanced by the bargaining leverage which withholding affords. Client agencies also should be urged to withhold pay and retirement benefits to Federal employees separated because of evidence of wrongdoing."

A. Evidentiary Pitfalls: Civil Case Admissions

On December 1, 2006, Federal Rule of Evidence 408 was amended to permit the government to introduce in a criminal case any "statements or conduct" made "during compromise negotiations regarding a civil dispute by a government regulatory, investigative or enforcement agency." Specifically, this may include "admissions of fault" made by a defendant in settlement of a civil enforcement action which are later introduced in a criminal prosecution of the same defendant. However, the balancing test under Rule 403, weighing the probative value of the statement against prejudice through its admission, still applies. However, the Advisory Committee notes to Amended Rule 408 fairly sum up the application of the rule: "Where an individual makes a statement in the presence of government agents, its subsequent admission in a criminal case should not be unexpected."

Prior to the amendment, in most federal circuits, parties could rely on Rule 408 to exclude statements made during settlement negotiations from admission to prove a party's liability. The rule provided that offers to compromise and "[e]vidence of conduct or statements made in compromise negotiations" offered to prove the validity or invalidity of a claim in both civil and criminal proceedings was "not admissible."

While seemingly ambiguous, most of the guidance for the application of the new rule is contained in the Advisory Committee notes. The notes consider at length the litany of preexisting rules developed by case law to elucidate what is and is not admissible. For example, the rule does not permit admission of: 1) statements made during settlement negotiations when offered to impeach by a prior inconsistent statement; 2) compromise offered to prove notice; 3) a party's own statement sought to be admitted by that party when made during settlement negotiations; or, 4) a statement to prove that a party made fraudulent statements during negotiations in order to settle litigation.

Additionally, the new rule distinguishes between statements and conduct that are a "direct admission of fault" from those that are "an offer or acceptance of compromise" of a claim. An offer or acceptance of a compromise of a civil claim is not admissible under the rule "if offered against the defendant as an admission of fault." Likewise, the rule does not apply when the negotiations are between private parties for the purpose of establishing liability for, invalidity of, or the amount of civil claims.

Chapter 7

TAX CONSEQUENCES AND PLANNING OPPORTUNITIES

CRIME DOESN'T PAY BUT IT MAY BE TAX-DEDUCTIBLE

The typical answer to the question about whether something is tax-deductible is "maybe, sometimes and it depends." The key concept is that there are general rules governing deductibility and then there are the exceptions and grey areas. Deductions for legal fees, costs, and expenses of settlement are on a surer footing than are deductions for fines, penalties, or restitution. However, structuring a plea or settlement agreement to include restitution may provide significant tax benefits to the corporation and ameliorate some of the consequences of economic sanctions.

Where ambiguity exists under the Internal Revenue Code,[1] advance tax planning may resolve the question. It should be emphasized that tax planning should be done *while* negotiating any plea or settlement agreement because in most instances, deductibility turns on the characterization of the payment in the agreement. The characterization of the payment in the court order, settlement, and/or plea agreement

1. Unless contraindicated, all future references to the Internal Revenue Code are to Title 26, U.S. Code.

is generally determinative in a dispute with the Internal Revenue Service[2] (IRS) and/or in a subsequent audit.

I. Legal Fees and Costs Paid to Defend the Corporation

Generally, legal fees incurred by the taxpayer corporation in the successful or unsuccessful defense of a criminal case are deductible if the subject crime under indictment or investigation involves the corporation's "trade or business." *Tellier v. Comm'r*, 383 U.S. 687 (1966). Section 162(a) provides the statutory authority: "There shall be allowed a deduction for all ordinary and necessary expenses paid or incurred during the taxable year in carrying on a trade or business." Treasury Regulation Section 1.162-21(b)(2) specifically exempts from the disallowance section under Section 162 "legal fees and related expenses paid or incurred in the defense of a prosecution or civil action." Likewise, the courts and the IRS have generally acquiesced when the corporate taxpayer's legal fees are related to its trade or business.[3]

The same rule of deductibility under Section 162 applies to other settlement expenses or costs where the acts that give rise to the litigation are again performed in the ordinary conduct of the corporate taxpayer's business.[4] However, "costs" do not include fines, penalties, or restitution. Fines and penalties are governed by Section 162(f), discussed later.

Note that the courts have construed the terminology "ordinary and necessary" under Section 162 to include legal fees and settlement costs, even though protecting the interests of the corporation in connection with a criminal prosecution may happen only once during the corporate existence. The courts have concluded that employment of counsel to protect a business from threatened destruction is a normal response ordinarily to be expected. *Kanne v. Am. Factors, Ltd.*, 190 F.2d 155, 159 (9th Cir. 1951); *Comm'r v. Heininger*, 320 U.S. 467, 471 (1943). The expenses are also deemed necessary in the sense that such expenses are "appropriate and helpful" to the development of the taxpayer's business. *Tellier*, 383 U.S. at 689. The bottom line is that a corporation can deduct legal fees incurred to defend itself.

---

2. *See* IRS Field Service Advisory (May 27, 1992), 1992 WL 1354910, citing Middle Atl. Distribs. Inc. v. Comm'r, 48 T.C. 15, 29 (1967).

3. *See id.*

4. Rev. Rul. 80-211, 1980-2 C.B. 57. *But see* United States v. Gilmore, 372 U.S. 39 (1963) wherein the Supreme Court disallowed a deduction for legal fees and costs incurred in protecting business property in a divorce proceeding. Formulating the "origin of the claim test," the Court concluded that the claim did not arise out of the taxpayer's trade or business but instead originated as part of personal divorce proceedings. Therefore, legal fees incurred in personal, nonbusiness activities are not deductible under the Code. Defending business property against the consequences of personal litigation does not fit under Section 162.

II. Legal Fees and Costs Paid to Defend a Corporate Employee

Under the Thompson Memo, advancing attorneys' fees to corporate employees was considered a form of "protection for culpable employees."[5] The current guidelines now instruct prosecutors that they cannot consider a corporation's advancement of attorneys' fees to employees when making a charging decision. A rare exception is created for those extraordinary instances where the advancement of fees, combined with other significant facts, shows that it was intended to impede the government's investigation. In those limited circumstances, fee advancement may be considered only with the authorization of the Deputy Attorney General.[6] Consequently, the tax consequences of such fee payments are significant, particularly in light of the significant fees charged by professionals.[7]

A corporate policy to pay the legal fees and costs for employees or directors and shareholders does not guarantee a deduction to the corporation under Section 162. The alleged wrongdoing must relate to the corporation's trade or business.[8] Unrelated litigation is not covered under Section 162.

Note that the tax treatment to the employee, director, or shareholder is covered under Section 62. As long as the fees are paid pursuant to a plan of formal reimbursement, the tax treatment to the employee is a "wash." The employee reports the reimbursement as additional compensation and then deducts the reimbursed fees as an above-the-line business expense from his or her gross income.[9]

---

5. Memorandum from Larry D. Thompson, Deputy Att'y Gen., U.S. Dep't of Justice, to Heads of Department Components and United States Attorneys, Principles of Federal Prosecution of Business Organizations (Jan. 20, 2003), at VI, cmt. B, http://www.usdoj.gov/dag/cftf/corporate_guidelines.htm.

6. Memorandum from Paul J. McNulty, Deputy Att'y Gen., U.S. Dep't of Justice, to Heads of Department Components and United States Attorneys, Principles of Federal Prosecution of Business Organizations (2006), http://www.usdoj.gov/dag/speeches/2006/mcnulty_memo.pdf.

7. Enron fees: Aegis Insurance Company filed a request with a New York bankruptcy court to pay up to $30 million in defense costs to individual defendants who were former or present Enron officers and/or directors. Press Release, Office of the Texas Attorney General, Texas Attorney General's Office Asks Court to Require Enron Officers and Directors to Post Collateral if Liability Insurance Proceeds Are Advanced for Legal Defense Fees (April 8, 2002), http://www.oag.state.tx.us/newspubs/newsarchive/2002/20020408enron.htm. In another recent example, business software maker CA Inc. sued convicted former chief executive Sanjay Kumar, seeking repayment of $14.9 million it says it fronted for his legal defense, according to court documents. William M. Bulkeley, *CA Sues Ex-CEO to Recoup Legal Fee*, Wall St. J. Online, Nov. 17, 2006, *reprinted at* Forum for Shareholders of CA, Inc., http://www.shareholderforum.com/CA/Library/20061117_WSJ.htm.

8. Rev. Rul. 68-662, 1968-2 C.B. 69.

9. Section 62(a)(2)(A). The limitations of Section 62(c) requiring substantiation and repayment of any amount in excess of the actual cost apply. Section 62(c) was added to the Internal Revenue Code by the Family Support Act of 1988, Pub. L. No. 100-485; H. R. Rep. No. 100-998, at 202–06 (Conf. Rep.).

III. Fines and Penalties

"Any fine or similar penalty paid to a government for the violation of any law" is not deductible.[10] While Section 162(f)[11] provides the unequivocal rule, it does not define what is meant by the terminology "fine or similar penalty." Treasury Regulation 1.162-21(b) defines and applies the general rule to four specific types of payments. Only three concern this discussion: a payment pursuant to a conviction, guilty plea, or nolo contendere plea in a criminal case; payment of a civil penalty imposed by federal state or local law; or a settlement payment involving "actual or potential liability for a fine or penalty (civil or criminal)."

The good news is that the definition is all-inclusive. When Congress enacted this provision in the code, it intended to limit the "fines and similar penalties" language to the four categories specified in the regulations. Consequently, where a deduction for a payment is not precluded by the express language of Section 162(f), a Section 162(a) deduction cannot be denied on nonstatutory "public policy grounds."[12] Consequently, the all-inclusive principle leaves open planning opportunities to structure an agreement to include otherwise nonpunitive forms of compensatory payments such as restitution, which is generally deductible.

The treasury regulations specifically exclude two types of payments from the definition of "fine and similar penalty." First, compensatory damages paid to the government do not constitute a fine or a penalty.[13] Second, legal fees and related expenses paid or incurred in the defense of a criminal or civil case arising from a violation of the law imposing the fine or penalty are deductible as ordinary and necessary business expenses under Section 162.

Some civil payments, labeled as penalties, are deductible if imposed to encourage "prompt compliance with the requirement of law" or as a "remedial measure" to compensate another party. *See Stephens v. Comm'r*, 905 F.2d 667, 673 (2d Cir. 1990), *rev'g* 93 T.C. 108 (1989); *Waldman v. Comm'r*, 88 T.C. 1384, 1387 (1987), *aff'd*, 850 F.2d 611 (9th Cir. 1988); *Huff v. Comm'r*, 80 T.C. 804, 824 (1983); *S. Pac. Transp. Co. v. Comm'r*, 75 T.C. 497, 646–54 (1980); *Allied-Signal, Inc. v. Comm'r*, T.C. Memo 1992-204. Where a payment may include both components, punitive (nondeductible) and

10. Section 162(f).

11. Section 162(f) was added to the Internal Revenue Code by Section 902(a) of the Tax Reform Act of 1969, Pub. L. No. 91-172, to codify the "public policy doctrine." That doctrine denied a deduction for any expense arising out of a statutory violation subjecting the taxpayer to civil or criminal penalties.

12. The report of the Senate Finance Committee states: "The provision added by the committee amendments denies deductions for four types of expenditures. . . . The provision for the denial of the deduction for payments in these situations which are deemed to violate public policy is intended to be all inclusive. Public policy, in other circumstances, generally is not sufficiently clearly defined to justify the disallowance of deductions." S. Rep. No. 91-552, at 273–75 (1969), *reprinted in* 1969-3 C.B. 423, at 596–98.

13. Treas. Reg. § 1.162-21 (b)(2) (1969).

compensatory (deductible), the court must determine which purpose the payment was designed to serve. It is here that tax planning at the settlement stage is critical.

The IRS and the courts have repeatedly acquiesced to the characterization of a settlement payment by the parties to the agreement. Thus, the characterization of the fines or penalties by the parties, rather than the origin of the claim to which the payments may relate, is determinative of deductibility.[14]

IV. Restitution

Restitution may be deductible under Section 165, the business and nonbusiness loss provision in the code.[15] However, restitution is not deductible as a business expense under Section 162. *Stephens,* 905 F.2d 667.[16] Section 165 is silent with regard to limitations on deductibility where public policy considerations might otherwise disqualify the deduction. However, the courts have rejected the IRS's contention that Section 165 includes a public policy exception to deductibility. *Id.* at 673. Instead, the courts have rejected the application of the public policy exception in favor of applying the requirements of Section 162 in determining tax treatment under Section 165. *Id.* at 672.

Under Section 165, losses are characterized as business or nonbusiness losses. The losses of corporations are generally deductible without statutory limitation as to character, while the deductibility of losses by individual taxpayers is restricted by the "business" or "profit" requirement unless the loss qualifies as a casualty loss. *Int'l Trading Co. v. CIR*, 484 F.2d 707, 710 (7th Cir. 1973); *accord* IRS Field Service Advisory (Apr. 20, 1995), 1995 WL 1770850 (no trade or business restriction on deductibility of corporate losses under Section 165, as corporations are presumptively engaged in profit-making activity). Consequently, restitution is a deductible loss under Section 165(c)(1) for a corporate taxpayer even though the tax character of restitution is essentially nonbusiness. *See Kraft v. United States*, 991 F.2d 292, 298 (6th Cir. 1993) (the repayment of "embezzled funds" is not a "trade or business" expense). Even where the deduction is allowable as a nonbusiness loss, the corporate taxpayer also qualifies for a net operating loss carryback. *Int'l Trading Co.,* 484 F.2d at 710.

However, individuals are not entitled to similar tax treatment, and so the courts have held. *United States v. Chernin*, 149 F.3d 805, 811 (8th Cir. 1998); *Kraft,* 991 F.2d at 295. For example, the repayment of stolen or embezzled funds is deductible by the

---

14. Middle Atl. Distribs. Inc. v. Comm'r, 48 T.C. 15, 29 (1967); Rev. Rul. 80-334, 1980-2 C.B. 61. *See also* IRS Field Service Advisory (May 27, 1992), *supra* note 2.

15. Section 165(c) provides for limitations on losses to individuals. The losses must be incurred in a trade or business or in a transaction entered into for profit. The third category, theft and casualty loss, has no application here.

16. The Second Circuit agreed with the Tax Court's interpretation of Section 162 that restitution payments are not deductible under that Code section. Numerous courts have followed the analysis in the wake of the *Stephens* decision. *See* United States v. Chernin, 149 F.3d 805, 811–12 (8th Cir. 1998); United States v. Wolf, 90 F.3d 191 (7th Cir. 1996); Kraft v. United States, 991 F.2d 292 (6th Cir. 1993).

individual taxpayer under Section 165(c)(2) as nonbusiness losses incurred in connection with a profit-seeking activity, not connected with a trade or business. The deductibility of nonbusiness losses under this section is limited to the amount of gross income not derived from a trade or business. If the taxpayer reports no nonbusiness income in the taxable year, Section 165(c)(2) offers no tax benefit. *Kraft*, 991 F.2d at 298. There is no authority allowing a deduction by a corporate taxpayer where the corporation assumes and pays the restitution liability of its officers, directors, or employees.

Restitution can be made in three ways: voluntary restitution; pursuant to court order; and pursuant to a settlement agreement. Voluntary restitution payments—those made not because a court orders it—are generally deductible in the year of repayment. *Int'l Trading Co.*, 484 F.2d at 671.

The sentencing court may also order a defendant to make restitution.[17] The court's statutory authority to order restitution does not include tax crimes charged under Title 26.[18] However, a sentencing court may order restitution in a criminal tax case to the extent agreed to by the parties in a plea agreement.[19] Restitution may be ordered for Title 18 criminal offenses such as mail fraud, *United States v. Helmsley*, 941 F.2d 71 (2d Cir. 1991), *cert. denied*, 502 U.S. 1091 (1992), and conspiracy, *United States v. Minneman*, 143 F.3d 274, 283–84 (7th Cir. 1998), *cert. denied sub nom. Punke v. United States*, 526 U.S. 1006 (1999), since the United States may also be a victim under the Victim Witness Protection Act.[20]

The sentencing court may also authorize restitution as a condition of probation, *United States v. Bok*, 156 F.3d 157, 166–67 (2d Cir. 1998), or supervised release.[21] However, the sentencing court's authority to order restitution is statutorily limited only to victims of the offense and the restitution amount cannot exceed the actual loss, *United States v. Wolf*, 90 F.3d 191, 194 (7th Cir. 1996).

The safest way to avoid any legal ambiguity regarding the nature or correctness of a restitution payment is to include specific restitution provisions in the plea or other settlement agreement between the parties. In some instances, the government has expressly provided in the agreement that the restitution payment shall not be deductible, in which case the restitution will be treated as a fine or similar penalty for tax purposes. This was done in the deferred prosecution agreement entered into

17. The Victim Witness Protection Act gave sentencing courts discretion to order a defendant to pay restitution to crime victims, taking into account "the amount of loss sustained by any victim as a result of the offense" and the defendant's financial resources and ability to pay. 18 U.S.C. § 3663(a)(1)(A) (1985).

18. IRS Practice & Procedure ¶ 7A.10 (Research Inst. of Am. (RIA) 2006).

19. 18 U.S.C. § 3662.

20. *Victim Witness Protection Act, 18 U.S.C.* §§ 3663–3664 (1985).

21. 18 U.S.C. § 3664(a) (1985).

between the accounting firm KPMG and the Department of Justice.[22] However, in the settlement between the Marsh & McLennan Cos. and the State of New York, the $850 million payment was structured as a fully deductible sanction.[23]

V. Tax Consequences to Fraud Victims

In direct response to the collapse of the Bernard Madoff investment "Ponzi" scheme in 2009, the IRS issued Revenue Ruling 2009-9[24] to provide detailed guidance on the uniform tax treatment of the losses suffered by the victims of certain "specified fraudulent arrangements." The IRS also issued Revenue Procedure 2009-20[25] providing optional "safe harbor" rules in conjunction with the issuance of the revenue ruling.

The Revenue Procedure also defines a "specified fraudulent arrangement" as an "arrangement in which a party (the lead figure) receives cash or property from investors; purports to earn income for the investors; reports income amounts to the investors that are partially or wholly fictitious; makes payments, if any, of purported income or principal to some investors from amounts that other investors invested in the fraudulent arrangement; and appropriates some or all of the investors' cash or property." Assuming the transaction fits the definition, Rev. Rul. 2009-9 answers the following questions:

(1) Is a loss from criminal fraud or embezzlement in a transaction entered into for profit a theft loss or a capital loss under § 165 of the Internal Revenue Code?

(2) Is such a loss subject to either the personal loss limits in § 165(h) or the limits on itemized deductions in §§ 67 and 68?

(3) In what year is such a loss deductible?

(4) How is the amount of such a loss determined?

(5) Can such a loss create or increase a net operating loss under § 172?

First, a loss from criminal fraud or embezzlement in a transaction entered into for profit is characterized as a theft loss, not a capital loss, under § 165. Thus, the § 1211 capital loss limitation is not applicable.

22. *See* KPMG Deferred Prosecution Agreement ¶ 4, http://www.usdoj.gov/usao/nys/pressreleases/August05/kpmgdpagmt.pdf. This agreement, along with other agreements entered into in similar white-collar prosecutions, can also be found on the website of the National Association of Criminal Defense Lawyers, http://www.nacdl.org/public.nsf/whitecollar/WC_DPA.

23. Stephen Taub, *Marsh's Settlement: Tax Deductible?*, CFO.com, Feb. 8, 2008, http://www.cfo.com/article.cfm/3642731?f=related.

24. 2009-1 C.B. 735, at http://www.irs.gov/pub/irs-drop/rr-09-09.pdf.

25. http://www.irs.gov/pub/irs-drop/rp-09-20.pdf.

This type of theft loss is deductible under § 165(c)(2), not § 165(c)(3), as an itemized deduction that is not subject to: the personal loss limits in § 165(h), or the limits on itemized deductions in §§ 67 (2 percent floor) and 68 (phase-out for losses that qualify as both personal theft losses and losses incurred in transactions entered into for a profit).

As far as the timing of the deduction, a theft loss in a transaction entered into for profit is deductible in the year the loss is discovered, provided that the loss is not covered by a claim for reimbursement recovery with respect to which there is a "reasonable prospect of recovery." Whether the taxpayer has a reasonable prospect for recovery is a fact-intensive determination. To aid in this determination, Revenue Procedure 2009-20 provides an optional safe harbor allowing taxpayers to claim a theft loss in the year that a criminal indictment, information or complaint is filed in respect of the arrangement, even if the taxpayer has an actual or potential claim for reimbursement or recovery.

The Revenue Procedure also allows victims to claim a theft loss deduction without having to meet certain evidentiary burdens. Typically, in order to claim a theft loss deduction, a taxpayer must show that the subject loss was the result of "theft;" that is, the loss "resulted from a taking of property that was illegal under the law of the jurisdiction in which it occurred and was done with criminal intent."

Instead, under the Revenue Procedure, a loss, defined as a "qualified loss," will be deemed to be the result of "theft" if the promoter was either: (1) charged by indictment or information (not withdrawn or dismissed) under state or federal law with the commission of fraud, embezzlement or a similar crime that, if proven, would meet the definition of "theft"; or (2) the subject of a state or federal criminal complaint (not withdrawn or dismissed) alleging the commission of such a crime and either (i) the complaint alleged an admission by the promoter, or the execution of an affidavit by that person admitting the crime; or (ii) a receiver or trustee was appointed with respect to the arrangement, or assets of the arrangement were frozen.

The amount of a theft loss in a transaction entered into for profit is generally the amount invested in the arrangement, less amounts withdrawn, if any, reduced by reimbursements or recoveries, and reduced by claims for which there is a reasonable prospect of recovery. Where an amount is reported to the investor as income prior to discovery of the arrangement and the investor includes that amount in gross income and reinvests this amount in the arrangement, the amount of the theft loss is increased by the purportedly reinvested amount.

A theft loss in a transaction entered into for profit may create or increase a net operating loss under § 172 that can be carried back up to three years and forward up to 20 years. An eligible small business may elect either a three, four, or five-year net operating loss carryback for an applicable 2008 net operating loss.

VI. Treasury Department Regulations Governing Practice Before the Internal Revenue Service

Not surprisingly, the Treasury Department, like the Securities and Exchange Commission, has "beefed up" its own rules and sanctions for attorneys, certified public accountants, enrolled agents, enrolled retirement plan agents, registered tax return preparers, and other persons representing taxpayers before the IRS in an effort to create accountability and transparency in financial and tax reporting. On August 2, 2011, the Treasury Department issued the latest round of amendments to Circular 230 entitled "Regulations Governing Practice Before the Internal Revenue Service."[26] Subpart B of the Circular outlines in detail the duties and restrictions relating to practice before the IRS and Subpart C outlines the sanctions for failure to follow the rules.

For example, when giving "written advice (including electronic communications) concerning one or more Federal tax issues," a practitioner is prohibited from: (1) basing the advice on "unreasonable factual or legal assumptions"; (2) engaging in unreasonable reliance upon "representations, statements, findings, or agreements of the taxpayer or any other person"; and, (3) failing to "consider all relevant facts that the practitioner knows or should know."[27] With respect to written advice in connection with tax shelters and other "tax-motivated transactions," the advice must satisfy certain new requirements designed to ensure that the practitioner has made "reasonable efforts" to obtain the relevant facts, that the written advice demonstrates well-considered reasoning, and that the written advice makes sufficient disclosure to adequately apprise any third party of all important limitations and risks and to ensure that the advice cannot be misrepresented or misused by the promoter.[28]

The most serious sanction for violating these rules includes disbarment from practice before the IRS. Financial sanctions include an amount up to the gross income derived by the practitioner arising out of the misconduct.[29]

26. 31 CFR Subtitle A, Part 10 at http://www.irs.gov/pub/irs-utl/pcir230.pdf.
27. 31 CFR § 10.37(a).
28. 31 CFR § 10.35.
29. 31 USC § 330.

CHAPTER 8

ACCOUNTING "HOCUS-POCUS" EARNINGS MANAGEMENT

Somebody saw it coming and said so. It's not clear who, if anyone, was listening. In 1998, Arthur Levitt, then chairman of the Securities and Exchange Commission (SEC), delivered his famous "Numbers Game" speech at New York University.[1]

Levitt expressed concern over a new "game of accounting hocus-pocus" among market participants: earnings management. This new game had brought about the "erosion in the quality of earnings" reported on company balance sheets to induce investor participation and increase the value of corporate stock. The game being played was an intensive effort to meet Wall Street earnings expectations through accounting manipulation and "illusions" reported as balance sheet transactions.

The problem was not simply caused by corporate management. Levitt described it as a "financial community" problem where corporate managers, auditors, and analysts became participants in a game of accounting and finance "nods and winks." The calculus for winning is where "trickery is employed to obscure actual financial volatility. This, in turn, masks the true consequences of management's decisions."

The new game also required a network of knowing participants, operating openly and notoriously with the consent of each other, to make the game succeed.

1. Arthur Levitt, Chairman, Sec. & Exchange Comm'n, The Numbers Game, Remarks at NYU Center for Law and Business (Sept. 28, 1998), http://www.sec.gov/news/speech/speecharchive/1998/spch220.txt.

As Levitt observed: "[The companies'] ability to do this depends on achieving the earnings expectations of analysts. And analysts seek constant guidance from companies to frame these expectations. Auditors, who want to retain their clients, are under pressure not to stand in the way."[2] The resulting conflicts of interest arguably evidence criminal intent and participation. Yet the most salient feature of earnings management is the number of willing players that must participate in order for the accounting scheme to succeed. As the Enron, WorldCom, and Refco debacles and the later subprime mortgage crisis demonstrate, the list of participants includes not only auditors and analysts, but also banks, underwriters, accounting firms, and law firms. "Community" is one way to describe the "new age" accounting scandals that have devastated the capital markets, or perhaps another way to describe it is as a new form of organized white-collar crime.

However, prosecuting earnings management is not so simple. The players, or coschemers, also represent many of the financial institutions that create domestic financial stability in the marketplace. The demise of Arthur Andersen brought attention to the possible draconian consequences of entity prosecution. The government is now very reticent to prosecute, for example, the banking industry, where the cure of enforcement may have more devastating economic consequences than the disease of the unlawful conduct. In short, entity prosecution could cripple or dismantle an entire segment of the domestic financial community. The stability of the banking system is as important to market stability as the preservation of its integrity through criminal prosecution.

This is a continuing debate that will not be resolved here. But the reality raises interesting questions for the practitioner. Armed with the knowledge that the Department of Justice (DOJ) is not interested in another Arthur Andersen, there is some additional flexibility under the USAM guidelines to avoid indictment and achieve a less heinous resolution in the form of a nonprosecution or deferred prosecution arrangements.[3] Again, the increase in entity "prosecution" through informal disposition, essentially "nonprosecution," is on the rise.

I. Hocus-Pocus: Five Accounting Tricks of Earnings Management

Earnings management is not per se illegal behavior. However, when earnings management is used to distort the true financial picture of the company and mislead the investing public, the participants cross over the line from legal to fraudulent conduct. Levitt identifies five popular "illusions" or tricks used to facilitate earnings

2. *Id.*
3. See Chapter 6.

management: large-charge restructuring charges; creative acquisition accounting; "cookie jar" reserves; materiality; and revenue recognition.[4]

A. Large-Charge Restructuring

Large-charge restructuring, also called "big bath" restructuring, is a one-time charge against earnings used to clean up the balance sheet. Firms use restructuring charge reversals to meet earnings targets. Here's how it works. A company undergoing a major organizational change or in the process of an acquisition anticipates incurring large expenses over a period of several years. Rather than recognizing these expenses as they actually occur, management reduces current income by at least the total amount of estimated expenses related to the entire transaction. In most instances, management will purposely overestimate the expenses and thereby create an excessive reserve. While the single large-charge write-off may dramatically reduce current earnings, income is boosted in subsequent years in the absence of these costs or by reversing an excessive reserve for expenses created in the prior year.

Levitt explains that the motivation for overestimating these expenses is the theory that Wall Street will overlook a one-time loss and focus only on future earnings estimates.[5] The conservative estimate is miraculously reborn as income in later years when estimates change or future earnings run short. Expenses overstated in one year can be reduced and added back into income in the next when the expenses never materialize. It creates a cushion for future years where performance may run short. (This has some similarities to the use of "cookie jar" reserves, explained shortly.)

The distortion is illustrated by Cisco Systems, Inc. In April 2001, Cisco announced charges against earnings of almost $4 billion. The bulk of the charge, $2.5 billion, consisted of an inventory write-down. However, Cisco wrote off an excessive amount that was almost equal to the cost of the entire inventory that was sold in the previous quarter. A current write-off of more than a billion dollars from inventory in the current year means more than a billion dollars of less cost in a future period.

At some point, Cisco could, theoretically, announce that business is starting to get better and the company could report results that confirm it, even if sales stay flat, by simply reversing some part of the overstated write-off reserve.[6] The numbers game produces ostensible earnings based only on balance sheet entries as opposed to actual earnings from performance. Restructuring or reversing write-offs helps in later years to meet earnings targets. That illustrates the "quality of earnings" problem identified by Levitt.[7] Earnings are based on paper and not actual performance.

4. Levitt, *supra* note 1.

5. *Id.*

6. Richard J. Kokoszka, *Recognizing the Signs: Internal Auditors Can Help Organizations Avoid the Risks Associated with Inappropriate Earnings Management by Understanding the Symptoms and Sharing Their Knowledge*, Internal Auditor, Apr. 1, 2003.

7. Levitt, *supra* note 1.

To counter this practice, in 1999, the SEC issued Accounting Bulletin No. 100 in an effort to rein in accountants.[8] Accounting Bulletin No. 100 requires companies to make full disclosure of the practice of restructuring charges and the impact on the specific line items on the balance sheet and the subsequent years' balance sheets so that investors have full knowledge regarding the practice. The policy is specially designed to "enhance financial statement transparency."[9] The Office of the Chief Accountant of the SEC sent out a letter to large public accounting firms that underscored the continuing importance of the policy.[10]

B. Creative Acquisition Accounting

Levitt refers to this trick as "merger magic."[11] During the course of a merger, purchasers may write off assets called in-process research and development (IPR&D). In merger accounting, the purchaser assigns values to acquired assets in order to properly capitalize the costs, which are then written off over future tax years. But the values assigned to IPR&D must be written off in total in the acquisition year and cannot be used to reduce earnings in the future. So, here's the trick. Purchasers overstate IPR&D accounts to take a large write-off and then restructure and reverse the write-off in future years when earnings do not meet targets.

This accounting illusion contributed to the downfall of WorldCom, the largest corporate bankruptcy in U.S. history.[12] WorldCom achieved its position as a significant player in the telecommunications industry through the successful completion of 65 acquisitions.[13] Between 1991 and 1997, WorldCom spent almost $60 billion in acquiring many of these companies and accumulated $41 billion in debt.[14] In an effort to make it appear that profits were increasing, WorldCom would write down in one quarter millions of dollars in assets it acquired while, at the same time, it "included in this charge against earnings the cost of company expenses expected in the future. The result was bigger losses in the current quarter but smaller ones in future quarters, so that its profit picture would seem to be improving."[15]

The acquisition of MCI gave WorldCom another accounting opportunity. While reducing the book value of some MCI assets by several billion dollars, the company

8. SEC Staff Accounting Bulletin No. 100 (Nov. 24, 1999), *available at* http://www.sec.gov/news/extra/sab100f.htm.

9. *Id.*

10. Office of the Chief Accountant: Sample Letter Sent to Large Public Accounting Firms (Mar. 22, 2001), http://www.sec.gov/info/accountants/staffletters/sampleletter.htm.

11. Levitt, *supra* note 1.

12. Dep't of Justice, Statement of the Attorney General Regarding WorldCom Bankruptcy (July 22, 2002), http://www.usdoj.gov/opa/pr/2002/July/02_ag_415.htm.

13. Kurt Eichenwald, *For WorldCom, Acquisitions Were Behind Its Rise and Fall*, N.Y. Times, Aug. 8, 2002.

14. Simon Romero & Rava D. Atlas, *WorldCom's Collapse: The Overview*, N.Y. Times, July 22, 2002.

15. Eichenwald, *supra* note 13.

increased the value of "goodwill." This enabled WorldCom each year to charge a smaller amount against earnings by spreading these large expenses over decades rather than years. The net result was WorldCom's ability to cut annual expenses, acknowledge all MCI revenue, and boost profits from the acquisition.[16]

C. Cookie Jar Reserves

Cookie jar reserves, sometimes referred to as rainy day reserves, are set up using unrealistic assumptions to estimate liability reserves for items such as expected sales returns, loan losses, or warranty costs. The overestimates allow companies to stash accruals in a reserve "cookie jar" during good times. In periods of weak financial performance, the cookie jar reserves can be used by reversing accruals, which will reduce current expenses and increase earnings. Again, the increase in earnings is as a result of an accounting entry only. There is no actual increase as a result of increased performance. Levitt provides an anecdote: "I'm reminded of one U.S. company who took a large one-time loss to earnings to reimburse franchisees for equipment. That equipment, however, which literally included the kitchen sink, had yet to be bought. And, at the same time, they announced that future earnings would grow an impressive 15 percent per year."[17]

The discretion to dip into the cookie jar is the key factor of the accounting manipulation. The company dips as needed to meet earnings expectations.

D. Materiality

No matter how good the accountant, not every financial statement is accurate to the penny. To deal with minor deviations or inaccuracies, auditors attest that financial statements are accurate "in all material respects." Materiality is another way that the accounting regulations build flexibility in financial reporting and financial statements. If a mistake is not "material," it need not be reported. Materiality is not defined in the accounting profession. That is where abuse finds its way into the process. Auditors and companies argue that a particular transaction was not material to the overall statement of financial condition and therefore need not be reported.

There are at least two problems that arise in this context. First, when each nonreported transaction is aggregated into a whole, the overall impact of numerous "immaterial transactions" may in the aggregate greatly affect the financial statement. Second, materiality is oftentimes in the eye of the beholder. While an auditor may use the materiality excuse for nonreporting, the transaction is in actuality material. Again, it is the discretion accorded the auditor that is the key factor in the manipulation.

---

16. Dennis Moberg & Edward Romar, *WorldCom* (case study, Markula Ctr. for Applied Ethics, Santa Clara Univ. 2003), http://www.scu.edu/ethics/dialogue/candc/cases/worldcom.html.

17. Levitt, *supra* note 1.

The inventory-reporting example of Sunbeam, Inc., the maker of small-home appliances, illustrates the point.[18] Sunbeam used a warehouse owned by EPI Printers to store its large inventory of warranty replacement parts. Sunbeam proposed selling its parts to EPI for $11 million and then booking an $8 million profit. EPI was not interested in the deal because its appraisal of the parts came in at only $2 million. To overcome the objection, Sunbeam agreed to have EPI buy the parts for $11 million on paper at the end of 1997. Sunbeam would then book the profit and allow EPI to later back out of the deal in January 1998. The deal was entered into, the profit booked in 1997, and then EPI backed out of the deal in the following month in the new tax year.

Sunbeam's auditor, Arthur Andersen, questioned the transaction but then did not reverse the entry on the basis that it was not "material" in terms of percentage of income. However, the total of this and other similar "nonmaterial" transactions equaled 16 percent of Sunbeam's profits for 1997, an obviously material percentage of profits.

With the passage of the Sarbanes-Oxley Act of 2002 and the creation of the Public Company Accounting Oversight Board (PCAOB), at least with respect to publicly traded companies, the SEC has attempted to tighten the accounting standards dealing with materiality determinations. On May 24, 2007, the PCAOB adopted Auditing Standard No. 5, "An Audit of Internal Control Over Financial Reporting That Is Integrated with An Audit of Financial Statements," to replace its previous internal control auditing standard, Auditing Standard No. 2. The Board also adopted the related Rule 3525, "Audit Committee Pre-Approval of Non-Audit Services Related to Internal Control Over Financial Reporting," and conforming amendments to certain of the Board's other auditing standards.[19]

The auditing standard adopted by the PCAOB is principles-based, meaning that strict compliance with accounting rules alone is not enough. The intentional or underlying principles governing the implementation of the rules must also be satisfied.[20] The auditing standard is designed to increase the likelihood that material weaknesses in internal control will be found before they result in material misstatement of a company's financial statements and, at the same time, eliminate procedures that are unnecessary. The final standard also focuses the auditor on the procedures necessary to perform a high quality audit that is tailored to the company's facts and circumstances. The PCAOB worked closely with the SEC to coordinate Auditing

18. Marianne Jennings, *The Ethics of Materiality in Financial Reporting*, Internal Auditing J. (2002).

19. For an explanation of the rules changes, see Pub. Co. Accounting Oversight Bd., Board Approves New Audit Standard For Internal Control Over Financial Reporting and, Separately, Recommendations on Inspection Frequency Rule (May 24, 2007), http://www.iasplus.com/usa/pcaob/0705as5pr.pdf.

20. For a quick primer on the differences between rules-based and principles-based accounting, see *Rebecca Shortridge & Mark Myring, Defining Principles-Based Accounting*, CPA J., Aug. 2004, *available at* http://www.nysscpa.org/cpajournal/2004/804/essentials/p34.htm. The SEC also provides a more complete discussion of the area on its website at http://www.sec.gov/news/studies/principlesbasedstand.htm.

Standard No. 5 with the guidance to public company management approved by the SEC. While the new rules still do not define materiality as such, they do provide guidance to auditors to prevent mere technical compliance with accounting rules as an excuse to mask financial statements that do not provide a true picture of the company's financial circumstances.

E. Revenue Recognition

Recording revenue before a sale is actually completed is premature revenue recognition. One common example is known as "channel stuffing," or shipping inventory before orders are placed by the customer. Coca-Cola is notorious for the practice. Some of the details came to light in a shareholder lawsuit filed in U.S. District Court in Atlanta in October 2000. The civil suit charged that Coca-Cola inflated its 1999 revenue by $600 million and boosted pretax earnings by $400 million by overloading bottles in Japan, the United States, Europe, and South Africa with "unneeded" concentrate. The lawsuit was filed after Coca-Cola reported $1.5 billion in write-offs and, in the first quarter of 2000, recorded its first quarterly loss in the recent history of the company.[21] Coca-Cola settled the allegations of channel stuffing with the SEC in 2005 after it was revealed that the company had engaged in the practice to meet earnings expectations for at least eight financial reporting quarters during 1997–1999.[22]

The practice is not limited to channel stuffing, although that is the most common. The revenue might also come from contingent sales that ultimately do not materialize, fictitious sales, subscription contracts, or other rebate and credit programs.

II. Warning Signs of Earnings Management: Spotting Accounting Frauds

On January 23, 2003, the SEC issued its "Report Pursuant to Section 704 of the Sarbanes-Oxley Act of 2002."[23] Section 704 directed the SEC "to study enforcement actions over the five years preceding its enactment in order to identify areas of issuer financial reporting that are most susceptible to fraud, inappropriate manipulation, or inappropriate earnings management."[24] The study period began July 31, 1997, and ended July 30, 2002.

---

21. Paul Klebnikov, *Coke's Sinful World*, 172(13) Forbes 86 (Dec. 22, 2003), *available at* http://www.forbes.com/forbes/2003/1222/086_print.html.

22. William Spain, *No Fine for Coke in "Channel-Stuffing,"* Mkt. Watch, Apr. 18, 2005, http://www.marketwatch.com/News/Story/Story.aspx?guid={669BE9B8-D05C-4B82-ADAD-234BF4637C26}.

23. Sec. & Exchange Comm'n, Report Pursuant to Section 704 of the Sarbanes-Oxley Act of 2002, Jan. 24, 2003, http://www.sec.gov/news/studies/sox704report.pdf.

24. Sarbanes-Oxley Act of 2002 § 704, Pub. L. No. 107-204, 116 Stat. 745.

Over the study period, the SEC filed 515 enforcement actions for financial reporting and disclosure violations arising out of 227 separate Division of Enforcement investigations. Those investigations fell into three categories:

- Revenue recognition, including fraudulent reporting of fictitious sales, inaccurate timing of revenue recognition, and improper valuation of revenue.
- Expense recognition, consisting of including improper capitalization or deferral of expenses, incorrect use of reserves, and other understatements of expenses.
- Business combinations relating to myriad improper accounting activities used to effect and report combined entities.

All but one of these 227 investigations included revenue-related issues, and many investigations identified violations in two or all three of these categories.[25] The importance of the study to practitioners is that it revealed relatively simple accounting warning signs that may either reveal a scam in progress or provide a road map in a case already under investigation.

To simplify any internal investigation, practitioners, investors, and auditors should consider these six relationships as early warning signs of abusive earnings management:[26]

- Cash flows that are not correlated with earnings;
- Receivables that are not correlated with revenues;
- Allowances for uncollectible accounts that are not correlated with receivables;
- Reserves that are not correlated with balance sheet items;
- Acquisitions with no apparent business purpose; and
- Earnings that consistently and precisely meet analysts' expectations.

Of course, the ability to identify the warning signs may be complicated by false financial statements generated internally or with the imprimatur of outside auditors. Yet common sense may prevail in the end. If the earnings growth sounds too good to be true, it probably isn't true. Never trust growth reported based on revenues alone. Growth from operations is the key and a truer measure of quality in earnings statements.

25. Leonard G. Weld, Peter M. Bergevin, & Lorraine Magrath, *Anatomy of a Financial Fraud*, CPA J., Aug. 2002, *available at* http://www.nysscpa.org/printversions/cpaj/2004/1004/p44.htm.

26. Lorraine Magrath & Leonard G. Weld, *Abusive Earnings Management and Early Warning Signs*, CPA J., Aug. 2002, *available at* http://www.nysscpa.org/cpajournal/2002/0802/features/f085002.htm.

III. Criminal Prosecutions: The Case of Bristol-Myers Squibb

Corporations may be held criminally liable for earnings management abuses. One recent case involved criminal charges filed against Bristol-Myers Squibb (BMS).[27] Under a deferred prosecution agreement, BMS agreed to pay $300 million in victim restitution and undertake a series of corporate reforms as part of an agreement with the government to defer prosecution on a charge of conspiring to commit securities fraud for the company's failure to disclose its "channel stuffing" activities in 2000 and 2001. The government charged individual corporate officers with planning and concealing the channel-stuffing scheme to meet aggressive internal sales and earnings targets and Wall Street consensus earnings estimates.

The government charged that throughout 2000 and 2001 BMS concealed from investors its use of "channel stuffing." BMS's channel stuffing consisted of enticing its wholesalers through use of financial incentives to buy and hold greater quantities of prescription drugs than were warranted by the demand for those products. By the end of 2001, BMS's channel stuffing resulted in nearly $2 billion in "excess inventory" at the wholesalers.

The two years at issue in the investigation—2000 and 2001—were the last year of BMS's "Double-Double" and the first year of its "Mega-Double" campaigns, publicly announced corporate goals to double sales and earnings, first in the seven years from 1994 to 2000, and then in the five years from 2001 to 2005. BMS's channel stuffing and other improper earnings management during 2000 and 2001 were part of an effort to report financial performance consistent with its Double-Double and Mega-Double public announcements. Without the channel stuffing, BMS also likely would have missed the Wall Street consensus estimates for its sales and earnings.

The charges alleged that BMS failed to disclose and made false and misleading statements to the investing public regarding: (1) the use of financial incentives to the wholesalers to generate sales in excess of demand; (2) the use of sales in excess of demand to hit budget targets; (3) the level of excess inventory at the wholesalers; and (4) the amount that excess inventory increased each quarter in 2000 and 2001. As a result, investors were misled regarding BMS's true sales and earnings, and did not have an accurate picture of the health of the company's business operations.

Under the deferred prosecution agreement, BMS agreed to pay an additional $300 million in restitution to victims of the fraud scheme, bringing the total that BMS was ordered to pay shareholders harmed by the fraudulent conduct to $839 million, including a $100 million civil penalty under an earlier consent agreement with the SEC, a $50 million Shareholder Fund payment, and monies paid in settlement

27. Bristol-Myers Squibb Deferred Prosecution Agreement (June 15, 2005), http://lib.law.virginia.edu/Garrett/prosecution_agreements/pdf/bristol-meyers.pdf.

of two class action proceedings. The monetary penalties provided full restitution for the losses sustained for shares traded in the four days after BMS announced its restatement in 2001.

The salient features of the agreement also required BMS to:[28]

- Accept and acknowledge responsibility for its conduct, as reflected in the factual statement accompanying the agreement;
- Appoint a current member of the board of directors, James Robinson III, as the nonexecutive chairman of the board, to ensure that BMS emphasizes openness, accountability, and integrity in corporate governance;
- Cooperate fully with the U.S. Attorney's Office in its ongoing investigation;
- Pay $300 million in additional restitution to shareholders;
- Adopt internal controls and other remedial measures designed to prevent and deter potential violations of the federal securities laws; and
- Engage an independent monitor, former U.S. Attorney and Federal Judge Frederick B. Lacey, as agreed upon by the DOJ and BMS, to monitor BMS's ongoing remediation efforts and report to the Department on a regular basis.

Other components of the deferred prosecution agreement include the following:[29]

- Requiring BMS to endow a chair at Seton Hall University Law School dedicated to the teaching of business ethics and corporate governance, which position shall include conducting at least one seminar on business ethics and corporate governance annually that members of BMS's executive and management staff may attend, as well as other corporate executives.
- Holding a meeting within 30 days of this agreement, for BMS senior executives and senior financial personnel and other BMS employees, to be conducted by U.S. Attorney Christie and others from his office for the purpose of communicating the goals and expected effect of the agreement.
- The appointment of an additional nonexecutive director acceptable to the U.S. Attorney's Office and the BMS Board of Directors within 60 days.

---

28. Deferred Prosecution Agreement Bristol-Myers Squibb Company at 2–3, http://www.usdoj.gov/usao/nj/press/files/pdffiles/deferredpros.pdf.

29. *Id.* at 6.

Chapter 9

THE FOREIGN CORRUPT PRACTICES ACT BRIBERY AS A GLOBAL MARKET ENTRY STRATEGY

"The proper governance of companies will become as crucial to the world economy as the proper governing of countries."[1] Many U.S. companies engage in some level of global commerce. The expectations about corporate governance and "business as usual" change as companies venture forth into a new and virtually unregulated global marketplace.

The first important lesson in international law is that the global marketplace is not subject to legal regulation in the same sense as domestic regulation. There is no such thing as a global statute or agreed-upon global set of regulations that govern corporate behavior in the course of conducting international business transactions, except that which is provided by treaty. Treaty observance is consensual by each signatory and the quality of treaty enforcement is the equivalent of the quality of voluntary self-restraint.

1. James Wolfensohn, former President of the World Bank, quoted in The World in 1999, at 38 (Economist 1998).

The second important lesson in international law is that not every country behaves in the same way. Different countries have different cultural and business mores. This is particularly true in commercial transactions where bribery is used to facilitate market entry strategy for multinational corporations. In many countries, bribery is the ordinary course of business and even tax-deductible. Of course, there is an international movement afoot to eliminate bribery as any kind of rational-choice market entry strategy, but progress tends to be slow and uneven. Even where countries, such as the United States, sign antibribery treaties, internal enforcement is perceived as little more than a cost of doing business to be avoided.

In the United States, law firms have entered the field to provide companies with compliance plans in the hopes of easing the pain in the event a client actually gets caught and prosecuted, which is generally unlikely based on the first 30 years of enforcement statistics under the Act. However, it is important to understand what business conduct the current global antibribery statute, the Foreign Corrupt Practices Act (FCPA), proscribes and what conduct is not covered under the Act.

To summarize the FCPA in a nutshell: U.S. corporations may not bribe foreign public officials to obtain or keep business. However, as far as issuers and nonissuers are concerned, private sector commercial bribery and "grease payments" are not prohibited. Payments made for any other purpose are likewise not prohibited. One word of caution. While the legal prohibitions of the FCPA may be limited, there is nothing to stop the Department of Justice (DOJ) from seeking criminal charges based on some other domestic criminal statute that might otherwise be applied to U.S. companies operating in foreign venues. Those statutes include the mail and wire fraud statutes, 18 U.S.C. §§ 1341 and 1343, money laundering, 18 U.S.C. § 1956, and the Travel Act, 18 U.S.C. § 1952, which provides for federal prosecution of violations of state commercial bribery statutes.

I. Understanding the Act

A. The "Watergate" Connection: The Enactment of the FCPA

In 1973, the Office of the Watergate Special Prosecutor uncovered more than a corrupt presidency. The investigation revealed a pattern of conduct involving the use of unaccounted-for corporate "slush" funds for questionable foreign payments.[2] The most famous case involved the criminal prosecution of Gulf Oil and its corporate vice president, Claude C. Wilde Jr., in connection with illegal political "gifts" of corporate funds to politicians, including one of $100,000 to President Richard Nixon. Securities and Exchange Commission (SEC) investigators found that from 1960 to

2. SEC Release No. 34-15570 (Feb. 15, 1979), *reprinted in* LawyerLinks Advantage, http://content.lawyerlinks.com/library/sec/sec_releases/34-15570.htm.

1973, Gulf Oil and Wilde spent more than $10 million on illegal political activities and in business transactions abroad.

The SEC filed a complaint against Gulf Oil and Wilde charging that the corporate balance sheets violated SEC disclosure rules for failing to include the value of the corporate slush fund as an asset.[3] It followed that company filings with the regulator, relied on by the public in making investment decisions, were false. Yet the case triggered a much larger concern for the SEC: How many other companies were engaged in the same conduct? Widespread corruption could easily frustrate the self-regulatory system of corporate accountability which mandated full and accurate disclosure of the use of corporate funds to the investment public through SEC filings.

Fearing a crisis in the self-reporting system, the SEC was determined to discover the magnitude of the practice of engaging in bribery by issuers. The only sure way to test the waters was to provide an amnesty program. Issuers were offered the opportunity to self-report their wrongdoing in the company's annual report, on Form 10-K, or on a supplemental Form 8-K, and thus there could be no claim that the information was merely anecdotal. The results astonished the SEC and Congress. More than 400 companies admitted to making questionable or illegal payments. The pay-outs exceeded $300 million in corporate "slush" funds to foreign officials, politicians, and political parties. Over 117 of the companies that self-reported ranked in the top Fortune 500 companies.[4]

It became immediately apparent that the same reasons for criminalizing domestic bribery existed to eradicate bribery as a global market entry strategy. It wasn't just that it was unethical; it was also "bad business." Bribery erodes public confidence in the markets and damages the integrity of the free market system. It distorts the rules of the marketplace by replacing competition with corruption and pressuring otherwise ethical enterprises to either behave corruptly or risk losing business. From the SEC's point of view, it threatens the self-regulatory system of corporate self-policing and mandatory disclosure, the glue that holds the securities acts together.

To combat this threat to stability in the domestic and international market infrastructures, the SEC proposed to Congress the criminalization of foreign bribery payments made to public officials and foreign political parties. The FCPA passed by unanimous vote in 1977.[5] The legislation included a permanent amendment to the Securities and Exchange Act of 1934,[6] designed to more strenuously regulate the conduct of issuers.

3. *Again, Political Slush Funds,* Time, Mar. 24, 1999, *available at* http://www.time.com/time/magazine/article/0,9171,946547-1,00.html.

4. H. R. Rep. No. 95-640 (1977), http://www.usdoj.gov/criminal/fraud/fcpa/history/1977/houseprt.html.

5. Foreign Corrupt Practices Act of 1977, 15 U.S.C. §§ 78dd-1, *et seq.* (1977), http://www.usdoj.gov/criminal/fraud/docs/statute.html.

6. *Id.*

B. Legislative Provisions and Limitations of Enforcement

In terms of enforcement, the SEC can institute civil injunctive and administrative proceedings to enforce all FCPA provisions against issuers. The DOJ can institute criminal actions against any person or company for any violation of the antibribery and against any issuer for violations of the recordkeeping provision. DOJ can also institute civil injunctive action against any domestic concern for violations of the antibribery provisions.

However, it is an important starting point to understand the limitations of enforcement under the FCPA. The act does not, and is not intended to, outlaw all forms of international bribery. Passed in 1977 and amended in 1988[7] and 1998, the FCPA includes two main provisions: the antibribery clause and the recordkeeping and accounting provisions. The antibribery clause prohibits payoffs to foreign public officials or political parties to "obtain or retain business."[8] However, payments made merely to seek "an improper advantage" may not be outlawed.[9]

In the same way that the FCPA does not proscribe all bribe payments, it also does not cover all companies under its prohibitions. While the antibribery clause applies to issuers, domestic concerns, and related individuals, the recordkeeping and accounting provisions, best thought of as "paper-trail" clauses or anticoncealment clauses designed to ensure an audit trail for all global expenditures, apply only to issuers. Only issuers are required to report, disclose, and account to the SEC for all payments made to foreign officials. Nonissuers are not required to make and keep such records. For nonissuers, self-regulation without disclosure is the only touchstone of compliance.

Without similar disclosure and accounting requirements for nonissuers, the enhanced ability of U.S. companies to conceal bribe payments becomes the self-fulfilling prophecy that bribery in foreign commerce is difficult to detect and prove. More important, without similar recordkeeping and accounting provisions, nonissuers fall through the enforcement net and undermine the decisive impact of the FCPA on market entry global behavior. The Organization for Economic Co-operation and Development (OECD), which monitors FCPA antibribery compliance by the United States, concluded: "It is at the level of non-issuer SMEs [small and medium-size enterprises] that the FCPA system may be at its least effective . . . these companies appear, as it were, to potentially slip through the net. The examiners could not avoid the conclusion that there may be a level of undetected foreign bribery taking place in the international operations of non-issuer SMEs, simply because there are insufficient

7. Foreign Corrupt Practices Act Amendments of 1988, Pub. L. No. 100-418, 5003(a), (c), 102 Stat. 1418, 1423–24 (1988).

8. Foreign Corrupt Practices Act, *supra* note 5.

9. *See* United States v. Kay, 539 F.3d 738 (5th Cir. 2004). Proscribed payments may include favorable tax or customs treatment.

compliance programs or other systems in place to deter it and insufficient bookkeeping, auditing or other control mechanisms in place to detect it."[10]

In 2005, the United States again declined to follow OECD recommendations to extend the coverage of the "paper trail" provisions to nonissuers, on the theory that current levels of FCPA deterrence were "generally reasonable."[11] However, the statistics show that the levels of enforcement in 2005 were less than "reasonable." No new cases were filed in 2005 and enforcement was practically nonexistent (see Appendix E: Foreign Corrupt Practices Case Statistics (1978–2011)).

Additionally, the exclusion of "grease payments" from the act's coverage was also intentional, as indicated by the legislative history.[12] Grease payments, also referred to as "facilitating payments," are those made to ensure that government functionaries discharge certain ministerial or clerical duties. While bribe payments are not deductible items, grease payments may be deductible as ordinary and necessary company business expenses under the Internal Revenue Code if certain conditions are satisfied.[13] Not surprisingly, the dividing line between bribe payments and facilitation payments remains somewhat unclear because with the absence of enforcement also comes the absence of a body of case law interpreting the scope of legislative application.

Finally, the other slippery slope is the limited scope of the application of the FCPA to foreign subsidiaries. The 1988 amendments to the act clarified responsibility for subsidiaries not wholly owned by U.S. parent companies. Where the parent-issuer owns 50 percent or less of voting power, neither the parent nor the subsidiary doing business in the foreign venue is covered by the FCPA. The issuer is required only to "proceed in good faith to use its influence, to the extent reasonable . . . to cause . . . [the subsidiary] to devise and maintain a system of internal accounting controls consistent with . . ." the section.[14] The legislative history notes

---

10. OECD, United States: Review of Implementation of the Convention and 1997 Recommendation (2002), http://www.oecd.org/dataoecd/16/50/2390377.pdf.

11. OECD, Follow-Up Report on the Implementation of the Phase 2 Recommendations on the Application of the Convention and the 1997 Recommendations on Combating Bribery of Foreign Public Officials in International Business Transactions (2005), http://www.oecd.org/dataoecd/7/35/35109576.pdf.

12. H. R Rep. No. 95-640 (1977), http://www.usdoj.gov/criminal/fraud/fcpa/history/1977/houseprt.html.

13. While the U.S. tax code denies a tax deduction for bribe payments per se, "grease payments," which remain legal under the FCPA, still qualify for favorable domestic tax treatment. Section 162(c)(1) of the Internal Revenue Code disallows deductions for illegal payments to officials or employees of any government. Facilitation payments, so-called grease payments, that are legal under the local law of a foreign jurisdiction may be deducted for tax purposes.

14. Foreign Corrupt Practices Act Amendments of 1988, *supra* note 7.

that "it is unrealistic to expect a minority owner to exert a disproportionate degree of influence."[15]

However, correlating control with ownership percentage alone may create another persistent source of undetected conduct. An example is the use by Enron of special purpose entities (SPEs) to transfer assets off Enron's balance sheet to conceal the true nature and extent of its liabilities. Enron was able to omit the SPE transactions from its balance sheet by merely structuring the SPE transactions to reflect that Enron held a lesser ownership interest than required by the accounting rules for balance sheet inclusion. To facilitate the accounting fraud, Enron placed majority ownership in "straw persons" and secretly financed capitalization through the extensive use of loan transactions. Similarly, an issuer holding 50 percent ownership or less may still exert actual control of a foreign operating entity even though ostensible percentage ownership is held by other real or fictitious parties. In this way, parent companies have avoided the reach of the FCPA. Congress is aware of the apparent loophole but has not acted to change the law.

II. Antibribery Provisions

Title 18 U.S.C. § 78dd-2 makes it unlawful for any issuer or domestic concern, or for any officer, director, employee, agent, or shareholder to make use of the mails or any means or instrumentality of interstate commerce corruptly in furtherance of an offer, payment, promise to pay, or authorization of the payment of any money, or offer, gift, promise to give, or authorization of the giving of anything of value to—

> (1) Any foreign official for purposes of—
>
> > (A) (i) influencing any act or decision of such foreign official in his official capacity, (ii) inducing such foreign official to do or omit to do any act in violation of the lawful duty of such official, or (iii) securing any improper advantage; or
> >
> > (B) inducing such foreign official to use his influence with a foreign government or instrumentality thereof to affect or influence any act or decision of such government or instrumentality; in order to . . . assist . . . in obtaining or retaining business for or with, or directing business to, any person;
>
> (2) Any foreign political party or official thereof or any candidate for foreign political office for purposes of [as stated above in (1)(A)&(B)] . . .

15. H.R. Conf. Rep. No. 100-576 (1987), http://www.usdoj.gov/criminal/fraud/fcpa/history/1988/tradeact.html.

(3) Any person, while knowing that all or a portion of such money or thing of value will be offered, given, or promised, directly or indirectly, to any foreign official, to any foreign political party or official thereof, or to any candidate for foreign political office, for purposes of [as stated above in (1)(A)&(B)] . . ."

The basic elements of the offense include:

1. Any U.S. person or entity—includes "issuers," "domestic concerns," officer, directors and agents
2. Jurisdictional means
3. Corruptly
4. Payment—anything of value including a promise to pay
5. Foreign government official—includes any official, member of party, or candidate
6. Receipt of thing of value—knowing that all or part of thing of value will be offered
7. Purpose—influence to do or omit
8. Obtain or retain business

"Issuer" is defined under 15 U.S.C. § 78dd-1(a) as including any U.S. public company subject to SEC reporting requirements including employees and foreign agents. "Domestic concern" is defined under 15 U.S.C. § 78dd-2(h)(10)(B) as including any business with its principal place of business in the United States. *See, e.g., United States v. Bodmer*, 342 F. Supp. 2d 176 (S.D.N.Y. 2004).

The FCPA applies to foreign agents of issuers or domestic concerns; however, it does not apply either directly or under conspiracy theory to foreign officials. *United States v. Blondek,* 741 F. Supp. 116 (N.D. Tex. 1990), *aff'd sub nom. United States v. Castle,* 925 F.2d 831 (5th Cir. 1991). Foreign corporations are not directly subject to the terms of the act. In short, there is no basis for the United States to exercise "international jurisdiction" in foreign venues.

The term "corruptly" is not defined by the statute, but the legislative history does provide guidance. "The word 'corruptly' is used in order to make clear that the offer, payment, promise, or gift, must be intended to induce the recipient to misuse his official position in order to wrongfully direct business to the payor or his client, or to obtain preferential regulation . . . [it] connotes an evil motive or purpose, an intent to wrongfully influence the recipient. It does not require that the act be fully consummated, or succeed in producing the desired outcome. . . . The defense that the payment was demanded on the part of a government official as a price for gaining entry into a market or to obtain entry into a market would not suffice. . . . That the payment may have been first proposed by the recipient rather than the U.S. company does not alter the corrupt purpose. . . . On the other hand true extortion situations would not be covered by this provision since a payment to an official to keep an oil rig from being dynamited should not be held to be made with the requisite corrupt purpose."[16]

There is not much decisional law under the statute, so guidance in determining exactly what constitutes a prohibited corrupt payment is limited. In *United States v. Liebo,* 923 F.2d 1308 (8th Cir. 1991), the court found sufficient evidence to establish the "corruptly" requirement where defendant paid for plane tickets for a public official's honeymoon, the company won the contract shortly after the honeymoon, and the defendant concealed the true nature of the payment, although the case was reversed on other grounds. The DOJ has charged a variety of payments including charitable donations, loans with favorable terms, transportation of household goods, college scholarships, and even the services of a prostitute.

In *United States v. Kay,* 513 F.3d 432 (5th Cir. 2007), *aff'd on reh'g en banc*, 513 F.3d 461 (2008), the court affirmed that bribes to obtain favorable tax treatment in that case were made to "obtain or retain business" and therefore violated the act. Specifically, the court held that any payments to foreign officials that might assist in obtaining or retaining business by lowering the costs of operations can fall within the FCPA, even where such a payment is not directly related to securing a contract. The judges rejected the defendants' claim that this broad interpretation of the business nexus requirement rendered the statute unconstitutionally vague. The court also ruled that in proving the "knowing" element of an FCPA offense, the United States need only prove the defendants understood that their actions were illegal. No specific knowledge about the FCPA or its prohibitions is required.

Note, however, not all such payments are automatically illegal, because the act expressly requires a corrupt purpose of obtaining or retaining business. The first *Kay* opinion, 359 F.3d 738, 749 (5th Cir. 2004), therefore cautions that not every bribe to reduce taxes is prohibited, because "it still must be shown that the bribery was intended to produce an effect—here, through tax savings—that would 'assist in obtaining or retaining business.'" Significantly, a motive to pay in order to achieve increased profit margins alone is insufficient to violate the act.[17]

The legislative history is clear that the act is to be strictly construed to prohibit payments to public officials for the limited purposes of obtaining or retaining

16. H.R. Rep. No. 95-640, at 8 (1977), S. Rep. No. 95-114, at 10–11 (1977), *reprinted in* 1977 U.S.C.C.A.N. 4098, 4108.

17. *See also* In re Bristow Group, Inc., SEC Release No. 34-56533 (Sep. 26, 2007), http://www.sec.gov/litigation/admin/2007/34-56533.pdf. This case involved a settled administrative proceeding in which the Cease and Desist Order alleged the Bristol Group made improper payments to Nigerian state government officials in return for a reduction in employment taxes. This issue still remains to be tested in the courts.

business.[18] The limitation is significant. The FCPA has no application to private sector bribery. The United States has politely but firmly refused any recommendation by the OECD to expand the coverage of the act in that regard.

The antibribery provisions do not apply to "grease" payments, defined as "any facilitating or expediting payment to a foreign official, political party or party official the purpose of which is to expedite or to secure the performance of routine government action by a foreign official, political party, or party official."[19] The statute defines routine government action to include the following:

An action which is ordinarily and commonly performed by a foreign official in—

i. obtaining permits, licenses, or other official documents to qualify a person to do business in a foreign country;
ii. processing governmental papers, such as visas and work orders;
iii. providing police protection, mail pick-up and delivery, or scheduling inspections associated with contract performance or inspections related to transit of goods across country;
iv. providing phone service, power and water supply, loading and unloading cargo, or protecting perishable products or commodities from deterioration; or
v. actions of a similar nature.[20]

The tax deductibility of grease payments is addressed below.

The application to foreign subsidiaries is also limited. Section 13(b)(6), added as part of the 1988 amendments, clarifies the scope of the parent's legal responsibility for subsidiaries not wholly owned, meaning the parent holds 50 percent or less of voting power. The parent is required only to "proceed in good faith to use its influence, to the extent reasonable . . . to cause . . . [the firm] to devise and maintain a system of internal accounting controls consistent with . . ." the section.

The general federal criminal five-year statute of limitations in 18 U.S.C. § 3282 applies. Under 18 U.S.C. § 3292, DOJ can seek a court order suspending the running of the statute for three years when a federal grand jury has been empanelled and an indictment has not yet been returned. The DOJ must file the request with the court where the grand jury is sitting and the court must then find by a preponderance of

---

18. Both houses of Congress at the time of passage rejected bills that would have prohibited payments unrelated to the award or renewal of business. A Conference Committee added language in the text. *See, e.g.*, Stephen F. Black & Roger M. Witten, Complying with the Foreign Corrupt Practices Act § 206, at 2–7 (1997). In 1988 amendments, the language remained the same. The legislative history does suggest that the statute may cover situations such as influencing legislation.

19. 15 U.S.C. §§ 78dd-1(b), 2(b) (1988).

20. 15 U.S.C. § 78dd-1(f)(3)(A) (1988).

the evidence that an official request has been made for the evidence and it appears reasonable at the time that the evidence is in the foreign country.

III. Recordkeeping Provisions

These provisions do not apply to nonissuers. They are intended not only to create a paper trail but also to ensure that self-reporting to the SEC is true and accurate so that correct financial information will be disseminated to the investing public.

Section 13(b)(2)(A) requires every SEC registrant or issuer to "make and keep books, records, and accounts, which, in reasonable detail, accurately and fairly reflect the transactions and dispositions of the assets of the issuer." The 1988 amendments further define "in reasonable detail" under Section 13(b)(7): "reasonable" means the degree of detail that "would satisfy prudent officials in the conduct of their own affairs." The prudent person is not required to engage in an "unrealistic degree of exactitude . . . [the] concept of reasonableness of necessity contemplates weighing a number of relevant factors, including the cost of compliance."[21]

There are two SEC regulations implementing the code section:

> Rule 13(b)2-1: "No person shall directly or indirectly, falsify or cause to be falsified, any book, record or account . . ."
>
> Rule 13(b)2-2: "No director or officer of any issuer shall, directly or indirectly . . . make any false statement" to any auditor.[22]

Regarding the internal controls provision, part of the recordkeeping provisions, Section 13(b)(5) provides: "No person shall knowingly circumvent or knowingly fail to implement a system of internal accounting controls or knowingly falsify any book, record or account. . . ." The system of internal accounting controls is roughly outlined in Section 13(b)(2)(B), which requires every issuer to devise and maintain a system of internal accounting controls sufficient to provide reasonable assurance that—

(i) Transactions are executed in accordance with management's general or specific authorization;

(ii) To maintain accountability for assets;

(iii) Access to assets is permitted only in accordance with management's general or specific authorization; and

(iv) The recorded accountability for assets is compared with the existing assets at reasonable intervals and appropriate action is taken with respect to any differences. . . .

---

21. H.R. CONF. REP. NO. 100-576, at 917 (1988), *reprinted in* 1988 U.S.C.C.A.N. at 1950.

22. *See, e.g.*, SEC v. Triton Energy Litig. Release No. 15266 (Feb. 27, 1997).

The law does not require any specific method of recordkeeping or internal controls other than those guidelines as set forth in the Act. Also, the recordkeeping and certification provisions of the Sarbanes-Oxley Act apply: Section 302 regarding chief executive officer or chief financial officer certification, Section 906 regarding criminal liability for certifications, and Section 404 regarding internal controls.[23]

IV. Enforcement Statistics: 1978–2011

A. The Prosecutive Policy of Nonenforcement: 1978-2006

Both the SEC and Congress had predicted the likelihood of a corporate pushback to the "new governance" embodied in the FCPA, particularly where the SEC sought to control extraterritorial activities. [24] U.S. companies cried foul based on anecdotal accounts that America had become disadvantaged in global markets where bribery was no longer part of business negotiations.[25]

Whether it was in response to U.S. concerns that the FCPA created an uneven economic playing field in world markets or simply a desire by the international community to rid the marketplace of bribery, the OECD drafted the OECD Anti-Bribery Convention of 1997. Opened for signature in 1977, the treaty came into force in 1999. This treaty prohibits OECD signatory members from making bribe payments in

---

23. Sarbanes-Oxley Act of 2002 §§ 302, 404, 906, Pub. L. No. 107-204 (July 30, 2002).

24. At the time of the passage of the FCPA and in later hearings before the Senate in 1981, the corporate community, fearing excessive SEC interference in global trade, argued that the SEC should not have an enforcement role under the statute at all. However, Congress had earlier recognized the SEC's "well deserved reputation for independence in its efforts. The committee would prefer to have investigations such as these, which may be politically sensitive, conducted by an independent agency responsive to Congress rather than the Executive branch." H.R. Rep. No. 95-640, at 6 (1977). In fact, the FCPA had become a highly sensitive political issue during the Reagan administration. The executive branch urged removal of the SEC from administering the act. William Brock, then U.S. Trade Representative, a cabinet position in the Reagan administration, criticized the SEC in testimony before the House Oversight Committee. Brock claimed that the SEC was improperly using the FCPA "as a Trojan horse to get an extension of accounting standards to all companies when [sic] they do foreign business at all or not." H.R. Conf. Rep. No. 100-576 (1988).

25. As part of Brock's testimony, the Reagan administration offered documentation ostensibly demonstrating examples of lost trade and increased business costs occasioned by compliance with the FCPA. The documentation was based on a report prepared by the U.S. Chamber of Commerce. Strangely, the Chamber was later unable to provide support for the conclusions in the report because it had destroyed the underlying documentation. H.R. Conf. Rep. No. 100-576, at 265 (1988), *supra* note 15. The House responded unfavorably to Brock's testimony, pointing out that the similar assertions made by the Carter administration of foreign business losses were rejected by the DOJ as "at best anecdotal" and that the claims were contradicted by the "reality" of economic trade figures. Those trade figures, supplied by the Department of Commerce, showed that America's share of free world exports had increased during 1977–80, immediately following the passage of the act. *Id.* at 253. Congress found no credible basis upon which to conclude that the FCPA represented a trade barrier in international commerce. Later, in a 1981 survey conducted by the Government Accounting Office, responded to by 200 companies in the Fortune 1000 category, two-thirds agreed that the FCPA "had little or no effect on business" *Id.* at 255.

global markets, leaving each nation to implement the treaty through domestic legislation. After the United States signed the treaty, the third round of amendments to the FCPA in 1998 followed in order to conform the act to treaty requirements. The FCPA became the means by which the treaty was to be applied domestically in the United States.

It is important to understand that no two countries have responded to the problem in the same way. Implementation of the treaty is left entirely to domestic legislation. That means that U.S. companies should be aware of the statutes in the OECD countries where they may be doing business. In any case, the OECD has monitored country compliance, including the United States, under the treaty. The results of FCPA compliance were published in 2002, 2005[26] and 2010.[27] The OECD also issued a report in 2008 reviewing the effectiveness of the treaty 10 years after its adoption.[28]

The continuing political interference created by the executive branch has been an effective detractor in terms of enforcement since the enactment. Beginning with the Reagan administration's foreign policy practices in the Iran-Contra affair, the FCPA was ignored. The Iran-Contra affair is a poignant example. U.S. government officials actually engaged in bribe payments to foreign institutions to facilitate the covert mission. Since then, the executive branch has generally followed a policy of nonenforcement across administrations, at least until recently. As explained in greater detail below, there has been some increased enforcement activity since 2006.

To illustrate the problem of nonenforcement, the statistics show that between 1977 and 2001, only 21 companies and 26 individuals were convicted for criminal violations of the FCPA. The OECD concluded, based on the enforcement figures supplied by the U.S. government in 2002, that "the number of prosecutions and civil enforcement actions for FCPA actions has not been great."[29]

The task of compiling actual statistics under the act is formidable because the United States does not publish public enforcement statistics. Nor do the responsible agencies (DOJ and SEC) report which opened cases are later closed without disposition. The DOJ claims that it maintains a nonpublic, computerized case tracking system that monitors the status of all cases that have been opened as formal investigations.[30] The SEC does list cases and investigations on its public website.[31] However,

---

26. OECD, United States: Review, *supra* note 10; OECD, Follow-Up Report, *supra* note 11.

27. OECD Phase 3 Report: United States Report on the Application of the Convention on Combating Bribery of Foreign Public Officials in International Business Transactions (2010) http://www.oecd.org/dataoecd/10/49/46213841.pdf.

28. OECD, Working Group on Bribery in Int'l Bus. Transactions, Consultation Paper: Review of the OECD Instruments on Combating Bribery of Foreign Public Officials in International Business Transactions Ten Years After Adoption (2008), http://www.oecd.org/dataoecd/18/25/39882963.pdf.

29. OECD, United States: Review, *supra* note 10, at 6.

30. OECD, Follow-Up Report, *supra* note 11.

31. See http://www.sec.gov/search/search.htm.

there is no public case-tracking system that monitors the status of cases, processing of allegations, or source of complaints.

In 2005, the OECD pointed to this failure to compile statistics as potentially undermining the working relationship between the United States and the OECD under the convention: "Enforcement of the FCPA still appears to be based mainly on informal arrangements, without any formal mechanism to review and evaluate the overall FCPA enforcement effort, or cross-institutional statistics as to the number, sources and subsequent processing of allegations of FCPA violations . . . this may in the long term undermine the efficiency of the working relationship between the agencies."[32]

In 2010, in response to the OECD criticism, the United States self-reported criminal enforcement statistics for the period 1998-September 2010 which were submitted as part of the U.S. responses to the Phase 3 questionnaire,[33] which the United States agreed to make public upon completion of the OECD Phase 3 audit report in 2010. Those statistics are included in Appendix F. Still, DOJ has made no commitment to establish a public case-tracking system.

Appendix E includes a compilation of statistics reporting enforcement activity for the 1978-2011 period, based on the amnesty figures in the House Report,[34] U.S. self-reported statistics provided to the OECD in 2002, 2005,[35] and 2010,[36] and statistics provided by the SEC on its website. These were cross-checked with the statistics published by two law firms specializing in the field on their respective websites.[37] The research for Appendix E also included statistics provided by a recent American Bar Association publication.[38] An analysis revealed that each of these sources—international, governmental, and private law firm publications—were incomplete in terms of annual case listings and case dispositions. Appendix E combines the sources in an effort to provide a more comprehensive case listing as of December 2011. The cases are indexed chronologically by case name and number, company name, a brief

---

32. OECD, Follow-Up Report, *supra* note 11, at 4.

33. Response of the United States: Questions Concerning OECD Working Group on Bribery (May 3, 2010), http://www.justice.gov/criminal/fraud/fcpa/docs/response3.pdf.

34. H.R. Rep. No. 95-640 (1977).

35. OECD, United States: Review, *supra* note 10; OECD, Follow-Up Report, *supra* note 11.

36. Response of the United States, *supra* note 33.

37. Shearman & Sterling LLP, FCPA Digest of Cases and Review Releases Relating to Bribes to Foreign Officials under the Foreign Corrupt Practices Act of 1977 (as of Feb. 13, 2008) (2008), http://www.shearman.com/files/upload/FCPA_Digest.pdf; WilmerHale, FCPA Developments Arising on a Variety of Fronts, http://www.wilmerhale.com/publications/whPubsDetail.aspx?publication=8385; GIBSON DUNN, 2010 Year-End Update on Corporate Deferred and Non-Prosecution Agreements (Jan. 4, 2011) http://www.gibsondunn.com/publications/pages/2010year-endupdate-corporatedeferredprosecutionandnon-prosecutionagreements.aspx.

38. John Gibeaut, *Battling Bribery Abroad*, A.B.A.J., Mar. 2007, *available at* http://www.abajournal.com/magazine/battling_bribery_abroad/.

description of the facts of the case, and disposition. Multiple case prosecutions arising out of the same investigation are also noted.

As an overview, Appendix E lists a total of 106 combined SEC and DOJ cases for the period 1978–2007. Fifteen of those cases arise out the same investigation but are charged as separate multiple case enforcement actions and may be used in other databases to increase case enforcement statistics. Eight cases arise out of the United Nations (U.N.) Oil for Food Program (OFFP) investigation involving American contractors doing business in Iraq.[39] This industrywide investigation was not initiated by the SEC or the DOJ. The DOJ cases were filed after a U.N. special investigation report was disclosed by former Federal Reserve Board Chief Paul Volcker, who headed the investigation. The report identified 2,253 companies that illicitly paid more than $1.8 billion to the Iraqi government. Yet, only eight cases had been prosecuted by the beginning of 2008. Six additional cases followed within the year.

The remaining 81 cases can be further broken down by year:

1978: 2 cases

1979: 3 cases

1980: 1 case

1981: 0 cases

1982: 5 cases

1983: 1 case

1984: 0 cases

1985: 2 cases

1986, 1987 and 1988: 1 case (Ashland Oil)

1989: 3 cases

1990: 5 cases (the fifth case was dismissed)

1991: 0 cases

1992: 0 cases

1993: 2 cases

1994: 2 cases

1995: 0 cases

1996: 1 case

1997: 1 case

---

39. *See* Indep. Inquiry Comm., The Management of the United Nations Oil-For-Food Programme (Sept. 7, 2005), http://www.iic-offp.org/documents/Sept05/Mgmt_V1.pdf (concluding that "Iraq manipulated the Program to dispense contracts on the basis of political preference and to derive illicit payments from companies that obtained oil and humanitarian goods contracts.").

1998: 3 cases

1999: 2 cases

2000: 1 case

2001: 5 cases

2002: 4 cases (2 individual cases dismissed)

2003: 2 cases (3 individual cases dismissed)

2004: 5 cases

2005: 6 cases (3 corporate nonprosecution agreements)

2006: 8 cases

2007: 13 cases (plus 7 of the OFFP cases, of which at least 4 have been resolved by corporate nonprosecution agreements)

2008: 2 cases (plus 1 OFFP case resolved by corporate nonprosecution agreement).

Between 1978 and 2002, the statistics further show that the SEC alone initiated a total of 13 cases, of which two were dismissed or disposed of without sanctions. Between 1978 and 1996, the SEC collected no fines or penalties in seven of the 13 cases, resolving most by injunction "against future violations," a slap on the wrist. The SEC sought injunctions in only five cases by 2002. Case filings included three cases under the antibribery clause and seven cases under accounting and recordkeeping provisions clauses. For at least 10 years, no actions were brought by the SEC under the accounting and recordkeeping provisions.[40]

Further analysis of this time period shows that between 1978 and 2001, 21 companies and 26 individuals were convicted for criminal violations. Corporate fines ranged from $1,500 to $3.5 million, with the exception of the Lockheed settlement for $21.8 million in 1994.[41]

Fines imposed on individuals ranged from $2,500 to $309,000. Until 1994, no one went to jail for an FCPA violation. In the period following the enactment of the Sarbanes-Oxley Act, between 2002 and 2005, 12 cases involving the criminal and recordkeeping and accounting provisions were filed, of which eight were civil and administrative SEC enforcement actions.[42]

For the period 1978–2002, the DOJ instituted only 32 criminal prosecutions under the antibribery provision of the FCPA. The OECD, based on the statistics self-reported by the United States as of 2002, observed: "Since only some 30 separate alleged bribery schemes have been prosecuted during 25 years under the FCPA, it is difficult to draw broad conclusions about enforcement. There are no statistics or

40. OECD, Follow-Up Report, *supra* note 11, at 23.

41. OECD, United States: Review, *supra* note 10 at 16.

42. OECD, Follow-Up Report, *supra* note 11.

other information available which would reveal the number of allegations received, the number of investigations commenced, terminated or abandoned, or that might shed light on the reasons which led to the decision not to proceed."[43]

Additionally, in terms of case magnitude, the largest case in 2007 was *United States v. Baker Hughes,* which resulted in combined cash penalties of $44 million. Though this is one of the largest monetary penalties in the history of FCPA enforcement, the parent corporation received a nonprosecution agreement from the DOJ, one of the many dispositions by "informal arrangements" in lieu of prosecution, highly criticized by the OECD. In an apparent effort to minimize financial damage to the parent, the wholly owned subsidiary, Baker Hughes Services International Inc., pled guilty to the same criminal offenses under the FCPA from which the parent was excused.

B. The "Cost of Doing Business" Enforcement Strategy: 2006-2011

In an effort to address this abysmal record of enforcement, the DOJ in 2006 formed a dedicated FCPA unit to handle prosecutions, issue opinion releases, participate in interagency anticorruption policy development, and engage in public education about the FCPA and OECD Anti-Bribery Convention. The unit consists of a deputy chief, two assistant chiefs, and a number of trial attorneys. Since the unit was established, prosecutions have increased, rising from an average of 4.6 prosecutions per year from 2001-2005 to 18.75 from 2006-2009. Thus, since 2005, the FCPA unit has prosecuted more cases than were prosecuted in the first 28 years of the FCPA's existence combined.[44]

While the U.S. Attorney General's Office and several private sector law firms have recently decried a significant increase in the number of FCPA prosecutions, the claim may be somewhat disingenuous based on the numbers. In 2010, the United States self-reported to the OECD, merely "opening" nine cases in 2005, 14 in 2006, 53 in 2007, 34 in 2008, 29 in 2009, and 28 as of April 30, 2010.[45] That is arguably "significant" when compared to a policy of nonprosecution of the statute for its first 28 years as illustrated by the statistics. However, when compared to the annual number of federal prosecutions or the sheer volume of global transactions involving U.S. corporations,[46] the number is hardly significant. The number of "opened" cases is

43. OECD, United States: Review, *supra* note 10 at 24.

44. OECD, United States Response, *supra,* note 33 at 12.

45. OECD, United States Response, *supra,* note 33 at 18; Appendix F.

46. The United States. is the largest foreign investor in the world with U.S. direct investment abroad that totaled $268.7 billion in 2009 and accounted for roughly 22 percent of total world foreign direct investment outflows, and exports that totaled $1.6 trillion (goods and services) and accounted for roughly 10 percent of world exports in 2009. OECD Phase 3 Report: United States Report on the Application of the Convention on Combating Bribery of Foreign Public Officials in International Business Transactions (2010), *supra* note 27. *http*://www.oecd.org/dataoecd/10/49/46213841.pdf

also not dispositive because neither the DOJ nor the SEC publicly disclose the number of investigations discontinued without sanctions.[47]

The statistics, broken down by year, reflect a policy of nonprosecution from 1978–2006. In 2008, the numbers begin to increase, reflecting a change in DOJ strategy in enforcing the FCPA. However, as shown below, the numbers reflect that the policy of increased prosecution is expressly facilitated by the increased use of non-prosecution agreements (NPAs) or deferred prosecution agreements (DPAs) accompanied by larger corporate fines and disgorgement of profits. In short, enforcement is an increased cost of doing business without criminal conviction.

Appendix E has been updated to include the combined cases prosecuted by the DOJ and SEC from 2008-2011:

> 2008: 6 additional OFFP cases prosecuted; 4 cases (Siemens company); 5 cases (Nexus Technologies)
>
> 2009: 55 cases (30 of the 55 separate cases reported arise out of the same case prosecution).
>
> 2010: 46 cases (17 of the 46 separate cases reported arise out of the same case prosecution).
>
> 2011: 11 cases (2 of the 11 separate cases reported arise out of the same case prosecution).

These statistics may be somewhat inflated because of the fact that the prosecution of multiple defendants arising out of the same transaction are reported and counted as separate case prosecutions. For example, in 2009, of the 55 total cases prosecuted by the DOJ and SEC combined, 30 were related cases but reported separately. Ten of the cases involved corporate defendants. In 2010, 46 total cases were prosecuted by the DOJ and SEC combined, of which 17 were related cases but reported separately. Three of the cases are related to a case prosecution initiated in 2009. Twenty-three of the cases involved corporate defendants.

Additionally, disgorgement of profits derived from bribery is reported to have increased. The United States recently self-reported updated case statistics to the OECD which indicate that since 2004, over $1 billion in foreign bribery proceeds have been recovered through disgorgement actions. The SEC also obtained civil penalties in addition to DOJ criminal fines. In the first nine months of 2010 alone, the SEC recovered over $404 million in disgorgement, interest, and civil penalties from 13 companies and eight individuals.[48]

An interesting feature of the updated prosecution statistics is the fact that several of the new cases involve corporate recidivists, such as Siemens and General Electric,

47. OECD, United States Response, *supra* note 33 at 18.
48. OECD, Phase 3 Report, *supra* note 27 at 10-11.

that have previously been punished for the same illegal behavior. It is indisputable that some in the corporate venue perceive the FCPA as a "cost of doing business" rather than a deterrent to illegal corporate behavior. That sentiment may be attributable to the increased use of DPAs and NPAs to dispose of FCPA actions. Indeed, this use of informal arrangements in lieu of prosecution has become a trend at the DOJ in dealing with corporate crime generally.[49]

Although DPAs and NPAs have existed since 1993, their use has grown dramatically in recent years. In FCPA cases, DPAs and NPAs were not used until 2004. As of the 2010 Phase 3 OECD audit report, they had been used in 30 out of 39 concluded criminal enforcement actions against companies.[50] One database reflects that in 2010, FCPA cases accounted for over 50 percent of the total reported NPA and DPA agreements entered into by the DOJ.[51]

Not surprisingly, the OECD is highly skeptical of what it perceives as disposition of global bribery through the use of informal arrangements, such as nonprosecution or deferred prosecution agreements. The OECD observes: "It seems quite clear that the use of these agreements is one of the reasons for the impressive FCPA enforcement record in the U.S. However, their actual deterrent effect has not been quantified; although the DOJ hears anecdotally from companies that their use has made FCPA compliance high priority."[52]

The new prosecutive model of global corporate governance caters to the same corporate pushback that resounded after the enactment of the FCPA. Corporate pressure nullified any meaningful enforcement of the Act for close to 30 years and is still a factor in fashioning case dispositions today. Whether the use of DPAs and NPAs, supported by heavy fines and disgorgement, accomplishes the goal of eradicating participation by U.S. companies in global bribery remains questionable. Certainly, the OECD remains unconvinced based on the numbers.

However, the real enforcement problem may center on the narrow application of the FCPA, which leaves much of bribery occurring in the private sector completely unregulated. Arguably, this regulation gap undermines the real success of deterrence.

---

49. See Chapter 6 for a detailed discussion.

50. OECD, Phase 3 Report, *supra* note 27 at p.32.

51. GIBSON DUNN, 2010 Year-End Update on Corporate Deferred and Non-Prosecution Agreements (Jan. 4, 2011) http://www.gibsondunn.com/publications/pages/2010year-endupdate-corporatedeferred prosecutionandnon-prosecutionagreements.aspx.

52. OECD, Phase 3 Report, *supra* note 27 at 19.

V. DOJ Investigations, Opinion Procedure, and Prosecutive Policy

A. Red Flags

In evaluating potential areas of concern, DOJ has prepared its own red-flags list that provides some guidance to companies and practitioners in determining those factors considered by law enforcement in pursuing investigations under the FCPA. DOJ cautions that

> [I]n negotiating a business relationship, the U.S. firm should be aware of so-called "red flags," i.e., unusual payment patterns or financial arrangements, a history of corruption in the country, a refusal by the foreign joint partner or representative to provide a certification that it will not take any action in furtherance of an unlawful offer, promise, or payment to a foreign public official and not take any act that would cause the U.S. firm to be in violation of the FCPA, unusually high commissions, lack of transparency in expenses and accounting records, apparent lack of qualifications or resources on the part of the joint venture partner or representative to perform the services offered, and whether the joint venture partner or representative has been recommended by an official of the potential governmental customer.[53]

DOJ further advises companies to engage in due diligence before entering into negotiations, which may include investigating third-party partners and representatives to determine whether they are qualified to perform services, whether they have personal or professional ties to the governmental official, the number and reputation of their clientele, and their reputation with banks and the U.S. Embassy or Consulate.[54] A true caveat emptor approach to enforcement!

As a final word of caution, many companies that have self-reported violations have done so only after discovering prohibited conduct in a postmerger situation. Consideration of possible FCPA violations should be undertaken during the due diligence acquisition process.[55] Seeking an opinion from the Attorney General's FCPA unit is advisable.

Opinion Procedure Release No. 08-02, included in the next section, is an example of the procedure as applied to mergers and acquisitions. In that matter, Halliburton intended to acquire a business in a foreign jurisdiction where it would not be able to conduct full due diligence preacquisition. The company provided a detailed procedure for conducting staged due diligence quickly after acquisition. The DOJ agreed to refrain from bringing an enforcement action against Halliburton in the transac-

---

53. U.S. Dep't of Justice, Lay-Person's Guide to FCPA, http://www.justice.gov/criminal/fraud/fcpa/docs/lay-persons-guide.pdf.

54. *Id.*

55. *See, e.g.*, SEC v. Delta & Pine Land Co. and Turk Deltapine, Inc., SEC Release No. 34-56138 (July 25, 2007) (conduct discovered by Monsanto during the acquisition process).

tion so long as it completed each of the steps detailed in the submission, including full disclosure of any discovered unlawful conduct to the Department. Additionally, the DOJ agreed not to initiate any enforcement action against Halliburton for any pre- or post-acquisition unlawful conduct engaged in by the business being acquired, if timely disclosed to the Department and halted in a timely fashion.

B. Department of Justice Guidance: Opinion Procedure

The DOJ Fraud Section provides an online "Lay-Person's Guide to the FCPA."[56] The guide provides links to legislative history, opinion procedures, regulations, and review procedure releases.

Pursuant to the DOJ FCPA Opinion Procedure, 28 C.F.R. part 80, DOJ provides guidance as to whether a specific, non-hypothetical, prospective transaction would violate the FCPA. If the Department affirms it will not take enforcement action based on the requestor's description of the transaction, and the transaction then takes place exactly as described, the requestor qualifies for a "safe harbor" and may not be prosecuted. Although the Department's opinions are nonbinding on other federal agencies, the SEC has stated that, as a matter of its prosecutorial discretion, it will not take enforcement action against an issuer with respect to a transaction concerning which the DOJ has rendered a favorable opinion.[57]

The DOJ did not issue any such opinions in 2005. However, the following are summaries of the opinions issued from 2006-2010. While relatively few in number, the opinions do illustrate various applications of the rules:

> *Opinion Procedure Release No. 10-10:* In April 2010, the Department responded to an opinion request regarding whether certain payments to a foreign government official would be appropriate under the FCPA. The requestor, who was contracting with a U.S. government agency to perform work overseas, was obligated to hire and compensate individuals at the direction of a U.S. government agency. One individual so identified, who was hired on the basis of the individual's qualifications, also served as a paid officer for an agency of the foreign country in a position unrelated to the work the individual would perform for the requestor. Based on all of the facts and circumstances, as represented by the requestor, the Department determined that while the individual was a foreign official within the meaning of the FCPA, and would receive compensation from the requestor through a subcontractor, the individual would not be in a position to influence any official act or decision affecting the requestor. In addition, the requestor is contractually bound to hire and compensate the individual as directed by the U.S. government agency, and the requestor did not play any role in selecting the individual. As such, the payment was not being corruptly

56. Lay-Person's Guide to FCPA, *supra* note 53.

57. *See* SEC Interpretative Release No. 34-17099 (Aug. 28, 1980).

made, was not made to obtain or retain business, and was not made to secure an improper advantage. Accordingly, the Department indicated that, based on the facts as presented, it would not take any enforcement action.

Opinion Procedure Release No. 09-01: In August 2009, the Department issued an opinion that donations of medical devices to a government agency, as opposed to individual government officials, through a program open to all medical device manufacturers, fell outside the scope of the FCPA, as the FCPA covers only the offering of things of value to individual government officials, not to a government itself.

Opinion Procedure Release No. 08-01: In January 2008, the Department issued an opinion in response to an inquiry from a U.S. public company regarding its intent to acquire a foreign company that managed public services for a foreign municipality. The foreign company was majority-owned by an individual determined to be a "foreign official" within the meaning of the FCPA. The U.S. company was concerned that payments to the owner of the foreign company in connection with the purchase might run afoul of the FCPA. The Department determined that, in light of the U.S. company's extensive due diligence, the transparency of the transaction, the undertakings of both the foreign owner and the U.S. company, and the terms of the transaction, it would not take enforcement action.

Opinion Procedure Release No. 08-02: In June 2008, the Department issued an opinion in response to an inquiry from a Halliburton company. Halliburton intended to acquire a business in a foreign jurisdiction where it would not be able to conduct full due diligence in advance of acquisition. The company provided a detailed procedure for conducting staged due diligence quickly after acquisition. The Department determined that, assuming Halliburton completed each of the steps detailed in the submission, including full disclosure to the Department, the Department would not take any enforcement action against Halliburton for the acquisition, any preacquisition unlawful conduct by the business being acquired, if timely disclosed to the Department, or any post-acquisition conduct by the business being acquired, if it is halted and disclosed to the Department in a timely fashion.

Opinion Procedure Release No. 08-03: In July 2008, the Department issued an opinion in response to an inquiry from TRACE International, a U.S. non-profit business membership organization, declining to take enforcement action if TRACE paid a limited stipend to cover certain travel expenses for Chinese journalists (who are employees of the state, and therefore foreign officials under the FCPA) to attend a press conference to be held by TRACE. TRACE represented that the journalists are not typically reimbursed by their employers for such costs; that stipends will be equally available to all journalists regardless of whether they later provide coverage of the conference and regardless of the nature of such coverage; that TRACE has no business pending with any government agency in China; and that it had obtained written assurances from an established international law firm that the payment of the stipends is not contrary to Chinese law.

Opinion Procedure Release No. 07-01: In July 2007, the Department issued an opinion in response to a private company in the United States, declining to take enforcement action if the company proceeded with sponsoring domestic expenses for a trip by a six-person delegation from an Asian government. The company represented that the purpose of the visit would be to familiarize the delegates with the nature and extent of the company's business operations; that it would not select the delegates; it would pay all costs directly to providers; and it did not currently conduct operations in the foreign country at issue.

Opinion Procedure Release No. 07-02: In September 2007, the Department issued an opinion in response to a private insurance company in the United States, declining to take enforcement action if the company proceeded with sponsoring domestic expenses for a trip by six officials from an Asian government for an educational program at the company's U.S. headquarters. The company represented that the purpose of the visit would be to familiarize the officials with the operation of a U.S. insurance company; that it would not select the officials who would participate; that it would pay costs directly to providers; and that it has no nonroutine business pending before the agency that employs the officials.

Opinion Procedure Release No. 07-03: In December 2007, the Department issued an opinion in response to a lawful permanent resident of the United States declining to take enforcement action if the requestor paid up-front expenses to a foreign court-appointed estate administrator. The Department noted that there were two primary reasons for declining enforcement: first, the requestor had represented that the payment would be made to a government entity (the court clerk's office) rather than directly to the foreign official; and second, that the payment in any event is lawful under the written laws and regulations of the country, according to an experienced attorney retained by the requestor in the country in question, which would be consistent with the affirmative defense of legality under local law enumerated in the FCPA.

Opinion Procedure Release No. 06-01: In October 2006, the Department issued an Opinion Procedure Release in response to a request from a Delaware corporation with headquarters in Switzerland, declining to take enforcement action if the corporation proceeded with a proposed contribution to the government of an African country. The company proposed to contribute $25,000 to the African country's regional customs department and/or Ministry of Finance as part of a pilot project to improve local enforcement of anticounterfeiting laws. The company represented that it would execute a formal memorandum of understanding with the country and would establish several procedural safeguards to ensure that the funds would be used as intended.

Opinion Procedure Release No. 06-02: In December 2006, the Department issued an opinion in response to a request from a subsidiary of a U.S. issuer declining to take enforcement action if the corporation retained a law firm in the foreign country and paid it substantial fees to aid the company in obtaining foreign exchange from a government agency of that country. The law firm would prepare its foreign exchange applications to that agency and represent the company during the review process. The Department's release was based on the company's representations regarding steps taken in conducting due diligence regarding the law firm and the inclusion in the agreement between the company and the law firm of several provisions designed to prevent corruption from occurring.

C. Prosecutive Policy

The government is offering leniency to those companies that voluntarily self-report FCPA violations. Here is a recent policy statement from the criminal division at the Justice Department:

> [I]t would not make sense for law enforcement to make one-size-fits-all promises about the benefits of voluntary disclosure before getting all of the facts. . . . But what I can say is that there is *always* a benefit to corporate cooperation, including voluntary disclosure, as contemplated by the Thompson memo.[58]

This policy position is evidenced by the use in most cases, even in the largest cases, of nonprosecution agreements to resolve charges of unlawful conduct. The policy is really no surprise. First, it is very difficult to detect unlawful bribery in foreign venues. The United States has no subpoena power abroad. Unless a treaty or other multilateral agreement provides a procedure to gain records access, the government is basically shut out from developing a paper trail. This, of course, was the SEC's reason for imposing a recordkeeping requirement on issuers. It is not hard to figure out that the absence of a similar recordkeeping requirement on nonissuers impairs the government's ability to investigate. As noted above, many cases come to the government's attention in the way that most corporate prosecutions do: whistleblowers. Somebody

58. Alice S. Fisher, Assistant Attorney Gen., U.S. Dep't of Justice, Prepared Remarks at the American Bar Association National Institute on the Foreign Corrupt Practices Act (Oct. 16, 2006) (emphasis in original), http://www.usdoj.gov/criminal/fraud/docs/reports/speech/2006/10-16-06AAGFCPASpeech.pdf.

on the inside provides the proof. Again, without subpoena power to compel witness testimony in foreign venues, a trial is almost impossible.

Second, the legislative history is instructive in many ways. Until 2006, the executive branch had not established the FCPA as a major prosecutive initiative in the same way that it had with healthcare, "deadbeat dad" legislation, and a host of other prosecutive priorities that change with each administration. Internal politics and corporate lobbyists contribute to the slow-paced enforcement.

Since the inception of the FCPA, the United States has assiduously declined any invitation to extend the reach of the statute to meaningfully prohibit global bribery in the marketplace by proscribing private sector bribery. The reasons are many: lack of prosecutive resources to detect and prosecute on a global level, proof problems occasioned by no subpoena power to obtain records or witnesses, and no jurisdiction over foreign companies or subsidiaries with 50 percent or less domestic ownership.

Voluntary self-reporting is a good idea for another reason: someone else may tell on the company first. While voluntary self-reporting has resulted in some prosecutions under the statute, it is not the major source of case referrals. Currently, the United States reports that investigations come to the attention of law enforcement from a wide variety of sources, including, but not limited to: corporate securities filings; suspicious activity reports from financial institutions; the media, including key word searches of the Internet; whistleblower complaints, including those pursuant to the Sarbanes-Oxley Act; *qui tam* and civil complaints; direct reporting to law enforcement by employees, customers, competitors, agents, and others; referral from other U.S. government agencies and their employees, including the various Inspectorates General; referral from state, local, and foreign law enforcement; referrals from international financial institutions such as the World Bank; reports through the "hotline" e-mail address that allows reporting directly to the FCPA unit of the Fraud Section; voluntary disclosures from companies; and investigations derived from traditional law enforcement methods, including sting operations.

In short, voluntary disclosure is a meaningful tool for corporate resolution of the problem, particularly where there is a risk of internal or third-party disclosure. The fine may be high but with the increased use of NPAs and DPAs, it is a more welcome cost of doing business than a criminal indictment.

VI. Tax Deductibility of "Grease Payments"

As noted above, grease payments, also referred to as facilitating payments, do not violate the FCPA or any other U.S. law. Nor do such payments contravene public policy. In fact, such payments are expressly sanctioned by the FCPA.

Grease payments are deductible under the Internal Revenue Code (IRC). IRC Section 162(a) provides the statutory authority for deductibility as an ordinary and necessary business expense[59]: "There shall be allowed a deduction for all ordinary and necessary expenses paid or incurred during the taxable year in carrying on a trade or business." Thus, grease payments made to employees in foreign countries are deductible unless there is a determination that the payment was made in violation of the FCPA.[60]

59. See Chapter 7 for a more complete discussion of this code secton.

60. Ephraim Smith, Philip Harmelink, and James Hasselback, 2009 CCH Federal Taxation: Comprehensive Topics 6-29, 6-30 (2008).

Chapter **10**

STATUTORY REFORMS POST-ENRON
THE NEW CORPORATE GOVERNANCE MODEL

I. The Failure of Credible Oversight

Credible oversight is a central component in achieving the goal of corporate governance. Behavioral finance literature, applying "rational choice theory," explains that "lure" more readily transforms into criminal "opportunity" where the corporate criminal perceives the absence of "credible oversight." It follows that credible oversight increases risk for the criminally predisposed, resulting in a decrease in the incidences of unlawful conduct. Congress, during the Enron hearings, credited the absence of credible oversight as one of the principal causes of the corporate failure. It concluded that the traditional "corporate watchdogs failed to bark."

Despite all of the rhetoric about the importance of credible oversight, there is almost nothing in the literature to explain exactly what it is. The failure to define credible oversight leaves a substantial gap in understanding how oversight should operate in the corporate environment and whether conclusions based on recent failed expectations about the quality of oversight are reasonable.

With the creation of the Securities and Exchange Commission (SEC) in 1934, pursuant to the Securities and Exchange Act, a conscious policy decision was made about the character of oversight that the new regulatory body was to exercise over issuers in the marketplace. The model was premised on self-regulation by issuers, a system of self-reporting under the supervision of the regulator. Here, supervision did not vest responsibility in the regulator to perform internal corporate auditing functions or other "hands-on" supervision. It was never intended that the SEC would become the issuer's accountant. Instead, it was the job of the issuer to hire credible third-party professionals, such as accountants and lawyers, to perform audits, issue opinion letters, and assist in the full and fair disclosure through a system of documentary reporting to the SEC.

Simply, the regulator was to review and inspect only the issuer's disclosure, to confirm that it was abiding by the rules. Critical to the model of self-regulation was trust. The regulator was supposed to be able to rely on the reporting disclosures of the issuer. That model also required the regulator to actually look at the materials being submitted by the issuer at least every three years to make such a determination. Credible oversight in this context meant a hands-off approach to issuers with, as former SEC Chairman and Supreme Court Justice William O. Douglas described, the "shot gun behind the door," in the event an issuer engaged in improper or unlawful behavior.

The SEC intended barebones regulation to avoid interference with natural market forces. The notion that respected third-party professionals would not maintain their independence was not accorded much weight. In this way, issuers were burdened with the obligation to provide corporate transparency and the regulator was able to rely on the watchful eye of third-party professionals to ensure that the issuer satisfied his burden. These third-party professionals were thought of as part of a class of corporate watchdogs, providing actual review and oversight. Indeed, the belief was that the marketplace had a pack of such watchdogs, including not only accountants and lawyers but also the self-regulatory organizations (SROs) such as the stock exchanges, investment advisors, banks, and market appraisers. Assuming each watchdog performed its functions in a conflict-free environment, the risk or opportunity for corporate wrongdoing would diminish.

There was nothing in this legislative model that contemplated anything more than a supervisory approach with reliance on information supplied by the issuer, combined with the reactive power to punish in the event of a breach of trust. Periodically, Congress considered increasing the powers of the regulator, and various statutes were added to the arsenal of regulatory enforcement tools. Yet the SEC and Congress remained at a respectful distance to avoid undue interference in the marketplace. The regulator was intended to supervise a system of self-regulation and enforce reactively in response to self-regulatory failure. That was the model of "credible oversight" created by Congress based on a myriad of policy considerations and political interests.

In October 2001, coinciding almost to the day that the SEC began an investigation of the Enron debacle, it issued a report known euphemistically as the "Seaboard Report," announcing a new 13-point policy directive concerning its enforcement activities.[1]

This itemized nonexhaustive list of criteria considered by the SEC in evaluating whether and how much to credit self-policing, self-reporting, and remediation includes the egregiousness and duration of the misconduct; the extent to which a lax corporate culture led to the misconduct; the extent of "front office" responsibility; the extent of investor harm; the extent to which internal corporate controls failed to detect the misconduct; the promptness and effectiveness of the company's response upon discovering misconduct; the promptness and thoroughness of the company's internal investigation of the misconduct; the effectiveness of the remedial measures to prevent recurrence; and the extent to which the company cooperated with the SEC in its investigation. Before the new policy could be fully implemented and tested, the SEC was blindsided by the Enron failure and the string of corporate debacles that were to follow in rapid succession.

In the wake of the Enron collapse, the SEC was severely chastised for its failure to have provided credible oversight. Given the model under which it operated, was the SEC remiss in its oversight duties? Was the expectation that the SEC should have caught the various fraudulent schemes through credible oversight a fair one?

There is no question that the SEC failed at least in its obligation to review the Enron disclosure documents in a timely fashion. The SEC's stubborn deference to industry self-regulation produced a reactive and untimely response to the crisis. Congress observed: "In short, the SEC's interactions with Enron reveal the downside to the Commission's largely reactive approach to market regulation . . . it has been less than proactive in attempting to address fraud at an earlier stage, before it becomes a corporate calamity."[2]

Enron supplies the proof. Not only did the SEC fail to look at Enron's Form 10-Ks for 1998–2000, the SEC staff confirmed before Congress that "Enron's 2000 Form 10K would not even have been flagged for review" under the SEC screening criteria.[3] Congress railed against the SEC for missing a critical opportunity to discover major

1. Report of Investigation Pursuant to Section 21(a) of the Securities Exchange Act of 1934 and Commission Statement on the Relationship of Cooperation to Agency Enforcement Decisions, SEC Release No. 34-44969, Accounting and Auditing Enforcement Release No. 1470 (Oct. 23, 2001), http://www.sec.gov/litigation/investreport/34-44969.htm.

2. Staff of Senate Comm. on Governmental Affairs, 107th Cong., Report on Financial Oversight of Enron, the SEC and the Private Sector Watchdog 31–36 (Comm. Print 2002).

3. *Id.* at 36.

aspects of the Enron fraud. If the SEC had simply looked at the Enron 2000 Form 10-K, it would have discovered some of Enron's wrongful practices, including the now-famous footnote 16 to Enron's financial statements. Footnote 16 ran for seven paragraphs in describing related-party transactions. Footnote 16 is equally famous for the "red flags" that littered the explanations: "[I]t is so lacking in information that it does not even name the related party in these transactions."[4] The Senate Enron Report concluded in disgust that "[b]y not reviewing Enron's last three Forms 10-K—or any of its recent registration statements, which incorporated much of this information [of wrongful practices]—the SEC missed potential opportunities to identify serious problems before the house of cards fell."[5]

The SEC argued in its defense that it lacked the human and financial resources to act as a policing authority. The statistics in earlier chapters of this book tend to support the SEC's claim that law enforcement personnel are scarce and are tied up with antiterrorism initiatives. Again, the system is designed to operate on trust with a protective layer of independent professionals between the SEC and the issuer. Having been stripped of this protective layer, at least when the third-party professionals joined in the criminal network, the regulatory model of credible oversight was severely crippled.

As a result, the post-Enron model of credible regulatory oversight was somewhat overhauled by the passage of the Sarbanes-Oxley Act of 2002 (SOX). The creation of the Public Company Accounting Oversight Board (PCAOB), to implement major reform, has added a stronger regulatory presence in terms of a rule-making authority imbued with supervisory authority to ensure compliance through periodic audit and reactive enforcement tools. Yet the SEC still remains dependent on the layer of third-party professionals hired by the issuer to provide accounting, financial, and legal information. The SEC remains a reviewer in a self-regulatory environment, perhaps with stricter rules, but still at a distance to avoid market interference.

On June 11, 2003, William J. McDonough became chairman of the PCAOB, after serving for 10 years as the president and chief executive officer of the Federal Reserve Bank of New York. McDonough's stated regulatory philosophy was that the quickest way for the professions to restore public confidence and trust shattered by recent corporate failures was for accountants to ensure that their actions remain consistent with moral principles. He emphasized that the centerpiece of the new regulatory system was predicated upon trust and morality—and a lot of new rules.

4. *Id.* at 37 n. 128.
5. *Id.* at 39.

II. Post-Enron Sarbanes-Oxley Reforms

A. Changes to Audit Standards[6]

SOX created the Public Company Accounting Oversight Board (PCAOB) to implement the new oversight mandates given to the SEC by the legislation. The SEC charged the PCAOB with establishing auditing and related attestation standards, quality control standards, ethics standards, and independence standards.

The PCAOB's first action on standards was to adopt the existing standards of the American Institute of Certified Public Accountants as interim standards, pending review of those standards. The PCAOB determined not to designate a professional group of accountants to formulate auditing standards for its approval. Instead, it formed its own staff of expert accountants to develop auditing and related professional practice standards at the PCAOB's direction. The staff was selected from a variety of backgrounds, including academia, professional practice, and government. It was initially composed of 30 individuals with experience in auditing, financial statement preparation, corporate governance, and investing, as well as other relevant fields. As part of its formal procedure, the PCAOB staff submitted proposed standards to the SEC for approval in accordance with SOX mandates. Then, the standards were released for public review and comment.

While SOX affirmatively requires auditors to follow PCAOB auditing standards only when they are performing public company audits, the hope was that, as with the Financial Accounting Standards Board's accounting standards, accountants would do the same in private industry as a "safe harbor" audit methodology. The PCAOB notes that while some public companies do go private, in many more cases private companies go public. In addition, stakeholders other than public investors, such as lenders, began to require auditors for nonpublic companies to provide audit reports according to issuer standards.

Specifically, the most significant revised auditing standards passed by the PCAOB include the following:

- Auditing Standard No. 1 requires that audits of publicly traded companies be conducted in compliance with the standards of the PCAOB, replacing the previous reference to generally accepted auditing standards, or GAAS.
- Auditing Standard No. 2 deals with auditors' responsibilities to audit a company's internal control over financial reporting. SOX required the PCAOB to develop this standard to complement the act's requirement that company management assess the quality of the company's internal controls.

6. For a summary of audit guideline changes, see the website for the Public Company Accounting Oversight Board at http://www.pcaobus.org/ and click "standards."

- Auditing Standard No. 3 deals with auditor document retention. This standard is important not just because it is expressly required by SOX (see 18 U.S.C. § 1520), but also because it was perceived as an integral piece in restoring investor confidence in the audit process. The PCAOB determined from a policy standpoint that good documentation is a critical component of an effective audit. The auditors' workpapers are central to accounting firms' quality control over their audit engagements. Investors rely on more than just the words of the audit report, which are standard. They also rely on the name and signature on the report. A firm's reputation for quality auditing is the most important asset it has, and its audit documentation defends that reputation.

Firms and regulators, including PCAOB inspectors, test quality control by examining audit workpapers to determine whether audits meet the standard of quality for which the firm's name stands. Inadequate workpapers are thus an early warning sign that audits may not be worthy of the firm's name, or of investors' reliance. Workpapers must be sufficiently specific to enable reviewers to understand the audit work performed, who performed and reviewed the work, and the nature of the audit evidence examined. In fact, the PCAOB determined that it was not enough to simply ask auditors to attest to and report on management's assessment of a company's internal controls. In its view, SOX clearly required more: that auditors self-determine that the internal controls are adequate to support reliable financial statements. The standards further require that auditors should make note of the effectiveness of the corporation's audit committee, including whether the committee is independent of management.

On October 21, 2008, in response to the financial crisis precipitated by the collapse of the mortgage market, the PCAOB announced seven proposed standards designed to crack down further on audit risk.[7] The PCAOB describes audit risk as one where the auditor violates its obligation of independence in the audit process and "issues an inappropriate opinion when the financial statements are materially misstated."[8] In other words, the protective layer of third-party professionals between the issuer and the SEC is once again corrupted through participation by the auditor in the scheme. The proposed standards were finally adopted in 2010 as Auditing Standards 8 through 15 (AS Nos. 8-15) and include the following salient features:[9]

- *Audit risk in an audit of financial statements.* AS No. 8 describes the components of audit risk and the auditor's responsibilities for reducing audit risk to an appropriately low level in order to obtain reasonable assurance in an audit of financial statements.

7. Pub. Co. Accounting Oversight Bd., Board Proposes New Auditing Standards Related to the Auditor's Assessment of and Responses to Risk, http://www.pcaobus.org/News_and_Events/News/2008/10-21.aspx.

8. *Id.*

9. AS Nos. 8-15 available at http://pcaobus.org/Standards/Auditing/Pages/default.aspx

- *Audit planning and supervision.* AS Nos. 9 and 10 describe the auditor's responsibilities for planning the audit, including assessing matters that are important to the audit, and establishing an appropriate audit strategy and audit plan and includes the responsibilities of the engagement partner and other engagement team members for supervising and reviewing the work of the engagement team.
- *Identifying and assessing risks of material misstatement.* AS No. 12 describes the auditor's responsibilities for identifying and assessing risks of material misstatement. The risk assessment process discussed in the proposed standard includes information-gathering procedures to identify risks (e.g., obtaining an understanding of the company, its environment, and its internal control) and analysis of the identified risks.
- *The auditor's responses to the risks of material misstatement.* AS No. 13 sets forth the auditor's responsibilities for responding to the risks of material misstatement in the general conduct of the audit and specific audit procedures.
- *Evaluating audit results.* AS No. 14 describes the auditor's responsibilities regarding the process of evaluating the results of the audit in order to form the opinion(s) to be presented in the auditor's report. This process includes evaluating uncorrected misstatements and control deficiencies identified during the audit.
- *Consideration of materiality in planning and performing an audit.* AS No. 11 sets forth the auditor's responsibilities for applying the concept of materiality, as described by the federal securities laws, in planning the audit and determining the scope of the audit procedures.
- *Audit evidence.* AS No. 15 sets forth the auditor's responsibilities regarding designing and applying audit procedures to obtain sufficient appropriate evidence to support the opinion(s) in the auditor's report. In particular, it discusses the principles for determining the sufficiency and appropriateness of audit evidence.

B. SOX Changes to Lawyers' Ethics: In-House and Outside Counsel Rules

While many have steadfastly held to the view that lawyers' ethics should not be "federalized," SOX changed the ethical landscape for attorneys, at least where they are licensed to appear on behalf of issuers before the SEC.[10] SOX provided a new ethical

10. For an in-depth discussion and analysis of the changes, see Miriam F. Miquelon-Weismann, *Corporate Transparency or Congressional Window-Dressing? The Case Against Sarbanes-Oxley as a Means to Avoid Another Corporate Debacle: The Failed Attempt to Revive Meaningful Regulatory Oversight,* 10 Stan. J.L. Bus. & Fin. 98 (2004); Stanley Keller, *SEC Implements Standards of Professional Conduct for Attorneys,* SJ014 ALI-ABA 1089 (2003).

framework that addresses the respective roles of in-house general counsel and outside counsel and the new disclosure requirements of financial improprieties. Section 307 of the act is implemented by 17 C.F.R. part 205.154. According to the SEC, Part 205 is intended to ensure that attorneys representing issuers before the Commission "are governed by standards of conduct that increase disclosure of potential impropriety within an issuer so that prompt intervention and remediation can take place. Doing so should boost investor confidence in the financial markets."[11]

Part 205 applies only to an attorney "appearing and practicing before the commission in the representation of the issuer." The rules have no application unless the attorney is providing legal advice and there is an attorney-client relationship. The distinction is an important one when considering where in-house general counsel fits in the statutory and ethical framework. Employees of an issuer who are licensed attorneys but do not practice law on behalf of their employer are not subject to the final rules. The rules, thus, exclude many in-house general counsel who typically provide a mix of legal and business advice. Indeed, in-house general counsel may, within the paradigm of the attorney-client relationship, fall more within the definition of the "client" as part of the corporate control group than on the side of the "attorney," depending on the circumstances of the transaction. Also excluded are attorneys for third parties who review part of an issuer's disclosure document or render a legal opinion to an issuer who is not their client; for example, attorneys who represent corporations that have related-party transactions with the issuer but have separate counsel.

There are two examples where an attorney may be subject to the rules even though not counsel for the issuer: (1) an attorney who is employed by an investment advisor for an investment company and knows that its report will be filed with the SEC; and (2) an attorney for a controlled subsidiary who is deemed to be appearing and practicing before the SEC in the representation of the parent.

Part 205.3 requires reporting by an attorney who is covered by the act and who becomes aware of "evidence of a material violation" by the issuer or any of its officers, directors, employees, or agents, which could include its underwriters. Under this standard, the attorney must be aware of a violation but is not obligated to conduct an inquiry. Evidence of a material violation means "credible evidence, based upon which it would be unreasonable, under the circumstances, for a prudent and competent attorney not to conclude that it is reasonably likely that a material violation has occurred, is ongoing, or is about to occur."[12] This is primarily an objective standard and it recognizes that there is a whole range of judgments an attorney can make

11. Final Rule, SEC Rel. Nos. 33-81, 85, 34-47276, 17 C.F.R. pt. 205, *Implementation of Standards of Professional Conduct for Attorneys*.

12. 17 C.F.R. § 205.3 (2003).

without being unreasonable. The materiality standard has not changed and remains the same as under existing law.

Assuming the attorney determines that evidence of a material violation must be reported, counsel has three alternatives for reporting that evidence. The basic requirement is for the attorney to "report up the ladder," starting with the issuer's chief legal officer (CLO). If the issuer has a Qualified Legal Compliance Committee (QLCC), the attorney may instead satisfy the reporting obligation by advising the QLCC. An attorney who reports to the existing QLCC fulfills the obligation and is not required to assess the issuer's response to the report. The attorney's role as the "gatekeeper" ends.

"Up the ladder" reporting is the most salient feature of the new regulations. The SEC remarks that this feature of the regulatory paradigm "responds fully to the mandate of Section 307 to require reporting of evidence of material violations up-the-ladder with an issuer, thereby allowing issuers to take necessary remedial action expeditiously and reduce any adverse impact upon investors. The final rule strikes an appropriate balance between our initial rule proposal on up-the-ladder reporting and the various views expressed by commentators while still achieving this important goal."[13]

Here, the SEC is prone to understatement. The initial proposed implementing regulations to Section 307 set off a maelstrom in the legal community. The American Bar Association (ABA) quickly formed a Task Force on Implementation of Section 307 of the Sarbanes-Oxley Act of 2002 in November 2002. The ABA summarized its views on ethical reforms in a letter to the SEC on December 18, 2002, in response to the issuance of proposed regulations. As a result of immense pressure, the ABA successfully backed the SEC away from promulgating regulations requiring an attorney to withdraw from representing a corporation, also referred to as the "noisy withdrawal" provision, where the issuer fails to appropriately respond to violations that threaten substantial injury to the investors of the issuer. Instead, the SEC proposed what it termed an alternative: "in the event that an attorney withdraws from representation of an issuer after failing to receive an appropriate response to reported evidence of a material violation, the issuer would be required to disclose its counsel's withdrawal to the commission."[14]

The ABA Task Force submitted a second letter to the SEC on April 2, 2003, notifying the SEC that the ABA intended to make changes to the ABA's Model Rules of Professional Conduct, strengthening attorney ethics provisions specifically in the area of noisy withdrawal. The final rule promulgated by the SEC does not mandate noisy withdrawal and instead, under Section 205, permits the attorney to decide, in

13. 17 C.F.R. pts 205, 240, and 249, 68 FR 6296, 6297 (2003).
14. *Id.* at 6297.

three limited circumstances, whether it is appropriate to report a material violation by the issuer to the SEC.

Significantly, the regulations also eliminate the requirement that a reporting attorney document the report of evidence of a material violation. Critics of the proposed regulations requiring documentation argued to the SEC that the requirement could chill the attorney-client relationship and possibly subject the issuer to increased discovery obligations detrimental to the issuer in the event of subsequent civil actions filed against the issuer.

Once the chief legal officer (CLO) receives the report of a material violation, the CLO must cause an inquiry to be made into the possible violations. If the CLO determines that there is no material violation, the reporting attorney must be provided the basis for the determination. It is unclear from the regulations whether the reporting attorney may rely on, as an "appropriate response," a simple statement from the CLO that no material violation exists. Apparently, the statement may be relevant to a determination of whether the CLO has given an appropriate response. However, it is not dispositive and there is no clarification about when the statement may be deemed dispositive.

The ambiguity in the definition of "appropriate response" is not insignificant. Whether something is deemed to be an appropriate response dictates the ethical and legal duties of the reporting attorney. This certainly makes attorneys uncomfortable. However, these regulations must be viewed in the context of implementing regulatory reform that achieves corporate transparency. If the reporting attorney is satisfied with taking "no" for an answer, because that answer can be defended based on a reasonableness standard, any obligation to protect the interests of the investors after that moment ceases. Again, the gatekeeper is done. More importantly, the SEC is completely out of the reporting loop at this point and cannot assess whether the issuer is acting reasonably. As long as the reporting attorney's mental processes were reasonable, there is no further recourse against the reporting attorney.

In the event that the CLO cannot reasonably make the determination about whether a material violation exists, the CLO must take all reasonable steps to cause the issuer to make an appropriate response. The regulations provide no definition of "appropriate response" here. If the CLO does not provide an appropriate response, the reporting attorney must disclose the evidence to the issuer's audit committee. If none exists, then the reporting attorney must disclose it to the independent members of the board of directors who are not employed directly or indirectly by the issuer.

The regulations fail to recognize, however, that the audit committee may not always be the appropriate committee to receive the report. It is not uncommon for the board of directors, of which the audit committee is a part, to be right in the middle of the scheme. Enron exemplifies this point. The Enron board of directors approved the faulty accounting and auditing procedures employed by management and the outside auditors. The Enron board of directors waived the company's code of ethics to permit management to "deconsolidate" certain investments by taking the bad investments off Enron's books and transferring them to related partnerships, Special Purpose Entities (SPEs), the straw purchasers of the bad investments. In the October 15, 2001, report issued by Vinson & Elkins (V&E),[15] the law firm hired by Enron to conduct an internal investigation of these and other claimed financial irregularities that had been reported "up the ladder" by Sherron Watkins, an Enron vice president, V&E notes that it was the board that established the "special procedures" authorizing the SPE transactions.

The regulations also provide that the up-the-ladder reporting requirements do not apply to outside counsel hired to conduct an internal legal audit, particularly where counsel has been retained to provide a colorable defense. V&E was hired by Enron to conduct such an internal legal audit regarding the claimed financial irregularities involving the related partnerships. As such, the current application of Sections 205.3(b)(6)(i)(A) and (B) would appear to exempt V&E from reporting evidence of a material violation to the board. Notably, V&E did report the results of its investigation to the CLO, through the issuance of its October 15 report. The CLO was to report this information to the directors, "except where the attorney and the CLO each reasonably believe[d] that no material violation ha[d] occurred."[16] V&E reported its findings to the issuer that no material violation had occurred and that no financial irregularity existed as claimed.

Under the new regulations, it is unlikely that V&E would be required as a matter of law to do anything differently unless V&E's beliefs at the time of the report were later proven to be unreasonable. V&E's claim that the firm had the right to rely on the expertise of Enron's outside auditors, Arthur Andersen, directly impacts the question of reasonableness in this context. Indeed, Enron's CLO specifically limited the scope of V&E's retention to conduct the internal legal audit without second-guessing the accounting advice and treatment provided by Enron's auditor, Arthur Andersen. The regulations probably do nothing to correct what the court-appointed examiner in bankruptcy concluded was V&E's mishandling of the internal legal audit.

Section 205 does permit an attorney to disclose confidential information related to representation without the issuer's consent in certain limited circumstances. First, confidential information may be disclosed where an "attorney reasonably believes [it is] necessary to prevent . . . a material violation that is likely to cause substantial injury to the financial interest . . . of the issuer or the investors."[17] Second, such information may be disclosed to prevent perjury or fraud in an SEC investigation or proceeding. Finally, a disclosure may be made to rectify a material violation in which

15. Letter from Max Hedrick III, Vinson & Elkins, to James Derrick, Executive Vice-President and Gen. Counsel, Enron Corp. (Oct. 15, 2001), http://news.findlaw.com/hdocs/docs/enron/veenron101501ltr.pdf.

16. *See* 17 C.F.R. § 205.3(b)(6)(i)(A), (B).

17. 17 C.F.R. § 205.3(d)(2)(i).

the attorneys' services were used in a way that caused or may cause financial injury. However, because the reporting is permissive only and not mandatory, an attorney will have to consider applicable state ethical rules that may circumscribe the attorney's ability to disclose client confidential information and decide whether the SEC's effort to override conflicting state ethics rules is effective. Even in those states where disclosure to the SEC is allowed, the reporting attorney may choose not to go to the SEC, and there may be no ethical disciplinary consequences for failing to do so.

Finally, there is no clear guidance whether the up-the-ladder reporting requirement applies where the evidence of a material violation is unrelated to the service for which the attorney has been hired. It is unlikely that an attorney's fiduciary obligation to its client can be extended beyond the scope of the firm's retention. A senior partner at V&E commented: "There is a misunderstanding of what outside counsel's role is. We would have no role in determining whether, or what, accounting treatment was appropriate [for a client]."[18] So, the question remains unanswered: is the attorney responsible to review the auditor's accounting treatment of corporate transactions, or is the attorney allowed to rely on the work product of other outside professionals, ostensibly more expert than legal counsel, engaged to provide audit and accounting services for the corporation? The regulations appear not to provide clarification to one of the most vexing problems in the Enron controversy.

The regulations also exclude immediate SEC intervention where material evidence of wrongdoing is uncovered. Instead, the issuer is left to internal remediation, with sole reliance on up-the-ladder reporting by employees who are dependent on the same corporation for their livelihoods or by law firms reaping lucrative legal fees from the issuer. In the case of V&E, the firm billed Enron between $27 and $30 million in legal fees in 2000. Enron provided nearly 7 percent of V&E's total annual billings.[19] Arguably, this might have a chilling effect on the success of the plan.

III. Wall Street Reform and Consumer Protection Act of 2010

There can be no question that the enactment of the Wall Street Reform and Consumer Protection Act of 2010 (Reform Act) was, in part, a recognition by Congress that there is a severe crisis in regulatory oversight. As the legislative history illustrates, Congress recognized that the existing regulatory oversight structure narrowly focused regulators on individual institutions and markets, which allowed supervi-

18. Dan Ackman, *It's the Lawyers' Turn to Answer for Enron*, Forbes, Mar. 14, 2002, *available at* http://www.forbes.com/2002/03/14/0314topnews.html.

19. Jill E. Fisch & Kenneth M. Rosen, *Lessons From Enron: Is There A Role for Lawyers in Preventing Future Enrons?*, 48 Vill. L. Rev. 1097, 1123–24 (2003).

sory gaps to grow and regulatory inconsistencies to emerge—in turn, allowing arbitrage and weakened standards. No single entity had responsibility for monitoring and addressing risks to financial stability posed by different types of financial firms operating in and across multiple markets. As a result, important parts of the system were left unregulated.

As Federal Reserve Board Chairman Ben Bernanke explained,[20] the purpose of the newly created Financial Stability Oversight Committee (FSOC), a central feature of the new Reform Act, is to provide a forum for agencies with differing responsibilities and perspectives to share information and approaches, and facilitate identification and mitigation of emerging threats to financial stability.[21] It is intended "that the lines of accountability for systemic oversight be clearly drawn, [but that] the council should not be directly involved in rule-writing and supervision. Rather, those functions should remain with the relevant supervisors, with the council in a coordinating role."

A. New Criminal Offense Conduct

The Reform Act describes the expansion of criminal offense conduct and the need for regulatory agencies to promulgate new regulations for the financial sector, many of which will be tied directly to criminal enforcement provisions. Promulgating these regulations is expected to take a great deal of time. Therefore, although Reform Act identifies numerous criminal offenses in its 848 pages, it will take some time to promulgate and define the actual number of criminal offenses that will result from enacting this legislation. It is apparent from the description of the offenses that most will be inserted into the securities acts. Chapter 3 of this publication does address some of the more salient changes affecting the security laws, including the changes to the insider trading laws, Rule 10b-5, and the whistleblower laws applicable to the securities acts. For a more complete listing of the new criminal offenses, see Appendix A.

B. Whistleblower Protections

The Reform Act also makes important changes to corporate whistleblower protections that affect publicly traded and nonpublicly traded companies. While SOX prohibited publicly traded companies from retaliating against employees who made reports of securities violations,[22] the Reform Act significantly expands the protections afforded to corporate whistleblowers, expands the companies subject to SOX's

20. Remarks of Chairman Ben Bernanke on the Squam Lake Report: Fixing the Financial System (2010) at http://www.federalreserve.gov/newsevents/speech/bernanke20100616a.htm.

21. Reform Act, 2010, Title I, Subtitle B, Section 1107.

22. 18 U.S.C. §1514A.

whistleblower provisions, provides informal rules concerning the timing and manner in which retaliation claims can be made, and harshens the penalties for retaliation.[23] The Reform Act also creates a new whistleblower cause of action that allows individuals to bring claims directly in federal court up to 10 years after the alleged retaliatory conduct, to seek extensive damages, including double back pay, and to receive up to 30 percent of SEC-imposed sanctions. The Act also amends the whistleblower protections created under SOX to include both publicly traded companies and their subsidiaries and affiliates, and it extends the statute of limitations for claims under SOX from 90 to 180 days.

This may not be the end of the story. The Reform Act expressly requires the Inspector General to explore current whistleblowing programs to determine if additional regulation is required, whether whistleblower awards are adequate, and whether sanctions to prevent retaliation should be increased.[24]

---

23. SEC. 922. WHISTLEBLOWER PROTECTION. (a) IN GENERAL.—The Securities Exchange Act of 1934 (15 U.S.C. 78a et seq.) is amended by inserting after section 21E the following: "SEC. 21F. SECURITIES WHISTLEBLOWER INCENTIVES AND PROTECTION..."(h) PROTECTION OF WHISTLEBLOWERS.— "(1) PROHIBITION AGAINST RETALIATION.— "(A) IN GENERAL.—No employer may discharge, demote, suspend, threaten, harass, directly or indirectly, or in any other manner discriminate against, a whistleblower in the terms and conditions of employment because of any lawful act done by the whistleblower— "(i) in providing information to the Commission in accordance with this section; "(ii) in initiating, testifying in, or assisting in any investigation or judicial or administrative action of the Commission based upon or related to such information; or "(iii) in making disclosures that are required or protected under the Sarbanes-Oxley Act of 2002 (15 U.S.C. 7201 et seq.), the Securities Exchange Act of 1934 (15 U.S.C. 78a et seq.), including section 10A(m) of such Act (15 U.S.C. 78f(m)), section 1513(e) of title 18, United States Code, and any other law, rule, or regulation subject to the jurisdiction of the Commission. "(B) ENFORCEMENT.— "(i) CAUSE OF ACTION.—An individual who alleges discharge or other discrimination in violation of subparagraph (A) may bring an action under this subsection in the appropriate district court of the United States for the relief provided in subparagraph (C).

24. "SEC. 21F. SECURITIES WHISTLEBLOWER INCENTIVES AND PROTECTION... (d) STUDY OF WHISTLEBLOWER PROTECTION PROGRAM.— (1) STUDY.—The Inspector General of the Commission shall conduct a study of the whistleblower protections established under the amendments made by this section, including— (A) whether the final rules and regulations issued under the amendments made by this section have made the whistleblower protection program (referred to in this subsection as the "program") clearly defined and user-friendly; (B) whether the program is promoted on the website of the Commission and has been widely publicized; (C) whether the Commission is prompt in—(i) responding to—(I) information provided by whistleblowers; and (II) applications for awards filed by whistleblowers; (ii) updating whistleblowers about the status of their applications; and (iii) otherwise communicating with the interested parties; (D) whether the minimum and maximum reward levels are adequate to entice whistleblowers to come forward with information and whether the reward levels are so high as to encourage illegitimate whistleblower claims; (E) whether the appeals process has been unduly burdensome for the Commission; (F) whether the funding mechanism for the Investor Protection Fund is adequate; (G) whether, in the interest of protecting investors and identifying and preventing fraud, it would be useful for Congress to consider empowering whistleblowers or other individuals, who have already attempted to pursue the case through the Commission, to have a private right of action to bring suit based on the facts of the same case, on behalf of the Government and themselves, against persons who have committee securities fraud; (H)(i) whether the exemption under section 552(b)(3) of title 5 (known as the Freedom of Information Act) established in section 21F(h)(2)(A) of the Securities Exchange Act of 1934, as added by this Act, aids whistleblowers in disclosing information to the Com-

IV. Expansion of the False Claims Act: Fraud Enforcement and Recovery Act of 2009

The United States has both statutory (e.g., the False Claims Act, 31U.S.C. §§ 3729–33)[25] and common law rights of action arising from fraud against the government and from the corruption of its officials. The Department of Justice (DOJ) has promulgated a useful explanatory memorandum summarizing the provisions of the False Claims Act (FCA) and the procedures for instituting suit and notification to the government.[26] Specifically, the FCA provides the United States with a civil cause of action[27] against any person who knowingly presents, or causes to be presented, a false or fraudulent claim for money or property to the United States; makes or causes to be made a false statement to get a false claim paid or approved; conspires to defraud the government by getting a false claim paid; or makes, uses, or causes to be made or used, a false statement to conceal, avoid, or decrease an obligation to the government. The statute provides for treble damages for the government's loss, plus penalties for each false claim.[28]

From a procedural standpoint, the FCA encourages the use of *qui tam* actions in which citizens are authorized to bring, as private attorneys general, lawsuits on behalf of the United States, alleging frauds upon the government. The plaintiff bringing the action, in most cases a former employee whistleblower, is referred to as a "relator." A relator shares in the money recovered for the government in the event that the lawsuit is successful in obtaining a recovery.

In 2009, the Fraud Enforcement and Recovery Act of 2009 (FERA) was signed into law, expanding the reach of the FCA. Under FERA, the DOJ may now share information with other government agencies, *qui tam* whistleblowers, and state agencies during the investigation of an FCA case. Prior to FERA, relators were often denied access to documents and information that a defendant in an FCA case or a party under investigation produced to the government in response to a Civil Investigative Demand (CID). The new law explicitly allows access by whistleblowers to such documents and information.[29] FERA also expands a whistleblower's ability to sue for employer retaliation under the FCA.

---

mission; (ii) what impact the exemption described in clause (i) has had on the ability of the public to access information about the regulation and enforcement by the Commission of securities; and (iii) any recommendations on whether the exemption described in clause (i) should remain in effect; and (I) such other matters as the Inspector General deems appropriate.

25. False Claims Act Amendments of 1986, Pub. L. No. 99-562, 100 Stat. 3153 (October 27, 1986).

26. U.S.Attorneys' Manual Title 9, Criminal Resource Manual 932, *available at* http://www.justice.gov/usao/eousa/foia_reading_room/usam/title9/crm00000.htm.

27. 31 U.S.C. § 3730.

28. 31 U.S.C. § 3729.

29. The government typically uses CIDs to obtain information when it is investigating FCA allegations and deciding whether it will join in a relator's case.

FERA overrules two recent court decisions that restricted the application of the FCA. Prior to FERA, the gist of 31 U.S.C. § 3729(a)(1) under the FCA was to make unlawful the presentation of false claims presented to the federal government. Courts uniformly interpreted this provision as requiring actual "presentment of a claim to the federal government." *United States ex rel. Totten v. Bombardier Corp.*, 380 F.3d 488, 492 (D.C. Cir. 2004). Therefore, merely submitting a false claim to a recipient of federal funds, such as a federal contractor or grantee, did not violate subsection (a)(1), even if the contractor or grantee paid the claim using government funds. Instead, a violation of subsection (a)(1) occurred only if the defendant submitted or caused another to submit a false or fraudulent claim to the federal government.

FERA now eliminates the requirement of presentment to the federal government and subjects to potential liability anyone who makes claims for payment to any recipient of federal funds. Thus, anyone doing business with a recipient of federal money now faces some risk of liability under the FCA, even if the allegedly false claim is not intended to induce payment by the government.

Again prior to FERA, 31 U.S.C. §3729(a)(2) prohibited anyone from using "a false record or statement to get a false or fraudulent claim paid or approved by the Government." Although subsection (a)(2) did not contain a presentment requirement similar to (a)(1), liability did not attach without a finding that the false record or statement was meant to induce payment by the government. And so the Supreme Court held in *Allison Engine Co. v. United States ex rel. Sanders*, 128 S.Ct. 2123, 2129–30 (2008). Mere payment by a federal grantee, absent some evidence of a claimant's intent to extract payment from the government, did not give rise to liability under subsection (a)(2), regardless of whether the federal grantee actually used federal funds to pay the claim.

Effectively overruling *Allison Engine Co.*, FERA removes the language relied on by the Court to limit the scope of the FCA and expands the language in subsection (a)(2) to cover false statements made to any recipient of federal money regardless of whether the entity making the statement knew about the source of the funds or expected the government to pay the claim.[30] Additionally, under FERA, contractors and fund recipients are now liable for a conspiracy to commit a violation of any substantive section of the False Claims Act. There is no longer a need for the false claim to be paid or approved in order to assess liability; merely conspiring to commit the violation is now covered.

30. FERA makes some substantive changes to subsection (a)(7) (now codified as 31 U.S.C. § 3729(a)(1)(G)), the "reverse false claims" provision. Specifically, it amends subsection (a)(7) to conform with the amended subsection (a)(2). Prior to FERA, subsection (a)(7) imposed liability on anyone who knowingly made a false record or statement "to conceal, avoid, or decrease an obligation to pay or transmit money or property to the Government." Under FERA, the FCA now imposes liability for false records or statements even if a business's allegedly false records or statements were never intended to result in the retention of a government payment.

V. Proposed Legislation

A. Public Corruption Prosecution Improvements Act of 2011

The legislative proposal currently pending proposes to amend the federal criminal code to revise and expand prohibitions against bribery, theft of public money, and other public corruption offenses. The movement behind the bill resulted from recent cases decided by the courts narrowing the definitions of prohibited conduct of public officials under the current bribery and illegal gratuity statutes. Thus, the bill is intended to clarify and expand the definition of what it means for a public official to perform an "official act," and amend the federal bribery statute to show that corrupt payment can be made to influence more than one official act. The legislation also proposes to amend the federal gratuities statute to make clear that public officials cannot accept anything of value given to them because of their official position other than as permitted by existing rules or regulations.

Specifically, it would establish a six-year limitation period for the prosecution of public corruption crimes involving bribery, extortion, theft of government property, mail fraud, and racketeering. It expands mail and wire fraud statutes to cover offenses involving any other thing of value (e.g., intangible rights and licenses). The proposed bill also modifies general venue rules for criminal prosecutions to allow prosecutions in any district in which an act in furtherance of an offense is committed and reduces from $5,000 to $1,000 the threshold amount for theft or bribery involving federally assisted programs and increases the maximum prison term for such offenses from 10 to 15 years. The maximum term of imprisonment for various offenses is also increased:

(1) theft and embezzlement of federal money, property, or records from 10 to 15 years; and (2) bribery offenses from 15 to 20 years. Increases to 10 years the maximum term of imprisonment for:

- (a) solicitation by federal officers and employees of political contributions from other federal officers and employees;
- (b) promise of employment made possible by an act of Congress for political activity;
- (c) deprivation of such employment for political activity;
- (d) intimidation to secure political contributions;
- (e) solicitation and acceptance of contributions in federal offices; and
- (f) coercion of political activity by federal employees.

The bill applies the prohibition against embezzlement or theft of federal money or property to government officials and employees of the District of Columbia and includes embezzlement or theft of government money or property as predicates for racketeering prosecutions and wiretaps.

It modifies elements relating to the crime of bribery of public officials and witnesses to:

(1) prohibit public officials from accepting anything of value, other than what is permitted by rule or regulation, for or because of the official's or person's official position;
(2) expand the definition of "official act" to include any conduct that falls within the range of official duty of a public official; and
(3) include a course of conduct involving multiple gifts, offers or promises designed to influence a public official.

It expands the types of perjury and obstruction of justice offenses for which venue lies in the district in which the official proceeding was intended to be affected or in which the conduct constituting the alleged offense occurred. The proposed bill also directs the U.S. Sentencing Commission to review and amend its guidelines and policy statements relating to public corruption offenses to reflect the intent of Congress that penalties for such offenses be increased. Finally, the bill would amend the federal judicial code to permit the disclosure of information regarding a potential criminal offense by a judge to the DOJ, a federal, state, or local grand jury, or federal, state, or local law enforcement agents.

VI. Conclusion

While a common theme in the new world of corporate governance appears to be more regulation and increased criminal punishment, it's not that simple. The economic philosophy of the marketplace—the system of free enterprise—depends on risk taking and innovation for growth. Risk taking is diminished as the consequences for failed risk increase. The struggle between self-regulation and increased government regulation is in the end a failure of corporations to engage in self-restraint. If trust is the cornerstone of a functional marketplace, the infrastructure has crumbled and is in need of rebuilding. It is back to business school for corporate executives to revisit the tried and true "Fisher Principle of Leadership." George Fisher, former CEO of Kodak and, prior to that, CEO of Motorola, urged business students to heed some useful business advice to avoid the increased presence of regulation and regulators in their business operations.[31] Simply, he advised business leaders to take an evolving problem in their own operation and fix it before the problem became regulated or

31. Thomas Kochan, *Rebuilding the Social Contract at Work: Lessons from Leading Cases*, Task Force Working Paper #WP09 (May 1999) at http://www.dol.gov/oasam/programs/history/herman/reports/futurework/conference/contract/eastman-kodak.htm.

litigated. Business people who voluntarily undertake self-correction are always ahead of the game. Lawyers and accountants might find this a useful lesson, too.

If corporate governance is to remain anchored in a system of self-regulation and governmental regulation held in abeyance, then self-restraint and self-correction will remain critical to the preservation of that independence and trust. It really is all about corporate ethics. In the end, ethical corporate practices tied to long-term growth in a sustainable business environment will generate substantially greater financial benefit for both corporations and their shareholders.

> "Really what we need now, is not laws against crime, but a law against insanity."[32]

32. Mark Twain, *A New Crime*, in SKETCHES, NEW AND OLD, 187, 191 (1875).

APPENDIX **A**

NEW CRIMINAL OFFENSES PROMULGATED BY THE WALL STREET REFORM AND CONSUMER PROTECTION ACT OF 2010

Excerpts from:
Criminal Provisions in the Dodd-Frank Wall Street Reform & Consumer Protection Act
Source: http://www.fed-soc.org/doclib/20101210_NFIPCrimProvisionDoddFrank.pdf

Disclosures: Section 202(a)(1)(C)[3]. Criminalizes Disclosures of Treasury Determinations or the pendency of court proceedings (Petitions of Orderly Liquidations).

Indexing of Swap transactions: Section 723(a)(2)[6]. Also, Sections 724, 728, 730, 731, 733, and 741. Makes it a criminal offense for any person, other than an eligible contract participant, to enter into a swap unless the swap is entered into on, or subject to the rules of, a board of trade designated as a contract market under section 5."

Swaps, Segregations and Bankruptcy Treatment: Section 724(a)[7]. Criminalizes accepting any money, securities, property or extending credit in lieu of money securities or property from, for, or on behalf of, a swaps customer to margin, guarantee, or secure a swap cleared by or through a derivatives clearing organization (including money, securities, or property accruing to the customer as the result of such a swap), unless the person shall have registered under this Act with the Commission as a futures commission merchant, and the registration shall not have expired nor been suspended nor revoked." This provision also prohibits any person, including any derivatives clearing organization and any depository institution, that has received any money, securities, or property for deposit in a separate account or accounts as provided in paragraph (2) to hold, dispose of, or use any such money, securities, or property as belonging to the depositing futures commission merchant or any person other than the swaps customer of the futures commission merchant."

Registration Requirement for Swap Data Repositories: Section 728. Creates a Registration Requirement in order to use the mails or any means or instrumentality of interstate commerce for swap data repositories without registering with the SEC. Criminal penalties apply for willful failure to do so.

Reporting Requirement for Large Swap Traders: Section 730[11]. Criminalizes the failure to report swap transactions that the SEC finds to perform a significant price discovery function with respect to registered entities if the trader enters a pre-designated amount into the swap in any one day (to be determined by the SEC) and the person obtains an amount in the swap in excess of an amount to be designated by the SEC. Such conduct will not be criminal if the person files reports regarding the transaction with the SEC (to be designated by SEC Rule or Regulation) and the person maintains records of all such swaps and transactions in any related commodity.

Registration Requirement for Swap Dealers and Major Swap Participants: Section 731[12]. Criminalizes the act of acting as a swap dealer or major swap participant while failing to have registered with the SEC.

Registration Requirement for Swap Execution Facilities: Section 733[13]. Prohibits the operation of a facility for the trading or processing of swaps unless the facility is registered as a swap execution facility or as a designated contract market under this section.

Fraud and False Statements: Section 741[14]. Criminalizes Fraud or Deceit in the use of the mails or means or instrumentality of interstate commerce in order to make any contract of sale of any commodity for future delivery (or option on such a contract), or any swap, on a group or index of securities (or any interest therein or based on the value thereof). This includes making any untrue statement of a material fact or failing to include a material fact necessary in order to make the statements made, in the light of the circumstances under which they were made, not misleading.

Broadens Insider Trading Ban and Adds New Categories to those Covered by the Statute: Section 753[17] which amends 7 U.S.C. § 136. Expands and criminalizes the conduct of *federal employees* and the prohibitions on their use of insider information. Expands coverage of the statute to *any person* who receives and uses insider information obtained from a federal employee. Makes it a criminal offense for "any person" to obtain insider information held by the federal government that may affect or tend to affect the price of any commodity in interstate commerce, or for future delivery, or any swap, where that person knew or should have known that such information has not been disseminated by a department of the federal government **and** uses such information, or imparts such information with the intent to assist another person, directly or indirectly, in using such information to enter into, or offer to enter into—(i) a contract of sale of a commodity for future delivery (or option on such a contract); (ii) an option (other than an option executed or traded on a national securities exchange registered pursuant to section 6(a) of the Securities Exchange Act of 1934 (15 U.S.C. 78f(a)); or (iii) a swap.

Antidisruptive Practices Provision: Section 747[16]. Criminalizes willful acts of disruption during transactional negotiating or the closing period including acts which demonstrate an intentional or reckless disregard for the orderly execution of transactions during the closing period. The statute particularly targets the practice known as in the trade as 'spoofing' (bidding or offering with the intent to cancel the bid or offer before execution). It also criminalizes the use of swaps to defraud including knowing or acting in reckless disregard of the fact, that its counterparty will use the swap as part of a device, scheme, or artifice to defraud any third party.

Securities Registration Requirement: Section 764[18]. Requires registration of all persons participating in securities based swaps and criminalizes the failure to register with the SEC. It also places the burden on securities based swap dealers and major securities based swap participants to not become associated with such unregistered persons in securities based swap transactions under criminal penalty for doing so.

Criminalizes Use of Mails or Interstate Commerce in Transactions with Ineligible Participants: Section 768[21]. Makes it a criminal offense to willfully use interstate commerce or the mails to trade in securities based swap transactions with any person not an eligible contract participant (as defined in section 1a(18) of the Commodity Exchange Act (7 U.S.C. § 1a(18))," unless a registration statement has been filed.

Criminalizes Margin Lending: Section 929[22] which amends 15 U.S.C. § 78g(c)(1)(A). Bars any member of a national securities exchange or any broker or dealer, directly or indirectly, from extending or maintaining credit or arranging for the extension or maintenance of credit to or for any customer on any security (with few exceptions) without collateral or on any collateral other than securities. It also prohibits any member of a national securities exchange or any broker or dealer from extending or maintaining credit in cases where the extension or maintenance of credit is not for the purpose of purchasing or carrying securities or of evading or circumventing these provisions. Thus creating two separate criminal violations where only one previously existed.

Violations Reporting Requirement for Rating Agencies: Section 934[23]. Requires each nationally recognized statistical rating organization shall refer to the appropriate law enforcement or regulatory authorities any information that the nationally recognized statistical rating organization receives from a third party and finds credible that alleges that an issuer of securities rated by the nationally recognized statistical rating organization has committed or is committing a material violation of law that has not been adjudicated by a Federal or State court. With no requirement that the nationally recognized statistical rating organization warranty the accuracy of the information.

Regulation of Municipal Advisors: Section 975(a)(1)[24]. Makes it a criminal offense for a municipal advisor to provide advice to or on behalf of a municipal entity or obligated person with respect to municipal financial products or the issuance of municipal securities, or to undertake a solicitation of a municipal entity or obligated person, unless the municipal advisor is registered in accordance with this subsection.

Municipal Advisor Fraud by Mail or Interstate Commerce: Section 975(a)(5)[25]. Criminalizes use of the mails or any means or instrumentality of interstate commerce to provide advice to or on behalf of a municipal entity or obligated person with respect to municipal financial products, the issuance of municipal securities, or to undertake a solicitation of a municipal entity or obligated person, in connection with which such municipal advisor engages in any fraudulent, deceptive, or manipulative act or practice by municipal advisors."

Bureau of Consumer Financial Protection (BCFP): Unlawful Acts: Section 1036[27]. Makes it a criminal offense for any covered person or service provider covered under the BCFP to offer or provide to a consumer any financial product or service not in conformity with Federal consumer financial law, or otherwise commit any act or omission in violation of a Federal consumer financial law; or to engage in any unfair, deceptive, or abusive act or practice. It also criminalizes the refusal or failure of any covered person or service provider who fails or refuses to permit access to or copying of records; to establish or maintain records; or to make reports or provide information to the Bureau when required by federal consumer financial law, or any rule or order issued by the Bureau thereunder. Additionally it criminalized providing substantial assistance to a covered person or service provider in violating these provisions.

APPENDIX **B**

EXCERPTS FROM USAM CHAPTER 9-27.000 PRINCIPLES OF FEDERAL PROSECUTION

9-27.000 (Excerpts)

PRINCIPLES OF FEDERAL PROSECUTION 9-27.001 Preface 9-27.110 Purpose 9-27.120 Application 9-27.130 Implementation 9-27.140 Modifications or Departures 9-27.150 Non-Litigability 9-27.200 Initiating and Declining Prosecution—Probable Cause Requirement 9-27.220 Grounds for Commencing or Declining Prosecution 9-27.230 Initiating and Declining Charges—Substantial Federal Interest 9-27.240 Initiating and Declining Charges—Prosecution in Another Jurisdiction 9-27.250 Non-Criminal Alternatives to Prosecution 9-27.260 Initiating and Declining Charges—Impermissible Considerations 9-27.270 Records of Prosecutions Declined 9-27.300 Selecting Charges—Charging Most Serious Offenses 9-27.320 Additional Charges 9-27.330 Pre-Charge Plea Agreements 9-27.400 Plea Agreements Generally 9-27.420 Plea Agreements—Considerations to be Weighed 9-27.430 Selecting Plea Agreement Charges 9-27.440 Plea Agreements When Defendant Denies Guilt 9-27.450 Records of Plea Agreements 9-27.500 Offers to Plead Nolo Contendere—Opposition

Except in Unusual Circumstances 9-27.520 Offers to Plead Nolo Contendere—Offer of Proof 9-27.530 Argument in Opposition of Nolo Contendere Plea 9-27.600 Entering into Non-prosecution Agreements in Return for Cooperation—Generally 9-27.620 Entering into Non-prosecution Agreements in Return for Cooperation—Considerations to be Weighed 9-27.630 Entering into Non-prosecution Agreements in Return for Cooperation—Limiting the Scope of Commitment 9-27.640 Agreements Requiring Assistant Attorney General Approval 9-27.641 Multi-District (Global) Agreement Requests 9-27.650 Records of Non-Prosecution Agreements 9-27.710 Participation in Sentencing—Generally 9-27.720 Establishing Factual Basis for Sentence 9-27.730 Conditions for Making Sentencing Recommendations 9-27.740 Consideration to be Weighed in Determining Sentencing Recommendations 9-27.745 Unwarranted Sentencing Departures by the Court 9-27.750 Disclosing Factual Material to Defense 9-27.760 Limitation on Identifying Uncharged Third-Parties Publicly

9-27.110 Purpose

The principles of Federal prosecution set forth herein are intended to promote the reasoned exercise of prosecutorial discretion by attorneys for the government with respect to:

1. Initiating and declining prosecution;
2. Selecting charges;
3. Entering into plea agreements;
4. Opposing offers to plead nolo contendere;
5. Entering into non-prosecution agreements in return for cooperation; and
6. Participating in sentencing.

B. Comment. Under the Federal criminal justice system, the prosecutor has wide latitude in determining when, whom, how, and even whether to prosecute for apparent violations of Federal criminal law. The prosecutor's broad discretion in such areas as initiating or foregoing prosecutions, selecting or recommending specific charges, and terminating prosecutions by accepting guilty pleas has been recognized on numerous occasions by the courts. *See, e.g., Oyler v. Boles,* 368 U.S. 448 (1962); *Newman v. United States,* 382 F.2d 479 (D.C. Cir. 1967); *Powell v. Ratzenbach,* 359 F.2d 234 (D.C. Cir. 1965), *cert. denied,* 384 U.S. 906 (1966). This discretion exists by virtue of his/her status as a member of the Executive Branch, which is charged under the Constitution with ensuring that the laws of the United States be "faithfully executed." U.S. Const. Art. § 3. *See Nader v. Saxbe,* 497 F.2d 676, 679 n. 18 (D.C. Cir. 1974).

Since Federal prosecutors have great latitude in making crucial decisions concerning enforcement of a nationwide system of criminal justice, it is desirable, in the interest of the fair and effective administration of justice in the Federal system, that all Federal prosecutors be guided by a general statement of principles that summarizes appropriate considerations to be weighed, and desirable practices to be followed, in discharging their prosecutorial responsibilities.

Although these principles deal with the specific situations indicated, they should be read in the broader context of the basic responsibilities of Federal attorneys: making certain that the general purposes of the criminal law—assurance of warranted punishment, deterrence of further criminal conduct, protection of the public from dangerous offenders, and rehabilitation of offenders—are adequately met, while making certain also that the rights of individuals are scrupulously protected.

[cited in USAM 9-2.031]

9-27.200 Initiating and Declining Prosecution—Probable Cause Requirement

A. If the attorney for the government has probable cause to believe that a person has committed a Federal offense within his/her jurisdiction, he/she should consider whether to:

1. Request or conduct further investigation;
2. Commence or recommend prosecution;
3. Decline prosecution and refer the matter for prosecutorial consideration in another jurisdiction;
4. Decline prosecution and initiate or recommend pretrial diversion or other non-criminal disposition; or
5. Decline prosecution without taking other action.

B. Comment. USAM 9-27.220 sets forth the courses of action available to the attorney for the government once he/she has probable cause to believe that a person has committed a Federal offense within his/her jurisdiction. The probable cause standard is the same standard as that required for the issuance of an arrest warrant or a summons upon a complaint (*See* Fed. R. Crim. P. 4(a)), for a magistrate' s decision to hold a defendant to answer in the district court (*See* Fed. R. Crim. P. 5.1(a)), and is the minimal requirement for indictment by a grand jury. *See Branzburg v. Hayes,* 408 U.S. 665, 686 (1972). This is, of course, a threshold consideration only. Merely because this requirement can be met in a given case does not automatically warrant prosecution; further investigation may be warranted, and the prosecutor should still take into account all relevant considerations, including those described in the following provisions, in deciding upon his/her course of action. On the other hand, failure to meet the minimal requirement of probable cause is an absolute bar to initiating a Federal prosecution, and in some circumstances may preclude reference to other prosecuting authorities or recourse to non-criminal sanctions as well.

9-27.220 Grounds for Commencing or Declining Prosecution

A. The attorney for the government should commence or recommend Federal prosecution if he/she believes that the person's conduct constitutes a Federal offense and that the admissible evidence will probably be sufficient to obtain and sustain a conviction, unless, in his/her judgment, prosecution should be declined because:

   1. No substantial Federal interest would be served by prosecution;
   2. The person is subject to effective prosecution in another jurisdiction; or
   3. There exists an adequate non-criminal alternative to prosecution.

B. Comment. USAM 9-27.220 expresses the principle that, ordinarily, the attorney for the government should initiate or recommend Federal prosecution if he/she believes that the person's conduct constitutes a Federal offense and that the admissible evidence probably will be sufficient to obtain and sustain a conviction. Evidence sufficient to sustain a conviction is required under Rule 29(a), Fed. R. Crim. P., to avoid a judgment of acquittal. Moreover, both as a matter of fundamental fairness and in the interest of the efficient administration of justice, no prosecution should be initiated against any person unless the government believes that the person probably will be found guilty by an unbiased trier of fact. In this connection, it should be noted that, when deciding whether to prosecute, the government attorney need not have in hand all the evidence upon which he/she intends to rely at trial: it is sufficient that he/she have a reasonable belief that such evidence will be available and admissible at the time of trial. Thus, for example, it would be proper to commence a prosecution though a key witness is out of the country, so long as the witness's presence at trial could be expected with reasonable certainty.

   The potential that—despite the law and the facts that create a sound, prosecutable case—the factfinder is likely to acquit the defendant because of the unpopularity of some factor involved in the prosecution or because of the overwhelming popularity of the defendant or his/her cause, is not a factor prohibiting prosecution. For example, in a civil rights case or a case involving an extremely popular political figure, it might be clear that the evidence of guilt—viewed objectively by an unbiased factfinder—would be sufficient to obtain and sustain a conviction, yet the prosecutor might reasonably doubt whether the jury would convict. In such a case, despite his/her negative assessment of the likelihood of a guilty verdict (based on factors extraneous to an objective view of the law and the facts), the prosecutor may properly conclude that it is necessary and desirable to commence or recommend prosecution and allow the criminal process to operate in accordance with its principles.

Merely because the attorney for the government believes that a person's conduct constitutes a Federal offense and that the admissible evidence will be sufficient to obtain and sustain a conviction, does not mean that he/she necessarily should initiate or recommend prosecution: USAM 9-27.220 notes three situations in which the prosecutor may property decline to take action nonetheless: when no substantial Federal interest would be served by prosecution; when the person is subject to effective prosecution in another jurisdiction; and when there exists an adequate non-criminal alternative to prosecution. It is left to the judgment of the attorney for the government whether such a situation exists. In exercising that judgment, the attorney for the government should consult USAM 9-27.230, 9-27.240, or 9-27.250, as appropriate.

[cited in USAM 6-4.210; USAM 9-10.060; USAM 9-27.200; USAM 9-28.300]

9-27.230 Initiating and Declining Charges—Substantial Federal Interest

A. In determining whether prosecution should be declined because no substantial Federal interest would be served by prosecution, the attorney for the government should weigh all relevant considerations, including:

    1. Federal law enforcement priorities;
    2. The nature and seriousness of the offense;
    3. The deterrent effect of prosecution;
    4. The person's culpability in connection with the offense;
    5. The person's history with respect to criminal activity;
    6. The person's willingness to cooperate in the investigation or prosecution of others; and
    7. The probable sentence or other consequences if the person is convicted.

B. Comment. USAM 9-27.230 lists factors that may be relevant in determining whether prosecution should be declined because no substantial Federal interest would be served by prosecution in a case in which the person is believed to have committed a Federal offense and the admissible evidence is expected to be sufficient to obtain and sustain a conviction. The list of relevant considerations is not intended to be all-inclusive. Obviously, not all of the factors will be applicable to every case, and in any particular case one factor may deserve more weight than it might in another case.

1. **Federal Law Enforcement Priorities.** Federal law enforcement resources and Federal judicial resources are not sufficient to permit prosecution of every alleged offense over which Federal jurisdiction exists. Accordingly, in the interest of allocating its limited resources so as to achieve an effective nationwide law enforcement program, from time to time the Department establishes national investigative and prosecutorial priorities. These priorities are designed to focus Federal law enforcement efforts on those matters within the Federal jurisdiction that are most deserving of Federal attention and are most likely to be handled effectively at the Federal level. In addition, individual United States Attorneys may establish their own priorities, within the national priorities, in order to concentrate their resources on problems of particular local or regional significance. In weighing the Federal interest in a particular prosecution, the attorney for the government should give careful consideration to the extent to which prosecution would accord with established priorities.
2. **Nature and Seriousness of Offense.** It is important that limited Federal resources not be wasted in prosecuting inconsequential cases or cases in which the violation is only technical. Thus, in determining whether a substantial Federal interest exists that requires prosecution, the attorney for the government should consider the nature and seriousness of the offense involved. A number of factors may be relevant. One factor that is obviously of primary importance is the actual or potential impact of the offense on the community and on the victim.

   The impact of an offense on the community in which it is committed can be measured in several ways: in terms of economic harm done to community interests; in terms of physical danger to the citizens or damage to public property; and in terms of erosion of the inhabitants' peace of mind and sense of security. In assessing the seriousness of the offense in these terms, the prosecutor may properly weigh such questions as whether the violation is technical or relatively inconsequential in nature and what the public attitude is toward prosecution under the circumstances of the case. The public may be indifferent, or even opposed, to enforcement of the controlling statute whether on substantive grounds, or because of a history of nonenforcement, or because the offense involves essentially a minor matter of private concern and the victim is not interested in having it pursued. On the other hand, the nature and circumstances of the offense, the identity of the offender or the victim, or the attendant publicity, may be such as to create strong public sentiment in favor of prosecution. While public interest, or lack thereof, deserves the prosecutor's careful attention, it should not be used to justify a decision to prosecute, or to take other action, that cannot be supported on other grounds. Public and professional responsibility sometimes will require the choosing of a particularly unpopular course.

Economic, physical, and psychological considerations are also important in assessing the impact of the offense on the victim. In this connection, it is appropriate for the prosecutor to take into account such matters as the victim's age or health, and whether full or partial restitution has been made. Care should be taken in weighing the matter of restitution, however, to ensure against contributing to an impression that an offender can escape prosecution merely by returning the spoils of his/her crime.

3. **Deterrent Effect of Prosecution.** Deterrence of criminal conduct, whether it be criminal activity generally or a specific type of criminal conduct, is one of the primary goals of the criminal law. This purpose should be kept in mind, particularly when deciding whether a prosecution is warranted for an offense that appears to be relatively minor; some offenses, although seemingly not of great importance by themselves, if commonly committed would have a substantial cumulative impact on the community.
4. **The Person's Culpability.** Although the prosecutor has sufficient evidence of guilt, it is nevertheless appropriate for him/her to give consideration to the degree of the person's culpability in connection with the offenses, both in the abstract and in comparison with any others involved in the offense. If, for example, the person was a relatively minor participant in a criminal enterprise conducted by others, or his/her motive was worthy, and no other circumstances require prosecution, the prosecutor might reasonably conclude that some course other than prosecution would be appropriate.
5. **The Person's Criminal History.** If a person is known to have a prior conviction or is reasonably believed to have engaged in criminal activity at an earlier time, this should be considered in determining whether to initiate or recommend Federal prosecution. In this connection particular attention should be given to the nature of the person's prior criminal involvement, when it occurred, its relationship if any to the present offense, and whether he/she previously avoided prosecution as a result of an agreement not to prosecute in return for cooperation or as a result of an order compelling his/her testimony. By the same token, a person's lack of prior criminal involvement or his/her previous cooperation with the law enforcement officials should be given due consideration in appropriate cases.
6. **The Person's Willingness to Cooperate.** A person's willingness to cooperate in the investigation or prosecution of others is another appropriate

consideration in the determination whether a Federal prosecution should be undertaken. Generally speaking, a willingness to cooperate should not by itself relieve a person of criminal liability. There may be some cases, however, in which the value of a person's cooperation clearly outweighs the Federal interest in prosecuting him/her. These matters are discussed more fully below, in connection with plea agreements and non-prosecution agreements in return for cooperation.

7. **The Person's Personal Circumstances.** In some cases, the personal circumstances of an accused may be relevant in determining whether to prosecute or to take other action. Some circumstances peculiar to the accused, such as extreme youth, advanced age, or mental or physical impairment, may suggest that prosecution is not the most appropriate response to his/her offense; other circumstances, such as the fact that the accused occupied a position of trust or responsibility which he/she violated in committing the offense, might weigh in favor of prosecution.
8. **The Probable Sentence.** In assessing the strength of the Federal interest in prosecution, the attorney for the government should consider the sentence, or other consequence, that is likely to be imposed if prosecution is successful, and whether such a sentence or other consequence would justify the time and effort of prosecution. If the offender is already subject to a substantial sentence, or is already incarcerated, as a result of a conviction for another offense, the prosecutor should weigh the likelihood that another conviction will result in a meaningful addition to his/her sentence, might otherwise have a deterrent effect, or is necessary to ensure that the offender's record accurately reflects the extent of his/her criminal conduct. For example, it might be desirable to commence a bail-jumping prosecution against a person who already has been convicted of another offense so that law enforcement personnel and judicial officers who encounter him/her in the future will be aware of the risk of releasing him/her on bail. On the other hand, if the person is on probation or parole as a result of an earlier conviction, the prosecutor should consider whether the public interest might better be served by instituting a proceeding for violation of probation or revocation of parole, than by commencing a new prosecution. The prosecutor should also be alert to the desirability of instituting prosecution to prevent the running of the statute of limitations and to preserve the availability of a basis for an adequate sentence if there appears to be a chance that an offender's prior conviction may be reversed on appeal or collateral attack. Finally, if a person previously has been prosecuted in another jurisdiction for the same offense or a closely related offense, the attorney for the government should consult existing departmental policy statements on the subject of "succes-

sive prosecution" or "dual prosecution," depending on whether the earlier prosecution was Federal or nonfederal. See USAM 9-2.031 (Petite Policy).

Just as there are factors that are appropriate to consider in determining whether a substantial Federal interest would be served by prosecution in a particular case, there are considerations that deserve no weight and should not influence the decision. These include the time and resources expended in Federal investigation of the case. No amount of investigative effort warrants commencing a Federal prosecution that is not fully justified on other grounds.
[cited in USAM 9-2.031; USAM 9-27.220]

9-27.240 Initiating and Declining Charges—Prosecution in Another Jurisdiction

A. In determining whether prosecution should be declined because the person is subject to effective prosecution in another jurisdiction, the attorney for the government should weigh all relevant considerations, including:

   1. The strength of the other jurisdiction's interest in prosecution;
   2. The other jurisdiction's ability and willingness to prosecute effectively; and
   3. The probable sentence or other consequences if the person is convicted in the other jurisdiction.

B. Comment. In many instances, it may be possible to prosecute criminal conduct in more than one jurisdiction. Although there may be instances in which a Federal prosecutor may wish to consider deferring to prosecution in another Federal district, in most instances the choice will probably be between Federal prosecution and prosecution by state or local authorities. USAM 9-27.240 sets forth three general considerations to be taken into account in determining whether a person is likely to be prosecuted effectively in another jurisdiction: the strength of the jurisdiction's interest in prosecution; its ability and willingness to prosecute effectively; and the probable sentence or other consequences if the person is convicted. As indicated with respect to the considerations listed in paragraph 3, these factors are illustrative only, and the attorney for the government should also consider any others that appear relevant to his/her in a particular case.

   1. **The Strength of the Jurisdiction's Interest.** The attorney for the government should consider the relative Federal and state characteristics of the criminal conduct involved. Some offenses, even though in violation of Federal law, are of particularly strong interest to the authorities of the state or local jurisdiction in which they occur, either because of the nature of the

offense, the identity of the offender or victim, the fact that the investigation was conducted primarily by state or local investigators, or some other circumstance. Whatever the reason, when it appears that the Federal interest in prosecution is less substantial than the interest of state or local authorities, consideration should be given to referring the case to those authorities rather than commencing or recommending a Federal prosecution.

2. **Ability and Willingness to Prosecute Effectively.** In assessing the likelihood of effective prosecution in another jurisdiction, the attorney for the government should also consider the intent of the authorities in that jurisdiction and whether that jurisdiction has the prosecutorial and judicial resources necessary to undertake prosecution promptly and effectively. Other relevant factors might be legal or evidentiary problems that might attend prosecution in the other jurisdiction. In addition, the Federal prosecutor should be alert to any local conditions, attitudes, relationships, or other circumstances that might cast doubt on the likelihood of the state or local authorities conducting a thorough and successful prosecution.
3. **Probable Sentence Upon Conviction.** The ultimate measure of the potential for effective prosecution in another jurisdiction is the sentence, or other consequence, that is likely to be imposed if the person is convicted. In considering this factor, the attorney for the government should bear in mind not only the statutory penalties in the jurisdiction and sentencing patterns in similar cases, but also, the particular characteristics of the offense or, of the offender that might be relevant to sentencing. He/she should also be alert to the possibility that a conviction under state law may, in some cases, result in collateral consequences for the defendant, such as disbarment, that might not follow upon a conviction under Federal law.

9-27.250 Non-Criminal Alternatives to Prosecution

A. In determining whether prosecution should be declined because there exists an adequate, non-criminal alternative to prosecution, the attorney for the government should consider all relevant factors, including:

   1. The sanctions available under the alternative means of disposition;
   2. The likelihood that an effective sanction will be imposed; and
   3. The effect of non-criminal disposition on Federal law enforcement interests.

B. Comment. When a person has committed a Federal offense, it is important that the law respond promptly, fairly, and effectively. This does not mean, however, that a criminal prosecution must be initiated. In recognition of the fact that resort to the criminal process is not necessarily the only appropriate response to serious forms of antisocial activity, Congress and state legislatures have provided civil and administrative remedies for many types of conduct that may also be subject to criminal sanction. Examples of such non-criminal approaches include civil tax proceedings; civil actions under the securities, customs, antitrust, or other regulatory laws; and reference of complaints to licensing authorities or to professional organizations such as bar associations. Another potentially useful alternative to prosecution in some cases is pretrial diversion. See USAM 9-22.000.

Attorneys for the government should familiarize themselves with these alternatives and should consider pursuing them if they are available in a particular case. Although on some occasions they should be pursued in addition to the criminal law procedures, on other occasions they can be expected to provide an effective substitute for criminal prosecution. In weighing the adequacy of such an alternative in a particular case, the prosecutor should consider the nature and severity of the sanctions that could be imposed, the likelihood that an adequate sanction would in fact be imposed, and the effect of such a non-criminal disposition on Federal law enforcement interests. It should be noted that referrals for non-criminal disposition may not include the transfer of grand jury material unless an order under Rule 6(e), Federal Rules of Criminal Procedure, has been obtained. *See United States v. Sells Engineering, Inc.*, 463 U.S. 418 (1983).

9-27.260 Initiating and Declining Charges—Impermissible Considerations

A. In determining whether to commence or recommend prosecution or take other action against a person, the attorney for the government should not be influenced by:

   1. The person's race, religion, sex, national origin, or political association, activities or beliefs;
   2. The attorney's own personal feelings concerning the person, the person's associates, or the victim; or
   3. The possible affect of the decision on the attorney's own professional or personal circumstances.

B. Comment. USAM 9-27.260 sets forth various matters that plainly should not influence the determination whether to initiate or recommend prosecution or take other action. They are listed here not because it is anticipated that any attorney for the government might allow them to affect his/her judgment, but in order to make clear that Federal prosecutors will not be influenced by such improper considerations. Of course, in a case in which a particular characteristic listed in subparagraph (1) is pertinent to the offense (for example, in an immigration case the fact that the offender is not a United States national, or in a civil rights case the fact that the victim and the offender are of different races), the provision would not prohibit the prosecutor from considering it for the purpose intended by the Congress.

9-27.270 Records of Prosecutions Declined

A. Whenever the attorney for the government declines to commence or recommend Federal prosecution, he/she should ensure that his/her decision and the reasons therefore are communicated to the investigating agency involved and to any other interested agency, and are reflected in the office files.

B. Comment. USAM 9-27.270 is intended primarily to ensure an adequate record of disposition of matters that are brought to the attention of the government attorney for possible criminal prosecution, but that do not result in Federal prosecution. When prosecution is declined in serious cases on the understanding that action will be taken by other authorities, appropriate steps should be taken to ensure that the matter receives their attention and to ensure coordination or follow-up.

9-27.300 Selecting Charges—Charging Most Serious Offenses

A. Except as provided in USAM 9-27.330, (precharge plea agreements), once the decision to prosecute has been made, the attorney for the government should charge, or should recommend that the grand jury charge, the most serious offense that is consistent with the nature of the defendant's conduct, and that is likely to result in a sustainable conviction. If mandatory minimum sentences are also involved, their effect must be considered, keeping in mind the fact that a mandatory minimum is statutory and generally overrules a guideline. The "most serious" offense is generally that which yields the highest range under the sentencing guidelines.

However, a faithful and honest application of the Sentencing Guidelines is not incompatible with selecting charges or entering into plea agreements on the basis of an individualized assessment of the extent to which particular charges fit the specific circumstances of the case, are consistent with the purposes of the Federal criminal code, and maximize the impact of Federal resources on crime. Thus, for example, in determining "the most serious offense that is consistent with the nature of the defendant's conduct that is likely to result in a sustainable conviction," it is appropriate that the attorney for the government consider, inter alia, such factors as the Sentencing Guideline range yielded by the charge, whether the penalty yielded by such sentencing range (or potential mandatory minimum charge, if applicable) is proportional to the seriousness of the defendant's conduct, and whether the charge achieves such purposes of the criminal law as punishment, protection of the public, specific and general deterrence, and rehabilitation. Note that these factors may also be considered by the attorney for the government when entering into plea agreements. USAM 9-27.400.

To ensure consistency and accountability, charging and plea agreement decisions must be made at an appropriate level of responsibility and documented with an appropriate record of the factors applied.

B. Comment. Once it has been determined to initiate prosecution, either by filing a complaint or an information, or by seeking an indictment from the grand jury, the attorney for the government must determine what charges to file or recommend. When the conduct in question consists of a single criminal act, or when there is only one applicable statute, this is not a difficult task. Typically, however, a defendant will have committed more than one criminal act and his/her conduct may be prosecuted under more than one statute. Moreover, selection of charges may be complicated further by the fact that different statutes have different proof requirements and provide substantially different penalties. In such cases, considerable care is required to ensure selection of the proper charge or charges. In addition to reviewing the concerns that prompted the decision to prosecute in the first instance, particular attention should be given to the need to ensure that the prosecution will be both fair and effective.

At the outset, the attorney for the government should bear in mind that at trial he/she will have to produce admissible evidence sufficient to obtain and sustain a conviction or else the government will suffer a dismissal. For this reason, he/she should not include in an information or recommend in an indictment charges that he/she cannot reasonably expect to prove beyond a reasonable doubt by legally sufficient evidence at trial.

In connection with the evidentiary basis for the charges selected, the prosecutor should also be particularly mindful of the different requirements of proof under different statutes covering similar conduct. For example, the bribe provisions of 18 U.S.C. § 201 require proof of "corrupt intent," while the "'gratuity" provisions do not. Similarly, the "two witness" rule applies to perjury prosecutions under 18 U.S.C. § 1621 but not under 18 U.S.C. § 1623.

As stated, a Federal prosecutor should initially charge the most serious, readily provable offense or offenses consistent with the defendant's conduct. Charges should not be filed simply to exert leverage to induce a plea, nor should charges be abandoned in an effort to arrive at a bargain that fails to reflect the seriousness of the defendant's conduct.

USAM 9-27.300 expresses the principle that the defendant should be charged with the most serious offense that is encompassed by his/her conduct and that is readily provable. Ordinarily, as noted above, this will be the offense for which the most severe penalty is provided by law and the guidelines. Where two crimes have the same statutory maximum and the same guideline range, but only one contains a mandatory minimum penalty, the one with the mandatory minimum is the more serious. This principle provides the framework for ensuring equal justice in the prosecution of Federal criminal offenders. It guarantees that every defendant will start from the same position, charged with the most serious criminal act he/she commits. Of course, he/she may also be charged with other criminal acts (as provided in USAM 9-27.320), if the proof and the government's legitimate law enforcement objectives warrant additional charges.

Current drug laws provide for increased maximum, and in some cases minimum, penalties for many offenses on the basis of a defendant's prior criminal convictions. *See, e.g.*, 21 U.S.C. §§ 841 (b)(1)(A),(B), and (C), 848(a), 960 (b)(1), (2), and (3), and 962. However, a court may not impose such an increased penalty unless the United States Attorney has filed an information with the court, before trial or before entry of a plea of guilty, setting forth the previous convictions to be relied upon 21 U.S.C. § 851.

Every prosecutor should regard the filing of an information under 21 U.S.C. § 851 concerning prior convictions as equivalent to the filing of charges. Just as a prosecutor must file a readily provable charge, he or she must file an information under 21 U.S.C. § 851 regarding prior convictions that are readily provable and that are known to the prosecutor prior to the beginning of trial or entry of plea. The only exceptions to this requirement are where: (1) the failure to file or the dismissal of such pleadings would not affect the applicable guideline range from which the sentence may be imposed; or (2) in the context of a negotiated plea, the United States Attorney, the Chief Assistant United States Attorney, the senior supervisory Criminal Assistant United States Attorney or within the Department of Justice, a Section Chief or Office Director has approved the negotiated agreement. The reasons for such an agreement must be set forth in writing. Such a reason might include, for example, that the United States Attorney's office is particularly overburdened, the case would be time-consuming to try, and proceeding to trial would significantly reduce the total number of cases disposed of by the office. The permissible agreements within this context include: (1) not filing an enhancement; (2) filing an enhancement which does not allege all relevant prior convictions, thereby only partially enhancing a defendant's potential sentence; and (3) dismissing a previously filed enhancement.

A negotiated plea which uses any of the options described in this section must be made known to the sentencing court. In addition, the sentence which can be imposed through the negotiated plea must adequately reflect the seriousness of the offense.

Prosecutors are reminded that when a defendant commits an armed bank robbery or other crime of violence or drug trafficking crime, appropriate charges include 18 U.S.C. § 924 (c).

[cited in USAM 9-27.400; USAM 9-28.1200; USAM 9-100.020]

9-27.320 Additional Charges

A. Except as hereafter provided, the attorney for the government should also charge, or recommend that the grand jury charge, other offenses only when, in his/her judgement, additional charges:

   1. Are necessary to ensure that the information or indictment:

      a. Adequately reflects the nature and extent of the criminal conduct involved; and

      b. Provides the basis for an appropriate sentence under all the circumstances of the case; or

   2. Will significantly enhance the strength of the government's case against the defendant or a codefendant.

B. Comment. It is important to the fair and efficient administration of justice in the Federal system that the government bring as few charges as are necessary to ensure that justice is done. The bringing of unnecessary charges not only complicates and prolongs trials, it constitutes an excessive—and potentially unfair—exercise of power. To ensure appropriately limited exercises of the charging power, USAM 9-27.320 outlines three general situations in which additional charges may be brought: (1) when necessary adequately to reflect the nature and extent of the criminal conduct involved; (2) when necessary to provide the basis for an appropriate sentence under all the circumstances of the case; and (3) when an additional charge or charges would significantly strengthen the case against the defendant or a codefendant.

   1. **Nature and Extent of Criminal Conduct.** Apart from evidentiary considerations, the prosecutor's initial concern should be to select charges that adequately reflect the nature and extent of the criminal conduct involved. This means that the charges selected should fairly describe both the kind and scope of unlawful activity; should be legally sufficient; should provide notice to the public of the seriousness of the conduct involved; and should negate any impression that, after committing one offense, an offender can commit others with impunity.

   2. **Basis for Sentencing.** Proper charge selection also requires consideration of the end result of successful prosecution—the imposition of an appropriate sentence under all the circumstances of the case. In order to achieve

this result, it ordinarily should not be necessary to charge a person with every offense for which he/she may technically be liable (indeed, charging every such offense may in some cases be perceived as an unfair attempt to induce a guilty plea). What is important is that the person be charged in such a manner that, if he/she is convicted, the court may impose an appropriate sentence. Under the sentencing guidelines, if the offense actually charged bears a true relationship with the defendant's conduct, an appropriate guideline sentence will follow. However, the prosecutor must take care to be sure that the charges brought allow the guidelines to operate properly. For instance, charging a significant participant in a major drug conspiracy only with using a communication facility would result in a sentence which, even if it were the maximum possible under the charged offense, would be artificially low given the defendant's actual conduct.

3. **Effect on the Government's Case.** When considering whether to include a particular charge in the indictment or information, the attorney for the government should bear in mind the possible effects of inclusion or exclusion of the charge on the government's case against the defendant or a codefendant. If the evidence is available, it is proper to consider the tactical advantages of bringing certain charges. For example, in a case in which a substantive offense was committed pursuant to an unlawful agreement, inclusion of a conspiracy count is permissible and may be desirable to ensure the introduction of all relevant evidence at trial. Similarly, it might be important to include a perjury or false statement count in an indictment charging other offenses, in order to give the jury a complete picture of the defendant's criminal conduct. Failure to include appropriate charges for which the proof is sufficient may not only result in the exclusion of relevant evidence, but may impair the prosecutor's ability to prove a coherent case, and lead to jury confusion as well. In this connection, it is important to remember that, in multi-defendant cases, the presence or absence of a particular charge against one defendant may affect the strength of the case against another defendant. In short, when the evidence exists, the charges should be structured so as to permit proof of the strongest case possible without undue burden on the administration of justice.

9-27.330 Pre-Charge Plea Agreements

Before filing or recommending charges pursuant to a precharge plea agreement, the attorney for the government should consult the plea agreement provisions of USAM 9-27.430, thereof, relating to the selection of charges to which a defendant should be required to plead guilty.
[cited in USAM 9-27.300]

9-27.400 Plea Agreements Generally

A. The attorney for the government may, in an appropriate case, enter into an agreement with a defendant that, upon the defendant's plea of guilty or nolo contendere to a charged offense or to a lesser or related offense, he/she will move for dismissal of other charges, take a certain position with respect to the sentence to be imposed, or take other action. Plea agreements, and the role of the courts in such agreements, are addressed in Chapter Six of the Sentencing Guidelines. See also USAM 9-27.300 which discusses the individualized assessment by prosecutors of the extent to which particular charges fit the specific circumstances of the case, are consistent with the purposes of the Federal criminal code, and maximize the impact of Federal resources on crime.

B. Comment. USAM 9-27.400 permits, in appropriate cases, the disposition of Federal criminal charges pursuant to plea agreements between defendants and government attorneys. Such negotiated dispositions should be distinguished from situations in which a defendant pleads guilty or nolo contendere to fewer than all counts of an information or indictment in the absence of any agreement with the government. Only the former type of disposition is covered by the provisions of USAM 9-27.400 et seq.

   Negotiated plea dispositions are explicitly sanctioned by Rule 11(e)(1), Fed. R. Crim. P., which provides that:

   The attorney for the government and the attorney for the defendant or the defendant when acting pro se may engage in discussions with a view toward reaching an agreement that upon the entering of a plea of guilty or nolo contendere to a charged offense or to a lesser or related offense, the attorney for the government will do any of the following:

A. Move for dismissal of other charges; or

B. Make a recommendation, or agree not to oppose, the defendant's request for a particular sentence, with the understanding that such recommendation or request shall not be binding upon the court; or

C. Agree that a specific sentence is the appropriate disposition of the case.

   Three types of plea agreements are encompassed by the language of USAM 9-27.400, agreements whereby in return for the defendant's plea to a charged offense or to a lesser or related offense, other charges are dismissed ("charge agreements"); agreements pursuant to which the government takes a certain position regarding the sentence to be imposed ("sentence agreements"); and agreements that combine a plea with a dismissal of charges and an undertaking by the prosecutor concerning the government's position at sentencing ("mixed agreements").

Once prosecutors have indicted, they should not find themselves bargaining about charges which they have determined are readily provable and reflect the seriousness of the defendant's conduct. Charge agreements envision dismissal of counts in exchange for a plea. As with the indictment decision, the prosecutor should seek a plea to the most serious readily provable offense charged. Should a prosecutor determine in good faith after indictment that, as a result of a change in the evidence or for another reason (e.g., a need has arisen to protect the identity of a particular witness until he or she testifies against a more significant defendant), a charge is not readily provable or that an indictment exaggerates the seriousness of an offense or offenses, a plea bargain may reflect the prosecutor's reassessment. There should be documentation, however, in a case in which charges originally brought are dropped.

The language of USAM 9-27.400 with respect to sentence agreements is intended to cover the entire range of positions that the government might wish to take at the time of sentencing. Among the options are: taking no position regarding the sentence; not opposing the defendant's request; requesting a specific type of sentence (e.g., a fine or probation), a specific fine or term of imprisonment, or not more than a specific fine or term of imprisonment; and requesting concurrent rather than consecutive sentences. Agreement to any such option must be consistent with the guidelines.

There are only two types of sentence bargains. Both are permissible, but one is more complicated than the other. First, prosecutors may bargain for a sentence that is within the specified United States Sentencing Commission's guideline range. This means that when a guideline range is 18 to 24 months, the prosecutor has discretion to agree to recommend a sentence of 18 to 20 months rather than to argue for a sentence at the top of the range. Such a plea does not require that the actual sentence range be determined in advance. The plea agreement may have wording to the effect that once the range is determined by the court, the United States will recommend a low point in that range. Similarly, the prosecutor may agree to recommend a downward adjustment for acceptance of responsibility if he or she concludes in good faith that the defendant is entitled to the adjustment. Second, the prosecutor may seek to depart from the guidelines. This is more complicated than a bargain involving a sentence within a guideline range. Departures are discussed more generally below.

Department policy requires honesty in sentencing; Federal prosecutors are expected to identify for the court departures when they agree to support them. For example, it would be improper for a prosecutor to agree that a departure is in order, but to conceal the agreement in a charge bargain that is presented to a court as a fait accompli so that there is neither a record of nor judicial review of the departure.

Plea bargaining, both charge bargaining and sentence bargaining, must honestly reflect the totality and seriousness of the defendant's conduct and any departure to which the prosecutor is agreeing, and must be accomplished through appropriate guideline provisions.

The basic policy is that charges are not to be bargained away or dropped, unless the prosecutor has a good faith doubt as to the government's ability readily to prove a charge for legal or evidentiary reasons. There are, however, two exceptions.

First, if the applicable guideline range from which a sentence may be imposed would be unaffected, readily provable charges may be dismissed or dropped as part of a plea bargain. It is important to know whether dropping a charge may affect a sentence. For example, the multiple offense rules in Part D of Chapter 3 of the guidelines and the relevant conduct standard set forth in Sentencing Guideline 1B1.3(a)(2) will mean that certain dropped charges will be counted for purposes of determining the sentence, subject to the statutory maximum for the offense or offenses of conviction. It is vital that Federal prosecutors understand when conduct that is not charged in an indictment or conduct that is alleged in counts that are to be dismissed pursuant to a bargain may be counted for sentencing purposes and when it may not be. For example, in the case of a defendant who could be charged with five bank robberies, a decision to charge only one or to dismiss four counts pursuant to a bar gain precludes any consideration of the four uncharged or dismissed robberies in determining a guideline range, unless the plea agreement included a stipulation as to the other robberies. In contrast, in the case of a defendant who could be charged with five counts of fraud, the total amount of money involved in a fraudulent scheme will be considered in determining a guideline range even if the defendant pleads guilty to a single count and there is no stipulation as to the other counts.

Second, Federal prosecutors may drop readily provable charges with the specific approval of the United States Attorney or designated supervisory level official for reasons set forth in the file of the case. This exception recognizes that the aims of the Sentencing Reform Act must be sought without ignoring other, critical aspects of the Federal criminal justice system. For example, approvals to drop charges in a particular case might be given because the United States Attorney's office is particularly over-burdened, the case would be time-consuming to try, and proceeding to trial would significantly reduce the total number of cases disposed of by the office.

In Chapter 5, Part K of the Sentencing Guidelines, the Commission has listed departures that may be considered by a court in imposing a sentence. Moreover, Guideline 5K2.0 recognizes that a sentencing court may consider a ground for departure that has not been adequately considered by the Commission. A departure requires approval by the court. It violates the spirit of the guidelines and Department policy for the prosecutor to enter into a plea bargain which is based upon the prosecutor's and the defendant's agreement that a departure is warranted, but that does not reveal to the court the existence of the departure and thereby afford the court an opportunity to reject it.

The Commission has recognized those bases for departure that are commonly justified. Accordingly, before the government may seek a departure based on a factor other than one set forth in Chapter 5, Part X, approval of the United States Attorney or designated supervisory officials is required. This approval is required whether or not a case is resolved through a negotiated plea.

Section 5K1.1 of the Sentencing Guidelines allows the United States to file a pleading with the sentencing court which permits the court to depart below the indicated guideline, on the basis that the defendant provided substantial assistance in the investigation or prosecution of another. Authority to approve such pleadings is limited to the United States Attorney, the Chief Assistant United States Attorney, and supervisory criminal Assistant United States Attorneys, or a committee including at least one of these individuals. Similarly, for Department of Justice attorneys, approval authority should be vested in a Section Chief or Office Director, or such official's deputy, or in a committee which includes at least one of these individuals.

Every United States Attorney or Department of Justice Section Chief or Office Director shall maintain documentation of the facts behind and justification for each substantial assistance pleading. The repository or repositories of this documentation need not be the case file itself. Freedom of Information Act considerations may suggest that a separate form showing the final decision be maintained.

The procedures described above shall also apply to Motions filed pursuant to Rule 35(b), Federal Rules of Criminal Procedure, where the sentence of a cooperating defendant is reduced after sentencing on motion of the United States. Such a filing is deemed for sentencing purposes to be the equivalent of a substantial assistance pleading.

The concession required by the government as part of a plea agreement, whether it be a "charge agreement," a "sentence agreement," or a "mixed agreement," should be weighed by the responsible government attorney in the light of the probable advantages and disadvantages of the plea disposition proposed in the particular case. Particular care should be exercised in considering whether to enter into a plea agreement pursuant to which the defendant will enter a nolo contendere plea. As discussed in USAM 9-27.500 and USAM 9-16.000, there are serious objections to such pleas and they should be opposed unless the responsible Assistant Attorney General concluded that the circumstances are so unusual that acceptance of such a plea would be in the public interest.

[updated September 2000] [cited in USAM 9-16.300; USAM 9-16.320; USAM 9-27.300; USAM 9-28.1300]

9-27.420 Plea Agreements—Considerations to be Weighed

A. In determining whether it would be appropriate to enter into a plea agreement, the attorney for the government should weigh all relevant considerations, including:

1. The defendant's willingness to cooperate in the investigation or prosecution of others;
2. The defendant's history with respect to criminal activity;
3. The nature and seriousness of the offense or offenses charged;
4. The defendant's remorse or contrition and his/her willingness to assume responsibility for his/her conduct;
5. The desirability of prompt and certain disposition of the case;
6. The likelihood of obtaining a conviction at trial;
7. The probable effect on witnesses;
8. The probable sentence or other consequences if the defendant is convicted;
9. The public interest in having the case tried rather than disposed of by a guilty plea;
10. The expense of trial and appeal;
11. The need to avoid delay in the disposition of other pending cases; and
12. The effect upon the victim's right to restitution.

B. Comment. USAM 9-27.420 sets forth some of the appropriate considerations to be weighed by the attorney for the government in deciding whether to enter into a plea agreement with a defendant pursuant to the provisions of Rule 11(e), Fed. R. Crim. P. The provision is not intended to suggest the desirability or lack of desirability of a plea agreement in any particular case or to be construed as a reflection on the merits of any plea agreement that actually may be reached; its purpose is solely to assist attorneys for the government in exercising their judgement as to whether some sort of plea agreement would be appropriate in a particular case. Government attorneys should consult the investigating agency involved and the victim, if appropriate or required by law, in any case in which it would be helpful to have their views concerning the relevance of particular factors or the weight they deserve.

1. **Defendant's Cooperation.** The defendant's willingness to provide timely and useful cooperation as part of his/her plea agreement should be given serious consideration. The weight it deserves will vary, of course, depending on the nature and value of the cooperation offered and whether the same benefit can be obtained without having to make the charge or sentence concession that would be involved in a plea agreement. In many situations, for example, all necessary cooperation in the form of testimony can be obtained through a compulsion order under 18 U.S.C.§§ 6001-6003. In such cases, that approach should be attempted unless, under the circumstances, it would seriously interfere with securing the person's conviction. If the defendant's cooperation is sufficiently substantial to justify the filing of a 5K1.1 Motion for a downward departure, the procedures set out in USAM 9-27.400(B) shall be followed.

2. **Defendant's Criminal History.** One of the principal arguments against the practice of plea bargaining is that it results in leniency that reduces the deterrent impact of the law and leads to recidivism on the part of some offenders. Although this concern is probably most relevant in non-federal jurisdictions that must dispose of large volumes of routine cases with inadequate resources, nevertheless it should be kept in mind by Federal prosecutors, especially when dealing with repeat offenders or "career criminals." Particular care should be taken in the case of a defendant with a prior criminal record to ensure that society's need for protection is not sacrificed in the process of arriving at a plea disposition. In this connection, it is proper for the government attorney to consider not only the defendant's past, but also facts of other criminal involvement not resulting in conviction. By the same token, of course, it is also proper to consider a defendant's absence of past criminal involvement and his/her past cooperation with law enforcement officials. Note that 18 U.S.C. § 924(e), as well as Sentencing Guidelines 4B1.1 and 4B1.4, address "career criminals" and "armed career criminals." 18 U.S.C. § 3559(c)—the so-called "three strikes" statute—addresses serious violent recidivist offenders. The application of these provisions to a particular case may affect the plea negotiation posture of the parties.

3. **Nature and Seriousness of Offense Charged.** Important considerations in determining whether to enter into a plea agreement may be the nature and seriousness of the offense or offenses charged. In weighing those factors, the attorney for the government should bear in mind the interests sought to be protected by the statute defining the offense (e.g., the national defense, constitutional rights, the governmental process, personal safety, public welfare, or property), as well as nature and degree of harm caused

or threatened to those interests and any attendant circumstances that aggravate or mitigate the seriousness of the offense in the particular case.

4. **Defendant's Attitude.** A defendant may demonstrate apparently genuine remorse or contrition, and a willingness to take responsibility for his/her criminal conduct by, for example, efforts to compensate the victim for injury or loss, or otherwise to ameliorate the consequences of his/her acts. These are factors that bear upon the likelihood of his/her repetition of the conduct involved and that may properly be considered in deciding whether a plea agreement would be appropriate. Sentencing Guideline 3E1.1 allows for a downward adjustment upon acceptance of responsibility by the defendant. It is permissible for a prosecutor to enter a plea agreement which approves such an adjustment if the defendant otherwise meets the requirements of the section.

It is particularly important that the defendant not be permitted to enter a guilty plea under circumstances that will allow him/her later to proclaim lack of culpability or even complete innocence. Such consequences can be avoided only if the court and the public are adequately informed of the nature and scope of the illegal activity and of the defendant's complicity and culpability. To this end, the attorney for the government is strongly encouraged to enter into a plea agreement only with the defendant's assurance that he/she will admit the facts of the offense and of his/her culpable participation therein. A plea agreement may be entered into in the absence of such an assurance, but only if the defendant is willing to accept without contest a statement by the government in open court of the facts it could prove to demonstrate his/her guilt beyond a reasonable doubt. Except as provided in USAM 9-27.440, the attorney for the government should not enter into a plea agreement with a defendant who admits his/her guilt but disputes an essential element of the government's case.

5. **Prompt Disposition.** In assessing the value of prompt disposition of a criminal case, the attorney for the government should consider the timing of a proffered plea. A plea offer by a defendant on the eve of trial after the case has been fully prepared is hardly as advantageous from the standpoint of reducing public expense as one offered months or weeks earlier. In addition, a last minute plea adds to the difficulty of scheduling cases efficiently and may even result in wasting the prosecutorial and Judicial time reserved for the aborted trial. For these reasons, governmental attorneys should make clear to defense counsel at an early stage in the proceedings that, if there are to be any plea discussions, they must be concluded prior to a certain date well in advance of the trial date. *See* USSG § 3E1.1(b)(1). However, avoidance of unnecessary trial preparation and scheduling disruptions are not the only benefits to be gained from prompt disposition of a case by means of a guilty plea. Such a disposition also saves the government

and the court the time and expense of trial and appeal. In addition, a plea agreement facilitates prompt imposition of sentence, thereby promoting the overall goals of the criminal justice system. Thus, occasionally it may be appropriate to enter into a plea agreement even after the usual time for making such agreements has passed.

6. **Likelihood of Conviction.** The trial of a criminal case inevitably involves risks and uncertainties, both for the prosecution and for the defense. Many factors, not all of which can be anticipated, can affect the outcome. To the extent that these factors can be identified, they should be considered in deciding whether to accept a plea or go to trial. In this connection, the prosecutor should weigh the strength of the government's case relative to the anticipated defense case, bearing in mind legal and evidentiary problems that might be expected, as well as the importance of the credibility of witnesses. However, although it is proper to consider factors bearing upon the likelihood of conviction in deciding whether to enter into a plea agreement, it obviously is improper for the prosecutor to attempt to dispose of a case by means of a plea agreement if he/she is not satisfied that the legal standards for guilt are met.
7. **Effect on Witnesses.** Attorneys for the government should bear in mind that it is often burdensome for witnesses to appear at trial and that sometimes to do so may cause them serious embarrassment or even place them in jeopardy of physical or economic retaliation. The possibility of such adverse consequences to witnesses should not be overlooked in determining whether to go to trial or attempt to reach a plea agreement. Another possibility that may have to be considered is revealing the identity of informants. When an informant testifies at trial, his/her identity and relationship to the government become matters of public record. As a result, in addition to possible adverse consequences to the informant, there is a strong likelihood that the informant's usefulness in other investigations will be seriously diminished or destroyed. These are considerations that should be discussed with the investigating agency involved, as well as with any other agencies known to have an interest in using the informant in their investigations.
8. **Probable Sentence.** In determining whether to enter into a plea agreement, the attorney for the government may properly consider the probable outcome of the prosecution in terms of the sentence or other consequences for the defendant in the event that a plea agreement is reached. If the proposed agreement is a "sentence agreement" or a "mixed agreement," the prosecutor should realize that the position he/she agrees to take with respect to sentencing may have a significant effect on the sentence that is actually imposed. If the proposed agreement is a "charge agreement,"

the prosecutor should bear in mind the extent to which a plea to fewer or lesser offenses may reduce the sentence that otherwise could be imposed. In either event, it is important that the attorney for the government be aware of the need to preserve the basis for an appropriate sentence under all the circumstances of the case. Thorough knowledge of the Sentencing Guidelines, any applicable statutory minimum sentences, and any applicable sentence enhancements is clearly necessary to allow the prosecutor to accurately and adequately evaluate the effect of any plea agreement.

9. **Trial Rather Than Plea.** There may be situations in which the public interest might better be served by having a case tried rather than by having it disposed of by means of a guilty plea. These include situations in which it is particularly important to permit a clear public understanding that "justice is done" through exposing the exact nature of the defendant's wrongdoing at trial, or in which a plea agreement might be misconstrued to the detriment of public confidence in the criminal justice system. For this reason, the prosecutor should be careful not to place undue emphasis on factors which favor disposition of a case pursuant to a plea agreement.
10. **Expense of Trial and Appeal.** In assessing the expense of trial and appeal that would be saved by a plea disposition, the attorney for the government should consider not only such monetary costs as juror and witness fees, but also the time spent by judges, prosecutors, and law enforcement personnel who may be needed to testify or provide other assistance at trial. In this connection, the prosecutor should bear in mind the complexity of the case, the number of trial days and witnesses required, and any extraordinary expenses that might be incurred such as the cost of sequestering the jury.
11. **Prompt Disposition of Other Cases.** A plea disposition in one case may facilitate the prompt disposition of other cases, including cases in which prosecution might otherwise be declined. This may occur simply because prosecutorial, judicial, or defense resources will become available for use in other cases, or because a plea by one of several defendants may have a "domino effect," leading to pleas by other defendants. In weighing the importance of these possible consequences, the attorney for the government should consider the state of the criminal docket and the speedy trial requirements in the district, the desirability of handling a larger volume of criminal cases, and the work loads of prosecutors, judges, and defense attorneys in the district.

9-27.430 Selecting Plea Agreement Charges

A. If a prosecution is to be concluded pursuant to a plea agreement, the defendant should be required to plead to a charge or charges:

1. That is the most serious readily provable charge consistent with the nature and extent of his/her criminal conduct;
2. That has an adequate factual basis;
3. That makes likely the imposition of an appropriate sentence and order of restitution, if appropriate, under all the circumstances of the case; and
4. That does not adversely affect the investigation or prosecution of others.

B. Comment. USAM 9-27.430 sets forth the considerations that should be taken into account in selecting the charge or charges to which a defendant should be required to plead guilty once it has been decided to dispose of the case pursuant to a plea agreement. The considerations are essentially the same as those governing the selection of charges to be included in the original indictment or information. See USAM 9-27.300.

1. **Relationship to Criminal Conduct.** The charge or charges to which a defendant pleads guilty should be consistent with the defendant's criminal conduct, both in nature and in scope. Except in unusual circumstances, this charge will be the most serious one, as defined in USAM 9-27.300. This principle governs the number of counts to which a plea should be required in cases involving different offenses, or in cases involving a series of familiar offenses. Therefore the prosecutor must be familiar with the Sentencing Guideline rules applicable to grouping offenses (Guideline 3D) and to relevant conduct (USSG § 1B1.3) among others. In regard to the seriousness of the offense, the guilty plea should assure that the public record of conviction provides an adequate indication of the defendant's conduct. With respect to the number of counts, the prosecutor should take care to assure that no impression is given that multiple offenses are likely to result in no greater a potential penalty than is a single offense. The requirement that a defendant plead to a charge that is consistent with the nature and extent of his/her criminal conduct is not inflexible. Although cooperation is usually acknowledged through a Sentencing Guideline 5K1.1 filing, there may be situations involving cooperating defendants in which considerations such as those discussed in USAM 9-27.600 take precedence. Such situations should be approached cautiously, however. Unless the government has strong corroboration for the cooperating defendant's testimony, his/her credibility may be subject to successful impeachment if he/she is permitted to plead to an offense that appears unrelated in seriousness or scope to the charges against the defendants on trial. It is also doubly important in such situations for the prosecutor to ensure that the public record of the plea demonstrates the full extent of the defendant's involvement in the criminal activity, giving rise to the prosecution.

2. **Factual Basis.** The attorney for the government should also bear in mind the legal requirement that there be a factual basis for the charge or charges to which a guilty plea is entered. This requirement is intended to assure against conviction after a guilty plea of a person who is not in fact guilty. Moreover, under Rule 11(f) of the Fed. R. Crim. P., a court may not enter a judgment upon a guilty plea "without making such inquiry as shall satisfy it that there is a factual basis for the plea." For this reason, it is essential that the charge or charges selected as the subject of a plea agreement be such as could be prosecuted independently of the plea under these principles. However, as noted, in cases in which Alford or nolo contendere pleas are tendered, the attorney for the government may wish to make a stronger factual showing. In such cases there may remain some doubt as to the defendant's guilt even after the entry of his/her plea. Consequently, in order to avoid such a misleading impression, the government should ask leave of the court to make a proffer of the facts available to it that show the defendant's guilt beyond a reasonable doubt.

   In addition, the Department's policy is only to stipulate to facts that accurately represent the defendant's conduct. If a prosecutor wishes to support a departure from the guidelines, he or she should candidly do so and not stipulate to facts that are untrue. Stipulations to untrue facts are unethical. If a prosecutor has insufficient facts to contest a defendant's effort to seek a downward departure or to claim an adjustment, the prosecutor can say so. If the presentence report states facts that are inconsistent with a stipulation in which a prosecutor has joined, the prosecutor should object to the report or add a statement explaining the prosecutor's understanding of the facts or the reason for the stipulation.

   Recounting the true nature of the defendant's involvement in a case will not always lead to a higher sentence. Where a defendant agrees to cooperate with the government by providing information concerning unlawful activities of others and the government agrees that self-incriminating information so provided will not be used against the defendant, Sentencing Guideline 1B1.8 provides that the information shall not be used in determining the applicable guideline range, except to the extent provided in the agreement. The existence of an agreement not to use information should be clearly reflected in the case file, the applicability of Guideline 1B1.8 should be documented, and the incriminating information must be disclosed to the court or the probation officer, even though it may not be used in determining a guideline sentence. Note that such information may still be used by the court in determining whether to depart from the guidelines and the extent of the departure. *See* US SG § 1B1.8.

3. **Basis for Sentencing.** In order to guard against inappropriate restriction of the court's sentencing options, the plea agreement should provide adequate scope for sentencing under all the circumstances of the case. To the extent that the plea agreement requires the government to take a position with respect to the sentence to be imposed, there should be little danger since the court will not be bound by the government's position. When a "charge agreement" is involved, however, the court will be limited to imposing the maxim term authorized by statue as well as the Sentencing Guideline range for the offense, to which the guilty plea is entered. Thus, as noted in USAM 9-27.320 above the prosecutor should take care to avoid a "charge agreement" that would unduly restrict the court's sentencing authority. In this connection, as in the initial selection of charges, the prosecutor should take into account the purposes of sentencing, the penalties provided in the applicable statutes (including mandatory minimum penalties), the gravity of the offense, any aggravating or mitigating factors, and any post conviction consequences to which the defendant may be subject. In addition, if restitution is appropriate under the circumstances of the case, the plea agreement should specify the amount of restitution. *See* 18 U.S.C. § 3663 *et seq.;* 18 U.S.C. §§ 2248, 2259, 2264 and 2327; *United States v. Arnold,* 947 F.2d 1236, 1237-38 (5th Cir. 1991); *and* USAM 9-16.320.
4. **Effect on Other Cases.** In a multiple-defendant case, care must be taken to ensure that the disposition of the charges against one defendant does not adversely affect the investigation or prosecution of co-defendants. Among the possible adverse consequences to be avoided are the negative jury appeal that may result when relatively less culpable defendants are tried in the absence of a more culpable defendant or when a principal prosecution witness appears to be equally culpable as the defendants but has been permitted to plead to a significantly less serious offense; the possibility that one defendant's absence from the case will render useful evidence inadmissible at the trial of co-defendants; and the giving of questionable exculpatory testimony on behalf of the other defendants by the defendant who has pled guilty.

9-27.450 Records of Plea Agreements

A. All negotiated plea agreements to felonies or to misdemeanors negotiated from felonies shall be in writing and filed with the court.

B. Comment. USAM 9-27.450 is intended to facilitate compliance with Rule 11 of the Federal Rules of Criminal Procedure and to provide a safeguard against misunderstandings that might arise concerning the terms of a plea agreement. Rule 11(e)(2), Fed. R. Crim. P., requires that a plea agreement be disclosed in open court (except upon a showing of good cause in which case disclosure may be made in camera), while Rule 11(e)(3) Fed. R. Crim. P. requires that the disposition provided for in the agreement be embodied in the judgment and sentence. Compliance with these requirements will be facilitated if the agreement has been reduced to writing in advance, and the defendant will be precluded from successfully contesting the terms of the agreement at the time he/she pleads guilty, or at the time of sentencing, or at a later date. Any time a defendant enters into a negotiated plea, that fact and the conditions of the agreement should also be maintained in the office case file. Written agreements will facilitate efforts by the Department or the Sentencing Commission to monitor compliance by prosecutors with Department policies and the guidelines. Documentation may include a copy of the court transcript at the time the plea is taken in open court.

There shall be within each office a formal system for approval of negotiated pleas. The approval authority shall be vested in at least a supervisory criminal Assistant United States Attorney, or a supervisory attorney of a litigating division in the Department of Justice, who will have the responsibility of assessing the appropriateness of the plea agreement under the policies of the Department of Justice pertaining to pleas. Where certain predictable fact situations arise with great frequency and are given identical treatment, the approval requirement may be met by a written instruction from the appropriate supervisor which describes with particularity the standard plea procedure to be followed, so long as that procedure is otherwise within Departmental guidelines. An example would be a border district which routinely deals with a high volume of illegal alien cases daily.

The plea approval process will be part of the office evaluation procedure.

The United States Attorney in each district, or a supervisory representative, should, if feasible, meet regularly with a representative of the district's Probation Office for the purpose of discussing guideline cases.

9-27.600 Entering into Non-prosecution Agreements in Return for Cooperation—Generally

A. Except as hereafter provided, the attorney for the government may, with supervisory approval, enter into a non-prosecution agreement in exchange for a person's cooperation when, in his/her judgment, the person's timely cooperation appears to be necessary to the public interest and other means of obtaining the desired cooperation are unavailable or would not be effective.

B. Comment.

1. In many cases, it may be important to the success of an investigation or prosecution to obtain the testimonial or other cooperation of a person who is himself/herself implicated in the criminal conduct being investigated or prosecuted. However, because of his/her involvement, the person may refuse to cooperate on the basis of his/her Fifth Amendment privilege against compulsory self-incrimination. In this situation, there are several possible approaches the prosecutor can take to render the privilege inapplicable or to induce its waiver.
   a. First, if time permits, the person may be charged, tried, and convicted before his/her cooperation is sought in the investigation or prosecution of others. Having already been convicted himself/herself, the person ordinarily will no longer have a valid privilege to refuse to testify and will have a strong incentive to reveal the truth in order to induce the sentencing judge to impose a lesser sentence than that which otherwise might be found appropriate.
   b. Second, the person may be willing to cooperate if the charges or potential charge against him/her are reduced in number or degree in return for his/her cooperation and his/her entry of a guilty plea to the remaining charges. An agreement to file a motion pursuant to Sentencing Guideline 5K1.1 or Rule 35 of the Federal Rules of Criminal Procedure after the defendant gives full and complete cooperation is the preferred method for securing such cooperation. Usually such a concession by the government will be all that is necessary, or warranted, to secure the cooperation sought. Since it is certainly desirable as a matter of policy that an offender be required to incur at least some liability for his/her criminal conduct, government attorneys should attempt to secure this result in all appropriate cases, following the principles set forth in USAM 9-27.430 to the extent practicable.
   c. The third method for securing the cooperation of a potential defendant is by means of a court order under 18 U.S.C. §§ 6001-6003. Those statutory provisions govern the conditions under which uncooperative witnesses may be compelled to testify or provide information notwithstanding their invocation of the privilege against compulsory self incrimination. In brief, under the so-called "use immunity" provisions of those statutes, the court may order the person to testify or provide other information, but neither his/her testimony nor the information he/she provides may be used against him/her, directly or indirectly, in any criminal case except a prosecution for perjury or other failure to comply with the order. Ordinarily, these "use immunity" provisions should be relied on in cases in which attorneys for the government

need to obtain sworn testimony or the production of information before a grand jury or at trial, and in which there is reason to believe that the person will refuse to testify or provide the information on the basis of his/her privilege against compulsory self-incrimination. See USAM 9-23.000. Offers of immunity and immunity agreements should be in writing. Consideration should be given to documenting the evidence available prior to the immunity offer.

d. Finally, there may be cases in which it is impossible or impractical to employ the methods described above to secure the necessary information or other assistance, and in which the person is willing to cooperate only in return for an agreement that he/she will not be prosecuted at all for what he/she has done. The provisions set forth hereafter describe the conditions that should be met before such an agreement is made, as well as the procedures recommended for such cases.

It is important to note that these provisions apply only if the case involves an agreement with a person who might otherwise be prosecuted. If the person reasonably is viewed only as a potential witness rather than a potential defendant, and the person is willing to cooperate, there is no need to consult these provisions.

USAM 9-27.600 describes three circumstances that should exist before government attorneys enter into non-prosecution agreements in return for cooperation: the unavailability or ineffectiveness of other means of obtaining the desired cooperation; the apparent necessity of the cooperation to the public interest; and the approval of such a course of action by an appropriate supervisory official.

2. **Unavailability or Ineffectiveness of Other Means.** As indicated above, non-prosecution agreements are only one of several methods by which the prosecutor can obtain the cooperation of a person whose criminal involvement makes him/her a potential subject of prosecution. Each of the other methods—seeking cooperation after trial and conviction, bargaining for cooperation as part of a plea agreement, and compelling cooperation under a "use immunity" order—involves prosecuting the person or at least leaving open the possibility of prosecuting him/her on the basis of independently obtained evidence. Since these outcomes are clearly preferable to permitting an offender to avoid any liability for his/her conduct, the possible use of an alternative to a non-prosecution agreement should be given serious consideration in the first instance.

   Another reason for using an alternative to a non-prosecution agreement to obtain cooperation concerns the practical advantage in terms of the person's credibility if he/she testifies at trial. If the person already has been convicted, either after trial or upon a guilty plea, for participating in the events about which he/she testifies, his/her testimony is apt to be far more credible than if it appears to the trier of fact that he/she is getting off "scot free." Similarly, if his/her testimony is compelled by a court order, he/she cannot properly be portrayed by the defense as a person who has made a "deal" with the government and whose testimony is, therefore, suspect; his/her testimony will have been forced from him/her, not bargained for.

In some cases, however, there may be no effective means of obtaining the person's timely cooperation short of entering into a non-prosecution agreement. The person may be unwilling to cooperate fully in return for a reduction of charges, the delay involved in bringing him/her to trial might prejudice the investigation or prosecution in connection with which his/her cooperation is sought and it may be impossible or impractical to rely on the statutory provisions for compulsion of testimony or production of evidence. One example of the latter situation is a case in which the cooperation needed does not consist of testimony under oath or the production of information before a grand jury or at trial. Other examples are cases in which time is critical, or where use of the procedures of 18 U.S.C. §[illegible]-6003 would unreasonably disrupt the presentation of evidence to the grand jury or the expeditious development of an investigation, or where compliance with the statute of limitations or the Speedy Trial Act precludes timely application for a court order.

Only when it appears that the person's timely cooperation cannot be obtained by other means, or cannot be obtained effectively, should the attorney for the government consider entering into a non-prosecution agreement.

3. **Public Interest.** If he/she concludes that a non-prosecution agreement would be the only effective method for obtaining cooperation, the attorney for the government should consider whether, balancing the cost of foregoing prosecution against the potential benefit of the person's cooperation, the cooperation sought appears necessary to the public interest. This "public interest" determination is one of the conditions precedent to an application under 18 U.S.C. § 6003 for a court order compelling testimony. Like a compulsion order, a non-prosecution agreement limits the government's ability to undertake a subsequent prosecution of the witness. Accordingly, the same "public interest" test should be applied in this situation as well. Some of the considerations that may be relevant to the application of this test are set forth in USAM 9-27.620.

4. **Supervisory Approval.** Finally, the prosecutor should secure supervisory approval before entering into a non-prosecution agreement. Prosecutors working under the direction of a United States Attorney must seek the approval of the United States Attorney or a supervisory Assistant United States Attorney. Departmental attorneys not supervised by a United States Attorney should obtain the approval of the appropriate Assistant Attorney General or his/her designee, and should notify the United States Attorney or Attorneys concerned. The requirement of approval by a superior is designed to provide review by an attorney experienced in such matters, and to ensure uniformity of policy and practice with respect to such agreements. This section should be read in conjunction with USAM 9-27.640, concerning particular types of cases in which an Assistant Attorney General or his/her designee must concur in or approve an agreement not to prosecute in return for cooperation.

9-27.620 Entering into Non-prosecution Agreements in Return for Cooperation—Considerations to be Weighed

A. In determining whether, a person's cooperation may be necessary to the public interest, the attorney for the government, and those whose approval is necessary, should weigh all relevant considerations, including:

   1. The importance of the investigation or prosecution to an effective program of law enforcement;
   2. The value of the person's cooperation to the investigation or prosecution; and
   3. The person's relative culpability in connection with the offense or offenses being investigated or prosecuted and his/her history with respect to criminal activity.

B. Comment. This paragraph is intended to assist Federal prosecutors, and those whose approval they must secure, in deciding whether a person's cooperation appears to be necessary to the public interest. The considerations listed here are not intended to be all-inclusive or to require a particular decision in a particular case. Rather they are meant to focus the decision-maker's attention on factors that probably will be controlling in the majority of cases.

   1. **Importance of Case.** Since the primary function of a Federal prosecutor is to enforce the criminal law, he/she should not routinely or indiscriminately enter into non-prosecution agreements, which are, in essence, agreements not to enforce the law under particular conditions. Rather, he/she should

reserve the use of such agreements for cases in which the cooperation sought concerns the commission of a serious offense or in which successful prosecution is otherwise important in achieving effective enforcement of the criminal laws. The relative importance or unimportance of the contemplated case is therefore a significant threshold consideration.

2. **Value of Cooperation.** An agreement not to prosecute in return for a person's cooperation binds the government to the extent that the person carries out his/her part of the bargain. *See Santobello v. New York*, 404 U.S. 257 (1971); *Wade v. United States,* 112 S. Ct. 1840 (1992). Since such an agreement forecloses enforcement of the criminal law against a person who otherwise may be liable to prosecution, it should not be entered into without a clear understanding of the nature of the quid pro quo and a careful assessment of its probable value to the government. In order to be in a position adequately to assess the potential value of a person's cooperation, the prosecutor should insist on an "offer of proof" or its equivalent from the person or his/her attorney. The prosecutor can then weigh the offer in terms of the investigation or prosecution in connection with which cooperation is sought. In doing so, he/she should consider such questions as whether the cooperation will in fact be forthcoming, whether the testimony or other information provided will be credible, whether it can be corroborated by other evidence, whether it will materially assist the investigation or prosecution, and whether substantially the same benefit can be obtained from someone else without an agreement not to prosecute. After assessing all of these factors, together with any others that may be relevant, the prosecutor can judge the strength of his/her case with and without the person's cooperation, and determine whether it may be in the public interest to agree to forego prosecution under the circumstances.

3. **Relative Culpability and Criminal History.** In determining whether it may be necessary to the public interest to agree to forego prosecution of a person who may have violated the law in return for that person's cooperation, it is also important to consider the degree of his/her apparent culpability relative to others who are subjects of the investigation or prosecution as well as his/her history of criminal involvement. Of course, ordinarily it would not be in the public interest to forego prosecution of a high-ranking member of a criminal enterprise in exchange for his/her cooperation against one of his/her subordinates, nor would the public interest be served by bargaining away the opportunity to prosecute a person with a long history of serious criminal involvement in order to obtain the conviction of someone else on less serious charges. These are matters with regard to which the attorney for the government may find it helpful to consult

with the investigating agency or with other prosecuting authorities who may have an interest in the person or his/her associates.

It is also important to consider whether the person has a background of cooperation with law enforcement officials, either as a witness or an informant, and whether he/she has previously been the subject of a compulsion order under 18 U.S.C. §§ 6001-6003 or has escaped prosecution by virtue of an agreement not to prosecute. The information regarding compulsion orders may be available by telephone from the Policy and Statutory Enforcement Unit in the Office of Enforcement Operations of the Criminal Division.

[updated October 2010]

9-27.630 Entering into Non-prosecution Agreements in Return for Cooperation—Limiting the Scope of Commitment

A. In entering into a non-prosecution agreement, the attorney for the government should, if practicable, explicitly limit the scope of the government's commitment to:

1. Non-prosecution based directly or indirectly on the testimony or other information provided; or
2. Non-prosecution within his/her district with respect to a pending charge, or to a specific offense then known to have been committed by the person.

B. Comment. The attorney for the government should exercise extreme caution to ensure that his/her non-prosecution agreement does not confer "blanket" immunity on the witness. To this end, he/she should, in the first instance, attempt to limit his/her agreement to non-prosecution based on the testimony or information provided. Such an "informal use immunity" agreement has two advantages over an agreement not to prosecute the person in connection with a particular transaction: first, it preserves the prosecutor's option to prosecute on the basis of independently obtained evidence if it later appears that the person's criminal involvement was more serious than it originally appeared to be; and second, it encourages the witness to be as forthright as possible since the more he/she reveals the more protection he/she will have against a future prosecution. To further encourage full disclosure by the witness, it should be made clear in the agreement that the government's forbearance from prosecution is conditioned upon the witness's testimony or production of information being complete and truthful, and that failure to testify truthfully may result in a perjury prosecution.

Even if it is not practicable to obtain the desired cooperation pursuant to an "informal use immunity" agreement, the attorney for the government should attempt to limit the scope of the agreement in terms of the testimony and transactions covered, bearing in mind the possible effect of his/her agreement on prosecutions in other districts.

It is important that non-prosecution agreements be drawn in terms that will not bind other Federal prosecutors or agencies without their consent. Thus, if practicable, the attorney for the government should explicitly limit the scope of his/her agreement to non-prosecution within his/her district. If such a limitation is not practicable and it can reasonably be anticipated that the agreement may affect prosecution of the person in other districts, the attorney for the government contemplating such an agreement shall communicate the relevant facts to the Assistant Attorney General with supervisory responsibility for the subject matter. United States Attorneys may not make agreements which prejudice civil or tax liability without the express agreement of all affected Divisions and/or agencies. See also 9-16.000 et seq. for more information regarding plea agreements.

Finally, the attorney for the government should make it clear that his/her agreement relates only to non-prosecution and that he/she has no independent authority to promise that the witness will be admitted into the Department's Witness Security program or that the Marshal's Service will provide any benefits to the witness in exchange for his/her cooperation. This does not mean, of course, that the prosecutor should not cooperate in making arrangements with the Marshal's Service necessary for the protection of the witness in appropriate cases. The procedures to be followed in such cases are set forth in USAM 9-21.000.

9-27.640 Agreements Requiring Assistant Attorney General Approval

A. The attorney for the government should not enter into a non-prosecution agreement in exchange for a person's cooperation without first obtaining the approval of the Assistant Attorney General with supervisory responsibility over the subject matter, or his/her designee, when:

   1. Prior consultation or approval would be required by a statute or by Departmental policy for a declination of prosecution or dismissal of a charge with regard to which the agreement is to be made; or
   2. The person is:
      a. A high-level Federal, state, or local official;
      b. An official or agent of a Federal investigative or law enforcement agency; or
      c. A person who otherwise is, or is likely to become, of major public interest.

B. Comment. USAM 9-27.640 sets forth special cases that require approval of non-prosecution agreements by the responsible Assistant Attorney General or his/her designee. Subparagraph (1) covers cases in which existing statutory provisions and departmental policies require that, with respect to certain types of offenses, the Attorney General or an Assistant Attorney General be consulted or give his/her approval before prosecution is declined or charges are dismissed. For example, see USAM 6-4.245 (tax offenses); USAM 9-41.010 (bankruptcy frauds); USAM 9-90.020 (internal security offenses); (see USAM 9-2.400 for a complete listing of all prior approval and consultation requirements). An agreement not to prosecute resembles a declination of prosecution or the dismissal of a charge in that the end result in each case is similar: a person who has engaged in criminal activity is not prosecuted or is not prosecuted fully for his/her offense. Accordingly, attorneys for the government should obtain the approval of the appropriate Assistant Attorney General, or his/her designee, before agreeing not to prosecute in any case in which consultation or approval would be required for a declination of prosecution or dismissal of a charge.

Subparagraph (2) sets forth other situations in which the attorney for the government should obtain the approval of an Assistant Attorney General, or his/her designee, of a proposed agreement not to prosecute in exchange for cooperation. Generally speaking, the situations described will be cases of an exceptional or extremely sensitive nature, or cases involving individuals or matters of major public interest. In a case covered by this provision that appears to be of an especially sensitive nature, the Assistant Attorney General should, in turn, consider whether it would be appropriate to notify the Attorney General or the Deputy Attorney General.

9-27.641 Multi-District (Global) Agreement Requests

A. No district or division shall make any agreement, including any agreement not to prosecute, which purports to bind any other district(s) or division without the express written approval of the United States Attorney(s) in each affected district and/or the Assistant Attorney General of the Criminal Division.

The requesting district/division shall make known to each affected district/division the following information:

1. The specific crimes allegedly committed in the affected district(s) as disclosed by the defendant. (No agreement should be made as to any crime(s) not disclosed by the defendant.)
2. Identification of victims of crimes committed by the defendant in any affected district, insofar as possible.

3. The proposed agreement to be made with the defendant and the applicable Sentencing Guideline range.

9-27.650 Records of Non-Prosecution Agreements

A. In a case in which a non-prosecution agreement is reached in return for a person's cooperation, the attorney for the government should ensure that the case file contains a memorandum or other written record setting forth the terms of the agreement. The memorandum or record should be signed or initialed by the person with whom the agreement is made or his/her attorney.

B. Comment. The provisions of this section are intended to serve two purposes. First, it is important to have a written record in the event that questions arise concerning the nature or scope of the agreement. Such questions are certain to arise during cross-examination of the witness, particularly if the existence of the agreement has been disclosed to defense counsel pursuant to the requirements of *Brady v. Maryland,* 373 U.S. 83 (1963) and *Giglio v. United States,* 405 U.S. 150 (1972). The exact terms of the agreement may also become relevant if the government attempts to prosecute the witness for some offense in the future. Second, such a record will facilitate identification by government attorneys (in the course of weighing future agreements not to prosecute, plea agreements, pre-trial diversion, and other discretionary actions) of persons whom the government has agreed not to prosecute.

   The principal requirements of the written record are that it be sufficiently detailed that it leaves no doubt as to the obligations of the parties to the agreement, and that it be signed or initialed by the person with whom the agreement is made and his/her attorney, or at least by one of them.

Appendix C

USAM CHAPTER 9-28.000 PRINCIPLES OF FEDERAL PROSECUTION OF BUSINESS ORGANIZATIONS

9-28.000 PRINCIPLES OF FEDERAL PROSECUTION OF BUSINESS ORGANIZATIONS [FN1]

9-28.100 Duties of Federal Prosecutors and Duties of Corporate Leaders
9-28.200 General Considerations of Corporate Liability
9-28.300 Factors to Be Considered
9-28.400 Special Policy Concerns
9-28.500 Pervasiveness of Wrongdoing Within the Corporation
9-28.600 The Corporation's Past History
9-28.700 The Value of Cooperation
9-28.710 Attorney-Client and Work Product Protections
9-28.720 Cooperation: Disclosing the Relevant Facts
9-28.730 Obstructing the Investigation

Source: http://www.justice.gov/usao/eousa/foia_reading_room/usam/title9/28mcrm.htm#FN1

9-28.740 Offering Cooperation: No Entitlement to Immunity
9-28.750 Qualifying for Immunity, Amnesty, or Reduced Sanctions Through Voluntary Disclosures
9-28.760 Oversight Concerning Demands for Waivers of Attorney-Client Privilege or Work Product By Corporations Contrary to This Policy
9-28.800 Corporate Compliance Programs
9-28.900 Restitution and Remediation
9-28.1000 Collateral Consequences
9-28.1100 Other Civil or Regulatory Alternatives
9-28.1200 Selecting Charges
9-28.1300 Plea Agreements with Corporations

9-28.100 Duties of Federal Prosecutors and Duties of Corporate Leaders

The prosecution of corporate crime is a high priority for the Department of Justice. By investigating allegations of wrongdoing and by bringing charges where appropriate for criminal misconduct, the Department promotes critical public interests. These interests include, to take just a few examples: (1) protecting the integrity of our free economic and capital markets; (2) protecting consumers, investors, and business entities that compete only through lawful means; and (3) protecting the American people from misconduct that would violate criminal laws safeguarding the environment.

In this regard, federal prosecutors and corporate leaders typically share common goals. For example, directors and officers owe a fiduciary duty to a corporation's shareholders, the corporation's true owners, and they owe duties of honest dealing to the investing public in connection with the corporation's regulatory filings and public statements. The faithful execution of these duties by corporate leadership serves the same values in promoting public trust and confidence that our criminal cases are designed to serve.

A prosecutor's duty to enforce the law requires the investigation and prosecution of criminal wrongdoing if it is discovered. In carrying out this mission with the diligence and resolve necessary to vindicate the important public interests discussed above, prosecutors should be mindful of the common cause we share with responsible corporate leaders. Prosecutors should also be mindful that confidence in the Department is affected both by the results we achieve and by the real and perceived ways in which we achieve them. Thus, the manner in which we do our job as prosecutors—including the professionalism we demonstrate, our willingness to secure the facts in a manner that encourages corporate compliance and self-regulation, and also our appreciation that corporate prosecutions can potentially harm blameless investors, employees, and others—affects public perception of our mission. Federal prosecutors recognize that they must maintain public confidence in the way in which they exercise their charging discretion. This endeavor requires the thoughtful analysis of all facts and circumstances presented in a given case. As always, professionalism and civility play an important part in the Department's discharge of its responsibilities in all areas, including the area of corporate investigations and prosecutions.

[new August 2008]

9-28.200 General Considerations of Corporate Liability

General Principle: Corporations should not be treated leniently because of their artificial nature nor should they be subject to harsher treatment. Vigorous enforcement of the criminal laws against corporate wrongdoers, where appropriate, results in great benefits for law enforcement and the public, particularly in the area of white collar crime. Indicting corporations for wrongdoing enables the government to be a force for positive change of corporate culture, and a force to prevent, discover, and punish serious crimes.

Comment: In all cases involving corporate wrongdoing, prosecutors should consider the factors discussed further below. In doing so, prosecutors should be aware of the public benefits that can flow from indicting a corporation in appropriate cases. For instance, corporations are likely to take immediate remedial steps when one is indicted for criminal misconduct that is pervasive throughout a particular industry, and thus an indictment can provide a unique opportunity for deterrence on a broad scale. In addition, a corporate indictment may result in specific deterrence by changing the culture of the indicted corporation and the behavior of its employees. Finally, certain crimes that carry with them a substantial risk of great public harm—*e.g.*, environmental crimes or sweeping financial frauds—may be committed by a business entity, and there may therefore be a substantial federal interest in indicting a corporation under such circumstances.

In certain instances, it may be appropriate, upon consideration of the factors set forth herein, to resolve a corporate criminal case by means other than indictment. Non-prosecution and deferred prosecution agreements, for example, occupy an important middle ground between declining prosecution and obtaining the conviction of a corporation. These agreements are discussed further in USAM 9-28.1000. Likewise, civil and regulatory alternatives may be appropriate in certain cases, as discussed in USAM 9-28.1100.

Where a decision is made to charge a corporation, it does not necessarily follow that individual directors, officers, employees, or shareholders should not also be charged. Prosecution of a corporation is not a substitute for the prosecution of criminally culpable individuals within or without the corporation. Because a corporation can act only through individuals, imposition of individual criminal liability may provide the strongest deterrent against future corporate wrongdoing. Only rarely should provable individual culpability not be pursued, particularly if it relates to high-level corporate officers, even in the face of an offer of a corporate guilty plea or some other disposition of the charges against the corporation.

Corporations are "legal persons," capable of suing and being sued, and capable of committing crimes. Under the doctrine of *respondeat superior,* a corporation may be held criminally liable for the illegal acts of its directors, officers, employees, and agents. To hold a corporation liable for these actions, the government must establish that the corporate agent's actions (i) were within the scope of his duties and (ii) were intended, at least in part, to benefit the corporation. In all cases involving wrongdoing by corporate agents, prosecutors should not limit their focus solely to individuals or the corporation, but should consider both as potential targets.

Agents may act for mixed reasons—both for self-aggrandizement (both direct and indirect) and for the benefit of the corporation, and a corporation may be held liable as long as one motivation of its agent is to benefit the corporation. *See United States v. Potter,* 463 F.3d 9, 25 (1st Cir. 2006) (stating that the test to determine whether an agent is acting within the scope of employment is "whether the agent is performing acts of the kind which he is authorized to perform, and those acts are motivated, at least in part, by an intent to benefit the corporation."). In *United States v. Automated Medical Laboratories, Inc.,* 770 F.2d 399 (4th Cir. 1985), for example, the Fourth Circuit affirmed a corporation's conviction for the actions of a subsidiary's employee despite the corporation's claim that the employee was acting for his own benefit, namely his "ambitious nature and his desire to ascend the corporate ladder." *Id.* at 407. The court stated, "Partucci was clearly acting in part to benefit AML since his advancement within the corporation depended on AML's well-being and its lack of difficulties with the FDA." *Id.; see also United States v. Cincotta,* 689 F.2d 238, 241-42 (1st Cir. 1982) (upholding a corporation's conviction, notwithstanding the substantial personal benefit reaped by its miscreant agents, because the fraudulent scheme required money to pass through the corporation's treasury and the fraudulently obtained goods were resold to the corporation's customers in the corporation's name).

Moreover, the corporation need not even necessarily profit from its agent's actions for it to be held liable. In *Automated Medical Laboratories,* the Fourth Circuit stated:

[B]enefit is not a "touchstone of criminal corporate liability; benefit at best is an evidential, not an operative, fact." Thus, whether the agent's actions ultimately redounded to the benefit of the corporation is less significant than whether the agent acted with the intent to benefit the corporation. The basic purpose of requiring that an agent have acted with the intent to benefit the corporation, however, is to insulate the corporation from criminal liability for actions of its agents which may be *inimical* to the interests of the corporation or which may have been undertaken solely to advance the interests of that agent or of a party other than the corporation.

770 F.2d at 407 (internal citation omitted) (quoting *Old Monastery Co. v. United States,* 147 F.2d 905, 908 (4th Cir. 1945)).

[new August 2008]

9-28.300 Factors to Be Considered

General Principle: Generally, prosecutors apply the same factors in determining whether to charge a corporation as they do with respect to individuals. *See* USAM 9-27.220 et seq. Thus, the prosecutor must weigh all of the factors normally considered in the sound exercise of prosecutorial judgment: the sufficiency of the evidence; the likelihood of success at trial; the probable deterrent, rehabilitative, and other consequences of conviction; and the adequacy of noncriminal approaches. *See id.* However, due to the nature of the corporate "person," some additional factors are present. In conducting an investigation, determining whether to bring charges, and negotiating plea or other agreements, prosecutors should consider the following factors in reaching a decision as to the proper treatment of a corporate target:

1. the nature and seriousness of the offense, including the risk of harm to the public, and applicable policies and priorities, if any, governing the prosecution of corporations for particular categories of crime (see USAM 9-28.400);
2. the pervasiveness of wrongdoing within the corporation, including the complicity in, or the condoning of, the wrongdoing by corporate management (see USAM 9-28.500);
3. the corporation's history of similar misconduct, including prior criminal, civil, and regulatory enforcement actions against it (see USAM 9-28.600);
4. the corporation's timely and voluntary disclosure of wrongdoing and its willingness to cooperate in the investigation of its agents (see USAM 9-28.700);
5. the existence and effectiveness of the corporation's pre-existing compliance program (see USAM 9-28.800);
6. the corporation's remedial actions, including any efforts to implement an effective corporate compliance program or to improve an existing one, to replace responsible management, to discipline or terminate wrongdoers, to pay restitution, and to cooperate with the relevant government agencies (see USAM 9-28.900);
7. collateral consequences, including whether there is disproportionate harm to shareholders, pension holders, employees, and others not proven personally culpable, as well as impact on the public arising from the prosecution (see USAM 9-28.1000);
8. the adequacy of the prosecution of individuals responsible for the corporation's malfeasance; and
9. the adequacy of remedies such as civil or regulatory enforcement actions (see USAM 9-28.1100).

Comment: The factors listed in this section are intended to be illustrative of those that should be evaluated and are not an exhaustive list of potentially relevant considerations. Some of these factors may not apply to specific cases, and in some cases one factor may override all others. For example, the nature and seriousness of the offense may be such as to warrant prosecution regardless of the other factors. In most cases, however, no single factor will be dispositive. In addition, national law enforcement policies in various enforcement areas may require that more or less weight be given to certain of these factors than to others. Of course, prosecutors must exercise their thoughtful and pragmatic judgment in applying and balancing these factors, so as to achieve a fair and just outcome and promote respect for the law.

In making a decision to charge a corporation, the prosecutor generally has substantial latitude in determining when, whom, how, and even whether to prosecute for violations of federal criminal law. In exercising that discretion, prosecutors should consider the following statements of principles that summarize the considerations they should weigh and the practices they should follow in discharging their prosecutorial responsibilities. In doing so, prosecutors should ensure that the general purposes of the criminal law—assurance of warranted punishment, deterrence of further criminal conduct, protection of the public from dangerous and fraudulent conduct, rehabilitation of offenders, and restitution for victims and affected communities—are adequately met, taking into account the special nature of the corporate "person."

[new August 2008]

9-28.400 Special Policy Concerns

General Principle: The nature and seriousness of the crime, including the risk of harm to the public from the criminal misconduct, are obviously primary factors in determining whether to charge a corporation. In addition, corporate conduct, particularly that of national and multi-national corporations, necessarily intersects with federal economic, tax, and criminal law enforcement policies. In applying these Principles, prosecutors must consider the practices and policies of the appropriate Division of the Department, and must comply with those policies to the extent required by the facts presented.

Comment: In determining whether to charge a corporation, prosecutors should take into account federal law enforcement priorities as discussed above. See USAM 9-27.230. In addition, however, prosecutors must be aware of the specific policy goals and incentive programs established by the respective Divisions and regulatory agencies. Thus, whereas natural persons may be given incremental degrees of credit (ranging from immunity to lesser charges to sentencing considerations) for turning themselves in, making statements against their penal interest, and cooperating in the government's investigation of their own and others' wrongdoing, the same approach may not be appropriate in all circumstances with respect to corporations. As an example, it is entirely proper in many investigations for a prosecutor to consider the corporation's pre-indictment conduct, *e.g.*, voluntary disclosure, cooperation, remediation or restitution, in determining whether to seek an indictment. However, this would not necessarily be appropriate in an antitrust investigation, in which antitrust violations, by definition, go to the heart of the corporation's business. With this in mind, the Antitrust Division has established a firm policy, understood in the business community, that credit should not be given at the charging stage for a compliance program and that amnesty is available only to the first corporation to make full disclosure to the government. As another example, the Tax Division has a strong preference for prosecuting responsible individuals, rather than entities, for corporate tax offenses. Thus, in determining whether or not to charge a corporation, prosecutors must consult with the Criminal, Antitrust, Tax, Environmental and Natural Resources, and National Security Divisions, as appropriate.

[new August 2008]

9-28.500 Pervasiveness of Wrongdoing Within the Corporation

General Principle: A corporation can only act through natural persons, and it is therefore held responsible for the acts of such persons fairly attributable to it. Charging a corporation for even minor misconduct may be appropriate where the wrongdoing was pervasive and was undertaken by a large number of employees, or by all the employees in a particular role within the corporation, or was condoned by upper management. On the other hand, it may not be appropriate to impose liability upon a corporation, particularly one with a robust compliance program in place, under a strict *respondeat superior* theory for the single isolated act of a rogue employee. There is, of course, a wide spectrum between these two extremes, and a prosecutor should exercise sound discretion in evaluating the pervasiveness of wrongdoing within a corporation.

Comment: Of these factors, the most important is the role and conduct of management. Although acts of even low-level employees may result in criminal liability, a corporation is directed by its management and management is responsible for a corporate culture in which criminal conduct is either discouraged or tacitly encouraged. As stated in commentary to the Sentencing Guidelines:

> Pervasiveness [is] case specific and [will] depend on the number, and degree of responsibility, of individuals [with] substantial authority . . . who participated in, condoned, or were willfully ignorant of the offense. Fewer individuals need to be involved for a finding of pervasiveness if those individuals exercised a relatively high degree of authority. Pervasiveness can occur either within an organization as a whole or within a unit of an organization.
>
> USSG § 8C2.5, cmt. (n. 4).
>
> [new August 2008]

9-28.600 The Corporation's Past History

General Principle: Prosecutors may consider a corporation's history of similar conduct, including prior criminal, civil, and regulatory enforcement actions against it, in determining whether to bring criminal charges and how best to resolve cases.

Comment: A corporation, like a natural person, is expected to learn from its mistakes. A history of similar misconduct may be probative of a corporate culture that encouraged, or at least condoned, such misdeeds, regardless of any compliance programs. Criminal prosecution of a corporation may be particularly appropriate where the corporation previously had been subject to non-criminal guidance, warnings, or sanctions, or previous criminal charges, and it either had not taken adequate action to prevent future unlawful conduct or had continued to engage in the misconduct in spite of the warnings or enforcement actions taken against it. The corporate structure itself (*e.g.*, the creation or existence of subsidiaries or operating divisions) is not dispositive in this analysis, and enforcement actions taken against the corporation or any of its divisions, subsidiaries, and affiliates may be considered, if germane. *See* USSG § 8C2.5(c), cmt. (n. 6).

[new August 2008]

9-28.700 The Value of Cooperation

General Principle: In determining whether to charge a corporation and how to resolve corporate criminal cases, the corporation's timely and voluntary disclosure of wrongdoing and its cooperation with the government's investigation may be relevant factors. In gauging the extent of the corporation's cooperation, the prosecutor may consider, among other things, whether the corporation made a voluntary and timely disclosure, and the corporation's willingness to provide relevant information and evidence and identify relevant actors within and outside the corporation, including senior executives.

Cooperation is a potential mitigating factor, by which a corporation—just like any other subject of a criminal investigation—can gain credit in a case that otherwise is appropriate for indictment and prosecution. Of course, the decision not to cooperate by a corporation (or individual) is not itself evidence of misconduct, at least where the lack of cooperation does not involve criminal misconduct or demonstrate consciousness of guilt (*e.g.*, suborning perjury or false statements, or refusing to comply with lawful discovery requests). Thus, failure to cooperate, in and of itself, does not support or require the filing of charges with respect to a corporation any more than with respect to an individual.

Comment: In investigating wrongdoing by or within a corporation, a prosecutor is likely to encounter several obstacles resulting from the nature of the corporation itself. It will often be difficult to determine which individual took which action on behalf of the corporation. Lines of authority and responsibility may be shared among operating divisions or departments, and records and personnel may be spread throughout the United States or even among several countries. Where the criminal conduct continued over an extended period of time, the culpable or knowledgeable personnel may have been promoted, transferred, or fired, or they may have quit or retired. Accordingly, a corporation's cooperation may be critical in identifying potentially relevant actors and locating relevant evidence, among other things, and in doing so expeditiously.

This dynamic—*i.e.,* the difficulty of determining what happened, where the evidence is, and which individuals took or promoted putatively illegal corporate actions—can have negative consequences for both the government and the corporation that is the subject or target of a government investigation. More specifically, because of corporate attribution principles concerning actions of corporate officers and employees (*see, e.g., supra* section II), uncertainty about exactly who authorized or directed apparent corporate misconduct can inure to the detriment of a corporation. For example, it may not matter under the law which of several possible executives or leaders in a chain of command approved of or authorized criminal conduct; however, that information if known might bear on the propriety of a particular disposition short of indictment of the corporation. It may not be in the interest of a corporation or the government for a charging decision to be made in the absence of such information, which might occur if, for example, a statute of limitations were relevant and authorization by any one of the officials were enough to justify a charge under the law. Moreover, and at a minimum, a protracted government investigation of such an issue could, as a collateral consequence, disrupt the corporation's business operations or even depress its stock price.

For these reasons and more, cooperation can be a favorable course for both the government and the corporation. Cooperation benefits the government—and ultimately shareholders, employees, and other often blameless victims—by allowing prosecutors and federal agents, for example, to avoid protracted delays, which compromise their ability to quickly uncover and address the full extent of widespread corporate crimes. With cooperation by the corporation, the government may be able to reduce tangible losses, limit damage to reputation, and preserve assets for restitution. At the same time, cooperation may benefit the corporation by enabling the government to focus its investigative resources in a manner that will not unduly disrupt the corporation's legitimate business operations. In addition, and critically, cooperation may benefit the corporation by presenting it with the opportunity to earn credit for its efforts.

[new August 2008]

9-28.710 Attorney-Client and Work Product Protections

The attorney-client privilege and the attorney work product protection serve an extremely important function in the American legal system. The attorney-client privilege is one of the oldest and most sacrosanct privileges under the law. *See Upjohn v. United States*, 449 U.S. 383, 389 (1981). As the Supreme Court has stated, "[i]ts purpose is to encourage full and frank communication between attorneys and their clients and thereby promote broader public interests in the observance of law and administration of justice." *Id.* The value of promoting a corporation's ability to seek frank and comprehensive legal advice is particularly important in the contemporary global business environment, where corporations often face complex and dynamic legal and regulatory obligations imposed by the federal government and also by states and foreign governments. The work product doctrine serves similarly important goals.

For these reasons, waiving the attorney-client and work product protections has never been a prerequisite under the Department's prosecution guidelines for a corporation to be viewed as cooperative. Nonetheless, a wide range of commentators and members of the American legal community and criminal justice system have asserted that the Department's policies have been used, either wittingly or unwittingly, to coerce business entities into waiving attorney-client privilege and work-product protection. Everyone agrees that a corporation may freely waive its own privileges if it chooses to do so; indeed, such waivers occur routinely when corporations are victimized by their employees or others, conduct an internal investigation, and then disclose the details of the investigation to law enforcement officials in an effort to seek prosecution of the offenders. However, the contention, from a broad array of voices, is that the Department's position on attorney-client privilege and work product protection waivers has promoted an environment in which those protections are being unfairly eroded to the detriment of all.

The Department understands that the attorney-client privilege and attorney work product protection are essential and long-recognized components of the American legal system. What the government seeks and needs to advance its legitimate (indeed, essential) law enforcement mission is not waiver of those protections, but rather the facts known to the corporation about the putative criminal misconduct under review. In addition, while a corporation remains free to convey non-factual or "core" attorney-client communications or work product—if and only if the corporation voluntarily chooses to do so—prosecutors should not ask for such waivers and are directed not to do so. The critical factor is whether the corporation has provided the facts about the events, as explained further herein.

[new August 2008]

9-28.720 Cooperation: Disclosing the Relevant Facts

Eligibility for cooperation credit is not predicated upon the waiver of attorney-client privilege or work product protection. Instead, the sort of cooperation that is most valuable to resolving allegations of misconduct by a corporation and its officers, directors, employees, or agents is disclosure of the relevant *facts* concerning such misconduct. In this regard, the analysis parallels that for a non-corporate defendant, where cooperation typically requires disclosure of relevant factual knowledge and not of discussions between an individual and his attorneys.

Thus, when the government investigates potential corporate wrongdoing, it seeks the relevant facts. For example, how and when did the alleged misconduct occur? Who promoted or approved it? Who was responsible for committing it? In this respect, the investigation of a corporation differs little from the investigation of an individual. In both cases, the government needs to know the facts to achieve a just and fair outcome. The party under investigation may choose to cooperate by disclosing the facts, and the government may give credit for the party's disclosures. If a corporation wishes to receive credit for such cooperation, which then can be considered with all other cooperative efforts and circumstances in evaluating how fairly to proceed, then the corporation, like any person, must disclose the relevant facts of which it has knowledge.[*FN2*]

(a) Disclosing the Relevant Facts—Facts Gathered Through Internal Investigation

Individuals and corporations often obtain knowledge of facts in different ways. An individual knows the facts of his or others' misconduct through his own experience and perceptions. A corporation is an artificial construct that cannot, by definition, have personal knowledge of the facts. Some of those facts may be reflected in documentary or electronic media like emails, transaction or accounting documents, and other records. Often, the corporation gathers facts through an internal investigation. Exactly how and by whom the facts are gathered is for the corporation to decide. Many corporations choose to collect information about potential misconduct through lawyers, a process that may confer attorney-client privilege or attorney work product protection on at least some of the information collected. Other corporations may choose a method of fact-gathering that does not have that effect—for example, having employee or other witness statements collected after interviews by non-attorney personnel. Whichever process the corporation selects, the government's key measure of cooperation must remain the same as it does for an individual: has the party timely disclosed the relevant facts about the putative misconduct? That is the operative question in assigning cooperation credit for the disclosure of information—*not* whether the corporation discloses attorney-client or work product materials. Accordingly, a corporation should receive the same credit for disclosing facts contained in materials that are not protected by the attorney-client privilege or attorney work product as it would for disclosing identical facts contained in materials that are so protected.[*FN3*] On this point the Report of the House Judiciary Committee, submitted in connection with the attorney-client privilege bill passed by the House of Representatives (H.R. 3013), comports with the approach required here:

> [A]n ... attorney of the United States may base cooperation credit on the facts that are disclosed, but is prohibited from basing cooperation credit upon whether or not the materials are protected by attorney-client privilege or attor-

> ney work product. As a result, an entity that voluntarily discloses should receive the same amount of cooperation credit for disclosing facts that happen to be contained in materials not protected by attorney-client privilege or attorney work product as it would receive for disclosing identical facts that are contained in materials protected by attorney-client privilege or attorney work product. There should be no differentials in an assessment of cooperation (i.e., neither a credit nor a penalty) based upon whether or not the materials disclosed are protected by attorney-client privilege or attorney work product.

H.R. Rep. No. 110-445 at 4 (2007).

In short, so long as the corporation timely discloses relevant facts about the putative misconduct, the corporation may receive due credit for such cooperation, regardless of whether it chooses to waive privilege or work product protection in the process.[*FN4*] Likewise, a corporation that does not disclose the relevant facts about the alleged misconduct—for whatever reason—typically should not be entitled to receive credit for cooperation.

Two final and related points bear noting about the disclosure of facts, although they should be obvious. First, the government cannot compel, and the corporation has no obligation to make, such disclosures (although the government can obviously compel the disclosure of certain records and witness testimony through subpoenas). Second, a corporation's failure to provide relevant information does not mean the corporation will be indicted. It simply means that the corporation will not be entitled to mitigating credit for that cooperation. Whether the corporation faces charges will turn, as it does in any case, on the sufficiency of the evidence, the likelihood of success at trial, and all of the other factors identified in Section III above. If there is insufficient evidence to warrant indictment, after appropriate investigation has been completed, or if the other factors weigh against indictment, then the corporation should not be indicted, irrespective of whether it has earned cooperation credit. The converse is also true: The government may charge even the most cooperative corporation pursuant to these Principles if, in weighing and balancing the factors described herein, the prosecutor determines that a charge is required in the interests of justice. Put differently, even the most sincere and thorough effort to cooperate cannot necessarily absolve a corporation that has, for example, engaged in an egregious, orchestrated, and widespread fraud. Cooperation is a relevant potential mitigating factor, but it alone is not dispositive.

(b) Legal Advice and Attorney Work Product

Separate from (and usually preceding) the fact-gathering process in an internal investigation, a corporation, through its officers, employees, directors, or others, may have consulted with corporate counsel regarding or in a manner that concerns the legal implications of the putative misconduct at issue. Communications of this sort, which are both independent of the fact-gathering component of an internal investigation and made for the purpose of seeking or dispensing legal advice, lie at the core of the attorney-client privilege. Such communications can naturally have a salutary effect on corporate behavior—facilitating, for example, a corporation's effort to comply with complex and evolving legal and regulatory regimes.[*FN5*] Except as noted in subparagraphs (b)(i) and (b)(ii) below, a corporation need not disclose and prosecutors may not request the disclosure of such communications as a condition for the corporation's eligibility to receive cooperation credit.

Likewise, non-factual or core attorney work product—for example, an attorney's mental impressions or legal theories—lies at the core of the attorney work product doctrine. A corporation need not disclose, and prosecutors may not request, the disclosure of such attorney work product as a condition for the corporation's eligibility to receive cooperation credit.

(i) Advice of Counsel Defense in the Instant Context

Occasionally a corporation or one of its employees may assert an advice-of-counsel defense, based upon communications with in-house or outside counsel that took place prior to or contemporaneously with the underlying conduct at issue. In such situations, the defendant must tender a legitimate factual basis to support the assertion of the advice-of-counsel defense. *See, e.g., Pitt v. Dist. of Columbia,* 491 F.3d 494, 504-05 (D.C. Cir. 2007); *United States v. Wenger,* 427 F.3d 840, 853-54 (10th Cir. 2005); *United States v. Cheek,* 3 F.3d 1057, 1061-62 (7th Cir. 1993). The Department cannot fairly be asked to discharge its responsibility to the public to investigate alleged corporate crime, or to temper what would otherwise be the appropriate course of prosecutive action, by simply accepting on faith an otherwise unproven assertion that an attorney—perhaps even an unnamed attorney—approved potentially unlawful practices. Accordingly, where an advice-of-counsel defense has been asserted, prosecutors may ask for the disclosure of the communications allegedly supporting it.

(ii) Communications in Furtherance of a Crime or Fraud

Communications between a corporation (through its officers, employees, directors, or agents) and corporate counsel that are made in furtherance of a crime or fraud are, under settled precedent, outside the scope and protection of the attorney-client privilege. *See United States v. Zolin,* 491 U.S. 554, 563 (1989); *United States v. BDO Seidman, LLP,* 492 F.3d 806, 818 (7th Cir. 2007). As a result, the Department may properly request such communications if they in fact exist.

[new August 2008]

9-28.730 Obstructing the Investigation

Another factor to be weighed by the prosecutor is whether the corporation has engaged in conduct intended to impede the investigation. Examples of such conduct could include: inappropriate directions to employees or their counsel, such as directions not to be truthful or to conceal relevant facts; making representations or submissions that contain misleading assertions or material omissions; and incomplete or delayed production of records.

In evaluating cooperation, however, prosecutors should not take into account whether a corporation is advancing or reimbursing attorneys' fees or providing counsel to employees, officers, or directors under investigation or indictment. Likewise, prosecutors may not request that a corporation refrain from taking such action. This prohibition is not meant to prevent a prosecutor from asking questions about an attorney's representation of a corporation or its employees, officers, or directors, where otherwise appropriate under the law.[*FN6*] Neither is it intended to limit the otherwise applicable reach of criminal obstruction of justice statutes such as 18 U.S.C. § 1503. If the payment of attorney fees were used in a manner that would otherwise constitute criminal obstruction of justice—for example, if fees were advanced on the condition that an employee adhere to a version of the facts that the corporation and the employee knew to be false—these Principles would not (and could not) render inapplicable such criminal prohibitions.

Similarly, the mere participation by a corporation in a joint defense agreement does not render the corporation ineligible to receive cooperation credit, and prosecutors may not request that a corporation refrain from entering into such agreements. Of course, the corporation may wish to avoid putting itself in the position of being disabled, by virtue of a particular joint defense or similar agreement, from providing some relevant facts to the government and thereby limiting its ability to seek such cooperation credit. Such might be the case if the corporation gathers facts from employees who have entered into a joint defense agreement with the corporation, and who may later seek to prevent the corporation from disclosing the facts it has acquired. Corporations may wish to address this situation by crafting or participating in joint defense agreements, to the extent they choose to enter them, that provide such flexibility as they deem appropriate.

Finally, it may on occasion be appropriate for the government to consider whether the corporation has shared with others sensitive information about the investigation that the government provided to the corporation. In appropriate situations, as it does with individuals, the government may properly request that, if a corporation wishes to receive credit for cooperation, the information provided by the government to the corporation not be transmitted to others—for example, where the disclosure of such information could lead to flight by individual subjects, destruction of evidence, or dissipation or concealment of assets.

[new August 2008]

9-28.740 Offering Cooperation: No Entitlement to Immunity

A corporation's offer of cooperation or cooperation itself does not automatically entitle it to immunity from prosecution or a favorable resolution of its case. A corporation should not be able to escape liability merely by offering up its directors, officers, employees, or agents. Thus, a corporation's willingness to cooperate is not determinative; that factor, while relevant, needs to be considered in conjunction with all other factors.

[new August 2008]

9-28.750 Qualifying for Immunity, Amnesty, or Reduced Sanctions Through Voluntary Disclosures

In conjunction with regulatory agencies and other executive branch departments, the Department encourages corporations, as part of their compliance programs, to conduct internal investigations and to disclose the relevant facts to the appropriate authorities. Some agencies, such as the Securities and Exchange Commission and the Environmental Protection Agency, as well as the Department's Environmental and Natural Resources Division, have formal voluntary disclosure programs in which self-reporting, coupled with remediation and additional criteria, may qualify the corporation for amnesty or reduced sanctions. Even in the absence of a formal program, prosecutors may consider a corporation's timely and voluntary disclosure in evaluating the adequacy of the corporation's compliance program and its management's commitment to the compliance program. However, prosecution and economic policies specific to the industry or statute may require prosecution notwithstanding a corporation's willingness to cooperate. For example, the Antitrust Division has a policy of offering amnesty only to the first corporation to agree to cooperate. Moreover, amnesty, immunity, or reduced sanctions may not be appropriate where the corporation's business is permeated with fraud or other crimes.

[new August 2008]

9-28.760 Oversight Concerning Demands for Waivers of Attorney-Client Privilege or Work Product Protection By Corporations Contrary to This Policy

The Department underscores its commitment to attorney practices that are consistent with Department policies like those set forth herein concerning cooperation credit and due respect for the attorney-client privilege and work product protection. Counsel for corporations who believe that prosecutors are violating such guidance are encouraged to raise their concerns with supervisors, including the appropriate United States Attorney or Assistant Attorney General. Like any other allegation of attorney misconduct, such allegations are subject to potential investigation through established mechanisms.

[new August 2008]

9-28.800 Corporate Compliance Programs

General Principle: Compliance programs are established by corporate management to prevent and detect misconduct and to ensure that corporate activities are conducted in accordance with applicable criminal and civil laws, regulations, and rules. The Department encourages such corporate self-policing, including voluntary disclosures to the government of any problems that a corporation discovers on its own. However, the existence of a compliance program is not sufficient, in and of itself, to justify not charging a corporation for criminal misconduct undertaken by its officers, directors, employees, or agents. In addition, the nature of some crimes, *e.g.*, antitrust violations, may be such that national law enforcement policies mandate prosecutions of corporations notwithstanding the existence of a compliance program.

Comment: The existence of a corporate compliance program, even one that specifically prohibited the very conduct in question, does not absolve the corporation from criminal liability under the doctrine of *respondeat superior. See United States v. Basic Constr. Co.*, 711 F.2d 570, 573 (4th Cir. 1983) ("[A] corporation may be held criminally responsible for antitrust violations committed by its employees if they were acting within the scope of their authority, or apparent authority, and for the benefit of the corporation, even if . . . such acts were against corporate policy or express instructions."). As explained in *United States v. Potter,* 463 F.3d 9 (1st Cir. 2006), a corporation cannot "avoid liability by adopting abstract rules" that forbid its agents from engaging in illegal acts, because "[e]ven a specific directive to an agent or employee or honest efforts to police such rules do not automatically free the company for the wrongful acts of agents." *Id.* at 25-26. *See also United States v. Hilton Hotels Corp.*, 467 F.2d 1000, 1007 (9th Cir. 1972) (noting that a corporation "could not gain exculpation by issuing general instructions without undertaking to enforce those instructions by means commensurate with the obvious risks"); *United States v. Beusch,* 596 F.2d 871, 878 (9th Cir. 1979) ("[A] corporation may be liable for acts of its employees done contrary to express instructions and policies, but . . . the existence of such instructions and policies may be considered in determining whether the employee in fact acted to benefit the corporation.").

While the Department recognizes that no compliance program can ever prevent all criminal activity by a corporation's employees, the critical factors in evaluating any program are whether the program is adequately designed for maximum effectiveness in preventing and detecting wrongdoing by employees and whether corporate management is enforcing the program or is tacitly encouraging or pressuring employees to engage in misconduct to achieve business objectives. The Department has no formulaic requirements regarding corporate compliance programs. The fundamental questions any prosecutor should ask are: Is the corporation's compliance program well designed? Is the program being applied earnestly and in good faith? Does the corporation's compliance program work? In answering these questions, the prosecutor should consider the comprehensiveness of the compliance program; the extent and pervasiveness of the criminal misconduct; the number and level of the corporate employees involved; the seriousness, duration, and frequency of the misconduct; and any remedial actions taken by the corporation, including, for example, disciplinary action against past violators uncovered by the prior compliance program, and revisions to corporate compliance programs in light of lessons learned. [*FN7*] Prosecutors should also consider the promptness of any disclosure of wrongdoing to the government. In evaluating compliance programs, prosecutors may consider whether the corporation has established corporate governance mechanisms that can effectively detect and prevent misconduct. For example, do the corporation's directors exercise independent review over proposed corporate actions rather than unquestioningly ratifying officers' recommendations; are internal audit functions conducted at a level sufficient to ensure their independence and accuracy; and have the directors established an information and reporting system in the organization reasonably designed to provide management and directors with timely and accurate information sufficient to allow them to reach an informed decision regarding the organization's compliance with the law. *See, e.g., In re Caremark Int'l Inc. Derivative Litig.*, 698 A.2d 959, 968-70 (Del. Ch. 1996).

Prosecutors should therefore attempt to determine whether a corporation's compliance program is merely a "paper program" or whether it was designed, implemented, reviewed, and revised, as appropriate, in an effective manner. In addition, prosecutors should determine whether the corporation has provided for a staff sufficient to audit, document, analyze, and utilize the results of the corporation's compliance efforts. Prosecutors also should determine whether the corporation's employees are adequately informed about the compliance program and are convinced of the corporation's commitment to it. This will enable the prosecutor to make an informed decision as to whether the corporation has adopted and implemented a truly effective compliance program that, when consistent with other federal law enforcement policies, may result in a decision to charge only the corporation's employees and agents or to mitigate charges or sanctions against the corporation.

Compliance programs should be designed to detect the particular types of misconduct most likely to occur in a particular corporation's line of business. Many corporations operate in complex regulatory environments outside the normal experience of criminal prosecutors. Accordingly, prosecutors should consult with relevant federal and state agencies with the expertise to evaluate the adequacy of a program's design and implementation. For instance, state and federal banking, insurance, and medical boards, the Department of Defense, the Department of Health and Human Services, the Environmental Protection Agency, and the Securities and Exchange Commission have considerable experience with compliance programs and can be helpful to a prosecutor in evaluating such programs. In addition, the Fraud Section of the Criminal Division, the Commercial Litigation Branch of the Civil Division, and the Environmental Crimes Section of the Environment and Natural Resources Division can assist United States Attorneys' Offices in finding the appropriate agency office(s) for such consultation.

[new August 2008]

9-28.900 Restitution and Remediation

General Principle: Although neither a corporation nor an individual target may avoid prosecution merely by paying a sum of money, a prosecutor may consider the corporation's willingness to make restitution and steps already taken to do so. A prosecutor may also consider other remedial actions, such as improving an existing compliance program or disciplining wrongdoers, in determining whether to charge the corporation and how to resolve corporate criminal cases.

Comment: In determining whether or not to prosecute a corporation, the government may consider whether the corporation has taken meaningful remedial measures. A corporation's response to misconduct says much about its willingness to ensure that such misconduct does not recur. Thus, corporations that fully recognize the seriousness of their misconduct and accept responsibility for it should be taking steps to implement the personnel, operational, and organizational changes necessary to establish an awareness among employees that criminal conduct will not be tolerated.

Among the factors prosecutors should consider and weigh are whether the corporation appropriately disciplined wrongdoers, once those employees are identified by the corporation as culpable for the misconduct. Employee discipline is a difficult task for many corporations because of the human element involved and sometimes because of the seniority of the employees concerned. Although corporations need to be fair to their employees, they must also be committed, at all levels of the corporation, to the highest standards of legal and ethical behavior. Effective internal discipline can be a powerful deterrent against improper behavior by a corporation's employees. Prosecutors should be satisfied that the corporation's focus is on the integrity and credibility of its remedial and disciplinary measures rather than on the protection of the wrongdoers.

In addition to employee discipline, two other factors used in evaluating a corporation's remedial efforts are restitution and reform. As with natural persons, the decision whether or not to prosecute should not depend upon the target's ability to pay restitution. A corporation's efforts to pay restitution even in advance of any court order is, however, evidence of its acceptance of responsibility and, consistent with the practices and policies of the appropriate Division of the Department entrusted with enforcing specific criminal laws, may be considered in determining whether to bring criminal charges. Similarly, although the inadequacy of a corporate compliance program is a factor to consider when deciding whether to charge a corporation, that corporation's quick recognition of the flaws in the program and its efforts to improve the program are also factors to consider as to appropriate disposition of a case.

[new August 2008]

9-28.1000 Collateral Consequences

General Principle: Prosecutors may consider the collateral consequences of a corporate criminal conviction or indictment in determining whether to charge the corporation with a criminal offense and how to resolve corporate criminal cases.

Comment: One of the factors in determining whether to charge a natural person or a corporation is whether the likely punishment is appropriate given the nature and seriousness of the crime. In the corporate context, prosecutors may take into account the possibly substantial consequences to a corporation's employees, investors, pensioners, and customers, many of whom may, depending on the size and nature of the corporation and their role in its operations, have played no role in the criminal conduct, have been unaware of it, or have been unable to prevent it. Prosecutors should also be aware of non-penal sanctions that may accompany a criminal charge, such as potential suspension or debarment from eligibility for government contracts or federally funded programs such as health care programs. Determining whether or not such non-penal sanctions are appropriate or required in a particular case is the responsibility of the relevant agency, and is a decision that will be made based on the applicable statutes, regulations, and policies.

Virtually every conviction of a corporation, like virtually every conviction of an individual, will have an impact on innocent third parties, and the mere existence of such an effect is not sufficient to preclude prosecution of the corporation. Therefore, in evaluating the relevance of collateral consequences, various factors already discussed, such as the pervasiveness of the criminal conduct and the adequacy of the corporation's compliance programs, should be considered in determining the weight to be given to this factor. For instance, the balance may tip in favor of prosecuting corporations in situations where the scope of the misconduct in a case is widespread and sustained within a corporate division (or spread throughout pockets of the corporate organization). In such cases, the possible unfairness of visiting punishment for the corporation's crimes upon shareholders may be of much less concern where those shareholders have substantially profited, even unknowingly, from widespread or pervasive criminal activity. Similarly, where the top layers of the corporation's management or the shareholders of a closely-held corporation were engaged in or aware of the wrongdoing, and the conduct at issue was accepted as a way of doing business for an extended period, debarment may be deemed not collateral, but a direct and entirely appropriate consequence of the corporation's wrongdoing.

On the other hand, where the collateral consequences of a corporate conviction for innocent third parties would be significant, it may be appropriate to consider a non-prosecution or deferred prosecution agreement with conditions designed, among other things, to promote compliance with applicable law and to prevent recidivism. Such agreements are a third option, besides a criminal indictment, on the one hand, and a declination, on the other. Declining prosecution may allow a corporate criminal to escape without consequences. Obtaining a conviction may produce a result that seriously harms innocent third parties who played no role in the criminal conduct. Under appropriate circumstances, a deferred prosecution or non-prosecution agreement can help restore the integrity of a company's operations and preserve the financial viability of a corporation that has engaged in criminal conduct, while preserving the government's ability to prosecute a recalcitrant corporation that materially breaches the agreement. Such agreements achieve other important objectives as well, like prompt restitution for victims.[*FN8*] Ultimately, the appropriateness of a criminal charge against a corporation, or some lesser alternative, must be evaluated in a pragmatic and reasoned way that produces a fair outcome, taking into consideration, among other things, the Department's need to promote and ensure respect for the law.

[new August 2008]

9-28.1100 Other Civil or Regulatory Alternatives

General Principle: Non-criminal alternatives to prosecution often exist and prosecutors may consider whether such sanctions would adequately deter, punish, and rehabilitate a corporation that has engaged in wrongful conduct. In evaluating the adequacy of non-criminal alternatives to prosecution—*e.g.*, civil or regulatory enforcement actions—the prosecutor may consider all relevant factors, including:

1. the sanctions available under the alternative means of disposition;
2. the likelihood that an effective sanction will be imposed; and
3. the effect of non-criminal disposition on federal law enforcement interests.

Comment: The primary goals of criminal law are deterrence, punishment, and rehabilitation. Non-criminal sanctions may not be an appropriate response to a serious violation, a pattern of wrongdoing, or prior non-criminal sanctions without proper remediation. In other cases, however, these goals may be satisfied through civil or regulatory actions. In determining whether a federal criminal resolution is appropriate, the prosecutor should consider the same factors (modified appropriately for the regulatory context) considered when determining whether to leave prosecution of a natural person to another jurisdiction or to seek non-criminal alternatives to prosecution. These factors include: the strength of the regulatory authority's interest; the regulatory authority's ability and willingness to take effective enforcement action; the probable sanction if the regulatory authority's enforcement action is upheld; and the effect of a non-criminal disposition on federal law enforcement interests. See USAM 9-27.240, 9-27.250.

[new August 2008]

9-28.1200 Selecting Charges

General Principle: Once a prosecutor has decided to charge a corporation, the prosecutor at least presumptively should charge, or should recommend that the grand jury charge, the most serious offense that is consistent with the nature of the defendant's misconduct and that is likely to result in a sustainable conviction.

Comment: Once the decision to charge is made, the same rules as govern charging natural persons apply. These rules require "a faithful and honest application of the Sentencing Guidelines" and an "individualized assessment of the extent to which particular charges fit the specific circumstances of the case, are consistent with the purposes of the Federal criminal code, and maximize the impact of Federal resources on crime." See USAM 9-27.300. In making this determination, "it is appropriate that the attorney for the government consider, *inter alia,* such factors as the [advisory] sentencing guideline range yielded by the charge, whether the penalty yielded by such sentencing range . . . is proportional to the seriousness of the defendant's conduct, and whether the charge achieves such purposes of the criminal law as punishment, protection of the public, specific and general deterrence, and rehabilitation." *Id.*

[new August 2008]

9-28.1300 Plea Agreements with Corporations

General Principle: In negotiating plea agreements with corporations, as with individuals, prosecutors should generally seek a plea to the most serious, readily provable offense charged. In addition, the terms of the plea agreement should contain appropriate provisions to ensure punishment, deterrence, rehabilitation, and compliance with the plea agreement in the corporate context. Although special circumstances may mandate a different conclusion, prosecutors generally should not agree to accept a corporate guilty plea in exchange for non-prosecution or dismissal of charges against individual officers and employees.

Comment: Prosecutors may enter into plea agreements with corporations for the same reasons and under the same constraints as apply to plea agreements with natural persons. See USAM 9-27.400-530. This means, *inter alia,* that the corporation should generally be required to plead guilty to the most serious, readily provable offense charged. In addition, any negotiated departures or recommended variances from the advisory Sentencing Guidelines must be justifiable under the Guidelines or 18 U.S.C. § 3553 and must be disclosed to the sentencing court. A corporation should be made to realize that pleading guilty to criminal charges constitutes an admission of guilt and not merely a resolution of an inconvenient distraction from its business. As with natural persons, pleas should be structured so that the corporation may not later "proclaim lack of culpability or even complete innocence." See USAM 9-27.420(b)(4),

9-27.440, 9-27.500. Thus, for instance, there should be placed upon the record a sufficient factual basis for the plea to prevent later corporate assertions of innocence.

A corporate plea agreement should also contain provisions that recognize the nature of the corporate "person" and that ensure that the principles of punishment, deterrence, and rehabilitation are met. In the corporate context, punishment and deterrence are generally accomplished by substantial fines, mandatory restitution, and institution of appropriate compliance measures, including, if necessary, continued judicial oversight or the use of special masters or *corporate monitors. See* USSG §§ 8B1.1, 8C2.1, *et seq.* In addition, where the corporation is a government contractor, permanent or temporary debarment may be appropriate. Where the corporation was engaged in fraud against the government (*e.g.*, contracting fraud), a prosecutor may not negotiate away an agency's right to debar or delist the corporate defendant.

In negotiating a plea agreement, prosecutors should also consider the deterrent value of prosecutions of individuals within the corporation. Therefore, one factor that a prosecutor may consider in determining whether to enter into a plea agreement is whether the corporation is seeking immunity for its employees and officers or whether the corporation is willing to cooperate in the investigation of culpable individuals as outlined herein. Prosecutors should rarely negotiate away individual criminal liability in a corporate plea.

Rehabilitation, of course, requires that the corporation undertake to be law-abiding in the future. It is, therefore, appropriate to require the corporation, as a condition of probation, to implement a compliance program or to reform an existing one. As discussed above, prosecutors may consult with the appropriate state and federal agencies and components of the Justice Department to ensure that a proposed compliance program is adequate and meets industry standards and best practices. See USAM 9-28.800.

In plea agreements in which the corporation agrees to cooperate, the prosecutor should ensure that the cooperation is entirely truthful. To do so, the prosecutor may request that the corporation make appropriate disclosures of relevant factual information and documents, make employees and agents available for debriefing, file appropriate certified financial statements, agree to governmental or third-party audits, and take whatever other steps are necessary to ensure that the full scope of the corporate wrongdoing is disclosed and that the responsible personnel are identified and, if appropriate, prosecuted. See generally USAM 9-28.700. In taking such steps, Department prosecutors should recognize that attorney-client communications are often essential to a corporation's efforts to comply with complex regulatory and legal regimes, and that, as discussed at length above, cooperation is not measured by the waiver of attorney-client privilege and work product protection, but rather is measured by the disclosure of facts and other considerations identified herein such as making witnesses available for interviews and assisting in the interpretation of complex documents or business records.

These Principles provide only internal Department of Justice guidance. They are not intended to, do not, and may not be relied upon to create any rights, substantive or procedural, enforceable at law by any party in any matter civil or criminal. Nor are any limitations hereby placed on otherwise lawful litigative prerogatives of the Department of Justice.

[new August 2008]

FN 1. While these guidelines refer to corporations, they apply to the consideration of the prosecution of all types of business organizations, including partnerships, sole proprietorships, government entities, and unincorporated associations.

FN 2. There are other dimensions of cooperation beyond the mere disclosure of facts, of course. These can include, for example, providing non-privileged documents and other evidence, making witnesses available for interviews, and assisting in the interpretation of complex business records. This section of the Principles focuses solely on the disclosure of facts and the privilege issues that may be implicated thereby.

FN 3. By way of example, corporate personnel are typically interviewed during an internal investigation. If the interviews are conducted by counsel for the corporation, certain notes and memoranda generated from the interviews may be subject, at least in part, to the protections of attorney-client privilege and/or attorney work product. To receive cooperation credit for providing factual information, the corporation need not produce, and prosecutors may not request, protected notes or memoranda generated by the lawyers' interviews. To earn such credit, however, the corporation does need to produce, and prosecutors may request, relevant factual information—including relevant factual information acquired through those interviews, unless the identical information has otherwise been provided—as well as relevant non-privileged evidence such as accounting and business records and emails between non-attorney employees or agents.

FN 4. In assessing the timeliness of a corporation's disclosures, prosecutors should apply a standard of reasonableness in light of the totality of circumstances.

FN 5. These privileged communications are not necessarily limited to those that occur contemporaneously with the underlying misconduct. They would include, for instance, legal advice provided by corporate counsel in an internal investigation report. Again, the key measure of cooperation is the disclosure of factual information known to the corporation, not the disclosure of legal advice or theories rendered in connection with the conduct at issue (subject to the two exceptions noted in USAM 9-28.720(b)(i-ii)).

FN 6. Routine questions regarding the representation status of a corporation and its employees, including how and by whom attorneys' fees are paid, sometimes arise in the course of an investigation under certain circumstances—to take one example, to assess conflict-of-interest issues. Such questions can be appropriate and this guidance is not intended to prohibit such limited inquiries.

FN 7. For a detailed review of these and other factors concerning corporate compliance programs, see USSG § 8B2.1.

FN 8. Prosecutors should note that in the case of national or multi-national corporations, multi-district or global agreements may be necessary. Such agreements may only be entered into with the approval of each affected district or the appropriate Department official. See USAM 9-27.641.

Appendix D

MORFORD MEMO

U.S. Department of Justice

Office of the Deputy Attorney General

The Deputy Attorney General

Washington, D.C. 20530

March 7, 2008

MEMORANDUM FOR HEADS OF DEPARTMENT COMPONENTS
UNITED STATES ATTORNEYS

FROM: Craig S. Morford CSM
Acting Deputy Attorney General

SUBJECT: Selection and Use of Monitors in Deferred Prosecution Agreements and Non-Prosecution Agreements with Corporations[1]

I. INTRODUCTION

The Department of Justice's commitment to deterring and preventing corporate crime remains a high priority. The Principles of Federal Prosecution of Business Organizations set forth guidance to federal prosecutors regarding charges against corporations. A careful consideration of those principles and the facts in a given case may result in a decision to negotiate an agreement to resolve a criminal case against a corporation without a formal conviction – either a deferred prosecution agreement or a non-prosecution agreement.[2] As part of some negotiated corporate agreements, there have been provisions pertaining to an independent corporate monitor.[3] The corporation benefits from expertise in the area of corporate compliance

[1] As used in these Principles, the terms "corporate" and "corporation" refer to all types of business organizations, including partnerships, sole proprietorships, government entities, and unincorporated associations.

[2] The terms "deferred prosecution agreement" and "non-prosecution agreement" have often been used loosely by prosecutors, defense counsel, courts and commentators. As the terms are used in these Principles, a deferred prosecution agreement is typically predicated upon the filing of a formal charging document by the government, and the agreement is filed with the appropriate court. In the non-prosecution agreement context, formal charges are not filed and the agreement is maintained by the parties rather than being filed with a court. Clear and consistent use of these terms will enable the Department to more effectively identify and share best practices and to track the use of such agreements. These Principles do not apply to plea agreements, which involve the formal conviction of a corporation in a court proceeding.

[3] Agreements use a variety of terms to describe the role referred to herein as "monitor," including consultants, experts, and others.

from an independent third party. The corporation, its shareholders, employees and the public at large then benefit from reduced recidivism of corporate crime and the protection of the integrity of the marketplace.

The purpose of this memorandum is to present a series of principles for drafting provisions pertaining to the use of monitors in connection with deferred prosecution and non-prosecution agreements (hereafter referred to collectively as "agreements") with corporations.[4] Given the varying facts and circumstances of each case – where different industries, corporate size and structure, and other considerations may be at issue – any guidance regarding monitors must be practical and flexible. This guidance is limited to monitors, and does not apply to third parties, whatever their titles, retained to act as receivers, trustees, or perform other functions.

A monitor's primary responsibility is to assess and monitor a corporation's compliance with the terms of the agreement specifically designed to address and reduce the risk of recurrence of the corporation's misconduct, and not to further punitive goals. A monitor should only be used where appropriate given the facts and circumstances of a particular matter. For example, it may be appropriate to use a monitor where a company does not have an effective internal compliance program, or where it needs to establish necessary internal controls. Conversely, in a situation where a company has ceased operations in the area where the criminal misconduct occurred, a monitor may not be necessary.

In negotiating agreements with corporations, prosecutors should be mindful of both: (1) the potential benefits that employing a monitor may have for the corporation and the public, and (2) the cost of a monitor and its impact on the operations of a corporation. Prosecutors shall, at a minimum, notify the appropriate United States Attorney or Department Component Head prior to the execution of an agreement that includes a corporate monitor. The appropriate United States Attorney or Department Component Head shall, in turn, provide a copy of the agreement to the Assistant Attorney General for the Criminal Division at a reasonable time after it has been executed. The Assistant Attorney General for the Criminal Division shall maintain a record of all such agreements.

This memorandum does not address all provisions concerning monitors that have been included or could appropriately be included in agreements. Rather this memorandum sets forth nine basic principles in the areas of selection, scope of duties, and duration.

This memorandum provides only internal Department of Justice guidance. In addition, this memorandum applies only to criminal matters and does not apply to agencies other than the

---

[4] In the case of deferred prosecution agreements filed with a court, these Principles must be applied with due regard for the appropriate role of the court and/or the probation office.

Department of Justice. It is not intended to, does not, and may not be relied upon to create any rights, substantive or procedural, enforceable at law by any party in any matter civil or criminal. Nor are any limitations hereby placed on otherwise lawful litigative prerogatives of the Department of Justice.

II. SELECTION

1. Principle: Before beginning the process of selecting a monitor in connection with deferred prosecution agreements and non-prosecution agreements, the corporation and the Government should discuss the necessary qualifications for a monitor based on the facts and circumstances of the case. The monitor must be selected based on the merits. The selection process must, at a minimum, be designed to: (1) select a highly qualified and respected person or entity based on suitability for the assignment and all of the circumstances; (2) avoid potential and actual conflicts of interests, and (3) otherwise instill public confidence by implementing the steps set forth in this Principle.

To avoid a conflict, first, Government attorneys who participate in the process of selecting a monitor shall be mindful of their obligation to comply with the conflict-of-interest guidelines set forth in 18 U.S.C. § 208 and 5 C.F.R. Part 2635. Second, the Government shall create a standing or *ad hoc* committee in the Department component or office where the case originated to consider monitor candidates. United States Attorneys and Assistant Attorneys General may not make, accept, or veto the selection of monitor candidates unilaterally. Third, the Office of the Deputy Attorney General must approve the monitor. Fourth, the Government should decline to accept a monitor if he or she has an interest in, or relationship with, the corporation or its employees, officers or directors that would cause a reasonable person to question the monitor's impartiality. Finally, the Government should obtain a commitment from the corporation that it will not employ or be affiliated with the monitor for a period of not less than one year from the date the monitorship is terminated.

Comment: Because a monitor's role may vary based on the facts of each case and the entity involved, there is no one method of selection that should necessarily be used in every instance. For example, the corporation may select a monitor candidate, with the Government reserving the right to veto the proposed choice if the monitor is unacceptable. In other cases, the facts may require the Government to play a greater role in selecting the monitor. Whatever method is used, the Government should determine what selection process is most effective as early in the negotiations as possible, and endeavor to ensure that the process is designed to produce a high-quality and conflict-free monitor and to instill public confidence. If the Government determines that participation in the selection process by any Government personnel creates, or appears to create, a potential or actual conflict in violation of 18 U.S.C. § 208 and 5

C.F.R. Part 2635, the Government must proceed as in other matters where recusal issues arise. In all cases, the Government must submit the proposed monitor to the Office of the Deputy Attorney General for review and approval before the monitorship is established.

Ordinarily, the Government and the corporation should discuss what role the monitor will play and what qualities, expertise, and skills the monitor should have. While attorneys, including but not limited to former Government attorneys, may have certain skills that qualify them to function effectively as a monitor, other individuals, such as accountants, technical or scientific experts, and compliance experts, may have skills that are more appropriate to the tasks contemplated in a given agreement.

Subsequent employment or retention of the monitor by the corporation after the monitorship period concludes may raise concerns about both the appearance of a conflict of interest and the effectiveness of the monitor during the monitorship, particularly with regard to the disclosure of possible new misconduct. Such employment includes both direct and indirect, or subcontracted, relationships.

Each United States Attorney's Office and Department component shall create a standing or *ad hoc* committee ("Committee") of prosecutors to consider the selection or veto, as appropriate, of monitor candidates. The Committee should, at a minimum, include the office ethics advisor, the Criminal Chief of the United States Attorney's Office or relevant Section Chief of the Department component, and at least one other experienced prosecutor.

Where practicable, the corporation, the Government, or both parties, depending on the selection process being used, should consider a pool of at least three qualified monitor candidates. Where the selection process calls for the corporation to choose the monitor at the outset, the corporation should submit its choice from among the pool of candidates to the Government. Where the selection process calls for the Government to play a greater role in selecting the monitor, the Government should, where practicable, identify at least three acceptable monitors from the pool of candidates, and the corporation shall choose from that list.

III. SCOPE OF DUTIES

A. INDEPENDENCE

2. Principle: A monitor is an independent third-party, not an employee or agent of the corporation or of the Government.

Comment: A monitor by definition is distinct and independent from the directors, officers, employees, and other representatives of the corporation. The monitor is not the corporation's attorney. Accordingly, the corporation may not seek to obtain or obtain legal advice from the monitor. Conversely, a monitor also is not an agent or employee of the Government.

While a monitor is independent both from the corporation and the Government, there should be open dialogue among the corporation, the Government and the monitor throughout the duration of the agreement.

B. MONITORING COMPLIANCE WITH THE AGREEMENT

3. Principle: A monitor's primary responsibility should be to assess and monitor a corporation's compliance with those terms of the agreement that are specifically designed to address and reduce the risk of recurrence of the corporation's misconduct, including, in most cases, evaluating (and where appropriate proposing) internal controls and corporate ethics and compliance programs.

Comment: At the corporate level, there may be a variety of causes of criminal misconduct, including but not limited to the failure of internal controls or ethics and compliance programs to prevent, detect, and respond to such misconduct. A monitor's primary role is to evaluate whether a corporation has both adopted and effectively implemented ethics and compliance programs to address and reduce the risk of recurrence of the corporation's misconduct. A well-designed ethics and compliance program that is not effectively implemented will fail to lower the risk of recidivism.

A monitor is not responsible to the corporation's shareholders. Therefore, from a corporate governance standpoint, responsibility for designing an ethics and compliance program that will prevent misconduct should remain with the corporation, subject to the monitor's input, evaluation and recommendations.

4. Principle: In carrying out his or her duties, a monitor will often need to understand the full scope of the corporation's misconduct covered by the agreement, but the monitor's responsibilities should be no broader than necessary to address and reduce the risk of recurrence of the corporation's misconduct.

Comment: The scope of a monitor's duties should be tailored to the facts of each case to address and reduce the risk of recurrence of the corporation's misconduct. Among other things, focusing the monitor's duties on these tasks may serve to calibrate the expense of the monitorship to the failure that gave rise to the misconduct the agreement covers.

Neither the corporation nor the public benefits from employing a monitor whose role is too narrowly defined (and, therefore, prevents the monitor from effectively evaluating the reforms intended by the parties) or too broadly defined (and, therefore, results in the monitor engaging in activities that fail to facilitate the corporation's implementation of the reforms intended by the parties).

The monitor's mandate is not to investigate historical misconduct. Nevertheless, in appropriate circumstances, an understanding of historical misconduct may inform a monitor's evaluation of the effectiveness of the corporation's compliance with the agreement.

C. COMMUNICATIONS AND RECOMMENDATIONS BY THE MONITOR

5. Principle: Communication among the Government, the corporation and the monitor is in the interest of all the parties. Depending on the facts and circumstances, it may be appropriate for the monitor to make periodic written reports to both the Government and the corporation.

Comment: A monitor generally works closely with a corporation and communicates with a corporation on a regular basis in the course of his or her duties. The monitor must also have the discretion to communicate with the Government as he or she deems appropriate. For example, a monitor should be free to discuss with the Government the progress of, as well as issues arising from, the drafting and implementation of an ethics and compliance program. Depending on the facts and circumstances, it may be appropriate for the monitor to make periodic written reports to both the Government and the corporation regarding, among other things: (1) the monitor's activities; (2) whether the corporation is complying with the terms of the agreement; and (3) any changes that are necessary to foster the corporation's compliance with the terms of the agreement.

6. Principle: If the corporation chooses not to adopt recommendations made by the monitor within a reasonable time, either the monitor or the corporation, or both, should report that fact to the Government, along with the corporation's reasons. The Government may consider this conduct when evaluating whether the corporation has fulfilled its obligations under the agreement.

Comment: The corporation and its officers and directors are ultimately responsible for the ethical and legal operations of the corporation. Therefore, the corporation should evaluate whether to adopt recommendations made by the monitor. If the corporation declines to adopt a recommendation by the monitor, the Government should consider both the monitor's recommendation and the corporation's reasons in determining whether the corporation is complying with the agreement. A flexible timetable should be established to ensure that both a monitor's recommendations and the corporation's decision to adopt or reject them are made well before the expiration of the agreement.

D. REPORTING OF PREVIOUSLY UNDISCLOSED OR NEW MISCONDUCT

7. **Principle: The agreement should clearly identify any types of previously undisclosed or new misconduct that the monitor will be required to report directly to the Government. The agreement should also provide that as to evidence of other such misconduct, the monitor will have the discretion to report this misconduct to the Government or the corporation or both.**

Comment: As a general rule, timely and open communication between and among the corporation, the Government and the monitor regarding allegations of misconduct will facilitate the review of the misconduct and formulation of an appropriate response to it. The agreement may set forth certain types of previously undisclosed or new misconduct that the monitor will be required to report directly to the Government. Additionally, in some instances, the monitor should immediately report other such misconduct directly to the Government and not to the corporation. The presence of any of the following factors militates in favor of reporting such misconduct directly to the Government and not to the corporation, namely, where the misconduct: (1) poses a risk to public health or safety or the environment; (2) involves senior management of the corporation; (3) involves obstruction of justice; (4) involves criminal activity which the Government has the opportunity to investigate proactively and/or covertly; or (5) otherwise poses a substantial risk of harm. On the other hand, in instances where the allegations of such misconduct are not credible or involve actions of individuals outside the scope of the corporation's business, the monitor may decide, in the exercise of his or her discretion, that the allegations need not be reported directly to the Government.

IV. DURATION

8. **Principle: The duration of the agreement should be tailored to the problems that have been found to exist and the types of remedial measures needed for the monitor to satisfy his or her mandate.**

Comment: The following criteria should be considered when negotiating duration of the agreement (not necessarily in this order): (1) the nature and seriousness of the underlying misconduct; (2) the pervasiveness and duration of misconduct within the corporation, including the complicity or involvement of senior management; (3) the corporation's history of similar misconduct; (4) the nature of the corporate culture; (5) the scale and complexity of any remedial measures contemplated by the agreement, including the size of the entity or business unit at issue; and (6) the stage of design and implementation of remedial measures when the monitorship commences. It is reasonable to forecast that completing an assessment of more extensive and/or complex remedial measures will require a longer period of time than completing an assessment of less extensive and/or less complex ones. Similarly, it is reasonable to forecast that a monitor who is assigned responsibility to assess a compliance program that has not been designed or implemented may take longer to complete that assignment than one who is assigned responsibility to assess a compliance program that has already been designed and implemented.

9. **Principle: In most cases, an agreement should provide for an extension of the monitor provision(s) at the discretion of the Government in the event that the corporation has not successfully satisfied its obligations under the agreement. Conversely, in most cases, an agreement should provide for early termination if the corporation can demonstrate to the Government that there exists a change in circumstances sufficient to eliminate the need for a monitor.**

Comment: If the corporation has not satisfied its obligations under the terms of the agreement at the time the monitorship ends, the corresponding risk of recidivism will not have been reduced and an extension of the monitor provision(s) may be appropriate. On the other hand, there are a number of changes in circumstances that could justify early termination of an agreement. For example, if a corporation ceased operations in the area that was the subject of the agreement, a monitor may no longer be necessary. Similarly, if a corporation is purchased by or merges with another entity that has an effective ethics and compliance program, it may be prudent to terminate a monitorship.

APPENDIX **E**

FOREIGN CORRUPT PRACTICES ACT CASE STATISTICS (1978–2011)

Case Name	Date of Prosecution	Company	Brief Case Description	Notes
SEC v. Katy Industries (N.D. Ill. 1978)	1978 (SEC)		Katy Industries is an oil production company that bribed Indonesian officials through an off-shore corporation in the amount of $250K. The purpose of the bribes was to secure an oil and gas contract in Indonesia. Two Katy directors were issued permanent injunctions and Katy was required to establish an outside compliance review committee.	
SEC v. Page Airways (D.D.C. 1978)	1978 (SEC)		Page sells and services aircrafts and paid $2.5 million in bribes to six Asian and African countries including Gabon, Morocco, and Saudi Arabia to sell its aircrafts and products. Page consented to a permanent injunction and charges against six of its officers were dismissed.	charges dismissed against individuals

Case Name	Date of Prosecution	Company	Brief Case Description	Notes
U.S. v. Kenny Int'l Corp.	1979 (DOJ)	Kenny Int'l Corp.	Kenny paid bribes to Sir Albert Henry and The Cook Islands Party to ensure the renewal of a stamp distribution agreement, whereby Kenny obtained exclusive rights to the promotion, distribution and sale of Cook Islands postage stamps through the world. The company paid restitution of $337,000 and fined $50,000, and permanent injunction against further FCPA violations. The chairman was permanently enjoined; the company entered into a settlement agreement with the foreign government.	
U.S. v. Carver (S.D. Fla. 1979)	1979 (DOJ)	Holcar Oil Corp.	In order to secure an oil drilling concession, Carver and Holley (officers of Holcar) paid $1.5 million to a Emirate of Qatar. Carver and Holley consented to permanent injunctions.	
SEC v. International Systems & Controls (D.D.C. 1979)	1979 (SEC)	ISC is a Del. Corp. and an issuer.	ISC paid $23 million in bribes to foreign officials in nearly a dozen countries including Saudi Arabia and Iran to secure energy and forestry processing contracts. Two ISC officers consented to permanent injunctions.	
SEC v. Tesoro Petroleum Corp.	1980	Tesoro Petroleum Corp.	Tesoro made a bribery payment to the worldwide foreign government officials or political leaders to obtain foreign oil and gas concessions from foreign governments. The company consented to the entry of a permanent injunction and agreed to appoint a new director to keep accurate books and records.	
U.S. v. Ruston Gas Turbines Inc.	1982 (DOJ)	Ruston Gas Turbines Inc.	Ruston made a bribery payment to two sub-directors of Pemex to obtain purchase order from Pemex for turbine compression systems and related equipment for Ruston and CEI. The company was fined $750,000 and two managers were fined 5,000.	

Case Name	Date of Prosecution	Company	Brief Case Description	Notes
U.S. v. Appl. Process Products Overseas Inc.; U.S. v. Gary Bateman	1982 (DOJ & SEC)	Appl. Process Products Overseas Inc.	Applied paid a bribe to the Administrative Secretary of the Chief of Purchasing at Pemex and other Pemex officials in Mexico to obtain a contract from Pemex for compression-related equipment and spare parts. The company was issued a permanent injunction and paid $229,512 civil penalty, $300,000 civil tax payments, and $5000 prosecution costs.	
U.S. v. Crawford Enterprise, Inc.	1982 (DOJ)	Crawford Enterprise, Inc.	CEI made a bribery payment to two sub-directors of Pemex to obtain purchase orders from Pemex for turbine compression systems and related equipment. The company was fined $3,450,000 and was charged with conspiracy, aiding, and abetting. Eight management persons were charged with conspiracy, aiding, and abetting and paid fines.	
U.S. v. C.E. Miller Corp.; U.S. v. Marquis King	1982, 1983 (DOJ)	C.E. Miller Corp.	CEMCO paid a bribe to two sub-directors of Pemex, Mexico, to obtain purchase orders from Pemex for turbine compression systems and related equipment for CEMCO and CEI. The company was fined $20,000 and charged with aiding and abetting. Two managers were charged and received probation and community service.	
U.S. v. Int'l Harvester co, (S.D. Tex. 1982); U.S. v. McLean; McLean v. Int'l Harvester Co.	1982,1985, 1987 (DOJ)	Int'l Harvester Co.	Harvester made bribery payment to two officials of Pemex to obtain from Pemex purchase orders for turbine compression systems and related equipment for Solar and CEI. The company was fined $10,000 and paid $40,000 prosecution costs and charged with conspiracy to violate FCPA. Two managers were charged with conspiracy, aiding and abetting.	

Case Name	Date of Prosecution	Company	Brief Case Description	Notes
U.S. v. Wallace; Rodriguez (D.P.R. 1983)	1983 (DOJ & SEC)	Wallace Company	Wallace Company is a Texas construction firm. Wallace senior officers allegedly paid $1.391 million in bribes to the Trinidad and Tobago Racing Authority to obtain a contract to build the racetrack's grandstand. Wallace Company paid a $530K fine. Rodriguez (president of Wallace) received three years probation and a $10K fine. The SEC also brought actions against Wallace and Rodriguez.	cases #12 and #13 arise out of the same investigation
U.S. v. Sam P. Wallace Co.; U.S. v. Carpenter Environmental Tectonics Corp Int'l. v. W.W. Kirkpatrick & Co. Inc.	1983 (DOJ & SEC)	Sam P. Wallace Co. and Carpenter Environmental Tectionics Corp.	The companies were charged with CFTRA (fines, $500,000) and SEC action. The president was fined $10,000 and suspended; ordered to perform community service.	same case
U.S. v. Harry G. Carpenter and W.S. Kirkpatrick, Inc.; U.S. v. Carpenter	1985 (DOJ)	W.S. Kirkpatrick, Inc	Kirkpatrick made a bribery payment to various Nigerian political and military officials to obtain a $10.8 million contract from the Nigerian government to furnish equipment for an Aero Medical Center at Kaduna Air Force Base in Nigeria.	
U.S. v. Silicon Contractors Inc.	1985 (DOJ)	Silicon Contractors Inc.	Silicon made a bribery payment to Mexican officials to obtain the award of a certain contract to manufacture and install radiation and fire-stop penetration seals for a nuclear power plant in Laguna Verde, Mexico. The company was fined $150,000 and permanent injunction. Three officers were permanently enjoined.	
SEC v. Ashland Oil, Inc.; Howes v. Atkins; Williams v. Hall	1986, 1987, 1988	Ashland Oil, Inc.	Ashland made a bribe to the Omani government official to obtain crude oil contracts with the Oman Refining Company, an instrumentality of the government of Oman. The company and the chairman both consented to the entry of a permanent injunction.	
U.S. v. Goodyear Intl Corp	1989 (DOJ)	Goodyear Int'l Corp	Goodyear made a bribery payment to an official of the Iraqi Trading Company to influence the Iraqi government to buy its car and truck tires. The company was fined $250,000.	Listed in SEC Self-Reporting Document

Case Name	Date of Prosecution	Company	Brief Case Description	Notes
U.S. v. Joaquin Pou, Alfred G. Duran and Jose Guarsch	1989 (DOJ)	no corp. charged	Rober Gurin, president of a Florida company, made a bribery payment to Dominican Republic officials to secure the release of an airplane confiscated for use in drug trafficking. Gurin was charged with conspiracy to violate FCPA.	
U.S. v. Napco Int'l Inc. and Venturian Corp.; U.S. v. Liebo	1989, 1991 (DOJ & SEC)	Napco Inc. and Venturian Corp.	Venturian and Napco made a bribery payment to two officials of the Niger government to obtain certain Foreign Military Service contracts for spare parts and maintenance for C-130 military aircraft from the Niger Ministry of Defense. The company was fined $785,000 and $140,000 settlement of civil liability and $75,000 settlement of civil tax liability and one manager received a 1.5 years suspended sentence and 600 hrs community work.	cases #19 and #20 arise out of the same investigation
U.S. v. Dornier GmbH (D. Minn. 1990)	1990 (DOJ)	Napco	Dornier gave a 5% kickback ($175K) to a Nigerian official in exchange for securing a contract for military aircraft parts and maintenance. The firm received a permanent injunction against future FCPA violations.	same case
U.S. v. Harris Corp	1990 (DOJ)	Harris Corp	Harris made a bribery payment to a Colombian legislator to obtain the telecommunications contracts from the Empress Nacional de Telecommunications via a consultant and a local company. The company was granted a motion for judgment of acquittal.	dismissed
U.S. v. F.G. Mason Eng'g Inc. and Grancis G. Mason	1990 (DOJ)	F.G. Mason Eng'g Inc.	MEI made a bribery payment to a German official to get the business of TSCM equipment. The company was fined $75,000 and restituted $160,000 and was charged with conspiracy to violate FCPA. The president was fined $75,000 and charged with conspiracy for FCPA.	

Case Name	Date of Prosecution	Company	Brief Case Description	Notes
U.S. v. Morton; U.S. v. Blondek et al; U.S. v. Eagle Bus., U.S. v. Castle et al.	1990, 1991 (DOJ)	Eagle Bus Mfg. Co. of Greyhound Lines Inc.	Morton, the Canadian agent of Eagle, made a bribery payment to two Canadian managers of Saskatchewan Transp. Co. to ensure that Eagle's bid to sell eleven buses to the STC would be accepted. Eagle consented to entry of a permanent injunction under FCPA. Morton pled guilty for conspiracy to commit FCPA offense. Castle and Lowry dismissed. Blondek and Tull acquitted.	
U.S. v. Young & Rubicam Inc.; Abrahams v. Young & Rubicam Inc.	1990, 1994 (DOJ)	Young & Rubicam Inc.	Y&R made a bribe to an advisor of the Jamaica Tourist Board and the Jamaican Minister of Tourism to obtain an advertising account with the Jamaica Tourist Board. The company was fined $500,000 and charged with conspiracy, RICO violations, and 33 alleged racketeering acts.	
U.S. v. American Tolalisator (D. Md. 1993)	1993 (DOJ)		Unspecified amount of bribes to Greek officials to secure a contract for sale of racetrack parts. ATC consented to a permanent injunction for future FCPA violations.	
U.S. v. Vitusa Corp.; Us v. Herzberg	1993, 1994 (DOJ)	Vitusa corp.	Vitusa made a bribery payment to a Dominican Republic official to collect its outstanding debt of $163,000 from the government contract. The company was fined with $20,000 and owner was fined $5,000.	
U.S. v. Steindler et al.	1994 (DOJ & SEC)	GE and National Airmotive Corp.	GE made a bribery payment to an Israelis Air Force officer to get the contract of $300 million via an Israeli attorney. GE was fined $69,000 in criminal and civil penalties and NA was fined $1.25 million, criminal penalties and $1.75 million, civil fines. Managers of two companies were charged with conspiracy, wire fraud, ML, mail fraud.	

Case Name	Date of Prosecution	Company	Brief Case Description	Notes
U.S. v. Lockheed Corp.; U.S. v. Love; U.S. v. Nassar	1994 (DOJ & SEC)	Lockheed Corp.	Lockheed made bribery payment through its Egyptian consultant to get the contract of $79 million for three aircraft. The company was fined $21.8 million and paid $3 million settlement. Two managers were sentenced to 1.5 years imprisonment and fined $20,000, respectively.	
U.S. v. Montedison, S.P.A.	1996	Montedison, S.P.A.	Montedison made a bribe to Italian politicians through a Rome real estate developer to ensure political backing to either change the terms of a contract or overturn the decision of a judge. The company was charged with committing financial fraud by falsifying documents to artificially inflate the company's financial statements as well as the corporate reporting. The company entered a settlement and agreed to pay a civil penalty of $3,000,000.	
SEC v. Triton Energy Corp.	1997	Triton Energy Corp.	Triton made a bribery payment to various officials of the Indonesian government to obtain favorable decisions from tax auditors, tax refund from the government and receive a favorable decision to revise rates paid under pipeline tariff. The company consented to an injunction and paid a $300,000 penalty.	
U.S. v. Saybolt North America Inc. U.S. v. Saybolt Inc.; U.S. v. David H. Mead, U.S. v. Frerik Pluimers	1998	Saybolt International (oil refinery company) http://www.saybolt.com/ index.htm		

Case Name	Date of Prosecution	Company	Brief Case Description	Notes
U.S. v. Herbert Tannebaum	1998 (DOJ)	Tanner Management Corp., no corp. charged	The company made bribery payment to obtain a contract for sale of a garbage incinerator to the government of Argentina. The president was fined $15,000 and charged with conspiracy to violate FCPA.	
U.S. v. Control Systems Specialist Inc.; U.S. v. Darrold Richard Cities	1998 (DOJ)	Control Systems Specialist Inc.	Richard made payment to BAF/Lt. Col. Z to obtain a contract for the company to sell surplus U.S. military equipment, including two gas turbine power units, to the BAC. The company was fined $1,500 and the president was fined $50 and sentenced to community service.	
U.S. v. Metcalf & Eddy (D. Ma. 1999)	1999 (DOJ)		Metcalf and Eddy gave travel advances and accommodation upgrades to Egyptian officials to enhance their bid for an architectural and engineering contract. The defendants paid $400K in fines and paid $50K towards the costs of the investigation in addition to agreeing to outside monitoring of their compliance.	
U.S. v. Int'l Material Solutions Corp. and Donald K. Qualey	1999 (DOJ)	Int'l Material Solutions Corp.	IMS paid $67,563 to Lt. Col. in the Brazilian Air Force to get the approval of a bid to sell ten forklift trucks. The company was fined $500 and the president was fined $2,500 and sentenced to three years probation, four months home confinement, and 150 hrs. community service.	
SEC v. International Business Machine Corp.	2000	IBM	IBM paid a bribe to several directors of Banco de La Nation Argentina to obtain awarding of the systems integration contract to IBM Argentina. The company was charged with violation of the FCPA accounting provisions and fined a civil penalty of $300,000.	

Case Name	Date of Prosecution	Company	Brief Case Description	Notes
SEC v. American Bank Note Holographics, Inc.	2001	American Bank Note Holographics (secure document identification products) http://www.abnh.com/	Former Chairman of the Board and Chief Executive Officer, as well as the former president of American Bank Note Holographics, Inc. ("ABNH") authorized ABNH to make a $239,000 payment to a foreign bank account for the benefit of one or more officials from a foreign government. ABNH then improperly accounted for this payment on its books and records as a consulting fee. The $239,000 payment comprised 40% of the contract's value and constituted an additional payment ABHN made to obtain business with the Saudi government.	Cases #37 and #38 arise out of the same investigation; SEC settled the case in 2001. American Bank Note Holographics, Inc. "consented to pay a $75,000 penalty in a separate federal court action relating specifically to ABNH's violation of Section 30A of the Exchange Act. At the same time, the Department of Justice announced criminal actions against former officers of ABNH, charging violations of the anti-bribery provisions, among other things." http://www.usdoj.gov/criminal/fraud/fcpa/append/ix/appendixb.pdf
U.S.. v. Cantor	2001 (DOJ)	ABNH	Cantor paid kickbacks, $239,000, for Saudi Arabian government officials to obtain the contract to produce holograms for Saudi Arabia. The managers' cases were pending.	Same case; United States v. Joshua Cantor (No. 01 Cr. 687) S.D.N.Y. 2001 "Defendant pled to conspiracy to violate the FCPA and various securities fraud charges. Sentencing is pending. Related SEC complaints and orders filed against American Banknote Holographics Inc., Cantor, and Morris Weissman" (see SEC Litigation Release 17068A). http://www.usdoj.gov/criminal/fraud/fcpa/append/appendixa.html

Case Name	Date of Prosecution	Company	Brief Case Description	Notes
U.S. v. Daniel Ray Rothrock	2001 (DOJ)	Allied Products Corp., no corp. charged	Daniel paid bribery payment to obtain sales contracts of work-over oil rigs. The vice president paid $100 for special assessment.	U.S. v. Daniel Ray Rothrock (No. SA01CR343OG), W.D. Tex. 2001. "In connection with authorizing the payment and entry on Allied Product's books of a false invoice to cover payments in Russia, the defendant agreed to plead guilty to a violation of the FCPA's books and records provision. Sentencing is pending." http://www.usdoj.gov/criminal/fraud/fcpa/append/appendixa.html
U.S. v. R.K. Halford; U.S. v. A.F. Feitz; U.S. v. P.B. Hernandez	2001 (DOJ)	Owl Securities and Investment Ltd., no corp. charged	OSI officials paid bribery payment to obtain favorable changes to Costa Rican law and regulations. Four officers were charged with violation to FCPA or Travel Act and the case is pending.	All of the accused were indicted by the U.S. Attorney for the Western District of MO in June 2001. No final resolution has yet been reached. http://www.fcpaenforcement.com/documents/document_detail.asp?ID=753&PAGE=2

Case Name	Date of Prosecution	Company	Brief Case Description	Notes
SEC v. KPMG-SSH; SEC v. Eric L. Mattson and James W. Harris	2001 (SEC)	KPMG	KPMG made a bribe to Indonesian tax official to reduce tax assessment for PT Eastman Christensen (PTEC) for the amount of $2.93 million. KPMG-SSH was joint civil injunctive action by the SEC and DOJ.	In the matter of Baker Hughes Inc. The first joint civil injunction action by SEC and DOJ. "In a joint complaint, the SEC & DOJ charged the defendants with violations of the FCPA. Without admitting or denying the allegations, the defendants consented to the entry of a Final Judgment that enjoined them from violating the antibribery and books and records provisions of the FCPA. See SEC Litigation Release 17127. For related SEC actions against Baker Hughes and two of its executives, see SEC Litigation Release 17126 and Administrative Action No. 3-10572." http://www.usdoj.gov/criminal/fraud/fcpa/append/appendixa.html
U.S. v. David Kay	2001-02 (DOJ & SEC)	American Rice, Inc. (rice) http://www.amrice.com/8-0.cfm	ARI has a Haitian subsidiary engaged in the import of rice to Haiti. The officials manipulated false shipping documents reducing the amount of customs duties and sales taxes due to Haitian authorities. Two managers' charges were dismissed on legal grounds.	Cases #42 and #43 arise out of the same investigation; January 10, 2008: In a remanded case, defendants were convicted in the United States District Court for the Southern District of Texas of violating the Foreign Corrupt Practices Act (FCPA). Their convictions were affirmed on appeal, and defendants filed a petition for a rehearing en banc. The petition for a rehearing was denied.

Case Name	Date of Prosecution	Company	Brief Case Description	Notes
SEC v. Douglas A. Murphy (S.D. Tex. 2002)	2002	American Rice, Inc. (rice) http://www.amrice.com/8-0.cfm	American Rice executives made approximately $500,000 in bribery payments to Haitian customs officials to reduce customs and duties taxes owed by the company. Joseph Schwartz (controller for Haiti operations), Joel Malebranche (customs clearance monitor), and Allen Sturdivant (preparer of shipping documents) were implicated in the improper payment scheme. Joseph A. Schwartz, Joel R. Malebranche, and Allen W. Sturdivant paid $1.5 million in improper payments to illegally reduce ARI's tax liability. In addition, the three defendants engaged in at least 12 separate bribe transactions with Haitian officials totaling $500,000. The purpose of the improper payments and bribes was to reduce the import taxes on ARI's rice shipments into Haiti. There were at least 12 $500,000 to Haitian officials. Schwartz, the controller for ARI Haiti, made false entries to cover the bribery payments in business expenditure account. Note: the bribes were authorized by Mr. Kay, who was indicted in 2004 in parallel proceedings (see Kay & Murphy brief).	2 individual cases dismissed.
U.S. v. Syncor (C.D. Cal. 2002); SEC v. Syncor	2002 (DOJ & SEC)	Syncor International (medical devices and pharmaceuticals) http://www.sec.gov/litigation/litreleases/lr17887.htm	Syncor paid $600K in bribes to Taiwanese officials to entice the government officials to retain Syncors medical services. Syncor agreed to pay a $2 million criminal fine in conjunction with the FCPA violation. In conjunction with the SEC action, Syncor agreed to pay a $500K fine and hire an outside consultant to monitor its compliance programs.	Cases #44 and #49 arise out of the same investigation; SEC came to a final judgment in February 2003 (2003 U.S. Dist. LEXIS 27742).
U.S. v. Pitchford (D.D.C. 2002)	2002 (DOJ)	Central Asia American Enterprise Fund (former U.S. vice-presidential fund)	Pitchford allegedly paid $400K in bribes to Turkmenistan officials to assist in efforts of obtaining CAAEF contracts totaling approximately $6 million. Pitchford also negotiated to allow several foreign nationals to buy Turkmenistanian goods at inflated prices. Pitchford pled guilty, was sentenced to one year and one day in prison, a $400K fine, 200 hours community service, and forfeiture of $142K and a luxury yacht.	

Case Name	Date of Prosecution	Company	Brief Case Description	Notes
U.S. v. Sengupta; Basu (D.D.C. 2002)	2002 (DOJ)		Sengupta and Basu were task managers for World Bank projects. They allegedly paid out $127K in bribes to secure three contracts for World Bank development projects. Both defendants pled guilty. Sengupta was sentenced to two months in prison and a $6K fine. Basu subsequently withdrew his guilty plea in May 2006.	
In the Matter of Chiquita Brands International, Inc.; SEC v. Chiquita Brands International, Inc. (D.D.C.)	2002 (SEC)	Chiquita Brands International, Inc. (food company) http://www.chiquita.com/	Banadex's chief administrative officer authorized the payment of the equivalent of approximately $30,000 to local officials to secure renewal of a license allowing Banadex to hold goods for customs inspection or "naturalization" at its Turbo, Colombia port facility. Payments were made without the knowledge or consent of any employees within the United States. Banadex is a subsidiary of Chiquita Brands in Colombia. Note: The FCPA record keeping and accounting provisions, not the antibribery provisions, were actually at issue in Chiquita. In order to maintain Turbo port facility, which is owned and operated by Banadex, licensed where goods could be stored pending inspection by custom officials; in 1995 and 1996 Banadex's chief administrative officer authorized a CEA agent—a Colombian entity licensed by the Colombian government to act as intermediary between corporations and Colombian customs officials—to make a $30,000 payment paid in two installments for renewal of license. Both payments were paid from a Banadex account used for discretionary expenses. The payments were incorrectly identified and recorded as an $18,000 maritime donation for the first payment and as a maritime agreement for the remainder in order to conceal payments. During an internal audit performed by Chiquita's internal staff, management was made aware of a number of instances in which Banadex had not provided documentation required by Chiquita's internal accounting control procedures regarding discretionary expenses.	In another DOJ action, Chiquita pled guilty in 2007 to supporting the terrorist organization in Columbia, Autodefensas Unidas de Colombia, and agreed to a $25 million fine. http://www .bis.doc.gov/news/2007/doj03_19_07.htm

Case Name	Date of Prosecution	Company	Brief Case Description	Notes
SEC v. Bellsouth Corp. (N.D. Ga. 2002)	2002 (SEC)	Bellsouth (telephone services) http://www.bellsouth.com/	In 1997 Bellsouth acquired a majority interest in Telcel of Venezuela and 49% ownership interest in Telefonia of Nicaragua, with an option granted by members of a Nicaraguan family to acquire an additional 40%. Bellsouth option could not be exercised due to a Nicaraguan law that prohibited foreign companies from acquiring a majority interest in Nicaraguan telecommunications companies. Telcel senior management authorized illegal payments to six offshore companies and in 1998 Telefonia retained the wife of the chairman of the Nicaraguan legislative committee to lobby for repeal of the foreign ownership law. Between 1997 and 2000 former Telcel senior management authorized improper payments totaling approximately $10.8 million to six offshore companies and recorded the disbursements in its books and records based on fictitious invoices that made it look as if payment had been provided for professional, computer and contracting services. NOTE: The complaint does not mention bribes or kickbacks explicitly. In 1997 Bellsouth also acquired 49% ownership interest in Telefonia of Nicaragua with an option to acquire an additional 40%; however, Nicaraguan law prevented Bellsouth from exercising this option. In connection with the acquisition Bellsouth's wholly-owned subsidiary Bellsouth International, Inc. obtained operational control of the company. Telefonia then retained the wife of the chairman of the Nicaraguan legislative committee and paid her $6,500 a month so that she would lobby for repeal of the foreign ownership law. In May 1999 Telefonia terminated the lobbyist and recorded the total sum of $60,000 paid to her as consulting services and as a severance payment. In 1999 the committee voted to repeal the restriction and Bellsouth increased its ownership in Telefonia to 89% in 2000.	The SEC settled the case in 2002 with a cease and desist order. http://www.sec.gov/litigation/litreleases/lr17310.htm

Case Name	Date of Prosecution	Company	Brief Case Description	Notes
Syncor	2002 (SEC)	Syncor International (medical devices and pharmaceuticals) http://www.sec.gov/litigation/litreleases/lr17887.htm	Monty Fu, a U.S. resident and former chairman and chief executive officer of Syncor, was charged in connection with improper payments made between 1985 and 2002. The improper payments were made by Syncor's subsidiary in Taiwan (Syncor Taiwan) to physicians employed by state-owned and state-controlled hospitals. Syncor, through Syncor Taiwan, paid commissions and referral fees to doctors employed by private and public hospitals in Taiwan. These improper payments were made for the purpose of influencing the doctors' decisions to purchase Syncor products and refer patients to Syncor Taiwan's medical imaging centers. Syncor Taiwan improperly recorded the payments in its accounting books and records as "Advertising and Promotions" expenses. Fu was Syncor's founder and at times Syncor's CEO and Chairman of Syncor's board of directors. Fu had the authority to maintain compliance with existing internal controls and to implement additional internal controls to comply with FCPA's books and records and internal controls provisions, yet failed to do so.	Same case; the SEC settled both actions in 2002 by administering a $500,000 civil penalty and a cease and desist order. Syncor's cooperation with the DOJ investigation was a major factor in the SEC leniency. http://www.sec.gov/litigation/litreleases/lr17887.htm
U.S. v. Giffen & Williams (S.D.N.Y. 2003)	2003 (DOJ)	Mercator (airline services) http://www.mercator.com/home/ default.aspx	Giffen was the chairman of Mercator and Williams was a former executive for Mobile Oil. The two negotiated millions of dollars (in excess of $2 million) in kickbacks for Kazakhstanian officials in conjunction with oil rights. Giffen's new trial date has yet to be set. Williams pled guilty to conspiracy and tax evasion and was sentenced to 46 months in prison and a $25K fine. Williams also had to pay taxes on the $2 million kickback he received.	In December 2006, Giffen's appeal was dismissed due to lack of jurisdiction. U.S. v. Giffen, 473 F.3d 30 (2d Cir. 2006)

Case Name	Date of Prosecution	Company	Brief Case Description	Notes
U.S. v. Bodmer (S.D.N.Y. 2003)	2003 (DOJ)	Oily Rock Group	Bodmer was an executive of an Oily Rock subsidiary and served as legal counsel. The five co-conspirators paid out millions in direct bribes, promises of profits, luxury items, and lavish trips to Azerbaijan officials. The purpose of these payments was to obtain a controlling interest in the privatization of the SOCAR. Bodmer's lawyers prevailed on the motion to dismiss. However, Bodmer did later plead guilty to money laundering.	Cases nos. 51–54 arise out of the same investigation
U.S. v. Omega Advisors (S.D.N.Y. 2003)	2003 (DOJ)	Oily Rock Group	Omega advisers were involved with an Oily Rock subsidiary. The five co-conspirators paid out millions in direct bribes, promises of profits, luxury items, and lavish trips to Azerbaijan officials. The purpose of these payments was to obtain a controlling interest in the privatization of the SOCAR. Omega signed a non-prosecution agreement and agreed to forfeit $500K in profits and continue to cooperate with the investigating authorities in the U.S. and abroad.	Same case; in July 2007, Omega reached a settlement with the DOJ that the firm would pay a $500K penalty, would pay the tax penalties the firm had incurred, and would continue to cooperate with the investigation. The DOJ offered Omega a non-prosecution agreement. skaddenpractices.skadden.com/fcpa//attach.php?uploadFileID=8 -
U.S. v. Clayton Lewis (S.D.N.Y. 2003)	2003 (DOJ)	Oily Rock Group	Lewis was an executive of an Oily Rock subsidiary. The five co-conspirators paid out millions in direct bribes, promises of profits, luxury items, and lavish trips to Azerbaijan officials. The purpose of these payments was to obtain a controlling interest in the privatization of the SOCAR.	Same case; Lewis plead guilty to all charges under the FCPA and as of July 7, 2007 was awaiting sentencing. skaddenpractices.skadden.com/fcpa//attach.php?uploadFileID=8

Case Name	Date of Prosecution	Company	Brief Case Description	Notes
U.S. v. Thomas Farrell (S.D.N.Y. 2003)	2003 (DOJ)	Oily Rock Group	Farrell was an executive of an Oily Rock subsidiary. The five co-conspirators paid out millions in direct bribes, promises of profits, luxury items, and lavish trips to Azerbaijan officials. The purpose of these payments was to obtain a controlling interest in the privatization of the SOCAR. Farrell pled guilty to conspiracy charges and was sentenced in 2004 (no information was given as to the length of his sentence).	Same case. Three individual defendants dismissed. (SDNY 2005).
U.S. v. ABB Vetco Gray (S.D. Tex. 2004)	2004 (SEC & DOJ)	Vetco International (oil company)	Vetco Gray executives paid $1.1 million in bribes to assist subsidiaries in Nigeria, Angola, and Kazakhstan to retain business. The SEC settlement involved $5.9 million in disgorgement and a $10.5 million civil penalty. Vetco agreed to a $10.5 million fine in conjunction with the DOJ charges.	Cases #55 and #74 arise out of the same investigation. According to one source, the combined fine of $26 million (paid by Vetco and its subisidiaries) is the largest criminal fine in the history of the FCPA. http://www.willkie.com/files/tbl_s29Publications%5CFileUpload5686%5C2393%5CVetco_Pays_Largest_Criminal_Fine.pdf. A memo from the DOJ confirms the combined $26 million in fines. http://www.usdoj.gov/opa/pr/2007/February/07_crm_075.html

Case Name	Date of Prosecution	Company	Brief Case Description	Notes
U.S. v. InVision Technologies; SEC v. InVision, Inc. (2005)	2004 (SEC & DOJ)	InVision Technologies	InVision sales agents and distributors allegedly paid more than $95K in bribes to Thai, Chinese, and Philippine officials to retain explosive devices sales. InVision entered into a non-prosecution agreement with the DOJ and agreed to pay a $800K criminal fine. InVision settled with the SEC to pay $589K in disgorgement and $500K in fines.	This is one of the few cases involving distributors rather than sales representatives of consultants. Cases #56 and #75 arise out of the same investigation. Non-prosecution agreement.
BJ Services	2004 (SEC)	BJ Services (chemical processes and machines) http://www.bjservices.com/	BJ Services Company, a Houston company that provides oilfield services, products, and equipment to worldwide petroleum producers, was charged with making illegal payments to Argentinian customs officials. In 2001, the controller for BJ Services, S.A. (BJSA), an Argentinian subsidiary of BJ Services, made illegal or questionable payments to Argentinean customs officials. BJSA negotiated with the customs official through a third party, and the bribery payments were made by issuing two checks to a lower-level BJSA employee who cashed the checks and gave the proceeds to the official. BJSA had improperly imported products, and the bribery payments were made in an effort to have these customs violations overlooked. These payments were improperly recorded in BJSA's books and records as a debit to the "Vendor Payable Account." Also, from 1998 through 2002 other improper payments to customs officials were made, and these payments were improperly recorded in BJSA's books and records in an effort to conceal them.	BJ Services entered into a cease and desist order with the SEC in 2004. Please see included link to view cease and desist order. http://www.sec .gov/litigation/admin/34-49390.htm

Case Name	Date of Prosecution	Company	Brief Case Description	Notes
SEC v. ABB, Ltd	2004 (SEC)	ABB U.S. (automation products) http://www.abb.us/	ABB is a Swiss company that manufactures automation technologies. Four former employees of an ABB Ltd. subsidiary allegedly bribed Nigerian officials in order to secure contracts for an offshore drilling project in Nigeria. ABB ultimately landed the contract that they sought to secure through the bribes. Between 1999 and 2001, four ABB executives paid the Nigerian state-owned agency responsible for oil exploration approximately $1 million in bribes in the form of cash and gifts. The purpose of the bribes was to obtain competitor bid information and secure favorable consideration of ABB's contract. One of the ABB executives (Campbell) received $50,000 in kickbacks on the oil drilling contract. The ABB executives covered up the bribes by recording them as false consulting invoices (books and recording keeping violation).	See also ABB Vetco above. ABB's portion of the $26 million in fines was $10.5 million to be paid to the DOJ. http://www.sec.gov/litigation/ litreleases/lr18775.htm. According to one source, the combined fine of $26 million (paid by Vetco and its subisidiaries) is the largest criminal fine in the history of the FCPA. http://www.willkie.com/files/tbl_s29Publications%5CFileUpload5686%5C2393%5CVetco_Pays_ Largest_Criminal_Fine.pdf. A memo from the DOJ confirms the combined $26 million in fines. http://www.usdoj.gov/opa/pr/2007/February/07_crm_075.html
SEC v. Schering Plough	2004 (SEC)	Schering Plough (pharmaceutical company) http://www.schering-plough.com/schering_ plough/index.jsp	A Polish subsidiary of Schering Plough allegedly paid $76,000 to a charity to induce the director of the fund to purchase Schering Plough pharmaceutical products. The Chudow Castle Foundation was run by the Polish government. The Schering Plough Poland subsidiary made improper payments between February 1999 and March 2002 to a charitable organization, Chudow Castle Foundation, which was run by the Polish government. The purpose of the payments was to induce the director of the foundation to buy Schering's pharmaceutical products. The complaint alleges that Schering Plough also had inadequate internal controls to prevent the fraudulent recording of the transactions.	Listed in SEC Self-Reporting Document. In June 2004, the SEC issued a cease and desist order against Schering Plough. No further penalties or disgorgement were required. http://www.sec .gov/litigation/admin/34-49838.htm

Case Name	Date of Prosecution	Company	Brief Case Description	Notes
U.S. v. Titan Corp (S.D. Cal. 2005); SEC v. Titan Corp.	2005 (DOJ & SEC)	L-3 Titan Group (radio and telephone services) http://www.dtsi.com/	Titan officials allegedly made $3.5 million in campaign contributions to the presidential campaign of a Benin official. The complaint also alleged that Titan had virtually no internal controls. Titan pled guilty in 2005 and agreed to a criminal fine of $13 million. The civil penalty (disgorgement and civil fine) was $15.5 million.	The combined fines (DOJ and SEC) were the largest in the history of the FCPA at $28.5 million.
U.S. v. DPC (Tianjin); In the Matter of Diagnostic Products (2005)	2005 (DOJ & SEC)	Subsidiary of Diagnostic Products Corp. Diagnostic Products, Corp. (medical devices acquired by Siemens in 2006). http://diagnostics.siemens.com/webapp/ wcs/stores/servlet/CategoryDisplay~q_ catalogId~e_-111~a_categoryId~e_ 1009304~a_catTree~e_100005,1009304~ a_langId~e_-111~a_storeId~e_10001.htm	Tianjin is a Chinese subsidiary of DPC. Tianjin paid $1.6 million in bribes to Chinese officials in exchange for an agreement that DPC would provide products and services to state-owned hospitals. DPC agreed to pay $2.8 million in disgorgement to the SEC and $2 million in fines to the DOJ. The firm also agreed to a 3rd party compliance monitoring, and a cease and desist order.	Corporate non-prosecution agreement; "Diagnostic Products disgorged $2.8 million in profit to the SEC and $2 million to the DOJ for incorrectly recording the bribes paid by its Chinese subsidiary of $1.6 million and because it lacked sufficient internal controls." http://www.metrocorpcounsel.com/current.php?artType=view&EntryNo=6627

Case Name	Date of Prosecution	Company	Brief Case Description	Notes
U.S. v. Amoako (D.N.J. 2005); SEC v. Amoako	2005 (DOJ & SEC)	IXTC Corp.	Amoako was a regional director of IXTC's African subsidiary and allegedly paid $267K in bribes to the Nigerian, Rwandan, and Senegalese government in order to secure $11.5 million in lucrative telephone contracts. Amoako eventually pled guilty and served 18 months in prison. He also paid a $7,500 fine. The SEC case is still pending.	Amoako's motion for a new trial was denied in February 2008. U.S. v. Amoako 2008, U.S. Dist. LEXIS 9553 (N.D. T.X. 2008). Amoako was sentenced to a $7,500 fine and an 18-month prison sentence. http://www.wilmerhale.com/publications/whPubsDetail.aspx?publication =8385
U.S. v. Monsanto; SEC v. Charles Martin; SEC v. Monsanto	2005 (DOJ & SEC)	Monsanto Corp (agriculture technology) http://www.monsanto.com/	Monsanto reported inconsistencies in their internal audits to the DOJ and SEC including a $50K bribe to Indonesian officials. The purpose of the bribe was to entice the Indonesian government to repeal a decree. Monsanto entered into a non-prosecution agreement with the DOJ and agreed to pay a $1.5 million fine to the SEC. The DOJ eventually dropped the charges.	Corporate non-prosecution agreement; Correction: Monsanto "entered into a deferred prosecution agreement with the Department of Justice under which it agreed to pay a $1 million fine and hire an 'independent compliance consultant.'" http://lawprofessors.typepad.com/whitecollarcrime_blog/2005/01/monsanto_ settle.html; The settlement with the DOJ is confirmed by a 2005 DOJ press release. http://www .usdoj.gov/opa/pr/2005/January/05_crm_008.htm
U.S. v. Micrus	2005 (DOJ)	Micrus Endovascular (medical devices) http://www.micrusendovascular.com/	Micrus employees paid $105K to state-run hospitals in France, Turkey, Spain, and Germany in order to bribe them to buy Micrus products. Micrus entered into a non-prosecution agreement with the DOJ, agreed to pay a $450K fine, and agreed to comply with an internal set of compliance controls.	Corporate non-prosecution agreement; Micrus obtained a non-prosecution agreement with DOJ due to the company's cooperation with the investigation. http://www.usdoj.gov/opa/pr/2005/March/05_crm_090.htm

Case Name	Date of Prosecution	Company	Brief Case Description	Notes
U.S. v. Thompson, et al (N.D. Al. 2005)	2005 (DOJ)	Health South	Thompson was the former COO of Health South and Reilly was the former VP of Health South's legal services department. Health South paid $2.5 million in bribes to the Saudi Government to secure a contract for staffing services for a state-owned hospital. The implicated officials have agreed to cooperate with the DOJ investigation. Thompson and Reilly were found not guilty at a jury trial in May 2005.	Individual defendants not guilty.
U.S. v. Kozeny et al. (S.D.N.Y. 2005)	2005 (DOJ)	Oily Rock Group (District Court dismissed co-defendant, Pinkerton—was a former AIG executive) http://www.lloyds.com/CMS-Phoenix/ Dow JonesArticle.aspix?id=396625	Kozeny was President and CEO of Oily Rock. The five co-conspirators paid out millions in direct bribes, promises of profits, luxury items, and lavish trips to Azerbaijan officials. The purpose of these payments was to obtain a controlling interest in the privatization of the SOCAR. Kozeny was charged and was expedited to the U.S. In June 2007, Bourke and Pinkerton had their charges dismissed along with their co-conspirator Kozeny.	Same case (nos. 51–54). In June 2007, the FCPA charges against Kozeny's co-conspirators were dropped due to the statute of limitations. However, as of June 2007, the DOJ was still attempting to extradite Kozeny from the Bahamas to the U.S. http://www.wilmerhale .com/files/Publication/36d5cbc0-b6a1-4774-9906-10ba6750ac5d/Presentation/PublicationAttachment/490ab1e4-6f36-434 a-8def-6cb0a7836484/FCPA%20Briefing%20Series%20August%202007.pdf
U.S. v. Statoil (S.D.N.Y 2006); In the Matter of Statoil USA	2006 (DOJ & SEC)	Statoil Hydro (oil company) http://www.statoilhydro.com/en/ Pages/default.aspx	Statoil is Norway's largest gas and oil company and allegedly agreed to pay Iranian officials $5.2 million to obtain "millions of dollars in profits." Statoil agreed to a 3-year deferred prosecution agreement and agreed to a $10.5 million penalty. Statoil also agreed to pay an additional $10.5 million disgorgement settlement to the SEC and a compliance monitor.	Statoil also paid a $3.045 million fine to the Norway National Authority for Investigation and Prosecution of Economic Crime. Corporate deferred prosecution agreement.

Case Name	Date of Prosecution	Company	Brief Case Description	Notes
U.S. v. SSI International Far East (D. Or. 2006); In the Matter of Schnitzer Steel Industries	2006 (DOJ & SEC)	Wholly owned South Korean subsidiary of Schnitzer Steel.	The Korean subsidiary allegedly paid $204K to foreign officials in South Korea and China in exchange for $6.28 million in profits from steel contracts. SSI agreed to pay a $7.5 million penalty. As part of the SEC settlement, Schnitzer Steel agreed to pay $7.7 million in disgorgement and retain a compliance monitor for three years.	Cases #68 and #82 arise out of the same investigation.
U.S. v. Brown (S.D. Tex. 2006); SEC v. Brown	2006 (DOJ & SEC)	Willbros	Brown worked for a wholly owned Willbros subsidiary in Panama and allegedly paid $1.8 million in bribes to Nigerian and Equadorian officials to secure $243.4 million in revenue for oil and gas pipeline construction contracts. Brown pled guilty in 2006 and is cooperating with the U.S. gov't. His sentencing hearing is set for Jan. 2008. The SEC was granted a motion to stay proceedings until the resolution of the DOJ matter.	Cases #69 and #86 arise out of the same investigation. In May 2008, Willbros agreed to pay $32 million in disgorgement, penalties, and back interest to settle the FCPA investigations with both the SEC and the DOJ. http://www.willkie.com/files/tbl_s29Publications%5CFileUpload5686%5C2608%5CWillbros_Group_Agrees_to_Pay_For_Violations.pdf. Brown plead guilty in 2006 and agree to pay a $250,000 fine and cooprate fully with the investigation. http://www.usdoj.gov/opa/pr/2006/September/06_crm_621.html. See also http://fcpacompliance.com/documents/document_detail.asp?ID =5055&PAGE=2
U.S. v. Lynwood Head (S.D. Cal. 2006)	2006 (DOJ)	Titan Corp.	Steven Lynwood Head was the manager of business activities in Benin and later became the CEO for Africa. He allegedly paid $2 million in bribes to Benin officials in an effort to secure a wireless service contract. Head pled guilty and was sentenced to six months in prison in 2007 and a $5,000 fine.	In 2006, Titan agreed to pay $28.5 million in disgorgement and penalties to settle the DOJ investigation. http://www.gibsondunn.com/publications/Pages/2006YearEndFCPAUpdate.aspx

Case Name	Date of Prosecution	Company	Brief Case Description	Notes
U.S. v. Sapsizian & Acosta (S.D. Fla. 2006)	2006 (DOJ)	Alcatel-Lucent (telecommunications)	Sapsizian was the VP for Latin America. Acosta was the manger of the Costa Rican subsidiary. Together, both officials paid roughly $2.56 million in bribes to Costa Rican officials to secure $250 million in business. Sapsizian pled guilty in Mar. 2007 and faces $250K in fines and up to ten years in prison. Acosta is still at large (fugitive status).	Acosta was indicted but remains at large. http://www.gibsondunn.com/publications/pages/2007Year-EndFCPAUpdate.aspx
U.S. v. Novak (E.D. Wash. 2006)	2006 (DOJ)		Novak was involved in "diploma mill" universities in Ghana, Liberia, and the U.S. He allegedly bribed officials at the National Commission on Higher Education in Liberia ($30K to $70K). The purpose of the payments was to obtain $2.3 million in fraudulent products. Novak pled guilty in 2006 and was scheduled to be sentenced in 2007.	
U.S. v. Salam (D.D.C. 2006)	2006 (DOJ)		Salam was a translator working for U.S. contractors in Iraq. He made a $60K bribe to an Iraqi official to try to get $1 million in business by selling armored vests to the Iraqi police. He pled guilty in Feb. 2007 and was sentenced to three years in prison and two years supervised release.	Salam was not acting on behalf of a company (similar to the Green case)
SEC v. Samson; Munro; Campbell; Whelan (D.D.C. 2006)	2006 (SEC)	Vetco International (oil company)	Samson was the former West Africa sales manager of the Nigerian subsidiary. Munro was the VP of operations for the UK. Campbell was VP of Finance for the UK. Whelan was the VP of Sales for the parent company Vetco Gray. Vetco paid $1 million in bribes to Nigerian officials for an oil contract worth $180 million. Each defendant agreed to a civil penalty of approximately $50K, and Samson was additionally ordered to disgorge $64K.	Same case (nos. 55 and 85). Samson is a British citizen who consented to judgment being entered against him for violation of the FCPA. http://www.shearman.com/files/upload/FCPA_Trends.pdf
SEC v. Pillor (N.D. Cal. 2006)	2006 (SEC)	InVision Technologies	Pillor authorized a $95K bribe to retain business for InVision. Pillor agreed to pay the SEC a $65K civil penalty and submit to a permanent injunction.	This action is related to the DOJ action for InVision. Same case (#56).

Case Name	Date of Prosecution	Company	Brief Case Description	Notes
In the Matter of Oil States International	2006 (SEC)	Hydraulic Well Control, LLC—subsidiary of Oil States International, which is traded on the NYSE	The subsidiary Hydraulic Well Control paid $348K to Venezuelan officials to avoid stoppage of work. Oil States agreed to a cease and desist order with the SEC.	
SEC v. Tyco (S.D.N.Y. 2006)	2006 (SEC)	Tyco is listed on the NYSE	Tyco's Bermuda subsidiary paid an unspecified amount of improper payments to Brazilian and South Korean officials to secure government contracts. Tyco agreed to a $50 million fine and $1 million in disgorgement.	
U.S. v. York International	2007 (DOJ & SEC)	York International (HVAC services—acquired by Johnson Controls in 2005) http://www.york.com/	$647,000 in payments to Iraqi, Bahraini, Egyptian, Indian, Turkish, and UAE gov't officials as part of the OFFP to secure $51 million in contracts. York agreed to a $10 million fine and an independent monitoring system for its compliance programs. In conjunction with the SEC action, York disgorged $10 million and paid a $2 million civil penalty.	OFFP case
U.S. v. Baker Hughes (S.D. Tex 2007); SEC v. Baker Hughes	2007 (DOJ & SEC)	Baker Hughes (oil refinement services) http://www.bakerhughesdirect.com/cgi/ bhi/myHomePage/myHomePage.jsp	$4.1 million in improper payments to Kazakhstan officials to secure $205 million in oil and gas services. Baker Hughes pled guilty and agreed to pay an $11 million criminal fine. The DOJ agreed not to bring any further charges provided that Baker Hughes continues to cooperate in the investigation for the next two years. As part of the SEC settlement, Baker agreed to pay $23 million in disgorgement, a $10 million civil penalty, and a cease and desist order.	The combined penalty of $44 million may be the largest ever in an FCPA case. Corporate non-prosecution agreement

Case Name	Date of Prosecution	Company	Brief Case Description	Notes
U.S. v. Ott (D.N.J. 2007); SEC v. Ott	2007 (DOJ & SEC)	IXTC; merged with Teleglobe	Ott was the Executive VP of Global Sales. The improper payments to Nigerian, Rwandan, and Senegalese officials totaled $267K in exchange for an undisclosed amount of business.	Cases #80 and #81 arise out of the same investigation; Ott's sentencing is still pending, but he faces a fine of up to $250K and up to five years in prison . http://www.wilmerhale.com/publications/whPubsDetail.aspx?publication=8385 Note: Ott and Young's co-conspirator, Amoako, received a 18-month prison sentence.
U.S. v. Young (D.N.J. 2007); SEC v. Young	2007 (DOJ & SEC)	IXTC; merged with Teleglobe	Young was the Managing Director for Africa and the Middle East. The improper payments to Nigerian, Rwandan, and Senegalese officials totaled $267K in exchange for an undisclosed amount of business. Young pled guilty. The SEC granted a six-month stay until the conclusion of the DOJ investigation.	Same case; Young's sentencing is still pending, but he faces a fine of up to $250K and up to five years in prison. http://www.wilmerhale.com/publications/whPubsDetail.aspx?publication=8385
U.S. v. Wooh; SEC v. Wooh	2007 (DOJ & SEC)	Schnitzer Steel (steel processing and trading) http://www.portlandsteel.com/	Improper payments of $204K to Chinese officials in exchange for approximately $102 million in profits. Wooh agreed to pay $40,000 in disgorgement (SEC) without admitting or denying the charges. His sentencing was set for Nov 19, 2007.	Wooh also paid $1.7 million in bribes to private parties in China and South Korea. Same case (#68).
U.S. v. Textron; SEC v. Textron	2007 (DOJ & SEC)	Textron (defense contractor) http://www.textron.com/	$600K in illegal payments in Iraq and $115K in illegal payments in other countries (Bangladesh, Indonesia, Egypt, and India). In exchange, Textron received $1.9 million in profits from Iraq and $328K in profits from other countries. Textron entered into a non-prosecution agreement and agreed to pay a $1.15 million fine (August 2007). As part of the SEC settlement, Textron paid $2.284 million in disgorgement and an $800K civil penalty.	OFFP case

Case Name	Date of Prosecution	Company	Brief Case Description	Notes
Panalpina World Transport	2007 (DOJ & SEC)	Swiss-based shipping company	In July 2007, the DOJ sent letters to eleven oil and oil service companies regarding illegal payments to customs agents (primarily Nigeria). The SEC is conducting its own independent investigation.	Investigation stage only; Panalpina was allegedly involved in some of the same bribes and kickback schemes that Vetco was involved in. http://goliath.ecnext.com/coms2/gi_ 0199-7819710/FCPA-Insights-To-Host-Or.html
U.S. v. Vetco (S.D. Tex 2007)	2007 (DOJ)	Vetco International (oil company) http://www.vetcointernational.com/	One of Vetco's U.S. subsidiaries (Gray Controls) paid $2.1 million in bribes to Nigerian officials for preferential treatment in the customs process. Vetco and Gray pled guilty and agreed to a collective fine of $26 million and agreed to hire an independent monitor of their compliance program.	Same case (nos. 55, 74)
U.S. v. Steph (S.D. Texas)	2007 (DOJ); 2008 (SEC)	Willbros	Steph was the manager of Willbros Nigerian off-shore operations. He allegedly paid $6 million in bribes to secure $387.5 million in construction contracts. Steph pled not guilty and a trial date was set for December 2007.	Same case (#69). Steph pled guilty to DOJ in November 2007, http://skaddenpractices.skadden.com/fcpa//attach.php?uploadFileID=47; DOJ plea agreement, http://skaddenpractices.skadden.com/fcpa//attach.php?uploadFileID=49; SEC charges Steph and the Willbros group in May 2008, http://www.sec.gov/litigation/complaints/2008/comp20571.pdf, Steph and Willbros agree to settle SEC action for 32 million, http://www.sec.gov/news/press/2008/2008-86.htm

Case Name	Date of Prosecution	Company	Brief Case Description	Notes
U.S. v. Jefferson (E.D. Va. 2007)	2007 (DOJ)	Jefferson is a current U.S. Representative	Jefferson allegedly paid $500K to Nigerian officials as part of a joint venture with NITEL, a telecommunications company. Jefferson pled not guilty and his trial was set for Jan. 2008.	Trial delayed pending appeal of procedural matters, i.e., whether his status as a congressman precludes this indictment, http://www.foxnews.com/story/0,2933,331733,00.html; http://www.sunnewsonline.com/webpages/news/national/2008/may/23/national-23-05-2008-006 .htm
U.S. v. Smith (C.D. Cal 2007)	2007 (DOJ)	Pacific Consolidated Industries	Smith paid $300K in bribes to the British Government to secure contracts with the Royal Air Force. Smith was indicted in April 2007 and was set to go to trial in July 2008.	No further updates. UK officials have already prosecuted and convicted a Ministry of Defense Official.
Pride International	2007 (DOJ)		Pride announced an internal investigation as to FCPA violations and the DOJ has requested information about the firm's dealings with Nigeria.	No further updates; investigation stage only.
SEC v. Monty Fu (D.D.C. 2007)	2007 (SEC)	Syncor International; Syncor Taiwan	Fu was the founder and former CEO of Syncor International. He allegedly authorized roughly $600K in bribes through illegal commission payments to doctors at private and public hospitals in Taiwan to get them to purchase radiopharmaceutical products. Fu agreed to settle with the SEC for $75K and a permanent injunction.	No further updates, SEC litigation release http://www.sec.gov/litigation/litreleases/2007/lr20310.htm
SEC v. El Paso Corp (S.D.N.Y. 2007)	2007 (SEC)	El Paso Corp. (oil company) http://www.elpaso.com	In violation of the UN OFFP, El Paso paid $5.5 million to Iraqi officials to obtain illegal surcharges. El Paso agreed to a $2.25 million civil penalty, $5.48 million in disgorgement, and an injunction.	OFFP Case No further updates, SEC litigation release http://www.sec.gov/litigation/litreleases/2007/lr19991.htm
SEC v. Dow Chemical	2007 (SEC)	Dow Chemical http://www.dow.com/	Dow paid $200K in bribes to Indian officials to expedite the registration of their pesticide products. Dow consented to a $325K civil penalty and a cease and desist order.	No further updates, SEC litigation release http://www.sec.gov/litigation/litreleases/2007/lr20000 .htm

Case Name	Date of Prosecution	Company	Brief Case Description	Notes
SEC v. Delta Pine (D.D.C. 2007)	2007 (SEC)	Subsidiary of Monsanto http://www.monsanto.com/dpl/default.asp	Delta Pine paid $43K in bribes to Turkish officials to secure government reports that would allow them to operate in Turkey. The SEC gave Delta Pine and Turk Deltapine, its subsidiary, a $300K joint fine, a cease and desist order, and required them to retain an independent consultant to review plan for their internal controls and compliance.	No further updates, SEC litigation release: http://www.sec.gov/litigation/litreleases/2007/lr20214.htm
In the Matter of Bristow	2007 (SEC)	Bristow Group (helicopter services) http://www.bristowgroup.com/	Bristow paid $423K in bribes to Nigerian officials to secure $873K in helicopter services business. Bristow also under-reported its payroll taxes. The SEC issued Bristow a cease and desist order.	No further updates, SEC cease and desist order, http://www.sec.gov/news/press/2007/2007-201.htm
Electronic Data Systems; SEC v. Srinivasan (D.D.C. 2007)	2007 (SEC)	EDS (IT services) http://www.eds.com/	Defendant Srinivasan was the president of the EDS Indian subsidiary A.T. Kearney. The D authorized $720K in probes to Indian officials to secure a $7.5 million government contract through phony invoices. The former CEO agreed to $70K in fines and EDS agreed to pay $490K in disgorgement in addition to a cease and desist order.	No further updates, SEC press release http://www.sec.gov/litigation/litreleases/2007/lr20296.htm
U.S. v. Paradigm BV	2007 (DOJ)	Paradigm BV (provides software services to oil companies) http://www.paradigmgeo.com/	$22,500 in bribes to Kazakhstan officials, approximately $200,000 in Mexico, and approximately $150,000 to Nigerian officials. The purpose of the payments was to secure a $1.48 million contract in Mexico and a $250K contract in Kazakhstan. Paradigm agreed to pay a $1 million penalty and implement internal controls. The govt agreed not to prosecute if all of the conditions were met within 18 months.	No further updates, DOJ release http://www .usdoj.gov/opa/pr/2007/September/07_crm_751.html

Case Name	Date of Prosecution	Company	Brief Case Description	Notes
U.S. v. King	2001 (DOJ)	Owl Securities & Investments (OSI) http://www.usdoj.gov/criminal/fraud/fcpa/append/ix/appendixg(iv).pdf	In order to secure a land concession to develop the Costa Rican project King and Barquero along with co-conspirator Stephen Kingsley, now deceased, President, Chief Executive Officer, and stockholder of OSI made or promised bribes to Costa Rican government officials, political parties, party officials, and candidates for public office from Fall 1997 to October 2000. King and Barquero would solicit investors in the United States for the Costa Rican Project and would represent to investors that a portion of the invested funds would be used to cultivate "friends" in the Costa Rican government. These payments were referred by using code words such as "political support money," "consulting fees," "tolls," "kiss money," and "closing costs." King and Barquero paid $1,000,000 for the bribes and the funds were not to be released until the concession agreement was granted and were referred to as "closing costs." The "closing costs" were to be put in an escrow by way of a letter of credit.	A jury later convicted King of one count of conspiracy and four counts under the FCPA. The district court sentenced King to thirty months' imprisonment and fined him $60,000; affirmed on appeal, 351 F.3d 859 (2003); denying ceriorari, 542 U.S. 905 (2004); Movant's Motion to Vacate, Set Aside, or Correct Sentence is denied, (not reported) 2006 WL 741904.
SEC v. Gioacchino De Chirico, Civil Action File No. 1:07-CV-2367 (N.D.GA)	2007 (SEC)	Immucor (medical devices) http://www.immucor.com/site/aum_ company_profile.jsp	In April 2004, Immucor, Inc. made an improper payment of $16,000 to the director of a public hospital in Milan, Italy as a quid pro quo for the hospital director favoring Immucor in selecting contracts for supplies and equipment. In addition, in order to help the director to avoid the Italian tax, De Chirico recorded the payment as a bogus consulting fee. Without admitting or denying the allegations in the SEC's complaint, De Chirico agreed to pay a civil penalty of $30,000. In addition, Immucor agreed to abide by the cease and desist order without admitting or denying the complaint allegations.	No further updates, SEC litigation release http://www.sec.gov/litigation/litreleases/2007/lr20316.htm

Case Name	Date of Prosecution	Company	Brief Case Description	Notes
SEC v. Ingersoll-Rand	2007 (SEC)	Ingersoll-Rand (manufacturing and construction services) http://company.ingersollrand.com/Pages/default.aspx	IR Italia and TKL entered into 12 contracts involving ASSF kickbacks to Iraqi officials as part of the Oil for Food Program. The kickbacks totaled roughly $1.5 million. The purpose of the kickbacks was to entice the Iraqi officials to select Ingersoll-Rand for several road construction contracts totaling $3.2 million. Many of the kickbacks utilized Jordanian Ministry officials as intermediaries. The kickbacks were recorded at 10% price mark-ups on the UN Oil for Food Bid paperwork; the proceeds of the price mark-ups went to Iraqi officials through the intermediary. In addition, IR Italia paid $11,000 in bribes in the form of "pocket money," travel expenses, and entertainment expenses to officials at the Iraqi Oil Ministry's Baiji refinery. Ingersoll-Rand agreed to pay $6.7 million in fines and penalties to settle the case. $4.2 million was for fines and penalties. $1.7 million was for disgorged profits. $1.95 million was for the civil penalty. The remaining $560,000 was for pre-judgment interest.	OFFP case. No further updates, SEC litigation release http://www.sec.gov/litigation/litreleases/2007/lr20353.htm
SEC v. Chevron	2007 (DOJ & SEC)	Chevron (oil and gas company) http://www.chevron.com/	Chevron paid $20 million in illegal surcharges (kickbacks) to third parties in conjunction with the UN OFFP. The surcharge proceeds were passed along to Iraqi officials for the purpose of inducing them to sell oil to Chevron. Some of the third party intermediaries were European shell companies. Chevron signed a non-prosecution agreement requiring that the company pay $30 million in fines and penalties: $20 million to U.S. Attorney's Office, $3 million to the SEC, $5 million to the NY DA's Office, and $2 million to the U.S. Treasury's Foreign Assets Control Office.	OFFP Case. No further updates, SEC litigation release, http://www.sec.gov/litigation/litreleases/2007/lr20363.htm; DOJ Agreement, http://skaddenpractices.skadden.com/fcpa//attach.php?uploadFileID=50

Case Name	Date of Prosecution	Company	Brief Case Description	Notes
Siemens Investigation	2007 (DOJ & SEC)	Siemens (broad services and technology) http://www.usa.siemens.com/entry/en/	The details in the Form 6-K are not specific, but the improper payments likely relate to bribes to Iraqi officials as part of the UN OFFP. The investigation was intiated by the French government, and the DOJ, the SEC, and the German government subsequently began investigating the allegations.	OFFP case. No further updates. Siemens is cooperating with the investigation, but bribery experts say Siemens is the biggest FCPA case—foreign or domestic—of all time, http://www .businessweek.com/globalbiz/content/nov2007/gb20071115_063908.htm?chan=top+news_top+news+index_global+business
Lucent	2007 (SEC & DOJ)	Merged with Alcatel (see above)	Lucent is charged with violating FCPA books and records and internal control provisions, and with improper recording of travel expenses and other things of value provided to authorities at Chinese state owned enterprises (SOEs). Between 2000 and 2003 Lucent spent $10 million on 315 trips to the U.S. for over 1,000 employees of Chinese SOEs to whom Lucent was seeking to sell equipment and services or to retain as existing customers. Lucent entered a two-year non-prosecution agreement with the Department of Justice (DOJ). As part of the DOJ agreement Lucent agreed to pay $1 million in fines and to enhance internal controls, policies, and procedures. In a related SEC action based on the same conduct, Lucent was charged with violating FCPA books and records and internal control provisions. Without admitting or denying the allegations, Lucent agreed to pay a civil penalty of $1.5 million.	No further updates, SEC litigation release http://www.sec.gov/litigation/litreleases/2007/lr20414 .htm; DOJ press release, http://www.usdoj.gov/opa/pr/2007/December/07_crm_1028.html

Case Name	Date of Prosecution	Company	Brief Case Description	Notes
Akzo Nobel	2007 (DOJ & SEC)	Akzo Nobel (medical products) http://www.akzonobel.com/com/	Akzo Nobel, through two of its subsidiaries, N.V. Organon and Intervet International B.V., is accused of making $280,000 in improper kickback payments to Iraqi government officials. The payments were made in the form of "after-sales-service-fees" (ASSFs) and were funded through inflated contracts and inflated commission payments. Akzo's subsidiaries were paying Iraqi ministers approximately 10% of the total contract price in illicit payments in order to secure and retain contracts related to the UN Oil For Food Program (OFFP). Akzo's subsidiaries negotiated these contracts and ASSFs through third party agents and consultants, and between 2000 and 2003 Akzo's total profits from contracts in which illegal payments were made totaled $1.6 million. These payments were mis-categorized in Intervet's and Organon's books and records as legitimate commission payments to agents. Akzo's subsidiaries failed to devise and maintain an effective system of internal accounting controls to protect against FCPA violations, and Akzo knew, or was reckless in not knowing, that these payments were being made. Department of Justice (DOJ). Akzo is expected to pay 381,000 euro in criminal fines to Dutch authorities, and if a timely resolution with Dutch authorities is not achieved, Akzo agreed to pay $800,000 to the U.S. treasury. The SEC settled FCPA books and records and internal control charges based on the same conduct. Without admitting or denying the allegations, Akzo agreed to pay $2.9 million in fees and penalties, including disgorgement of $1.6 million in profits on the tainted contracts and a $750,000 civil penalty.	OFFP Case. No further updates, SEC litigation release http://www.sec.gov/litigation/litreleases/2007/lr20410 .htm

Case Name	Date of Prosecution	Company	Brief Case Description	Notes
U.S. v. Green	2007–2008 (DOJ)	Film Festival Management http://www.festivalmanagementinc.com/insidefm.html	Gerald and Patricia Green are charged with making more than $900,000 in improper payments to the senior government authority (the Governor) of the Tourism Authority of Thailand (TAT). These bribes were made in order to secure film festival contracts and other contracts from TAT. In January 2007 the Department of Justice (DOJ) announced the indictment of the Greens for conspiracy to bribe and for making improper payments to the TAT official.	Complaint filed December 2007; Green indicted January 2008; trial set for February 2008.
SEC v. Westinghouse	2008 (SEC & DOJ)	Westinghouse (electronics and services provider) http://www.westinghouse.com/	Wabtec, through its Indian subsidiary, Pioneer, is charged with making approximately $135,000 in improper payments to various Ministry of Railroad officials between 2001 and 2005. These bribes were made in order to have its bids for government business granted or considered, as well as in scheduling pre-shipping product inspections, obtaining product delivery certificates, and curbing what it viewed as excessive tax audits. Wabtec entered a three-year non-prosecution agreement with the Department of Justice (DOJ) who agreed not to prosecute if Wabtec pays a $300,000 penalty and adopts "rigorous" internal controls. The SEC charged Wabtec with violating the FCPA's anti-bribery provisions as well as its books and records and internal control provisions. Without admitting or denying the allegations, Wabtec agreed to pay a $87,000 civil penalty. Based on the same conduct, the SEC filed an administrative order finding that Wabtec violated the FCPA, and pursuant to that order Wabtec is required to pay approximately $290,000 in disgorgement and prejudgment interest and engage an independent compliance consultant.	Listed in SEC Self-Reporting Document. Corporate compliance monitor. No further updates, SEC litigation release http://www.sec.gov/litigation/litreleases/2008/lr20457.htm

Case Name	Date of Prosecution	Company	Brief Case Description	Notes
U.S. v. Flowserve Corp.	2008 (SEC & DOJ)	Flowserve (pump, valve, and services provider and manufacturer) http://www.flowserve.com/eim/index.html	Flowserve, through two of its foreign subsidiaries, Flowserve Pompes and Flowserve B.V., is charged with making $820,000 in improper kickback payments via agents in connection with twenty contracts with the Iraqi government under the OFFP. The kickbacks were made in the form of "after-sales-service-fees" and funded through inflated contracts and inflated commission payments to the agents. Flowserve entered a three-year DOJ deferred prosecution agreement, where Flowserve acknowledged responsibility for the actions of its subsidiaries and agreed to pay a $4 million penalty. The SEC filed FCPA books and records and internal control charges. Without admitting or denying the SEC allegations, Flowserve agreed to pay approximately $6.5 million, of which approximately $2.7 million is disgorgement from profits on the contracts and pre-judgment interest and a $3 million civil penalty.	OFFP case. Corporate non-prosecution agreement. No further updates, SEC litigation release http://www.sec.gov/litigation/litreleases/2008/lr20461.htm
U.S. vs. James K. Tillery	2008 (DOJ)		James Tillery authorized bribery payments to government officials in Nigerian and Equador. These payments were made with the intent to secure an imporper advantaging in gaining oil and gas pipeline construction contracts.	
U.S. vs. Paul G. Novak	2008 (DOJ)		Paul Novak authorized bribery payments to government officials in Nigerian and Equador. These payments were made with the intent to secure an imporper advantaging in gaining oil and gas pipeline construction contracts. Paul pleaded guilty to one count of conspiracy to violate the Foreign Corrupt Practices Act and to one substantive count of violating the FCPA.	

Case Name	Date of Prosecution	Company	Brief Case Description	Notes
SEC vs. AB Volvo	2008 (SEC)(DOJ)	AB Volvo	AB Volvo, through two of its subsidiaries and agents, made kick-back payments to government officials in Iraq through the Oil for Food Program. These payments were made to influence the sales of humanitarian goods. As a result of these transactions, AB Volvo violated the books and records and internal controls provisions of the FCPA. AB consented to a final judgment permanently enjoining it from future violations of the FCPA, to disgorge $7,299,208, in profits plus $1,303,441 in pre-judgment interest, and to pay a civil penalty of $4,000,000. AB Volvo has also agreed to pay a $7,000,000 penalty pursuant to a deferred prosecution agreement with the U.S. Department of Justice.	see below
U.S. vs. Renault Trucks SAS	2008 (DOJ)	Renault Trucks SAS	Renault Trucks SAS, a subsidiary of AB Volvo, paid approximately $4.8 million in kickbacks to the government of Iraq under the Oil for Food Program. These payments were made to gain contracts to supply several types of Renault Trucks vehicles and other equipment to Iraq. See AB Volvo for penalties.	see above
U.S. vs. Martin Eric Self	2008 (DOJ)	Pacific Consolidated Industries	Martin Self, President and part owner of Pacific Consolidated Industries, made bribery payments to a U.K Ministry of Defense. These payments were made to obtain business contracts with the U.K. royal airforce. Martin pleaded guilty to a two-count information charging him with violating the FCPA. Martin shall pay to the United States a total fine of $20,000 and is placed on Probation for a term of two years for each count that he pled guilty to.	

Case Name	Date of Prosecution	Company	Brief Case Description	Notes
U.S. vs. AGA Medical Corporation	2008 (DOJ)	AGA Medical Corporation	AGA Medical Croporation, through its distributors, made kickback payments to physicians of government-owned hospitals. These payments were made to pursuade the hospitals to purchace AGA's equipment over their competitors. AGA has agreed to pay a $2 million criminal penalty and has entered into a deferred prosecution agreement with the Department of Justice.	
U.S. vs. Nam Nguyen	2008 (DOJ)	Nexus Technologies Inc	Nam Nguyen, President and founder of Nexus Technologies, negotiated contracts and bribes with a number of Vietnamese government officials. These bribes were made with the intent to secure contracts to supply equipment and technology to the government agencies. Nam pled quilty and was sentenced to 16 months in prison and a $400 assesment penalty.	
U.S. vs. Joseph Lukas	2008 (DOJ)	Nexus Technologies Inc	Joseph Lukas comspired to pay bribes to Vietnamese government officials to influence their decisions to engage in contracts to supply equipment and technology to Vietnamese government agencies. Joseph plead guilty and is sentenced to probation for a term of 2 years and pay a special assessment of $200.00, perform 200 hours of community service, and will pay a fine in the amount of $1000.00.	
U.S. vs. Kim Nguyen	2008 (DOJ)	Nexus Technologies Inc	Kim Nguyen arranged for the transfer of funds to bribe a number of Vietnamese government officials with the intention to obtain contracts to supply equipment and technology to the government agencies. Kim pled guilty and is sentenced to probation for a term of 2 years, perform 200 hours of community service, pay a special assessment of $300.00, and pay a $20,000 fine.	

Case Name	Date of Prosecution	Company	Brief Case Description	Notes
U.S. vs. An Nguyen	2008 (DOJ)	Nexus Technologies Inc	An Nguyen arranged for the transfer of funds to bribe a number of Vietnamese government officials with the intention to obtain contracts to supply equipment and technology to the government agencies. An pled guilty and was sentenced to 9 months in prison and pay a special assessment of $400.00.	
U.S. vs. Nexus Technologies	2008 (DOJ)	Nexus Technologies Inc	Nexus Technologies made bribery payments to Vietnamese government officials. The payments were made in exchange for contracts to sell equipment and technology to Vietnamese government agencies. Nexus Technologies pled guilty and was sentenced to 1 year of probation, to pay a special assessment of $11,200.00, and to cease all operations permanently and tum over all net assets to the Clerk of Court as a fine.	
U.S. vs. Shu Quan-Sheng	2008 (DOJ)		Shu Quan-Sheng, an employee of AMAC, made bribery payments to Chinese government officials. These payments were made to obtain contracts of a hydrogen liquefier project for a French company that Shu represented. Shu pled guilty and was sentenced to 51 months in prison and a special assesment of $300.00.	
U.S. vs. Misao Hioki	2008 (DOJ)		Misao Hioki, who was the general manager of the International engineered products department of a company in Tokyo, made bribery payments to government officials in Latin America and other places with the intent to retain business for the internation engineered products department. He also arranged to rig bids and fix prices. Misao pled guilty to the accusations made against him. Misao was sentenced to 24 months in prison, to pay a $200 assessment, and an $80,000 fine.	

Case Name	Date of Prosecution	Company	Brief Case Description	Notes
DOJ vs. Siemens Venezuela	2008 (DOJ)	Siemens Venezuela	Siemens Venezuela paid bribery payments to government officials in Venezuela. These payments were made to influence their decisions to award business related to mass rail transit projects with government entities. Siemens pled guilty and agreed to pay a $500,000 fine.	case related to Argentina, Bangladesh, and Aktiengesellschaft
SEC vs. Siemens Aktiengesellschaft	2008 (SEC) (DOJ)	Siemens Aktiengesellschaft	Siemens Aktiengesellschaft engaged in numerous bribery payments to government officials all around the world. These payments were made with the intent to unfairly obtain or retain business for Siemens. Siemens has consented to the entry of a court order permanently enjoining it from future violations of the anti-bribery, books and records, and internal controls provisions of the FCPA, to pay $350 million in disgorgement of wrongful profits, and comply with its FCPA compliance program that includes an independent monitor for a period of four years. Siemens AG also agreed to pay a $448.5 million criminal fine.	case related to Argentina, Bangladesh, and Venezuela
U.S. vs. Siemens Bangladesh Limited	2008 (DOJ)	Siemens Bangladesh Limited	Siemens Bangladesh Limited made or authorized over $10 million in bribery payments to Bangladeshi government officials or their families to obtain business, including the Bangladesh Telegraph Telephone Board project. Siemens Bangladesh pled guily and agreed to pay a $500,000 criminal fine in connection with the violation of the Foreign Corrupt Practices Act.	case related to Argentina, Aktiengesellschaft, and Venezuela
U.S. vs. Siemens S.A Argentina	2008 (DOJ)	Siemens S.A Argentina	Siemens S.A Argentina agreed made and concealed about $32 million in bribery payments to Argentine government officials. They made these payments to obtain or retain business for Siemens, including the national identity card project. Siemens Argentina pled guilty to the accusations and agreed to pay a $500,000 criminal fine.	case related to Bangladesh, Aktiengesellschaft, and Venezuela

Case Name	Date of Prosecution	Company	Brief Case Description	Notes
U.S. vs. Mario Covino	2008 (DOJ)		Mario Covino, director of worldwide factory sales for a company, authorized and paid a number of bribery payments to officials of many state-owned enterprises. Mario made these payments to ensure business for the company he was employeed with. Mario pled guilty to the charges.	case related to Richard Molak and Control Components
SEC vs. Yaw Osei Amoako	2008 (SEC)	ITEX Corp	Yaw Osei Amoako violated the anti-bribery provison of the Foreign Corrupt Practices Act by making bribe payments to government officials in Nigeria, Rwanda, and Senegal to obtain or retain business with government-owned telephone companies. Amoako concealed these payments in ITEX's books and therefore aided and abetted ITEX's violations of the books and records provisions of the FCPA. Amoako has consented to enjoin from future violations of the anti-bribery provision of the FCPA and from aiding and abetting the books and records provision and to pay $188,453 in disgorgement and prejudgment interest.	
SEC vs. Faro Technologies	2008 (SEC) (DOJ)	Faro Technologies	Faro Technologies made a number of bribery payments to employees of multiple Chinese state-owned companies. These payments were made with the intent to obtain or retain sales with these companies. Faro Technologies is ordered to cease and desist from violating the anti-bribery, books and records, and internal controls provisions of the FCPA, and to pay disgorgement of $1,411,306 and prejudgment interest of $439,637.32. Faro also agreed to pay a $1.1 million criminal penalty in connection with charges brought on by the Department of Justice.	

Case Name	Date of Prosecution	Company	Brief Case Description	Notes
SEC vs. Baker Hughes Incorporated	2008 (SEC)	Baker Hughes Incorporated	Baker Hughes Incorporated authorized and made illicit payments to government officials in Indonesia, Brazil, and India. These payments were made to secure business for Baker Hughes. Baker Hughes is ordered to cease and desist from violating the FCPA.	
SEC vs. Con-Way Inc.	2008 (SEC)	Con-Way Inc.	Con-way Inc., violated the books and records and internal controls provisons of the Foreign Corrupt Practice Act. The violations are a result of bribery payments made by Emery Transnational to customs officials in the Philippines and to officials of state-owned airlines. The bribery payments were made with the intent to influence the officials to help Emery to obtain or retain business. Con-way consented to an order that requires Con-way to cease and desist from any future violations of the books and records and internal controls provisoins of the FCPA.	
SEC vs. Albert Jackson Stanley	2008 (SEC) (DOJ)	KBR Inc	Albert Jackson Stanley violated the anti-bribery provision of the FCPA. As an employee of KBR, Inc., Albert, along with others, authorized a series of bribery payments to government officials in Nigeria. These payments were made to obtain contracts to build liquified natural gas production facilities. Albert consented to the entry of a final judgment that permanently enjoins him from violating the anti-bribery provision of the FCPA.	In a related criminal proceeding announced today, the United States Department of Justice filed criminal charges against Stanley for conspiring to violate the FCPA and conspiring to commit mail and wire fraud. Stanley has pleaded guilty to one count of conspiring to violate the FCPA and one count of conspiring to commit mail and wire fraud (unrelated to the FCPA charge). He faces seven years in prison and payment of $10.8 million in restitution.

Case Name	Date of Prosecution	Company	Brief Case Description	Notes
SEC vs. Fiat S.p.A.	2008 (SEC) (DOJ)	Fiat S.p.A.	Fiat S.p.A., through their subsidiaries, agents, and distributors, violated the books and records and internal control provisions of the Foreign Corrupt Practices Act. Fiat's subsidiaries and agents made a number of kickback payments to Iraq during the United Nations Oil for Food Program in order to sell humanitarian goods in Iraq. These payments were improperly recorded as "after sales service fees." Resulting from these transactions, Fiat's books and records inaccurately reflected these transactions and they failed to implement an effective control system to prevent or detect them. Fiat consented to a final judgment permanently enjoining them from future violations of the books and records and internal controls provisions of the FCPA, to disgorge $5,309,632 in profits plus $1,899,510 in pre-judgment interest plus a civil penalty of $3,600,000. Fiat will also pay a total of $7,000,000 criminal penalty pursuant to a deferred prosecution agreement with the U.S. Department of Justice.	case related to CNH France and CNH Italia, Iveco, and CNH Global.
SEC vs. CNH Global N.V.	2008 (SEC)	CNH Global N.V.	CNH Global N.V., a wholly-owned subsidiary of Fiat S.p.A., through its subsidiaries, made kickback payments to officials in Iraq during the United Nations Oil for Food Program. These payments were made to obtain an unfair advantage in the sale of humanitarian goods in Iraq. CNH Global consented to a final judgment permanently enjoining them from future violations of the books and records and internal controls provisions of the FCPA.	case related to CNH France and CNH Italia, Iveco, and Fiat
U.S. vs. CNH France S.A	2008 (DOJ)	CNH France S.A	CNH France S.A, a wholly owned subsidiary of CNH Global, paid approximately $188,000 in kickbacks to the Ministry of Oil in Iraq to obtain contracts to supply CNH's construction vehicles and spare parts through the United Nations Oil for Food Program. See Fiat S.p.A. for sentencing.	case related to CNH Global, CNH Italia, Iveco, and Fiat.

Case Name	Date of Prosecution	Company	Brief Case Description	Notes
U.S. vs. CNH Italia S.p.A.	2008 (DOJ)	CNH Italia S.p.A.	CNH Italia S.p.A., a wholly owned subsidiary of CNH Global, paid about $1 million in kickback payments to the Ministry of Agriculture in Iraq during the Oil for Food Program. These payments were made to obtain contracts to supply agricultural products. See Fiat for sentencing.	case related to CNH France and CNH Italia, Iveco, Fiat S.p.A., and CNH Global
U.S. vs. Iveco S.p.A.	2008 (DOJ)	Iveco S.p.A.	Iveco S.p.A., a wholly-owned subsidiary of Fiat S.p.A., paid about $3.17 million dollars in kickback payments to the Government of the Republic of Iraq under the United Nations Oil for Food Program. They made these payments to secure business to supply Iveco trucks and parts. See Fiat for sentencing.	case related to CNH France and CNH Italia, CNH Global, and Fiat S.p.A.
U.S. vs. Richard Morlok	2009 (DOJ)		Richard Morlok, as the Financing Director of a company, made a number of bribery payments to officials of government-owned enterprises in order to obtain or retain business for the company. Richard pled guilty to the charges.	case related to Mario Covino and Control Components
U.S. vs. Juthamas Siriwan	2009 (DOJ)		Juthamas Siriwan was the senior government officer for the Tourism Authority of Thiland (TAT). He was responsible for selecting the business that would provide goods and services for the TAT. Juthamas accepted bribery payments and as a result of being bribed, awarded Green business with business contracts.	case related to Gerald Green (2008)
U.S. vs. Jittisopa Siriwan	2009 (DOJ)		Jittisopa Siriwan, daughter of Juthamas Siriwan and an employee of the Thailand Privilege Card Co. (TPC) which was controlled by the TAT. Bank accounts were set up in Juttispoa's name to collect bribery paymens made from Gerald and Patricia Green to Juthamas Siriwan.	case related to Gerald and Patricia Green (2008)

Case Name	Date of Prosecution	Company	Brief Case Description	Notes
SEC vs. Halliburton Company	2009 (SEC)	Halliburton Company	Halliburton Company is accused of violating the books and records and internal controls provisions of the Foreign Corrupt Practices Act. A Halliburton subsidiary, KBR, through a four-company joint venture, made bribery payments to Nigerian government officials to obtain contracts to build liquified natural gas production facilities. Halliburton has consented to the entry of a court order that permanently enjoins Halliburton from violating the record-keeping and internal control provisions of the Exchange Act, orders Halliburton and KBR to disgorge $177 million in ill-gotten profits derived from the scheme, and imposes an independent consultant for Halliburton to review its policies and procedures as they relate to compliance with the FCPA. The proposed settlements are subject to the court's approval.	
SEC vs. KBR, Inc.	2009 (SEC) (DOJ)	KBR, Inc.	KBR, Inc., through a four-company joint venture, paid a series of bribery payments to Nigerian government officials to obtain contracts worth over $6 billion to build liquified natural gas facilities. KBR violated the anti-bribery provision of the FCPA and aided and abbetted Halliburton to violate the books and records and internal controls provisions of the FCPA. KBR consented to the entry of a court order that permanently enjoins KBR from violating the anti-bribery and records falsification provisions and from aiding and abetting violations of the record-keeping and internal control provisions, and imposes an independent monitor for KBR for a period of three years to review its FCPA compliance program. Between KBR and Halliburton, they have to pay $177 million in ill-gotten profits derived from the scheme. KBR pled guilty to the criminal charges brought against them and will pay a $402 million criminal fine.	see case related to Halliburton Company.

Case Name	Date of Prosecution	Company	Brief Case Description	Notes
U.S. vs. Jeffrey Tesler	2009 (DOJ)		Jeffrey Tesler was hired by the joint-venture of KBR, Technip, Snamprogetti, and to act as an agent to help them bribe Nigerian government officials to obtain contracts to build liquefied natural gas plants.	related to KBR and Wojciech Chodan.
U.S. vs. Wojciech Chodan	2009 (DOJ)		Wojciech Chodan, an employee of M.W. Kellogg Ltd. (a subsidiary of KBR), assisted in the bribery scheme to obtain business contracts to build liquefied natural gas plants in Nigeria. Wojciech pled guilty and as part of his plea agreement, Chodan agreed to forfeit $726,885.	related to KBR and Jeffrey Tesler.
U.S. vs. Latin Node, Inc.	2009 (DOJ)	Latin Node, Inc.	Latin Node, Inc. paid approximately $2.25 million to government officials in Honduras and Yemen. These payments were made to obtain business, reduce per minuute rates, and to gain favorable interconnection agreements. Latin Node pled guilty and agreed to pay a $2 million fine during a three-year period.	
U.S. vs. Stuart Carson	2009 (DOJ)	No Company	Stuart Carson was the CEO of a California-based valve company. Stuart was involved in a bribery scheme within his company to bribe a number of government officials of state-owned and privately owned companies worldwide. These payments were made to secure contracts for the valve company.	this case is related to the next 5 cases.
U.S. vs. Hong (Rose) Carson	2009 (DOJ)	No Company	Hong Carson was the director of sales for China and Taiwan for the valve company, and Stuart's wife. Hong was involved in a bribery scheme within his company to bribe a number of government officials of state-owned and privately owned companies worldwide. These payments were made to secure contracts for the valve company.	

Case Name	Date of Prosecution	Company	Brief Case Description	Notes
U.S. vs. Paul Cosgrove	2009 (DOJ)	No Company	Paul Cosgrove was the director of worldwide sales for the valve company. Paul was involved in a bribery scheme within his company to bribe a number of government officials of state-owned and privately owned companies worldwide. These payments were made to secure contracts for the valve company.	
U.S. vs. David Edmonds	2009 (DOJ)	No Company	David Edmonds was Vice President of Worldwide Customer Service at the valve company. David was involved in a bribery scheme within his company to bribe a number of government officials of state-owned and privately owned companies worldwide. These payments were made to secure contracts for the valve company.	
U.S. vs. Flavio Ricotti	2009 (DOJ)	No Company	Flavio Ricotti was Vice President and head of Sales for Europe, Africa, and the Middle East. Flavio was involved in a bribery scheme within his company to bribe a number of government officials of state-owned and privately owned companies worldwide. These payments were made to secure contracts for the valve company.	
U.S. vs. Han Yong Kim	2009 (DOJ)	No Company	Han Yong Kim was Vice President of the valve company's Korean office. Han was involved in a bribery scheme within his company to bribe a number of government officials of state-owned and privately owned companies worldwide. These payments were made to secure contracts for the valve company.	
U.S. vs. Antonio Perez	2009 (DOJ)	No Company	Antonio Perez was a controller of a company and along with others, made a number of bribes in exchange for business for his company. The bribes were also exchanged for a reduction in telecommunication rates, reduction in the number of minutes used before payment was needed, and to obtain credits towards amounts owed. Antonio pled guilty and was sentenced to 24 months in prison, must serve two years of supervised release following his prison term, and to forfeit $36,375.	Related to Juan Diaz, Carlos Rodriguez, and Marguerite Grandison, Jean Fourcand and Joel Esquenazi.

Case Name	Date of Prosecution	Company	Brief Case Description	Notes
U.S. vs. Juan Diaz	2009 (DOJ)	No Company	Juan Diaz, along with others, conspired to pay, and paid bribery payments to government officials to obtain an unfair advantage for three companies. Some of these advantages included a reduction in telecommunication rates, reduction in the number of minutes used before payment was needed, and to obtain credits towards amounts owed. Juan pled guilty and was sentenced to 57 months in prison, to pay $73,824 in restitution, and to forfeit $1,028,851.	related to Antonio Perez, Carlos Rodriguez, and Marguerite Grandison, Jean Fourcand and Joel Esquenazi.
U.S. vs. Fernando Maya Basurto	2009 (DOJ)	No Company	Fernando Maya Basurto was a principal at a Mexican company that acted as a sales agent on behalf of other companies. Fernando was involved in helping to carry out bribery payments to help obtain business for his clients. Fernando pled guilty to the charges brought against him on November 16, 2009.	
U.S. vs. Control Components Inc.	2009 (DOJ)	Control Components Inc.	Control Components Inc. paid approximately $4.9 million in bribery payments to officials of state-owned and privately-owned companies in thirty-six countries in violation of the Foreign Corrupt Practices Act. These payments were made to obtain business for Control Components Inc. Control Components pled guilty to the charges and agreed to pay a criminal fine of $18.2 million.	Related to Richard Morlok, Mario Covino, and Stuart Carson.
U.S. vs. Charles Paul Edward Jumet	2009 (DOJ)	No Company	Charles Paul Edward Jumet was the President of Ports Engineering Consultants Corporation and Vice President of Overman de Panama, a subsidiary of Overman Associates. While in these positions, Charles made payments to governmet officials in Panama to obtain contracts to maintain lighthouses and bouys along Panama's waterways. Charles pled guilty and was sentenced to 87 months in prison, to pay a $15,000 fine, and to serve three years of supervised release following the prison term.	case related to John W. Warwick

Case Name	Date of Prosecution	Company	Brief Case Description	Notes
U.S. vs. John Joseph O'Shea	2009 (DOJ)	No Company	John Joseph O'Shea made and authorized over $900,000 in bribery payments to Mexican government officials to secure business with state-owned utility companies.	Case related to Fernando Maya Baustro.
U.S. vs. Joel Esquenazi	2009 (DOJ)	No Company	Joel Esquenazi, along with others, made a series of bribery payments to employees of Haiti Telco. These payments were made to gain unfair privileges. These privileges were reduced telecommunication rates, a reduction in the number of minutes used before payment was needed, and obtaining credits towards amounts owed. Joel was sentenced for 180 months for charges of 8 counts of violating the FCPA and 13 counts of money laundering. He will also be on supervised release for a term of 3 years, and pay criminal monetary penalties of $2,200,000 of restitution and 2,100 special assesment fees.	Related to Juan Diaz, Antonio Perez, Carlos Rodriguez, Jean Fourcand and Marguerite Grandison.
U.S. vs. Carlos Rodriguez	2009 (DOJ)	No Company	Carlos Rodriguez was part of a bribery scheme to bribe government officials in exhange for special treatment. This special treatment was in regards to reduced telecommunication rates, a reduction in the number of minutes used before payment was needed, and obtaining credits towards amounts owed. Carlos was sentenced to 84 months in prison based on 8 counts of violating the FCPA and 13 counts of money laundering. He will also be on supervised release for a term of 3 years, and pay monetary penalties of $2,200,000 in restitution and a $2,100 special assessment fee.	Related to Juan Diaz, Antonio Perez, Marguerite Grandison, Jean Fourcand and Joel Esquenazi.
U.S. vs. Marguerite Grandison	2009 (DOJ)	No Company	Marguerite Grandison was involved in the payment of bribes to government officials in exchange for reduced telecommunication rates, a reduction in the number of minutes used before payment was needed, and credits towards amounts owed.	Related to Juan Diaz, Antonio Perez, Carlos Rodriguez, Jean Fourcand, Marguerite Grandison, and Joel Esquenazi.

Case Name	Date of Prosecution	Company	Brief Case Description	Notes
U.S. vs. Jonathan M. Spiller	2009 (DOJ)	No Company	Johnathan M. Spiller was the owner of two companies, one a consulting company and the other sold and marketed military and police enforcement equipment. Jonathan made bribery payments to an agent with the intent of a portion of the money to be given to the Ministry of Defense of a country in Africa. These payments were made to obtain business for his consulting business and to sell equipment. The agent was actually an undercover FBI agent.	
U.S. vs. John Gregory Godsey	2009 (DOJ)	No Company	John Gregory Godsey was the owner of a company that was in the business of selling ammunition and other military and law enforecement equipment. John made a deal to make bribery payments to sales agents with the intent that these payments would be passed to the country's Ministry of Defense. These payments were made to secure business for the company. In reality, the sales agents that they paid the bribes to were undercover FBI agents.	case related to Mark Fredrick Morales
U.S. vs. Mark Fredrick Morales	2009 (DOJ)	No Company	Mark Fredrick Morales was a business associate of John Gregory Godsey and was involved in the deal making for Godsey's company. Mark was involved in arranging a scheme to make payments through agents to the Ministy of Defense of a certain country. The agents Mark thought they were dealing with were undercover FBI agents.	case related to John Gregory Godsey
U.S. vs. Daniel Alvirez	2009 (DOJ)	No Company	Daniel Alvarez was the President of an Arkansas based company that was in the business of selling law enforcement and military equipment. Daniel Alvares and Lee Allen Tolleson conspired to and made bribery payments to an agent who was to pay a portion of that to the Ministy of Defense of a country in Africa. The agents were really undercover FBI agents.	case related to Lee Allen Tolleson

Case Name	Date of Prosecution	Company	Brief Case Description	Notes
U.S. vs. Lee Allen Tolleson	2009 (DOJ)	No Company	Lee Allen Tolleson was the Director of Acquisitions and Logistics at the same Arkansas company as Daniel Alvirez. Lee and Daniel conspired to pay and paid bribery payments to agents that were then to pay a potrion to the Ministry of Defense in a country in Africa. The agents were really undercover FBI agents.	case related to Daniel Alvarez
U.S. vs. Helmie Ashiblie	2009 (DOJ)	No Company	Helmie Ashiblie was the Founder and Vice President of a company based in Virginia that supplied tactical bags and security related articles to law enforcement and governments all around the world. Helmie was involved in a scheme to bribe the Ministry of Defense to obtain business for the comapny. These bribes were to be paid to agents who would then pay the Ministry, and these agents were actually undercover FBI agnets.	
U.S. vs. Andrew Bigelow	2009 (DOJ)	No Company	Andew Bigelow was the Managing Partner and Director of Government Programs for a company that sold machine guns, grenade launchers, and other small arms and accessories. They were involved in an undercover operation by the FBI to persue allegations of bribery in the law enforcement and militaty industry. Andrew Bigelow conspired to make payments to secure business for his company by paying agents that were, in reality, FBI agents.	
U.S. vs. Patrick Caldwell	2009 (DOJ)	No Company	Patrick Caldwell was the Senior Vice President of Sales and Marketing, and later became CEO, of a Florida corporation. The corporation's main business was manufacturing and selling tactical body armor. Patrick was arrested in connection with an undercover FBI operation for attempting to bribe the Ministry of Defense in an African country to sell their products.	

Case Name	Date of Prosecution	Company	Brief Case Description	Notes
U.S. vs. Stephen Gerard Giordanella	2009 (DOJ)	No Company	Stephen Gerard Giordanella was the CEO of the Florida based corporation that Patick Caldwell later became CEO of. Stephen was also involved in the FBI undercover operation for bribing foreign officials to obtain business for the company.	
U.S. vs. Saul Mishkin	2009 (DOJ)	No Company	Saul Mishkin was CEO of a Florida company that sold law enforcement and military equipment. Saul was arrested for a bribery scheme set up to make payments to the Ministry of Defense in an African country. The payments he made were paid to undercover FBI agents working under an operation to persue allegations of bribery in the law enforcement and military industry.	
U.S. vs. Yochanan R. Cohen	2009 (DOJ)	No Company	Yochanan R. Cohen was CEO of a San Francisco company who's main business was manufacturing security equipment, including body armor and hard armor ballistic plates. Yochanan set up bribes to be paid, through agents, to the Ministry of Defense of an African country. The agents were undercover FBI agents persuing allegations of bribery in the law enforcement and military industry.	
U.S. vs. Haim Geri	2009 (DOJ)	No Company	Haim Geri was President of a company in North Miami Beach. The company was in the business of serving as a consultant to companies in the law enforcement and military industry. Hiam was arrested in connection with an undercover FBI operation to persue allegations of bribery in the law enforcement and military industry. Hiam made payments, through agents and those agents were undercover FBI agents.	

Case Name	Date of Prosecution	Company	Brief Case Description	Notes
U.S. vs. John Benson Weir III	2009 (DOJ)	No Company	John Benson Weir III was President of a St. Petersberg company who was in the business of selling tactical and ballistic equipment. John is accused of bribery of the Ministry of Defense to obtain business for his company. He made these payments to agents with the intent that the payments would be passed along to the officials. The agents were, in fact, undercover FBI agents persuing bribery in the law enforcement and military industry.	
U.S. vs. Israel Weisler	2009 (DOJ)	No Company	Isreal Weisler was the owner and CEO of a Kentuky company who was in the business of manufacturing and selling armor products. Isreal, along with Michael Sacks and other conspirators, made payments to bribe the Minsitry of Defense through agents. These agents were undercover FBI agents that were persuing allegations of bribery in the law enforcement and military industry.	case related to Michael Sacks
U.S. vs. Michael Sacks	2009 (DOJ)	No Company	Michael Sacks was co-owner and CEO of the Kentucky company mentioned in the case relating to Israel Weisler. Michael Sacks is accused of FCPA violations in connection with an undercover FBI operation to persue bribery in the law enforcement and military industry. Michael Sacks made bribery payments to agents that would ensure the improper advatage in obtaining business. The agents were in fact undercover FBI agents.	case related to Israel Weisler
U.S. vs. Ofer Paz	2009 (DOJ)	No Company	Ofer Paz was President and CEO of an Isreal-based copmany. This company acted as a sales agent for companies in the law enforcement and military products industry. Ofer Paz was arrested for making bribery payments in connection with an undercover FBI operation to persue bribery in the law enforcement and military industries.	

Case Name	Date of Prosecution	Company	Brief Case Description	Notes
U.S. vs. Pankesh Patel	2009 (DOJ)	No Company	Pankesh Patel was the Managing Director of a United Kingdom company in the business of acting as a sales agent to companies in the law enforcement and military products industries. Pankesh unknowingly made bribery payments to undercover FBI agents involved in an operation to investigate allegations of bribery in the military and law enforcement industries.	
U.S. vs. John M. Mushriqui	2009 (DOJ)	No Company	John M. Mushriqui was Owner and Director of International Development for a company in Pennsylvania. The company was in the business of manufacturing and exporting bulletproof vests and other law enforcement and military equipment. John, through agents, made bribery payments to the Ministry of Defense to obtain business for his comapny. The agents were in reality undercover FBI agents pursuing allegations of bribery in the law enforcement and military industries.	case related to Jenna Mushriqui
U.S. vs. Jenna Mushriqui	2009 (DOJ)	No Company	Jenna Mushriqui, sister of John. M. Mushruqui, was the General Cousel and U.S. manager of the Pennsylvania company. Jenna was also involved in the bribery scheme to bribe the Ministry of Defense that was part of the FBI's undercover operation.	case related to John M. Mushriqui
U.S. vs. David R. Painter	2009 (DOJ)	No Company	David R. Painter was the Chairman of a United Kingdom company that was in the business of marketing armored vehicles. David made bribery payments that he thought would lead to obtaining business for his company. In reality, he was involved in an undercover FBI operation and made the payments to undercover FBI agents.	related to Lee M. Wares

Case Name	Date of Prosecution	Company	Brief Case Description	Notes
U.S. vs. Lee M. Wares	2009 (DOJ)	No Company	Lee M. Wares was Director of the United Kingdom that marketed armored vehicles. Lee was also involved in the bribery of undercover FBI agents posing as agents that would pass along the bribe payments to the Ministry of Defense of a company.	related to David R. Painter
U.S. vs. Amaro Goncalves	2009 (DOJ)	No Company	Amaro Goncalves was the Vice President of Sales for a Springfield, Massachusetts company in the business of maunfacturing firearms, firearm safety/security products, rifles, firearms systems, and accessories. Amaro was involved in a scheme that was meant to bribe the Ministry of Defense of a country to obtain business. In reality, it was an undercover FBI operation and the agents used to pass along the payments were undercover FBI agents.	
U.S. vs. John W. Warwick	2009 (DOJ)	No Company	John W. Warwick the former President of Ports Engineering Consultants Corporation made bribery payments to governmet officials in Panama to obtain contracts to maintain lighthouses and bouys along Panama's waterways. John pled guilty to the allegations and was sentenced to 37 months in prison, two years of supervised release following his prison term, and to forfeit $331,000 in proceeds of the crime.	case related to Charles Paul Edward Jumet
SEC vs. ITT Corporation	2009 (SEC)	ITT Corporation	ITT Corporation violated the books and records provision of the FCPA by imporperly recording approximately $200,000 in bribery payments. These payments were made by ITT's subsidiary to Chinese state-owned entities to secure business. ITT consented to the entry of a final judgment permanently enjoining it from future violations of the FCPA, to pay disgorgement of $1,041,112, together with prejudgment interest thereon of $387,538.11; and imposing a $250,000 civil penalty.	

Case Name	Date of Prosecution	Company	Brief Case Description	Notes
SEC vs. Novo Nordisk A/S	2009 (SEC) (DOJ)	Novo Nordisk A/S	Novo Nordisk A/S is charged with violating the books and records and internal controls provisions of the Foreign Corrupt Practices Act. Novo improperly recorded kickback payments made to Iraq during the United Nations Oil for Food Program. These payments were made to obtain sales of humanitarian goods. Novo consented to the entry of a final judgment permanently enjoining it from future violations of Sections of the FCPA, to disgorge $4,321,523 in profits plus $1,683,556 in pre-judgment interest, and a civil penalty of $3,025,066. Novo Nordisk has agreed to pay a $9 million criminal penalty pursuant to a deferred prosecution agreement with the U.S. DOJ.	
SEC vs. United Industrial Corporation	2009 (SEC)	United Industrial Corporation	United Industrial Corporation, through its subsidiary and employees, made a series of bribery payments to Egyptian Air Force officials to obtain or retain business of a military aircraft depot being built by United Industrial Corporation through ACL. UIC is ordered to cease and desist from committing or causing any violations and any future violations of the Foreign Corrupt Practices Act, pay disgorgement of $267,571.00 and prejudgment interest of $70,108.42.	
SEC vs. Thomas Wurzel	2009 (SEC)	No Company	Thomas Wurzel was president of ACL Technologies, a wholly-owned subsidiary of United Industrial Corporation. Thomas authorized multiple payments to Egyptian Air Force officials to obtain or retain business for United Industrial Corporation through ACL. ACL was awarded the contracts becuase of these payments. Thomas is charged with violating the anti-bribery provision of the Foreign Corrupt Practices Act and also aiding and abetting United Industrial's violations of the ant-bribery and books and records provisions of the FCPA. Wurzel has consented to the entry of a final judgment permanently enjoining him from future violations of the FCPA and from aiding and abetting violations of the FCPA and to pay a $35,000 civil penalty.	

Case Name	Date of Prosecution	Company	Brief Case Description	Notes
SEC vs. Avery Dennison Corporation	2009 (SEC)	Avery Dennison Corporation	Avery Dennison Corporation is charged with violating the books and records and internal controls provisions of the FCPA. Avery's subsidiary and other aquired compnies gave kickbacks, sightseeing trips, and gifts to Chinese government officials to obtain or retain business for the corporation. Avery consented to the ordered relief and within ten business days of the entry of the order, must pay disgorgement of $273,213 and prejudgment interest of $45,257 to the United States Treasury.	
SEC vs. Helmerich & Payne, Inc.	2009 (SEC) (DOJ)	Helmerich & Payne, Inc.	Helmerich & Payne, Inc., through its subsidiaries made multiple bribery payments to customs officials in Latin America. These payments were made with the intent to obtain an improper advantage in regards to international transport of their drilling equipment. As a result of these actions, Helmerich & Payne violated the books and records and internal controls provisions of the Foreign Corrupt Practices Act. Helmerich & Payne are ordered to cease and desist from committing or causing any violations and any future violations of the FCPA and to pay disgorgement of $320,604 and prejudgment interest of $55,077.22. Helmerich & Payne must also pay a $1 million criminal penalty.	

Case Name	Date of Prosecution	Company	Brief Case Description	Notes
SEC vs. Oscar Meza	2009 (SEC)	No Company	Oscar Meza authorized a number of bribery payments on behalf of Faro Technologies, Inc. These payments were made to Chinese state-owned companies to obtain contracts for Faro. As a result of his actions, Oscar violated the anti-bribery provision of the Foreign Corrupt Practices Act. He also aided and abetted Faro's violations of the anti-bribey and books and records provisions of the FCPA. Meza has consented to the entry of a final judgment permanently enjoining him from violating the anti-bribery provision of the FCPA, from aiding and abetting violations of the anti-bribery and books and records provisions of the FCPA, and to pay a $30,000 civil penalty, as well as $26,707 in disgorgement and prejudgment interest.	
SEC vs. AGCO Corporation	2009 (SEC) (DOJ)	AGCO Corporation	AGCO Corporation, through its subsidiaries, made approximately $5.9 million in kickback payments to Iraq in connection with the United Nations Oil for Food program. These payments were made to secure sales of their products in Iraq. AGCO impropoerly recorded these transactions as after sales service fees and failed to implement an internal control system that would prevent or detect these payments. AGCO consented to the entry of a final judgment permanently enjoining AGCO from future violations of the FCPA, to disgorge $13,907,393 in profits plus $2,000,000 in pre-judgment interest plus a civil penalty of $2,400,000. Relating to a criminal investigation AGCO must pay a $1,600,000 penalty pursuant to a deferred prosecution agreement with the DOJ.	

Case Name	Date of Prosecution	Company	Brief Case Description	Notes
SEC vs. Bobby Benton	2009 (SEC)	No Company	Bobby Benton, while working at Pride International, authorized and concealed bribery payments made to government officials in Mexico and Venezuela. These payments were made to extend drilling contracts, for favorable treatment in regards to customs, and to export rigs. Bobby aided and abetted Pirdes violations of the books and records and internal controls provisions of the Foreign Corrupt Practices Act. The SEC's action seeks a permanent injunction, a civil penalty, and the disgorgement of ill-gotten gains plus prejudgment interest.	
SEC vs. UTStarcom, Inc.	2009 (SEC) (DOJ)	UTStarcom, Inc.	UTStarcom, Inc. paid approximately $7 in bribery payments to government owned telecommunications companies in China and Mongolia that were customers of UTStarcom. These payments were made in the form of trips, gifts, and training. UTStarcom agreed to the entry of a permanent injunction against FCPA violations, to provide the SEC with FCPA compliance reports and certifications for four years, and to pay the $1.5 million penalty. UTStarcom must also pay a $1.5 million criminal penatly to the DOJ in connection with a non-prosecution agreement.	

Case Name	Date of Prosecution	Company	Brief Case Description	Notes
U.S. vs. Richard T. Bistrong	2010 (DOJ)		Richard T. Bistrong was Vice President for international sales for a Florida-based company in the business of manufacturing and selling various law enforcement and military equipment. Richard made bribery payments in connection with an undercover FBI operation. Richard thought the bribery payments being made to agents would be passed along to the Ministry of Defense to obtain sales, but in reality those agents were undercover FBI agents.	
U.S. vs. Jean Fourcand	2010 (DOJ)	Fourcand Enterprises, Inc.	Jean Fourcand was the President and Director of Fourcand Enterprises, Inc. Jean was the receipent of the bribery payments made by Juan Diaz, Antonio Perez, Carlos Rodriguez, Marguerite Grandison, and Joel Esquenazi. Jean pled guilty and was senttenced to 6 months in prison, supervised release for a term of 2 years, and a $100 assessment.	Related to Juan Diaz, Antonio Perez, Carlos Rodriguez, Marguerite Grandison, and Joel Esquenazi.
U.S. vs. BAE Systems plc	2010 (DOJ)	BAE Systems plc	BAE Systems plc made false statements to the United States government about its Foreign Corrupt Practices Act Compliance Program. BAE pled guilty and agreed to pay a $400 million criminal fine.	
SEC vs. NATCO Group Inc.	2010 (SEC)	NATCO Group Inc.	NATCO Group Inc., through its subsidiary, violated the books and records and internal controls provisions of the Foreign Corrupt Practices Act. These violations came about when NATCOs books and records failed to accurately reflect bribery payments made by its subsidiary to officials of the Republic of Kazakhstan. These payments were made to obtain immigration visas based on false documentation. NATCO is ordered to cease and desist from violating the books and records and internal controls provisions of the FCPA.	

Case Name	Date of Prosecution	Company	Brief Case Description	Notes
SEC vs. Innospec Inc.	2010 (SEC) (DOJ)	Innospec Inc.	Innospec Inc., from 2000 to 2007, made a series of bribery payments to government-owned oil refineries and oil companies in Iraq and Indonesia. These payments were made to obtain sales contracts of Tetra Ethyl Lead, a feul additive, which have lost sales since the enactment of the Clean Air Act of 1970 and similar legislation in other countries. Based on their actions, Innospec violated the anti-bribery, books and records, and internal controls provisions of the Foreign Corrupt Practices Act. Innospec has consented to the entry of a court order permanently enjoining it from future violations of the FCPA, to pay $60,071,613 in disgorgement and to comply with its FCPA compliance program, including an independent monitor for a period of three years. In connection with an investigation by the DOJ, Innospec must also pay a $14.1 million criminal fine.	
SEC vs. Daimler AG	2010 (SEC) (DOJ)	Daimler AG	Daimler AG, through its subsidiaries and affiliates, violated the anti-bribery, books and records, and internal controls provisions of the FCPA. Daimler made illicit payments, related to 51 transactions, to government officials worldwide with the intention to secure or maintain business for the company. Daimler AG agreed to pay $91.4 million in disgorgement of profits relating to the civil case violations. In total, Daimler AG and its subsidiaries will pay $93.6 million in criminal fines and penalties relating to the DOJ investigation.	related to Daimler CAR, Daimler CCL, and Daimler ETF
U.S. vs. DaimlerChrysler Automotive Russia SAO	2010 (DOJ)	DaimlerChrysler Automotive Russia SAO	DaimlerChrysler Automotive Russia SAO made bribery payments to Russian Federal and Municipal government officicials in order to sell their vehicles. Daimler pled guilty and was sentenced to pay criminal fines of $27.26 million.	related to Daimler AG, Daimler CCL, and Daimler ETF

Case Name	Date of Prosecution	Company	Brief Case Description	Notes
U.S. vs. Daimler Export and Trade Finance GmbH	2010 (DOJ)	Daimler Export and Trade Finance GmbH	Daimler Export and Trade Finance GmbH made bribery payments to Croatian government officials and to third parties, to obtain business to sell their products in Croatia. Daimler pled guilty and was sentenced to pay $29.12 million.	related to Daimler AG, Daimler CCL, and Daimler CAR
U.S. vs. DaimlerChrysler China Ltd.	2010 (DOJ)	DaimlerChrysler China Ltd.	DaimlerChrysler China Ltd. made bribery payments to government officials in China to obtain business to sell their products. Daimler pled guilty to the allegations against them. See Daimler AG for sentencing.	related to Daimler AG, Daimler ETF, and Daimler CAR
SEC vs. Bobby J. Elkin, Jr.	2010 (SEC) (DOJ)	No Company	Bobby J. Elkin, Jr., country manager of Dimon (now Alliance One), authorized, directed, and made bribery payments to government officials in Kyrgyzstan in order to purchase tobacco to resell to customers of Dimon. Bobby consented to the entry of final judgment permanently enjoining him from violating the anti-bribery provisions of the FCPA and aiding and abetting violations of the books and records and internal control provisoins of the FCPA. Bobby pled guilty to a relating DOJ case and was sentenced to probation for 3 years, pay a $5000 criminal fine, and pay an assessment of $100.	

Case Name	Date of Prosecution	Company	Brief Case Description	Notes
SEC vs. Baxter J. Myers	2010 (SEC)	No Company	Baxter J. Myers, Dimon's Regional Financial Manager, made all money transfers from a Dimon subsidiary to a special account that was used to make bribery payments to government officials in Kyrgyzstan. As a result of his actions, Baxter violated the anti-bribery provsion of the Foreign Corrupt Practices Act and aided and abetted Dimon's (now Alliance One) violations of the books and records provisons of the FCPA. Baxter consented to the entry of final judgment permanently enjoining him from violating the anti-bribery provisions of the FCPA and aiding and abetting violations of the books and records and internal control provisions of the FCPA, and to pay a civil monetary penalty of $40,000.	
SEC vs. Thomas G. Reynolds	2010 (SEC)	No Company	Thomas G. Reynolds was the International Controller for Dimon (now Alliance One). Thomas formalized the account procedure to conceal bribery payments made to government officials in Kyrgyzstan. As a result of his actions, Thomas violated the anti-bribery provsion of the Foreign Corrupt Practices Act and aided and abetted Alliance One's violations of the books and records and internal controls provisons of the FCPA. Thomas consented to the entry of final judgment permanently enjoining him from violating the anti-bribery provisions of the FCPA and aiding and abetting violations of the books and records and internal control provisions of the FCPA and to pay a civil monetary penalty of $40,000.	

Case Name	Date of Prosecution	Company	Brief Case Description	Notes
SEC vs. Tommy Lynn Williams	2010 (SEC)	No Company	Tommy Lynn Williams, Dimon's Senior Vice President of Sales, authorized bribery payments to the Thiland Tobacco Monopoly officials to obtain sales. Tommy improperly recorded these transactions as commission payments to Dimon's agent in Thiland. As a result of his actions, Tommy violated the anti-bribery provision of the Foreign Corrupt Practices Act and aided and abetted Dimon's (now Alliance One) violations of the books and records and internal controls provisons of the FCPA. Tommy consented to the entry of final judgment permanently enjoining him from violating the anti-bribery provisions of the FCPA and aiding and abetting violations of the books and records and internal control provisions of the FCPA.	
SEC vs. Technip	2010 (SEC) (DOJ)	Technip	Technip violated the anti-bribery, books and records, and internal controls provisions of the FCPA. A four-company joint venture called "TSKJ," of which Technip was a member, won contracts to build liquified natural gas production facilities in Nigeria by paying bribes to government officials. Technip has consented to the entry of a court order permanently enjoining it from violating provisions of the FCPA and ordering Technip to disgorge $98 million in ill-gotten profits derived from the scheme and prejudgment interest. The proposed settlement is subject to court approval. Technip agreed to pay a criminal penalty of $240 million and has entered into a deferred prosecution agreement with the DOJ.	

Case Name	Date of Prosecution	Company	Brief Case Description	Notes
SEC vs. VerazNetworks, Inc.	2010 (SEC)	VerazNetworks, Inc.	VerazNetworks, Inc., violated the books and records and internal controls provisions of the Foreign Corrupt Practices Act when they made payments to employees of government-owned telecommunications companies in China and Vietnam. These payments were made with the intention to influence the employees' decisions to grant or continue business with Veraz. Veraz consented to the entry of a final judgment permanently enjoining Veraz from future violations of the books and records and internal controls provisions of the FCPA and ordering Veraz to pay a penalty of $300,000.	
SEC vs. ENI, S.p.A.	2010 (SEC)	ENI, S.p.A.	ENI, S.p.A., through Snamprogetti Netherlands B.V., violated the books and records and internal controls provisions of the Foreign Corrupt Practices Act. Snamprogetti was included in a four-company joint venture, made bribery payments to Nigerian government officials to obtain contracts to build liquified natural gas production facilities. ENI has consented to the entry of a court order permanently enjoining it from violating the recordkeeping and internal controls provisions of the FCPA, to pay $125 million in disgorgement jointly and severally with Snamprogetti. The proposed settlements are subject to court approval.	see Snamprogetti

Case Name	Date of Prosecution	Company	Brief Case Description	Notes
SEC vs. Snamprogetti Netherlands B.V.	2010 (SEC)	Snamprogetti Netherlands B.V.	Snamprogetti Netherlands B.V., through a four-company joint venture, paid a series of bribery payments to Nigerian government officials to obtain contracts worth over $6 billion to build liquified natural gas facilities. Snamprogetti violated the anti-bribery provision of the FCPA and knowingly falsified the books of ENI, S.p.A. Snamprogetti has consented to the entry of a court order permanently enjoining it from violating the anti-bribery and recordkeeping and internal controls provisions of the Securities Exchange Act of 1934 and Rule 13b2-1, to pay $125 million in disgorgement jointly and severally with ENI. The proposed settlements are subject to court approval. Snamprogetti agreed to pay $240 million in criminal penalties in a related DOJ case.	see Halliburton, KBR, Technip
SEC vs. General Electric Company	2010 (SEC)	General Electric Company	General Electric Company, through two of its subsidiaries, violated the books and records and internal controls provisions of the Foreign Corrupt Practices Act by making kickback payments of approximately $2.04 million to Iraqi Health Ministry under the United Nations Oil for Food Program. These payments were made in the form of computer equipment, medical supplies, and services. GE consented to the entry of a final judgment permanently enjoining them from future violations of the FCPA, to disgorge $18,397,949 in wrongful profits, pay $4,080,665 in pre-judgment interest, and pay a civil penalty of $1,000,000.	

Case Name	Date of Prosecution	Company	Brief Case Description	Notes
SEC vs. Ionics Inc.	2010 (SEC)	Ionics Inc.	Ionics Inc., through its subsidiaries, violated the books and records and internal controls provisions of the Foreign Corrupt Practices Act. Kickback payments of $795,000 were paid to obtain sales contracts to the Iraqi Ministry of Health under the Unitied Nations Oil for Food program. Ionics failed to properly record these payments and failed to adequately maintain proper internal controls to prevent or detect these transactions. Ionics consented to the entry of a final judgment permanently enjoining them from future violations of the FCPA	GE acquired Ionics Inc. after the kickbacks were paid. See General Electrics for settlement payments.
SEC vs. Amersham plc	2010 (SEC)	Amersham plc	Amersham plc, through its subsidiaries, paid approximately $750,000 in kickback payments to the Iraqi Ministry of Health to obtain business contracts. Based on this information, Amersham violated the books and records and internal controls provisions of the Foreign Corrput Practices Act. Amersham consented to the entry of a final judgment permanently enjoining them from future violations of the FCPA.	GE acquired Amersham plc after the kickbacks were paid. See General Electrics for settlement payments.
SEC vs. Joe Summers	2010 (SEC)	No Company	Joe Summers, an employee of Pride International, authorized illicit payments of approximately $414,000. These payments were made with the intentions that they would be given to a Venezuelan state-owned oil company. These payments were made to secure drilling contracts and to secure imporper payments of receivables. Joe is being charged with violatin the anti-bribery provision of the FCPA, knowingly falsifying books and records, and aiding and abetting Prides violations of the books and records and internal controls provisions of the FCPA. Joe Summers consented to the entry of a permanent injunction and a civil penalty of $25,000.	

Case Name	Date of Prosecution	Company	Brief Case Description	Notes
SEC vs. David P. Turner	2010 (SEC)	No Company	David P. Turner, an employee of Innospec Inc., violated the anti-bribery provision of the FCPA and also aided and abetted Innospecs violations of the anti-bribery, books and records, and internal controls provisions. David made multiple bribery payments in connection with the sale of TEL, a fuel additive, to officials in Iraq and Indonesia. David has consented to the entry of final judgments that permanently enjoins him from violating the anti-bribery provision of the FCPA and aiding and abetting the violations and the books and records and internal controls provisions, to disgorge $40,000.	
SEC vs. Ousarna M. Naarnan	2010 (SEC) 2008 (DOJ)	No Company	Ousarna M. Naarnan, an employee of Innospec Inc., violated the anti-bribery provision of the FCPA and also aided and abetted Innospecs violations of the anti-bribery, books and records, and internal controls provisions. Ousarna engaged in bribery of the Iraqi Oil Ministry during the post-Oil for Food period. These payments were made to ensure sales of TEL, a fuel additive sold by Innospec. Ousarna has consented to the entry of final judgments that permanently enjoins him from violating the anti-bribery provision of the FCPA and aiding and abetting the violations and the books and records and internal controls provisions, to disgorge $810,076 plus prejudgment interest of $67,030, and pay a civil penalty of $438,038.	

Case Name	Date of Prosecution	Company	Brief Case Description	Notes
SEC vs. Universal Corporation	2010 (SEC)	Universal Corporation	Universal Corporation, through its subsidiaries, violated the anti-bribery, books and records, and internal controls provisions of the FCPA. Bribery payments were made to government officials in Thiland, Mozambique, and Malawi. These payments were made to secure sales contracts and rights to purchase tobacco. Universal Corporation consented to the entry of final judgments permanently enjoining them from violating the anti-bribery, books and records, and internal control provisions of the FCPA, to pay disgorgement of $4,581,276.51. See Universal Leaf Tobacco for related DOJ sentencing.	related to Universal Leaf Tobaccos
U.S. vs. Universal Leaf Tobaccos Ltda.	2010 (DOJ)	Universal Leaf Tobaccos Ltda	Universal Leaf Tobaccos Ltda, a subsidiary of Universal Corporation, made bribery payments to Thailand Tobacco Monopoly employees for the sale of Brazilian tobacco. ULTL was sentenced to 3 years of probation, to pay a $4,400,000 criminal penalty and an $800 assessment.	related to Universal Corporation
SEC vs. Alliance One International, Inc.	2010 (SEC)	Alliance One International, Inc.	Alliance One International, Inc. was formed after a merger between Dimon Incorporated and Standard Commercial Corporation. Both Dimon and Standard made bribery payments to government officials in Thailand, Greece, Indonesia and Kyrgyzstan. These payments were made with the intention to purchase tobacco to resell to their customers, to obtain sales contracts, and to influence decisions not to disclose tax irregularities. Alliance One consented to the entry of final judgments permanently enjoining them from violating the anti-bribery, books and records, and internal control provisions of the FCPA, to pay disgorgement of $10,000,000. In a related DOJ case, Alliance One pled guilty and was sentenced to pay 5,250,000 in criminal penalites and a $1,200 assessment.	case related to Universal Corporation. DOJ case $9,450,000 (see universal)

Case Name	Date of Prosecution	Company	Brief Case Description	Notes
U.S. vs. Alliance One Tobacco OSH, LLC	2010 (DOJ)	Alliance One Tobacco OSH, LLC	Alliance One Tobacco OSH, LLC, a wholly owned subsidiary of Alliance One, made bribery payements to governmet officials to obtain business and improper tax advantages. Alliance One pled guilty to these allegations and was sentenced to pay $4,200,000 in criminal penalties and a $1,200 assessment.	
U.S. vs. Enrique Aguilar	2010 (DOJ)	No Company	Enrique Aguilar, as a sales representative, accepted bribery payments from clients to help them obtain and maintain business in Mexico.	related to Angela Aguilar
U.S. vs. Angela Aguilar	2010 (DOJ)	No Company	Angela Aguilar accepted bribery payments from clients to help them obtain and retain business in Mexico.	related to Enrique Aguilar
SEC vs. ABB Ltd.	2010 (SEC)	ABB Ltd.	ABB Ltd., through its subsidiaries, made a number of bribery payments to government officials in Mexico to obtain business with government-owned power companies and to Iraqi officials to obtain contracts through the United Nations Oil for Food Program. ABB has agreed to settle the SEC's action by consenting to the entry of a final judgment that permanently enjoins the company from future violations of the FCPA, to pay $22,804,262 in disgorgement and prejudgment interest, orders the company to pay a $16,510,000 civil penalty, and requires the company to comply its FCPA compliance program. In a related case with the DOJ, ABB entered into a deferred prosecution agreement and agreed to pay a criminal penalty of $1.9 million related to its subsidiary ABB Jordan.	related to ABB Inc and ABB Ltd-Jordan
ABB Inc.	2010 (DOJ)	ABB Inc.	ABB Inc, a subsidiary of ABB Ltd, made bribery payments to government officails in Iraq under the United Nations Oil for Food Program. ABB Inc. pled guilty and was sentenced to pay a criminal penalty of $17.1 million.	related to ABB Ltd and ABB Ltd-Jordan

Case Name	Date of Prosecution	Company	Brief Case Description	Notes
U.S. vs. ABB Ltd—Jordan	2010 (DOJ)	ABB Ltd-Jordan	ABB Ltd—Jordan paid kickbacks to the former Iraqi government in connection with contracts to sell vehicles to Iraq under the U.N.'s Oil for Food program. These payments were made to obtain business to sell electrical equipment and services worth over $5.9 million. See ABB Ltd for sentencing.	related to ABB Ltd and ABB Inc.
SEC vs.Transocean Inc.	2010 (SEC) (DOJ)	Transocean Inc.	Transocean Inc., through its customs agent, Panalpina, made illicit payments to Nigerian government officials to secure improper importation of Transoceans drills and to obtain false paperwork regarding the drill imports. Transocean has consented to the entry of a court order permanently enjoining it from future violations of the FCPA, and to pay $5,981,693 in disgorgement, plus prejudgment interest of $1,283,387. In a related DOJ case, Transocean enter into a deferred prosecution agreement and agreed to pay a $13.44 million criminal penalty.	
SEC vs. Pride International Inc.	2010 (SEC) (DOJ)	Pride International Inc.	Pride International Inc., through its employees and or agents, violated the anti-bribery, books and records, and internal controls provisions of the FCPA. Payments were made on behalf of Pride International to government officials in many countries with the intention to obtain drilling contracts and an unfair advantage in regards to imports, customs, and receivables. Pride consented to the entry of permanently enjoining it from violating the anti-bribery, books and records, and internal controls provisions of the FCPA, to pay disgorgement of $19,341,870 plus pre-judgment interest of $4,187,848. In a related DOJ case, Pride International entered into a deferred prosecution agreement and agreed to pay a $32.625 million criminal penalty.	

Case Name	Date of Prosecution	Company	Brief Case Description	Notes
U.S. vs. Pride Forasol S.A.S	2010 (DOJ)	Price Forasol S.A.S	Pride Forasol, a subsidiary of Pride International, made bribery payments to obtain drilling contracts and an unfair advantage in regards to imports, customs, and receivables. Pride Forasol pled guilty. See Pride International for criminal sentencing.	
SEC vs. Panalpina, Inc.	2010 (SEC) (DOJ)	Panalpina, Inc.	Panalpina, Inc. is charged with violating the anti-bribery provision of the Foreign Corrupt Practices Act by making bribery payments to government officials in Nigeria, Angola, Brazil, Russia, and Kazakhstan on behalf of their customers. These payments were made in order to gain an unfair treatment in regards to imports, duties, and customs. Panalpina is also charged with aiding and abetting the violations of the anti-bribery, books and records, and internal controls provisions of the FCPA. Panalpina consented to the entry of a final judgment ordering disgorgement and permanently enjoining it from violating the FCPA's anti-bribery provisions and aiding and abetting violations of the FCPA's books and records and internal controls provisions. The proposed settlement is subject to court approval. In a related DOJ case, Panalpina pled guilty and will pay a $70.56 million criminal penalty.	
SEC vs. Noble Corporation	2010 (SEC) (DOJ)	Noble Corporation	Noble Corporation authorized, and their subsidiary paid, bribery payments to government officials in Nigeria. These payments were made to obtain temporary import papers that were based on false documentation. Noble has agreed to the entry of a Court order enjoining it from violating the anti-bribery, books and records, and internal controls provisions, to disgorge ill-gotten gains of $4,294,933 and pay prejudgment interest of $1,282,065. In a related DOJ case, Noble entered into a non-prosecution agreement and will pay a $2.59 million criminal penalty.	

Case Name	Date of Prosecution	Company	Brief Case Description	Notes
SEC vs. GlobalSantaFe Corp	2010 (SEC)	GlobalSantaFe Corp	GlobalSantaFe Corp violated the anti-bribery, books and records, and internal controls provisions of the Foreign Corrupt Practices Act by making illicit payments to officials of the Nigerian Customs Service. These payments were made to obtain false paperwork during the customs process to give GlobalSantaFe an unfair advantage. GSF has consented to the entry of a court order permanently enjoining it from violating the anti-bribery and record keeping and internal controls provisions of the FCPA, to pay disgorgement of $2,694,405, prejudgment interest of $1,063,760, and a civil penalty of $2.1 million. The proposed settlement is subject to court approval.	
SEC vs. Royal Dutch Shell plc	2010 (SEC) (DOJ)		Royal Dutch Shell plc, as a result of its subsidiary's violation of the anti-bribery provision of the FCPA, has violated the books and records and internal controls provisions of the FCPA. Shell's subsidiary, Shell International Exploration and Production Inc., made bribery payments to customs officials in Nigeria to secure business in regards to Shell's Bongo Project. Shell's books and records did not accurately reflect these payments and they did not maintain adequate controls to detect or prevent them at the time. Shell has been ordered to cease and desist from future violations of the books and records and internal controls provisions of the FCPA and to jointly and severally (with Shell International Exploration and Production Inc.) pay disgorgement of $14,153,536 and prejudgment interest thereon of $3,995,923.	

Case Name	Date of Prosecution	Company	Brief Case Description	Notes
SEC vs. Shell International Exploration and Production Inc.	2010 (SEC) (DOJ)		Shell International Exploration and Production Inc., violated the anti-bribery provision of the FCPA by engaging in a number of payments made to customs officials in Nigeria. These payments were made with the intention to gain unfair treatment in the customs process so Shell could obtain or retain business in Nigeria on Shell's Bonga Project. Shell International Exploration and Production Inc. is ordered to cease and desist from future violations of the anti-bribery provision of the FCPA and to jointly and severally (with Royal Dutch Shell) pay disgorgement of $14,153,536 and prejudgment interest thereon of $3,995,923. In a related DOJ case, Shell was sentenced to pay a $30 million criminal penalty.	
SEC vs. Tidewater Inc.	2010 (SEC) (DOJ)	Tidewater Inc.	Tidewater Inc., through its subsidiaries, employees, and agents, made a series of bribery payments to government officials in Nigeria and Azerbaijan. The Nigerian payments were made to the Nigerian Customs Service in order to ignore regulatory requirements related to temporary import papers. The payments to Azerbaijan officials were made to Azeri tax officials to influence the outcome of audits. Tidewater has consented to a court order permanently enjoining it from future violations of the FCPA, to pay $7,223,216 in disgorgement plus prejudgment interest of $881,146, and a $217,000 civil penalty. In a related DOJ case, Tidewater entered into a deferred prosecution agreement and agreed to pay a $7.35 million criminal penalty.	

Case Name	Date of Prosecution	Company	Brief Case Description	Notes
SEC vs. RAE Systems Inc.	2010 (SEC) (DOJ)	RAE Systems Inc.	RAE Systems Inc., through two joint-ventures, made bribery payments to government officials in China to influence the officials' decisions to obtain or retain business for RAE. RAE was aware of the illicit payments. RAE has consented to the entry of a court order permanently enjoining it from future violations, to pay $1,147,800 in disgorgement, plus $109,212 in prejudgment interest, and to comply with its FCPA compliance program. RAE entered into an agreement with the Department of Justice to pay $1.7 million in a related criminal case.	
U.S. vs. Jorge Granados	2010 (DOJ)	Latin Node, Inc.	Jorge Grandos was the founder, CEO, and Chairman of the Board at Latin Node. Jorge made more than $500,000 in bribery payments to government officials in Hondorus to obtain unfair business advantages. Jorge pled guilty to the DOJ allegations and was sentenced to 46 months in prison and to serve two years of supervised release following the prison term.	
U.S. vs. Manuel Caceres	2010 (DOJ)	Latin Node, Inc.	Manuel Caceres was a senior executive at Latin Node. Manuel made bribery payments to government officails in Hondorus to obtain unfair business advantages. Manuel pled guilty to the DOJ allegations.	
U.S. vs. Manuel Salvoch	2010 (DOJ)	Latin Node, Inc.	Manuel Salvoch was CFO of Latin Node. He is accused of being involved in a $500,000 bribery scheme to pay to Hondorus government officials to obtain unfair business advantages to Latin Node. Manuel pled guilty and entered into a plea agreement with the DOJ.	

Case Name	Date of Prosecution	Company	Brief Case Description	Notes
U.S. vs. Juan Pablo Vasquez	2010 (DOJ)	Latin Node, Inc.	Juan Pablo Vasquez was the Chief Commercial Officer of Latin Node. Juan was a part of a scheme to bribe government officials in Hondorus to obtain unfair business advantages for Latin Node. Juan pled guilty to the DOJ allegations and entered into a plea agreement with the DOJ.	
SEC vs. Alcatel-Lucent, S.A.	2010 (SEC) (DOJ)	Alcatel-Lucent, S.A.	Alcatel-Lucent, S.A., through its subsidiaries (Alcatel-Lucent France, S.A, Alcatel-Lucent Trade International, A.G.), Alcatel Centroamerica, S.A.), violated the anti-bribery, books and records, and internal controls provisions of the FCPA. Alcatels subsidiaries made a number of bribery payments to government officials all over the world to influence the officials' decisions to extend Alcatel telecommunications contracts. Alcatel has consented to a court order permanently enjoining it from future violations of the provisions, to pay $45.372 million in disgorgement of wrongfully obtained profits, and to comply with certain undertakings, including an independent monitor for a three year term. In a related DOJ case, Alcatel-Lucent has agreed to pay a $92 million criminal penalty (includes penalty for the 3 subsidiaries involved).	
SEC vs. Paul W. Jennings	2011 (SEC)	No Company	While working for Innospec, Inc., Paul assisted the company in making a number of bribery payments to government officials in Iraq and Indonesia. These payments were made to gain an unfair advantage to sell their fuel additive products. Jennings signed false documents stating that the books and records of the company were correct. Jennings will disgorge $116,092 plus prejudgment interest of $12,945, and pay a civil penalty of $100,000.	see case related to Innospec Inc.

Case Name	Date of Prosecution	Company	Brief Case Description	Notes
SEC vs. Maxwell Technologies Inc.	2011 (SEC) (DOJ)	Maxwell Technologies Inc.	Maxwell Technologies Inc., through its agents, employees, and subsidiaries, violated the Foreign Corrupt Practices Act by making $2.5 million in bribery payments to Chinese officials. These payments were made under the assumption that they would influence the decisions of the officials to retain contracts to sell high voltage capacitors. Maxwell is to pay $5,654,576 in disgorgement, and $696,314 in prejudgment interest to be paid in two installments over one year. In a related DOJ case, Maxwell Technologies was sentenced to pay an $8 million criminal penalty.	
SEC vs. Tyson Foods, Inc.	2011 (SEC) (DOJ)	Tyson Foods, Inc.	Tyson Foods, Inc., through its wholly-owned subsidiary, made illicit payments to two Mexican-state veterinarians. These payments were made with the understanding that they would influence the decisions of the veterinarians responsible for certifying Tyson de Mexico products for export. Tyson Foods consented to the entry of a final judgment ordering disgorgement plus pre-judgment interest of more than $1.2 million and permanently enjoining it from violating the anti-bribery, books and records, and internal controls provisions of the FCPA. In a related DOJ case, Tyson Foods has entered into a deferred prosecution agreement and has agreed to pay a $4 million criminal penalty.	
U.S. vs. JGC Corporation	2011 (DOJ)	JGC Corporation	JGC Corporation was a member of a four-company joint venture called "TSKJ." As part of the joint venue, JGC made bribery payments to government officials in Nigeria to win contracts to build liquified natural gas production facilities. JGC entered into a deferred prosecution agreement and has agreed to pay a $218.8 million criminal penalty.	See KBR, Technip, and Snamprogetti.

Case Name	Date of Prosecution	Company	Brief Case Description	Notes
SEC vs. International Business Machines Corp.	2011 (SEC)	Intemational Business Machines Corp. (IBM)	International Business Machines Corp violated the books and records and internal controls provisions of the Foreign Corrupt Practices Act when their employees of IMB's subsidiaries and a majority-owned joint-venture provided bribery payments in the form of cash, gifts, and travel and entertainment to government officials in South Korea and China. These payments were made with the intention to secure the sale of IBM's products. IBM consented to the entry of a final judgment that permanently enjoins the company from violating the books and records and internal control provisions of the FCPA and to pay disgorgement of $5,300,000, $2,700,000 in prejudgment interest, and a $2,000,000 civil penalty.	
SEC vs. Ball Corporation	2011 (SEC)	Ball Corporation	Ball Corporation, through its subsidiary, made a series of bribery payments to government officials in Argentina. These payments were made to gain an improper advantage in the import of prohibited use machines and in the export of raw materials at lower tariffs. Ball Corporation failed to accurately record these payments and failed to maintain an adequate control system that would prevent or detect them. Ball Corporation is ordered to cease and desist from future violations of the books and records and internal controls provisions of the FCPA and to pay a civil penalty of $300,000.	

Case Name	Date of Prosecution	Company	Brief Case Description	Notes
SEC vs. Comverse Technology, Inc.	2011 (SEC) (DOJ)	Comverse Technology, Inc.	Comverse Technology, Inc. violated the books and records and internal controls provisions of the Foreign Corrupt Practices Act when its subsidiary Comverse Limited made illicit payments to obtain or retain business. Comverse has consented to a conduct-based injunction that prohibits Comverse from having books and records that do not accurately reflect improper payments, or from having internal controls that do not prevent or detect them. Also, Comverse consented to pay $1,249,614 in disgorgement and $358,887 in prejudgment interest. In a related DOJ case, Comverse has entered into a non-prosecution agreement and has agreed to pay a $1.2 million criminal penalty.	
SEC vs. Johnson & Johnson	2011 (SEC) (DOJ)	Johnson & Johnson	Johnson & Johnson violated the Foreign Corrupt Practices Act when its subsidiaries made bribery payments to doctors in Greece, Poland, and Romania. They also provided kickbacks to government officials in Iraq under the Oil for Food Program. These payments were made for the purpose of influencing the decisions to use Johnson & Johnson products. J&J has consented to the entry of a court order permanently enjoining it from future violations of the FCPA, to pay $38,227,826 in disgorgement and $10,438,490 in prejudgment interest, and to comply with the FCPA compliance program. In a related DOJ case, J&J has agreed to pay a $21.4 million criminal penalty as part of a deferred prosecution agreement.	

Case Name	Date of Prosecution	Company	Brief Case Description	Notes
SEC vs. Rockwell Automation	2011 (SEC)	Rockwell Automation	Rockwell Automations' subsidiary made bribery payments to state-owned Design Institutes that provide design engineering and technical integration services. These services can influence end-users' decisions to enter into contracts with Rockwell. Rockwell is ordered to cease and desist from future violations of the books and records and internal control provisions of the Foreign Corrupt Practices Act and to pay disgorgement of $1,771,000, prejudgment interest of $590,091, and a civil money penalty of $400,000.	
SEC vs. Armor Holdings, Inc.	2011 (SEC) (DOJ)	Armor Holdings, Inc.	Armor Holdings, Inc., through its agents, violated the anti-bribery, books and records, and internal controls provisions of the Foreign Corrupt Practices Act by making corrupt payments to an official of the United Nations. These payments were made with the intent to secure business with the U.N. Armor Holdings has consented to a court order permanently enjoining it from violating the FCPA, to pay disgorgement of $1,552,306, together with prejudgment interest of $458,438; imposing on it a civil penalty of $3,680,000, and to comply with the FCPA compliance program. The settlement is subject to court approval. In a related DOJ case, Armor Holdings has entered into a non-prosecution agreement and has agreed to pay a $10.29 million criminal penalty.	

Case Name	Date of Prosecution	Company	Brief Case Description	Notes
SEC vs. Diageo plc	2011 (SEC)	Diageo plc	Diageo plc, through its subsidiaries, made a number of bribery payments to government officials in Thiland, India, and South Korea. These payments were made with the intent to obtain sales and tax benefits. Diageo is ordered to cease and desist from future violation of the books and records and internal controls provisions of the Foreign Corrupt Practices Act, to pay disgorgement of $11,306,081 and prejudgment interest of $2,067,739, and to pay a civil money penalty in the amount of $3,000,000.	
U.S. vs. Bridgestone Corporation	2011 (DOJ)	Bridgestone Corporation	Bridgestone Corporation made bribery payments to government officials in Latin America. These payments were made with the intention to rig bids and obtain business to sell marine hoses and other industrial products manufactured by the company. Bridgestone pled guilty and was sentenced to pay a $28 million criminal fine.	

Appendix 

U.S. Self-Reported FCPA Enforcement Statistics to the OECD (1998-2010), as reported in *Response of the United States Questions Concerning Phase 3 OECD Working Group on Bribery May 3, 2010 (Appendix B)*

The charts in this report will display as "Appendix B"

Source: http://www.justice.gov/criminal/fraud/fcpa/docs/response3-appx-b.pdf

APPENDIX B – CHART 1A

FCPA Criminal Enforcement Statistics (1998-2010)
Natural Persons

	Prosecutions of Natural Persons																					
	Total No. Charged[1]	No. Charged with:[2]			Pending as of end of calendar year[3]			Discontinued without Sanctions[4]			Guilty Pleas			Trial Convictions			Acquittals			No. Sentenced		
Year		FB	AM	ML	FB	AM	ML	FB	AM	ML	FB	AM	ML	FB	AM	ML	FB	AM	ML	FB	AM	ML
1998	4	4	0	0	7	1	2	0	0	0	2	0	0	1	0	0	0	0	0	0	0	0
1999	1	1	0	0	4	1	2	0	0	0	1	0	0	0	0	0	0	0	0	4	0	0
2000	0	0	0	0	4	1	2	0	0	0	0	0	0	0	0	0	0	0	0	0	0	0
2001	7	6	2	0	10	2	2	0	0	0	3	2	0	0	0	0	0	0	0	0	1	0
2002	4	4	0	0	11	2	2	0	0	0	3	0	0	1	0	0	0	0	0	4	0	0
2003	4	4	0	3	15	2	5	0	0	0	1	0	0	0	0	0	0	0	0	0	0	0
2004	2	0	2	0	14	4	5	0	0	0	2	0	2	2	0	0	0	0	0	0	0	0
2005	5	5	0	3	19	2	8	0	0	0	0	0	0	0	0	0	0	2	0	2	0	0
2006	4	3	1	1	21	3	9	0	0	0	4	1	0	0	0	0	0	0	0	1	0	0
2007	9	9	0	6	28	2	15	0	0	0	5	0	2	0	0	0	0	0	0	2	1	0
2008	12	12	1	5	30	3	18	1	0	1	4	0	0	0	0	0	0	0	0	7	0	1
2009	44	40	0	33	70	3	51	0	0	0	9	0	5	4	0	4	0	0	0	3	0	2
2010[5]	5	3	1	3	62	4	45	0	0	0	8	2	6	0	0	0	0	0	0	11	0	9
Total	**101**	**91**	**7**	**54**	--	--	--	**1**	**0**	**1**	**42**	**5**	**15**	**8**	**0**	**4**	**0**	**2**	**0**	**34**	**2**	**12**

[1] In this column, each natural person was only counted once, so the numbers represent the actual number of natural persons charged with FCPA violations in each year.

[2] For the purposes of this chart, the Department counted a natural person in each applicable column according to the conduct with which the defendant was charged. For instance, if a defendant was charged with both foreign bribery (FB) and foreign bribery related accounting misconduct (AM), the person was counted in both the applicable FB and AM columns.

[3] For the purposes of this column, cases were deemed to still be pending if any of the following was true: (1) the defendant was charged, but not yet convicted; (2) the defendant was convicted, but not yet sentenced; (3) the defendant was sentenced, but had filed an appeal, which was still open; or, (4) the defendant was a fugitive, as of the end of the calendar year.

[4] Since 1998, there has not been a case in which the Department discontinued the prosecution of a natural person for foreign bribery or a related offense while imposing sanctions. Therefore, this category was excluded from this table.

[5] For 2010, the numbers in this chart are current through September 30, 2010.

APPENDIX B – CHART 1B

FCPA Criminal Enforcement Statistics (1998-2010)
Legal Persons

Prosecutions of Legal Persons																										
	Total No. Charged[6]	No. Charged with:[7]			Pending as of end of calendar year[8]			Discontinued with Sanctions			Discontinued without Sanctions			Guilty Pleas			Trial Convictions			Acquittals			No. Sentenced		
Year		FB	AM	ML	FB	AM	ML	FB	AM	ML	FB	AM	ML	FB	AM	ML	FB	AM	ML	FB	AM	ML	FB	AM	ML
1998	3	3	0	0	3	0	0	0	0	0	0	0	0	3	0	0	0	0	0	0	0	0	0	0	0
1999	1	1	0	0	0	0	0	0	0	0	0	0	0	1	0	0	0	0	0	0	0	0	4	0	0
2000	1	0	1	0	0	0	0	0	0	0	0	0	0	0	1	0	0	0	0	0	0	0	0	1	0
2001	0	0	0	0	0	0	0	0	0	0	0	0	0	0	0	0	0	0	0	0	0	0	0	0	0
2002	1	1	0	0	0	0	0	0	0	0	0	0	0	1	0	0	0	0	0	0	0	0	1	0	0
2003	0	0	0	0	0	0	0	0	0	0	0	0	0	0	0	0	0	0	0	0	0	0	0	0	0
2004	3	3	1	0	0	0	0	1	1	0	0	0	0	2	0	0	0	0	0	0	0	0	2	0	0
2005	4	4	2	0	0	0	0	2	1	0	0	0	0	2	1	0	0	0	0	0	0	0	2	1	0
2006	2	2	2	0	0	0	0	2	2	0	0	0	0	1	1	0	0	0	0	0	0	0	1	1	0
2007	15	13	8	0	0	0	0	9	7	0	0	0	0	4	1	0	0	0	0	0	0	0	4	1	0
2008	16	9	13	1	1	0	1	5	7	0	0	0	0	3	4	0	0	0	0	0	0	0	3	4	0
2009	7	5	4	0	1	0	1	2	4	0	0	0	0	3	0	0	0	0	0	0	0	0	3	0	0
2010[9]	15	13	8	0	3	2	0	5	4	0	0	0	0	9	4	1	0	0	0	0	0	0	6	2	1
Total	**68**	**54**	**39**	**1**	--	--	--	**26**	**26**	**0**	**0**	**0**	**0**	**29**	**12**	**1**	**0**	**0**	**0**	**0**	**0**	**0**	**26**	**10**	**1**

[6] In this column, each legal person was only counted once, so the numbers represent the actual number of legal persons charged with FCPA violations in each year.

[7] For the purposes of this chart, the Department counted a legal person in each applicable column according to the conduct with which the defendant was charged. For instance, if a defendant was charged with both foreign bribery (FB) and foreign bribery related accounting misconduct (AM), the person was counted in both the applicable FB and AM columns.

[8] For the purposes of this column, cases were deemed to still be pending if any of the following was true: (1) the defendant was charged, but not yet convicted; (2) the defendant was convicted, but not yet sentenced; or, (3) the defendant was sentenced, but had filed an appeal, which was still open, as of the end of the calendar year.

[9] For 2010, the numbers in this chart are current through September 30, 2010.

APPENDIX B – CHART 2A

FCPA Administrative/Civil Enforcement Statistics (1998-2010)
Natural Persons

	Administrative/Civil Enforcement Actions Against Natural Persons																					
	Total No. of Enforcement Actions[1]	Due to Conduct Involving:			Pending as of end of calendar year[2]			Discontinued with Sanctions			Discontinued without Sanctions[3]			Discontinued as a Result of Civil Settlements			Decisions with Sanctions			Decisions Finding No Liability		
Year		FB	AM	ML	FB	AM	ML	FB	AM	ML	FB	AM	ML	FB	AM	ML	FB	AM	ML	FB	AM	ML
1998	0	0	0	0	0	0	0	0	0	0	0	0	0	0	0	0	0	0	0	0	0	0
1999	0	0	0	0	0	0	0	0	0	0	0	0	0	0	0	0	0	0	0	0	0	0
2000	0	0	0	0	0	0	0	0	0	0	0	0	0	0	0	0	0	0	0	0	0	0
2001	3	3	3	0	2	2	0	0	0	0	0	0	0	0	0	0	1	1	0	0	0	0
2002	3	3	1	0	5	3	0	0	0	0	0	0	0	0	0	0	0	0	0	0	0	0
2003	1	1	1	0	5	3	0	0	0	0	2	2	0	0	0	0	1	1	0	0	0	0
2004	0	0	0	0	4	3	0	0	0	0	0	0	0	0	0	0	1	0	0	0	0	0
2005	1	1	1	0	5	4	0	0	0	0	0	0	0	0	0	0	0	0	0	0	0	0
2006	8	7	8	0	8	7	0	0	0	0	0	0	0	0	0	0	5	6	0	0	0	0
2007	8	5	8	0	10	9	0	0	0	0	0	0	0	0	0	0	3	6	0	0	0	0
2008	6	4	6	0	5	4	0	0	0	0	0	0	0	0	0	0	8	10	0	0	0	0
2009	3	3	3	0	6	5	0	0	0	0	0	0	0	0	0	0	2	2	0	0	0	0
2010[4]	7	7	5	0	5	5	0	0	0	0	0	0	0	0	0	0	8	5	0	0	0	0
Total	**40**	**34**	**36**	**0**	--	--	--	**0**	**0**	**0**	**2**	**2**	**0**	**0**	**0**	**0**	**29**	**31**	**0**	**0**	**0**	**0**

[1] This column lists the number of enforcement actions taken against a natural person in each year from 1998 through 2010. If a natural person was subject to both an administrative proceeding and a civil enforcement action, these are counted as separate enforcement actions for the purposes of this chart. Also, if an enforcement action targeted more than one natural person, the number of enforcement actions recorded in this chart reflects the number of natural persons subject to the enforcement action.

[2] For the purposes of this column, cases were deemed to still be pending if any of the following was true: (1) a final judgment or settlement had not been reached; or, (2) the matter had been stayed pending the resolution of an ongoing criminal enforcement action against the defendant in question.

[3] This column includes cases in which the civil charges against the natural person were dismissed by the Court.

[4] For 2010, the numbers in this chart are current through September 30, 2010.

APPENDIX B – CHART 2B

FCPA Administrative/Civil Enforcement Statistics (1998-2010)
Legal Persons

Administrative/Civil Enforcement Actions Against Legal Persons																						
	Total No. of Enforcement Actions[5]	Due to Conduct Involving:			Pending as of end of calendar year[6]			Discontinued with Sanctions[7]			Discontinued without Sanctions			Discontinued as a Result of Civil Settlements			Decisions with Sanctions			Decisions Finding No Liability		
Year		FB	AM	ML	FB	AM	ML	FB	AM	ML	FB	AM	ML	FB	AM	ML	FB	AM	ML	FB	AM	ML
1998	0	0	0	0	0	0	0	0	0	0	0	0	0	0	0	0	0	0	0	0	0	0
1999	1	1	0	0	0	0	0	0	0	0	0	0	0	0	0	0	1	0	0	0	0	0
2000	2	0	2	0	0	0	0	0	0	0	0	0	0	0	0	0	0	2	0	0	0	0
2001	6	3	6	0	0	0	0	0	0	0	0	0	0	0	0	0	3	6	0	0	0	0
2002	4	2	4	0	0	0	0	0	0	0	0	0	0	0	0	0	2	4	0	0	0	0
2003	0	0	0	0	0	0	0	0	0	0	0	0	0	0	0	0	0	0	0	0	0	0
2004	3	2	3	0	0	0	0	0	0	0	0	0	0	0	0	0	2	3	0	0	0	0
2005	6	6	6	0	0	0	0	0	0	0	0	0	0	0	0	0	6	6	0	0	0	0
2006	4	3	4	0	0	0	0	0	0	0	0	0	0	0	0	0	3	4	0	0	0	0
2007	18	7	15	1	0	2	0	0	0	1	0	0	0	0	0	0	7	13	0	0	0	0
2008	11	5	11	0	0	0	0	0	0	0	0	0	0	0	0	0	5	13	0	0	0	0
2009	12	5	11	1	1	0	1	0	0	0	0	0	0	0	0	0	4	11	0	0	0	0
2010[8]	12	7	12	0	0	0	0	0	0	0	0	0	0	0	0	0	8	12	1	0	0	0
Total	**79**	**41**	**74**	**2**	--	--	--	**0**	**0**	**1**	**0**	**0**	**0**	**0**	**0**	**0**	**41**	**74**	**1**	**0**	**0**	**0**

[5] This column lists the number of enforcement actions taken against a legal person in each year from 1998 through 2010. If a legal person was subject to both an administrative proceeding and a civil enforcement action, these are counted as separate enforcement actions for the purposes of this chart. Also, if an enforcement action targeted more than one legal person, the number of enforcement actions recorded in this chart reflects the number of legal persons subject to the enforcement action.

[6] For the purposes of this column, cases were deemed to still be pending if any of the following was true: (1) a final judgment or settlement had not been reached; or, (2) the matter had been stayed pending the resolution of an ongoing criminal enforcement action against the defendant in question.

[7] This column includes one case in which the Department of Justice filed a civil forfeiture action against a certain monetary amount, plus interest, being held in a foreign bank account belonging to a foreign government, alleging that the money was the proceeds of criminal conduct including violations of the FCPA, as well as wire fraud and money laundering. The Department reached an agreement with the foreign government whereby, if the money is not claimed, it will be used to fund social and civil society programs in that country.

[8] For 2010, the numbers in this chart are current through September 30, 2010.

APPENDIX B - CHART 3
SENTENCES OF NATURAL PERSONS CONVICTED AT TRIAL OF FCPA VIOLATIONS

	DEFENDANT	CASE NUMBER	AMOUNT OF BRIBES	SENTENCE (excluding monetary penalties)
1	**Gerald Green** (Owner/Film Executive)	United States v. Green, *et al.*, 08-CR-059 (C.D. Cal. 2008)	~ 1.8M	6 months' imprisonment; 6 months' home confinement
2	**Patricia Green** (Owner/Film Executive)	United States v. Green, *et al.*, 08-CR-059 (C.D. Cal. 2008)	~ 1.8M	6 months' imprisonment; 6 months' home confinement
3	**William Jefferson** (Congressperson)	United States v. Jefferson, 07-CR-209 (E.D. Va. 2007)	~ 500K + Equities	13 years' imprisonment
4	**Frederick Bourke, Jr.** (Investor)	United States v. Kozeny, *et al.*, 05-CR-518 (S.D.N.Y. 2005)	~ Millions	1 year and 1 day's imprisonment
5	**David Kay**[1] (Vice President)	United States v. Kay, *et al.*, 01-CR-914 (S.D. Tex. 2002)	~ 528K	37 months' imprisonment
6	**Douglas Murphy**[1] (President)	United States v. Kay, *et al.*, 01-CR-914 (S.D. Tex. 2002)	~ 528K	63 months' imprisonment
6	**Robert R. King**[1] (Employee)	United States v. King, *et al.*, 01-CR-190 (W.D. Mo. 2001)	~ 1.5M	30 months' imprisonment
7	**David H. Mead**[1, 2] (President, CEO, and Executive Vice President)	United States v. Mead, *et al.*, 98-Cr-240 (D. N.J. 1998)	~ 50K	4 months' imprisonment; 4 months' home detention
8	**Richard H. Liebo**[1, 2] (Vice President)	United States v. Liebo, 89-CR-076 (D. Minn. 1989)	~ 131K	18 months' imprisonment (suspended); 60 days' home detention

[1] United States Sentencing Guidelines Section 2B4.1, with a base offense level of 8, was the applicable U.S.S.G. Section at this time. After 2002, Section 2C1.1, with a base offense level of 12, became the applicable U.S.S.G. Section in accordance with international treaty obligations.

[2] In addition, corporate guilty pleas to FCPA violations resulted in over $2.2 million in fines.

APPENDIX B – CHART 4
SENTENCES OF NATURAL PERSONS WHO PLEADED GUILTY TO FCPA VIOLATIONS SINCE 1998

	DEFENDANT	CASE NUMBER	SENTENCE REDUCTION FOR COOPERATION	AMOUNT OF BRIBES	SENTENCE (excluding monetary penalties)
1	**Nam Quoc Nguyen** (President/Owner)	United States v. Nguyen, *et al.*, 08-CR-522 (E.D. Pa. 2008)	NO	~ 690K	16 months' imprisonment
2	**An Quoc Nguyen** (Employee)	United States v. Nguyen, *et al.*, 08-CR-522 (E.D. Pa. 2008)	NO	~ 325K	9 months' imprisonment
3	**Kim Anh Nguyen** (Employee)	United States v. Nguyen, *et al.*, 08-CR-522 (E.D. Pa. 2008)	YES	~ 399K	2 years' probation
4	**Joseph T. Lukas** (Joint Venture Partner)	United States v. Nguyen, *et al.*, 08-CR-522 (E.D. Pa. 2008)	YES	~ 180K	2 years' probation
5	**Juan Diaz** (Intermediary)	United States v. Diaz, 09-CR-20346 (S.D. Fla. 2009)	NO	~ 1M	57 months' imprisonment
6	**John W. Warwick**[1] (President)	United States v. Warwick, 09-CR-449 (E.D. Va. 2009)	NO	~ 200K	37 months' imprisonment
7	**Charles Paul Edward Jumet** (Vice President; President)	United States v. Jumet, 09-CR-397 (E.D. Va. 2009)	NO	~ 200K	87 months' imprisonment
8	**Misao Hioki** (General Manager)	United States v. Hioki, 08-CR-795 (S.D. Tex. 2008)	YES	~ 1M	24 months' imprisonment
9	**Shu Quan-Sheng** (President, Secretary, and Treasurer)	United States v. Quan-Sheng, 08-CR-194 (E.D. Va. 2008)	NO	~ 189K	51 months' imprisonment
10	**Martin Eric Self**[2] (CEO)	United States v. Self, 08-CR-110 (C.D. Cal. 2008)	NO	~ 70K	2 years' probation
11	**Jason Edward Steph** (General Manager)	United States v. Steph, 07-CR-307 (S.D. Tex. 2007)	YES	~ 6M	15 months' imprisonment
12	**Jim Bob Brown** (Managing Director)	United States v. Brown, 06-CR-316 (S.D. Tex. 2006)	YES	~ 6M	1 year and 1 day's imprisonment

[1] United States Sentencing Guidelines Section 2B4.1, with a base offense level of 8, was the applicable U.S.S.G. Section at this time. After November 2002, Section 2C1.1, with a base offense level of 12, became the applicable U.S.S.G. Section in accordance with international treaty obligations.
[2] Self pleaded guilty to the "willful blindness" provision of the FCPA.

APPENDIX B – CHART 4
SENTENCES OF NATURAL PERSONS WHO PLEADED GUILTY TO FCPA VIOLATIONS SINCE 1998

	DEFENDANT	CASE NUMBER	SENTENCE REDUCTION FOR COOPERATION	AMOUNT OF BRIBES	SENTENCE (excluding monetary penalties)
13	**Steven J. Ott** (Executive Vice President)	United States v. Ott, 07-CR-608 (D. N.J. 2007)	YES	~ 267K	6 months' home confinement; 5 years' probation
14	**Yaw Osei Amoako**[3] (Regional Director)	United States v. Amoako, 06-CR-702 (D. N.J. 2006)	YES	~ 267K	18 months' imprisonment
15	**Christian Sapsizian** (Vice President)	United States v. Sapsizian, *et al.*, 06-CR-20797 (S.D. Fla. 2006)	YES	~ 2.4M	30 months' imprisonment
16	**Roger Michael Young** (Managing Director)	United States v. Young, 07-CR-609 (D. N.J. 2007)	YES	~ 267K	3 months' home confinement; 5 years' probation
17	**Steven Lynwood Head**[4] (Program Manager)	United States v. Head, 06-CR-1380 (S.D. Cal. 2006)	YES	~ 2M	6 months' imprisonment
18	**Richard John Novak** (Employee)	United States v. Randock, *et al.*, 05-CR-180 (E.D. Wash. 2005)	YES	~ 30K-70K	3 years' probation
19	**Faheem Mousa Salam** (Translator/Contractor)	United States v. Salam, 06-CR-157 (D.D.C. 2006)	YES	~ 60K	36 months' imprisonment
20	**Richard G. Pitchford**[1] (Vice President; Country Manager)	United States v. Pitchford, 02-CR-365 (D.D.C. 2002)	YES	~ 400K	1 year and 1 day's imprisonment
21	**Gautam Sengupta**[1] (Task Manager)	United States v. Sengupta, 02-CR-040 (D.D.C. 2002)	YES	~ 50K[5]	2 months' imprisonment; 4 months' home confinement
22	**Ramendra Basu**[1] (Trust Funds Manager)	United States v. Basu, 02-CR-475 (D.D.C. 2002)	NO	~ 50K[5]	15 months' imprisonment

[3] Judgment states "defendant is hereby committed to the custody of the United States Bureau of Prisons to be imprisoned for a term of 18 months, including 6 months to be served in a halfway house." [Docket Entry 35]

[4] Defendant pleaded guilty to violating the books and records provisions of the FCPA, not the anti-bribery provisions.

[5] The defendants admitted to having taken steps in furtherance of the payment of a $50,000 bribe to a Kenyan government official, in violation of the FCPA. The defendants also admitted to having received $127,000 in kickbacks in exchange for using their positions with the World Bank to give favorable treatment to a consultant.

APPENDIX B – CHART 4
SENTENCES OF NATURAL PERSONS WHO PLEADED GUILTY TO FCPA VIOLATIONS SINCE 1998

	DEFENDANT	CASE NUMBER	SENTENCE REDUCTION FOR COOPERATION	AMOUNT OF BRIBES	SENTENCE (excluding monetary penalties)
23	**Richard K. Halford**[1] (CFO)	United States v. Halford, 01-CR-221 (W.D. Mo. 2001)	YES	~ 1.5M	5 years' probation
24	**Albert Reitz**[1] (Vice President and Secretary)	United States v. Reitz, 01-CR-222 (W.D. Mo. 2001)	YES	~ 1.5M	6 months' home confinement; 5 years' probation
25	**Daniel Ray Rothrock**[1, 4] (Vice President)	United States v. Rothrock, 01-CR-343 (W.D. Tex. 2001)	--[6]	~ 300K	1 year's probation
26	**Thomas K. Qualey** (President)	United States v. Qualey, 99-CR-008 (S.D. Ohio 1999)	NO	~70K	4 months' home confinement; 3 years' probation
27	**Darrold Richard Crites** (President)	United States v. Crites, 98-CR-073 (S.D. Ohio 1998)	YES	~260K[7]	6 months' home confinement; 3 years' probation
28	**Herbert Tannenbaum** (President)	United States v. Tannenbaum, 98-CR-784 (S.D.N.Y. 1998)	NO	~ 120K – 200K[8]	1 year and 1 day's imprisonment
29	**Albert Jackson "Jack" Stanley**[9] (Officer/Director)	United States v. Stanley, 08-CR-597 (S.D. Tex. 2008)	--	~ 10.8M	84 months' imprisonment; Rule 11(c)(1)(C)

[6] There is no indication on the docket.
[7] Crites was charged with paying a total of $257,139 in bribes to a Brazilian government official. In addition, Crites was charged with paying a total of $99,000 in bribes to an American government official as part of the same scheme.
[8] Tannenbaum's plea agreement states that the value of the bribe was greater than $120,000, but less than $200,000.
[9] Stanley has not been sentenced, but he was included in this chart since his plea was pursuant to Rule 11(c)(1)(C), with an agreed upon sentence of 84 months and restitution of $10.8 million. The plea agreement also provides for the possibility of a sentence reduction below 84 months.

APPENDIX B – CHART 5
SANCTIONS IMPOSED UPON LEGAL PERSONS FOR FCPA VIOLATIONS SINCE 1998

CORPORATE ENTITY	DATE OF DISPOSITION	DISPOSITION			CRIMINAL MONETARY PENALTIES	LENGTH OF CORPORATE COMPLIANCE MONITOR	OTHER MONETARY PENALTIES
		GUILTY PLEA	DPA	NPA			
ABB Ltd (and two subsidiaries)	09/29/2010	1	1		$19,020,000	--	$22,804,262 (disgorgement); $16,510,000 (civil penalty)
Alliance One International (and two subsidiaries)	08/06/2010	2		1	$9,450,000[1] (anticipated)	3 Years	$10,000,000 (disgorgement)
Universal Corporation (and one subsidiary)	08/06/2010	1		1	$4,400,000	3 Years	$4,581,276.51 (disgorgement)
The Mercator Corporation[2]	08/06/2010	1			--	--	--
Snamprogetti Netherlands	07/07/2010		1		$240,000,000	--	$125,000,000 (disgorgement)
Technip S.A.	06/28/2010		1		$240,000,000	2 Years	$98,000,000 (disgorgement)
Daimler AG (and three subsidiaries)	04/01/2010	2	2		$93,600,000	3 Years	$91,432,867 (disgorgement)
Innospec Inc.	03/18/2010	1			$14,100,000	3 Years	$11,200,000 (disgorgement); $2,200,000 (civil penalty - OFAC)

[1] Two subsidiaries of Alliance One International, Inc. are scheduled to be sentenced on October 21, 2010. As part of their plea agreements, the two subsidiaries agreed to pay a total criminal monetary penalty of $9.45 million.
[2] The Mercator Corporation is currently scheduled to be sentenced on November 19, 2010.

APPENDIX B – CHART 5
SANCTIONS IMPOSED UPON LEGAL PERSONS FOR FCPA VIOLATIONS SINCE 1998

CORPORATE ENTITY	DATE OF DISPOSITION	DISPOSITION			CRIMINAL MONETARY PENALTIES	LENGTH OF CORPORATE COMPLIANCE MONITOR	OTHER MONETARY PENALTIES
		GUILTY PLEA	DPA	NPA			
Nexus Technologies Inc.	03/16/2010	1			--[3]	--	--
BAE Systems plc	03/01/2010	1			$400,000,000	3 Years	--
UTStarcom Inc.	12/31/2009			1	$1,500,000	--	$1,500,000 (civil penalty)
AGCO Corp. (and one subsidiary)	09/30/2009		1		$1,600,000	--	$2,400,000 (civil penalty); $16,000,000 (disgorgement)
Control Components, Inc.	07/31/2009	1			$18,200,000	3 Years	--
Helmerich & Payne, Inc.	07/30/2009			1	$1,000,000	--	$375,000 (disgorgement)
Novo Nordisk A/S	05/11/2009		1		$9,000,000	--	$3,025,066 (civil penalty); $6,005,079 (disgorgement)
Latin Node Inc.	04/07/2009	1			$2,000,000	--	--
Kellogg Brown & Root LLC	02/11/2009	1			$402,000,000	3 Years	$177,000,000 (disgorgement)

[3] As part of its plea agreement, Nexus Technologies Inc. admitted to having operated primarily through criminal means and agreed to dissolve itself and turn over all assets to the Court. Accordingly, on September 15, 2010, Nexus was sentenced and ordered to permanently cease all operations and turn all net assets over to the Clerk of Court as a fine.

APPENDIX B – CHART 5
SANCTIONS IMPOSED UPON LEGAL PERSONS FOR FCPA VIOLATIONS SINCE 1998

CORPORATE ENTITY	DATE OF DISPOSITION	DISPOSITION			CRIMINAL MONETARY PENALTIES	LENGTH OF CORPORATE COMPLIANCE MONITOR	OTHER MONETARY PENALTIES
		GUILTY PLEA	DPA	NPA			
Fiat S.p.A. (and three subsidiaries)	12/22/2008		1		$7,000,000	--	$3,600,000 (civil penalty); $7,209,142 (disgorgement)
Siemens AG (and three subsidiaries)	12/15/2008	4			$450,000,000	4 Years	$350,000,000 (disgorgement)
Aibel Group Limited	11/21/2008	1			$4,200,000	2 Years	--
Faro Technologies, Inc.	06/05/2008			1	$1,100,000	2 Years	$1,850,000 (disgorgement)
AGA Medical Corporation	06/03/2008		1		$2,000,000	3 Years	--
Willbros Group Inc. (and one subsidiary)	05/14/2008		2		$22,000,000	3 Years	$10,300,000 (disgorgement)
AB Volvo (and two subsidiaries)	03/20/2008		1		$7,000,000	--	$4,000,000 (civil penalty); $8,600,000 (disgorgement)
Flowserve Corporation (and one subsidiary)	02/21/2008		1		$4,000,000	--	$3,000,000 (civil penalty); $3,500,000 (disgorgement)
Westinghouse Air Brake Technologies Corporation	02/14/2008			1	$300,000	--	$87,000 (civil penalty); $288,000 (disgorgement)
Lucent Technologies Inc.	12/21/2007			1	$1,000,000	--	$1,500,000 (civil penalty)

APPENDIX B – CHART 5
SANCTIONS IMPOSED UPON LEGAL PERSONS FOR FCPA VIOLATIONS SINCE 1998

CORPORATE ENTITY	DATE OF DISPOSITION	DISPOSITION			CRIMINAL MONETARY PENALTIES	LENGTH OF CORPORATE COMPLIANCE MONITOR	OTHER MONETARY PENALTIES
		GUILTY PLEA	DPA	NPA			
Akzo Nobel N.V.	12/20/2007			1	$800,000 (contingent upon Dutch disposition)	--	$750,000 (civil penalty); $2,200,000 (disgorgement)
Chevron Corporation	11/14/2007		1		$20,000,000 (forfeiture); $5,000,000 (to NYC District Attorney's Office)	--	$3,000,000 (civil penalty-SEC) $2,000,000 (civil penalty-OFAC)
Ingersoll-Rand Company Ltd. (and two subsidiaries)	10/31/2007		1		$2,500,000	--	$1,950,000 (civil penalty); $2,270,000 (disgorgement)
Baker Hughes Incorporated (and one subsidiary)	04/26/2007	1	1		$11,000,000	3 Years	$10,000,000 (civil penalty); $24,000,000 (disgorgement)
El Paso Corporation	02/07/2007			1	$5,482,363 (forfeiture)	--	$2,250,000 (civil penalty)
Vetco Gray Inc. (and three related subsidiaries)	02/06/2007	3	1		$26,000,000	3 Years	--
Schnitzer Steel Industries, Inc. (and one subsidiary)	10/16/2006	1	1		$7,500,000	3 Years	$7,700,000 (disgorgement)
Statoil, ASA	10/13/2006		1		$10,500,000[4]	3 Years	$10,500,000 (disgorgement)

[4] Of the $10.5 million criminal penalty imposed upon Statoil, $3 million was deemed to have been satisfied by a prior penalty paid to Norwegian authorities.

APPENDIX B – CHART 5
SANCTIONS IMPOSED UPON LEGAL PERSONS FOR FCPA VIOLATIONS SINCE 1998

CORPORATE ENTITY	DATE OF DISPOSITION	DISPOSITION			CRIMINAL MONETARY PENALTIES	LENGTH OF CORPORATE COMPLIANCE MONITOR	OTHER MONETARY PENALTIES
		GUILTY PLEA	DPA	NPA			
DPC (Tianjin) Co. Ltd.	05/20/2005	1			$2,000,000	3 Years	$2,800,000 (disgorgement)
Micrus Corporation	03/02/2005			1	$450,000	3 Years	--
Titan Corporation	03/01/2005	1			$13,000,000	3 Years	$15,479,000 (disgorgement); $13,000,000 (civil penalty)[5]
Monsanto Company	01/06/2005		1		$1,000,000	3 Years	$500,000 (civil penalty)
InVision Technologies, Inc.	12/06/2004			1	$800,000	18 Months	$500,000 (civil penalty); $617,703.57 (disgorgement)
ABB Vetco Gray, Inc. (and one related subsidiary)	07/06/2004	2			$10,500,000	90 Days[6]	$5,915,405.64 (disgorgement)
Syncor Taiwan, Inc. (and its parent company)	12/10/2002	1			$2,000,000	130 Days[7]	$500,000 (civil penalty)
UNC/Lear Services Inc.	03/10/2000	1			$75,000	--	$132,000 (civil penalty); $768,000 (restitution)

[5] Titan was ordered to pay a civil penalty of $13,000,000, but this obligation was deemed satisfied by the payment of a criminal fine in the same amount.

[6] As part of the plea agreements and the judgment issued in the SEC's civil action, ABB Ltd. and its subsidiaries were required to retain an independent compliance consultant for a period 90 days. During this period, the consultant was to review and make recommendations regarding ABB's compliance programs. Except in certain circumstances, ABB was then required to implement the consultant's recommendations within 90 days of having received the consultant's report.

[7] As part of the administrative cease-and-desist order issued by the SEC, Syncor International Corporation was required to retain an independent compliance consultant for a period 130 days. During this period, the consultant was to review and make recommendations regarding Syncor's compliance programs. Except in certain circumstances, Syncor was then required to implement the consultant's recommendations within 90 days of having received the consultant's report.

APPENDIX B – CHART 5
SANCTIONS IMPOSED UPON LEGAL PERSONS FOR FCPA VIOLATIONS SINCE 1998

CORPORATE ENTITY	DATE OF DISPOSITION	DISPOSITION			CRIMINAL MONETARY PENALTIES	LENGTH OF CORPORATE COMPLIANCE MONITOR	OTHER MONETARY PENALTIES
		GUILTY PLEA	DPA	NPA			
International Materials Solutions Corporation	10/04/1999	1			$1,000	--	--
Control Systems Specialist, Inc.	03/08/1999	1			$1,500	--	--
Saybolt Inc. (and one subsidiary)	01/26/1999	2			$1,500,000[8]	--[9]	--
TOTALS		33	21	14	$2,086,729,863	--	$1,104,834,842

[8] Saybolt Inc. was also fined $3,400,000 in a related criminal case involving the falsification of data from certain environmental tests of its products.
[9] As part of its plea agreement, Saybolt Inc. was required to institute a compliance program related to its environmental testing program.

APPENDIX B – CHART 6A

Enforcement Actions with Regard to Alleged Foreign Bribery and Related Accounting Misconduct (Entries in columns 3-6 by number of investigations; entries in columns 7-8 by number of persons)

				Investigations							
Working Group member	Alleged misconduct at issue	Date of latest information supplied by WG member	Date of entry into force of the Convention for WG member	Investigations		Number of investigations in which assets seized or frozen pretrial	Number of investigations to date having led to one or more proceedings	Number of investigations to date not yet having led to any proceedings	Number of discontinued investigations without sanctions	Persons sanctioned in connection with discontinued investigation (settlement, mediation, etc...)	
		1	2	3 ongoing	4 total to date	5	6.a	6.b	6.c	7 NP	8 LP
United States	Foreign bribery	31 Dec 2009	15 Feb 1999	More than 150[1]							
	Foreign bribery related accounting misconduct	31 Dec 2009	15 Feb 1999	--[2]							

NP – Natural Person
LP – Legal Person

☐ Reported by all Working Group members
☐ Reported on a voluntary basis

[1] The number of ongoing investigations reported here includes all open investigations into allegations of foreign bribery and/or foreign bribery related accounting misconduct.
[2] The SEC, as a matter of policy, does not report on the number of ongoing, active investigations.

Notes by the United States:
i) The Department of Justice (DOJ) is providing statistics for all criminal and civil enforcment actions undertaken by DOJ since: (a) the enactment of the OECD Anti-Bribery Convention (February 15, 1999 - December 31, 2009); and (b) the enactment of the Foreign Corrupt Practices Act (FCPA) (1977-December 31, 2009). The Securities and Exchange Commission (SEC) has reported numbers since the enactment of the Convention through December 31, 2009. Therefore, the numbers contained within parentheses represent all DOJ enforcement actions since 1977 combined with all SEC enforcement actions since 1999.
ii) For those DOJ and SEC enforcement actions in which a natural or legal person was charged with both "foreign bribery" and "foreign bribery related accounting misconduct," one entry was made in each row under the applicable columns.
iii) For both criminal and civil enforcement actions, DOJ and SEC counted as separate, in every applicable column, each individual legal person that was subject to enforcement actions and/or sanctions. This includes instances in which multiple subsidiaries of single corporation (or a parent corporation and one or more subsidiaries) were individually and/or jointly subject to criminal prosecution, administrative/civil proceedings, and/or criminal or civil sanctions. For example, in 2007, Vetco Gray Controls, Inc., Vetco Gray Controls Limited, and Vetco Gray UK Limited were charged in a criminal information with violations of the anti-bribery provisions of the FCPA. All three companies pleaded guilty and were individually sentenced to a monetary penalty (in the amount of $6 million, $8 million, and $12 million respectively) and a term of organizational probation. Accordingly, in this instance, three legal persons were counted in each of the following columns: 12, 18, 34, 37, and 52. Due to the size of the respective fines, two legal persons were counted in column 48d while only one legal person was counted in column 48e.

APPENDIX B – CHART 6B

Enforcement Actions with Regard to Alleged Foreign Bribery and Related Accounting Misconduct (Entries in columns 9-32 by number of persons)

WG member	Alleged misconduct at issue	Date of latest information supplied by WG member	Date of entry into force of the Convention for WG member	Proceedings: Criminal Prosecutions (with formal charges): Prosecutions (with formal charges)				Discontinued prosecutions without sanctions/ condition		Discontinued prosecutions with sanctions[3]		Criminal convictions with sanctions[4]		Acquittals		Administrative/Civil proceedings: Administrative/ civil enforcement seeking imposition of sanctions				Discontinued administrative/ civil proceedings without sanctions		Discontinued administrative/ civil proceedings with sanctions		Administrative/ civil enforcement decisions with sanctions		Administrative / civil decisions finding no liability	
				Ongoing		Total to date										Ongoing		Total to date									
		1	2	9	10	11	12	13	14	15	16	17	18	19	20	21	22	23	24	25	26	27	28	29	30	31	32
				NP	LP	NP	LP	NP	LP	NP	LP	NP	LP	NP	LP	NP	LP	NP	LP	NP	LP	NP	LP	NP	LP	NP	LP
United States	Foreign bribery	31 Dec 2009	15 Feb 1999	63 (67)	1 (1)	83 (121)	39 (58)	1 (8)	0 (0)	0 (0)	21 (21)	38 (57)	17 (35)	0 (6)	0 (1)	3 (3)	0 (0)	36 (44)	28 (35)	4[5] (4)	0 (0)	0 (0)	0 (0)	29 (37)	28 (35)	0 (0)	0 (0)
	Foreign bribery related accounting misconduct	31 Dec 2009	15 Feb 1999	1 (2)	0 (0)	5 (11)	32 (35)	0 (0)	0 (0)	0 (0)	22 (22)	3 (8)	8 (10)	2 (4)	0 (1)	3 (3)	0 (0)	38 (38)	50 (50)	4[5] (4)	0 (0)	0 (0)	0 (0)	31 (31)	50 (50)	0 (0)	0 (0)

NP – Natural Person
LP – Legal Person

☐ Reported by all Working Group members
☐ Reported on a voluntary basis

[3] Those criminal prosecutions recorded as "Discontinued with sanctions" (columns 15-16) include instances in which DOJ entered into either Non-Prosecution or Deferred Prosecution Agreements with the parties involved in the case.

[4] Those criminal prosecutions recorded as "Convictions with sanctions" (columns 17-18) include instances in which the defendants either pleaded guilty or were found guilty at trial. These columns also include those persons that have been convicted but that are still awaiting sentencing.

[5] Voluntarily dismissed with prejudice; that is, SEC asked the court to dismiss the action, while agreeing not to prosecute the defendants at a later date as a result of the same conduct.

Notes by the United States:

i) The Department of Justice (DOJ) is providing statistics for all criminal and civil enforcment actions undertaken by DOJ since: (a) the enactment of the OECD Anti-Bribery Convention (February 15, 1999 - December 31, 2009); and (b) the enactment of the Foreign Corrupt Practices Act (FCPA) (1977-December 31, 2009). The Securities and Exchange Commission (SEC) has reported numbers since the enactment of the Convention through December 31, 2009. Therefore, the numbers contained within parentheses represent all DOJ enforcement actions since 1977 combined with all SEC enforcement actions since 1999.

ii) For those DOJ and SEC enforcement actions in which a natural or legal person was charged with both "foreign bribery" and "foreign bribery related accounting misconduct," one entry was made in each row under the applicable columns.

iii) For both criminal and civil enforcement actions, DOJ and SEC counted as separate, in every applicable column, each individual legal person that was subject to enforcement actions and/or sanctions. This includes instances in which multiple subsidiaries of single corporation (or a parent corporation and one or more subsidiaries) were individually and/or jointly subject to criminal prosecution, administrative/civil proceedings, and/or criminal or civil sanctions. For example, in 2007, Vetco Gray Controls, Inc., Vetco Gray Controls Limited, and Vetco Gray UK Limited were charged in a criminal information with violations of the anti-bribery provisions of the FCPA. All three companies pleaded guilty and were individually sentenced to a monetary penalty (in the amount of $6 million, $8 million, and $12 million respectively) and a term of organizational probation. Accordingly, in this instance, three legal persons were counted in each of the following columns: 12, 18, 34, 37, and 52. Due to the size of the respective fines, two legal persons were counted in column 48d while only one legal person was counted in column 48e.

APPENDIX B – CHART 6C

Sanctions for Alleged Foreign Bribery and Related Accounting Misconduct
(Except where noted, entries by number of persons sanctioned)

WG member	Alleged misconduct at issue	Criminal Cases																									
		Total imposed or agreed sanctions[6]		Combined prison/-monetary sanctions	Monetary sanctions only		Prison only	Prison sentences								Monetary penalties imposed (USD)									Exclusions or limitations on access to public procurement or benefits[7]		Other penalties[8]	
		33	34	35	36	37	38	<1 year		1-2 years		2-5 years		>5 years		Natural Persons				Legal Persons					49	50	51	52
		NP	LP	NP	NP	LP	NP	39	40	41	42	43	44	45	46	47a	47b	47c	47d	48a	48b	48c	48d	48e	NP	LP	NP	LP
								Total	Suspended	Total	Suspended	Total	Suspended	Total	Suspended	<10K	10K-50K	50K-250K	>250K	0K-50K	50K-250K	250K-1M	1M-10M	>10M				
United States	Foreign bribery	20 (39)	38 (56)	13 (18)	1 (10)	34 (52)	4 (7)	4 (7)	0 (1)	5 (7)	0 (2)	6 (6)	0 (0)	2 (3)	0 (0)	5 (8)	2 (7)	2 (6)	5 (7)	1 (6)	0 (3)	6 (12)	18 (21)	9 (10)	--	--	18 (31)	11 (15)
	Foreign bribery related accounting misconduct	2 (5)	30 (32)	1 (3)	0 (1)	27 (29)	0 (0)	1 (1)	0 (0)	0 (1)	0 (0)	0 (0)	0 (0)	0 (1)	0 (0)	1 (1)	0 (1)	0 (1)	0 (1)	0 (0)	0 (0)	6 (7)	13 (13)	8 (9)	--	--	2 (4)	7 (7)

NP – Natural Person
LP – Legal Person

☐ Reported by all Working Group members
☐ Reported on a voluntary basis

[6] Criminal convictions are only recorded in columns 33 and 34 if the defendant has been sentenced.
[7] Debarment from public procurement processes is not handled by DOJ or SEC.
[8] For criminal cases, DOJ counted under "Other penalties" those natural and legal persons whose imposed or agreed sanctions included terms of community service, supervised release, and/or probation.

Notes by the United States:
i) The Department of Justice (DOJ) is providing statistics for all criminal and civil enforcment actions undertaken by DOJ since: (a) the enactment of the OECD Anti-Bribery Convention (February 15, 1999 - December 31, 2009); and (b) the enactment of the Foreign Corrupt Practices Act (FCPA) (1977-December 31, 2009). The Securities and Exchange Commission (SEC) has reported numbers since the enactment of the Convention through December 31, 2009. Therefore, the numbers contained within parentheses represent all DOJ enforcement actions since 1977 combined with all SEC enforcement actions since 1999.
ii) For those DOJ and SEC enforcement actions in which a natural or legal person was charged with both "foreign bribery" and "foreign bribery related accounting misconduct," one entry was made in each row under the applicable columns.
iii) For both criminal and civil enforcement actions, DOJ and SEC counted as separate, in every applicable column, each individual legal person that was subject to enforcement actions and/or sanctions. This includes instances in which multiple subsidiaries of single corporation (or a parent corporation and one or more subsidiaries) were individually and/or jointly subject to criminal prosecution, administrative/civil proceedings, and/or criminal or civil sanctions. For example, in 2007, Vetco Gray Controls, Inc., Vetco Gray Controls Limited, and Vetco Gray UK Limited were charged in a criminal information with violations of the anti-bribery provisions of the FCPA. All three companies pleaded guilty and were individually sentenced to a monetary penalty (in the amount of $6 million, $8 million, and $12 million respectively) and a term of organizational probation. Accordingly, in this instance, three legal persons were counted in each of the following columns: 12, 18, 34, 37, and 52. Due to the size of the respective fines, two legal persons were counted in column 48d while only one legal person was counted in column 48e.

APPENDIX B – CHART 6D

Sanctions for Alleged Foreign Bribery and Related Accounting Misconduct (Except where noted, entries by number of persons sanctioned)

		Administrative/Civil cases																			Confiscation	
WG member	Alleged misconduct at issue	Total imposed or agreed sanctions		Monetary sanctions		Monetary penalties imposed (USD)									Exclusions or limitations on access to public procurement or benefits[9]		Other penalties[10]		Suspended sentences		Confiscation or forfeiture of assets	
		53	54	55	56	Natural Persons				Legal Persons					59	60	61	62	63	64	65	66
		NP	LP	NP	LP	57a	57b	57c	57d	58a	58b	58c	58d	58e	NP	LP	NP	LP	NP	LP	NP	LP
						<10K	10K-50K	50K-250K	>250K	<50K	50K-250K	250K-1M	1M-10M	>10M								
United States	Foreign bribery	29 (37)	28 (35)	16 (17)	23 (23)	0 (0)	11 (11)	4 (4)	1 (2)	0 (0)	1 (1)	8 (8)	4 (4)	10 (10)	--	--	29 (37)	28 (35)	0 (0)	0 (0)	16 (16)	22 (22)
	Foreign bribery related accounting misconduct	31 (31)	50 (50)	19 (19)	44 (44)	0 (0)	12 (12)	6 (6)	1 (1)	0 (0)	3 (3)	14 (14)	13 (13)	14 (14)	--	--	31 (31)	50 (50)	0 (0)	0 (0)	19 (19)	44 (44)

NP – Natural Person
LP – Legal Person

☐ Reported by all Working Group members
☐ Reported on a voluntary basis

[9] Debarment from public procurement processes is not handled by the DOJ or SEC.

[10] For civil cases, DOJ and SEC counted under "Other penalties" those natural and legal persons who were subject to permanent injunctions or cease and desist orders against further violations of the FCPA.

Notes by the United States:

i) The Department of Justice (DOJ) is providing statistics for all criminal and civil enforcement actions undertaken by DOJ since: (a) the enactment of the OECD Anti-Bribery Convention (February 15, 1999 - December 31, 2009); and (b) the enactment of the Foreign Corrupt Practices Act (FCPA) (1977-December 31, 2009). The Securities and Exchange Commission (SEC) has reported numbers since the enactment of the Convention through December 31, 2009. Therefore, the numbers contained within parentheses represent all DOJ enforcement actions since 1977 combined with all SEC enforcement actions since 1999.

ii) For those DOJ and SEC enforcement actions in which a natural or legal person was charged with both "foreign bribery" and "foreign bribery related accounting misconduct," one entry was made in each row under the applicable columns.

iii) For both criminal and civil enforcement actions, DOJ and SEC counted as separate, in every applicable column, each individual legal person that was subject to enforcement actions and/or sanctions. This includes instances in which multiple subsidiaries of single corporation (or a parent corporation and one or more subsidiaries) were individually and/or jointly subject to criminal prosecution, administrative/civil proceedings, and/or criminal or civil sanctions. For example, in 2007, Vetco Gray Controls, Inc., Vetco Gray Controls Limited, and Vetco Gray UK Limited were charged in a criminal information with violations of the anti-bribery provisions of the FCPA. All three companies pleaded guilty and were individually sentenced to a monetary penalty (in the amount of $6 million, $8 million, and $12 million respectively) and a term of organizational probation. Accordingly, in this instance, three legal persons were counted in each of the following columns: 12, 18, 34, 37, and 52. Due to the size of the respective fines, two legal persons were counted in column 48d while only one legal person was counted in column 48e.

AUTHORITIES

Attorney-Client Privilege Protection Act. 81
C.F.R.
Title 5
§2635. 228–229
Title 17
§202.12 . . . . 76n10
§205. . . . . 147nn13–14
§205.3 146
§205.3(b)(6)(i)(A). 149n16
§205.3(b)(6)(i)(B) 149n16
§205.3(d)(2)(i). 149n17
§205.154 146
§240. . . . . 147nn13–14
§240.14e-3 . . . . 19, 19n5
§249. . . . . 147nn13–14
Title 28
§80. 132
Title 31
§10.35 . . . . 101n28
§10.37(a). 101n27
Subtitle A, Part 10 . . . . 101n26
Title 68
§6296. . . . . 147nn13–14
§6297. . . . . 147nn13–14
Clayton Act. 69
Code of Federal Regulations (*see* C.F.R.)
Commodity Exchange Act. 161
Criminal Justice Act 54
False Claims Act 14, 153–154
Family Support Act. 95n9
Federal Labor Standards Act 50–51
Federal Rules of Civil Procedure
§26(b)(5)(B). 62n19

Federal Rules of Criminal Procedure
§4(a) 165
§5.1(a) 165
§6(3) 173
§11 190
§11(e) 183
§11(e)(1) 179
§11(e)(2) 191
§11(e)(3) 191
§11(f) 189
§16 71
§17(c) 51, 71
§26 60–61
§29(a) 166
§35 192
§35(b) 182
§44 60
Federal Rules of Evidence
§403 91
§408 91
§501 55
§502 62–63
§801(d)(2)(A) 55n11
§801(d)(2)(E) 28n16, 67n1
§803(3)(b) 28
Foreign Corrupt Practices Act 75n7, 88, 114–137, 235–314, 315–333
§13(b)(2)(A) 122
§13(b)(2)(B) 122
§13(b)(5) 122
§13(b)(6) 121
§13(b)(7) 122
Fraud Enforcement and Recovery Act 37, 40, 153–154
Freedom of Information Act 152n24, 182
Hobbs Act 34
Internal Revenue Code .... 93–94, 93n1, 95, 96, 97–98, 99–100, 117n13, 136–137 *(see also* U.S.C., Title 26 *for sections)*
IRS Field Service Advisory
(April 20, 1995), 1995 WL 1770850 97
(May 27, 1992), 1992 WL 1354910 .... 94n2, 97n14
Jenks Act 71
N.Y. Stock Exchange Listed Company Manual
§303A.10 .... 9n20

Opinions
38 Op. Att'y Gen. 98 90
Procedure Release 06-01. 134–135
Procedure Release 06-02. 135
Procedure Release 07-01. 134
Procedure Release 07-02. 134
Procedure Release 07-03. 134
Procedure Release 08-01. 133
Procedure Release 08-02. . . . . 131, 133
Procedure Release 08-03. 133–134
Procedure Release 09-01. 133
Procedure Release 10-10. 132–133
PCAOB Auditing Standards
No. 1 143
No. 2 . . . . . 108, 143
No. 3 144
No. 5 108–109
No. 8 144
No. 9 145
No. 10 145
No. 11 145
No. 12 145
No. 13 145
No. 14 145
No. 15 145
Rule 3525 108
Public Corruption Prosecution Improvements Act (2011). 35, 155–156
Restatement (Second) of Agency
§403. . . . . 16n2
Restatement (Third) of the Law Governing Lawyers
§§128-131. . . . . 59n15
Rev. Rule
§68-662, 1968-2 C.B. 69 . . . . . 95n8
§80-211, 1980-2 C.B. 57 . . . . . 94n4
§80-334, 1980-2 C.B. 61 . . . . . 97n14
§2009-9. 99
§2009-20. . . . . 99, 100
Sarbanes-Oxley Act (2002) 2–3, 5, 9, 17, 19, 30, 40–41, 42–43, 71, 108, 109, 123, 142, 143–150, 151–152
§205. . . . . 147–148, 149
§302. 123
§307. . . . . 146, 147
§404. 123

§406(a) 9n19
§704 109
§906 123
Title V 19
SEC Accounting Bulletin
No. 100 106
No. 1470 .... 141n1
SEC Enforcement Manual 76
SEC Regulation
Rule 13(b)2-1 122
Rule 13(b)2-2 122
SEC Releases
No. 33-81 .... 146n11
No. 33-85 .... 146n11
No. 34-17099 .... 132n57
No. 34-44969 .... 141n1
No. 34-47276 .... 146n11
No. 34-56138 .... 131n55
No. 34-56533 .... 120n17, 263
No. 15266 .... 122n22, 241
Securities Act (1933)
§17(a) 38
Securities Exchange Act (1934) 2n1, 19, 38, 40, 115, 141n1, 152–153nn23–24, 161
§6(a) 161
§10(b) 38, 40
§15D 19
§21(a) 141n1
§21(f) 152nn23–24
Sentencing Reform Act 181
Sherman Antitrust Act 29n18
Tax Reform Act 96n11
Travel Act 34, 114
Treasury Regulation
§1.162-21(b) 96
§1.162-21(b)(2) 94, 96n13
Circular 230 101
U.S. Attorneys Manual
Title 6
§6-4.245 199
Title 9 .... 88n55
§9-2.031 171
§9-2.400 199
§9-16.000 182

§§9-16.000, *et seq.* . . . 198
§9-16.320 . . . 190
§9-21.000 . . . 198
§9-22.000 . . . 173
§9-23.000 . . . 193
§§9-27.000, *et seq.* . . . 78, 163–200
§9-27.110 . . . 164–165
§9-27.200 . . . 165–166
§9-27.220 . . . 75n8, 165, 166–167
§9-27.230 . . . 167–171, 206
§9-27.240 . . . 167, 171–172, 220
§9-27.250 . . . 86, 86n45, 87, 87n49, 167, 172–173, 220
§9-27.260 . . . 173–174
§9-27.270 . . . 174
§9-27.300 . . . 174–177, 179, 188, 221
§9-27.320 . . . 176, 177–178, 190
§9-27.330 . . . 174, 178
§9-27.400 . . . 82, 82n31, 175, 179–183
§9-27.400-500 . . . 79n17
§§9-27.400-530 . . . 221
§9-27.420 . . . 78, 78n16, 83, 83n35, 85, 85n39, 183–187
§9-27.420(b)(4) . . . 79n20, 221
§9-27.430 . . . 178, 187–190, 192
§9-27.440 . . . 79n20, 185, 222
§9-27.450 . . . 190–191
§9-27.500 . . . 79n17, 79n20, 182, 222
§9-27.600 . . . 86, 86n43, 188, 191–195
§9-27.620 . . . 86, 86n44, 194, 195–197
§9-27.630 . . . 86, 86n42, 197–198
§9-27.640 . . . 195, 198–199
§9-27.641 . . . 85, 85n40, 199–200, 224
§9-27.650 . . . 86, 86n42, 200
§§9-28.000, *et seq.* . . . 59n14, 70, 77, 81, 201–224
§9-28.100 . . . 202–203
§9-28.200 . . . 203–204
§9-28.300 . . . 205–206
§9-28.400 . . . 41, 205, 206–207
§9-28.500 . . . 205, 207
§9-28.600 . . . 205, 208
§9-28.700 . . . 205, 208–209, 222
§9-28.710 . . . 209–210
§9-28.720 . . . 210–213
§9-28.720(b)(i-ii) . . . 223

§9-28.730 213–214
§9-28.740 214–215
§9-28.750 215
§9-28.760 215
§9-28.800 .... 83, 83nn36–37, 205, 215–217, 222
§9-28.900 .... 205, 218
§9-28.1000 .... 74n2, 203, 205, 219–220
§9-28.1100 .... 203, 205, 220
§9-28.1200 221
§9-28.1300 221–224
§9-41.010 199
§9-42.010 .... 90, 90nn59–64
§9-90.020 199
§932 .... 153n26

U.S.C.

Title 1

§1 .... 54n9

Title 5

§552(b)(3) 152n24

Title 7

§1a(18) 161
§13(a)(5) 39
§13(e) 39
§136 161

Title 15

§§78a, *et seq.* 152n23
§§78dd-1, *et seq.* 115n5
§78dd-1(a) 119
§78dd-1(b) 121n19
§78dd-1(f)(3)(A) 121n20
§78dd-2(b) 121n19
§78dd-2(h)(10)(B) 119
§78f(a) 161
§78f(iii) 161
§78f(m) 152n23
§78g(c) 161
§78o-6(a)(3) 19n9
§§7201, *et seq.* 152n23

Title 18

§78dd-2 118
§201 .... 34–35, 175
§208 228–229
§371 26–30
§666 35–36

§924(c) 177
§924(e) 184
§1341 . . . . . 16, 30, 31, 114
§1343 . . . . . 30n21, 31, 114
§1344 . . . . . 30n21, 33, 41
§1346 31–32
§1348 40–41
§1350 41
§§1501, *et seq.* 42
§1503 214
§1505 43
§1512 . . . . . 43–44, 70, 71, 74
§1513(e) 152n23
§1514A 40, 151n22
§1519 . . . . . 42–43, 71
§1520 . . . . . 71, 144
§1621 . . . . . 42, 175
§1623 . . . . . 42, 175
§1951 34
§1952 . . . . . 34, 114
§1956 . . . . . 36–38, 114
§1957 36–38
§1961(1) 36
§2248 190
§2259 190
§2264 190
§2327 190
§3006A 54
§3282 121
§3292 121
§§3500, *et seq.* 71
§3553 221
§3559(c) 184
§3662 . . . . . 98n19
§§3663, *et seq.* 190
§3663-3664 . . . . . 98n20
§3663(a)(1)(A) 98n17
§3664(a) 98n21
§§6001-6003 . . . . . 184, 192, 194, 197
Title 21
§841(b)(1)(A) 176
§841(b)(1)(B) 176
§841(b)(1)(C) 176
§848(a) 176

§851 . . . 176
§960(b)(1) . . . 176
§960(b)(2) . . . 176
§960(b)(3) . . . 176
§962 . . . 176
Title 26 . . . 93n1
§62 . . . 95
§62(a)(2)(A) . . . 95n9
§67 . . . 99, 100
§68 . . . 99, 100
§162 . . . 94n4, 95, 97, 97n16
§162(a) . . . 94, 96, 136–137
§162(c)(1) . . . 117n13
§162(f) . . . 96, 96nn10–11
§165 . . . 97–98, 97n15, 99–100
§172 . . . 99, 100
§1211 . . . 99
§7206(1) . . . 42
Title 28
§1738 . . . 63
Title 31 . . . 36
§330 . . . 101n29
§§3327-33 . . . 153
§3729 . . . 153n28
§3729(a)(1) . . . 154
§3729(a)(2) . . . 154
§3730 . . . 153n27
U.S. Sentencing Guidelines
§1 B1.3 . . . 188
§1 B1.3(a)(2) . . . 181
§1 B1.8 . . . 189
§2 B4.1 . . . 320n1, 321n1
§2 C1.1 . . . 320n1, 321n1
§3 E1.1(b)(1) . . . 185
§4 B1.1 . . . 184
§4 B1.4 . . . 184
§5 K . . . 181–182
§5 K1.1 . . . 188, 192
§5 X . . . 182
§7 . . . 10
§8 Amendments . . . 9–10, 9n22, 84
§8 B1.1 . . . 79n23, 222
§8 B2.1 . . . 224
§8 C2.1 . . . 222

§§8C2.1, *et seq.* . . . 79n23
§8 C2.2 . . . 8n17
§8 C2.5, cmt. (n.4) . . . 207
§8 C2.5(c), cmt. (n.6) . . . 208
§8 C3.1 . . . 9n18
§8 introductory comment . . . 8n16
generally . . . 8–10, 84–85
Victim Witness Protection Act . . . 98
Wall Street Reform and Consumer Protection Act (2010) . . . 3, 39, 40, 84, 150–152, 159–162
§202(a)(1)(C)[3] . . . 159
§723(a)(2)[6] . . . 159
§724 . . . 159
§724(a)[7] . . . 159
§728 . . . 159, 160
§730 . . . 159
§730[11] . . . 160
§731 . . . 159
§731[12] . . . 160
§733 . . . 159
§733[13] . . . 160
§741 . . . 159
§741[14] . . . 160
§746 . . . 39
§747[16] . . . 161
§753[17] . . . 161
§764[18] . . . 161
§768[21] . . . 161
§922 . . . 152n23
§929[22] . . . 161
§929O(b) . . . 40
§934[23] . . . 162
§975(a)(1)[24] . . . 162
§975(a)(5)[25] . . . 162
§1036[27] . . . 162
Title I, Subtitle B, §1107 . . . 3n6, 151n21

Cases

ABB, Inc., *In re* (2010) . . . 303
ABB Ltd-Jordan, United States v. (2010) . . . 304
Abboud, United States v., 438 F.3d 554 (6th Cir.), *cert. denied,* 127 S. Ct. 446 (2006) . . . 33
ABB Vetco Gray, United States v. (S.D. Tex. 2004) . . . 251

Abrahams v. Young & Rubicam, Inc. (1994) 240
Abuhouran, United States v., 162 F.3d 230 (3d Cir. 1998) 37
Ackert, United States v., 169 F.3d 136 (2d Cir. 1999) 56
Adlman, United States v., 68 F.3d 1495 (2d Cir. 1995) 56
AGA Medical Corporation, United States v. (2008) 271
Aguilar, United States v., 295 F.3d 1018 (8th Cir. 2002) 28
Aguilar, United States v., 515 U.S. 593 (1995) 43–44
Angela Aguilar, United States v. (2010) 303
Enrique Aguilar, United States v. (2010) 303
Akzo Nobel, *In re* (2007) 267
Alameida, United States v., 341 F.3d 1318 (11th Cir. 2003) 59, 60
Alliance One Tobacco OSH, LLC, United States v. (2010) 303
Allied Freight Forwarding Inc., United States v. 80n28
Allied-Signal, Inc. v. Comm'r, T.C. Memo 1992-204 96
Allison Engine Co. v. United States *ex rel.* Sanders, 128 S. Ct. 2123 (2008) . . . 154
Daniel Alvirez, United States v. (2009) 283
Am. Airways Charters, Inc. v. Regan, 746 F.2d 865 (D.C. Cir. 1984) 52
American Tolalisator, United States v. (D. Md. 1993) 240
Amoako, United States v. (D.N.J. 2005) 255
Amoako, United States v., 06-CR-702 (D.N.J. 2006) 322
An Nguyen, United States v. (2008) 272
Appl. Process Products Overseas Inc., United States v. (1982) 237
Aramony, United States v., 88 F.3d 1369 (4th Cir. 1996) 58
Arch Trading Co., United States v., 987 F.2d 1087 (4th Cir. 1992) 27
Arias, United States v., 431 F.3d 1327 (11th Cir. 2005) 67
Armored Transp., Inc., United States v., 629 F.2d 1313 (9th Cir.), *cert. denied,* 450 U.S. 965 (1981) 48
Arnold, United States v., 947 F.2d 1236 (5th Cir. 1991) 190
Aronson v. Lewis, 473 A.2d 805 (Del. 1984) 16
Arthur Andersen, LLP, United States v., 374 F.3d 281 (5th Cir. 2004), *rev'd,* 544 U.S. 696 (2005) 5n9, 14
Arthur Andersen, LLP v. United States, 544 U.S. 696 (2005) 5n9, 14, 43, 70–71, 74
Helmie Ashiblie, United States v. (2009) 284
Automated Med. Labs., Inc. United States v., 770 F.2d 399 (4th Cir. 1985), *aff'd,* 526 U.S. 398 (1999) 13, 204
BAE Systems plc, United States v. (2010) 293
Bailey, United States v., 444 U.S. 394 (1980) 25
Baker Hughes, United States v. 128
Baker Hughes, United States v. (S.D. Tex. 2007) 259
Bank of New England, N.A., United States v., 821 F.2d 844 (1st Cir. 1987) . 13–14
Bank of Nova Scotia v. United States, 487 U.S. 250 (1988) 53
Basic Constr. Co., United States v., 711 F.2d 570 (4th Cir. 1983) 216

Basu, United States v., 02-CR-475 (D.D.C. 2002) 247, 322
Fernando Maya Basurto, United States v. (2009) 281
Gary Bateman; United States v. (1982). 237
BDO Seidman LLP, United States v., 492 F.3d 806 (7th Cir. 2007). 58, 213
Bellis v. United States, 417 U.S. 85 (1974) 46
Beneficial Franchise Co., Inc. v. Bank One, N.A.,
205 F.R.D. 212 (N.D. Ill. 2001). 59
Beusch, United States v., 596 F.2d 871 (9th Cir. 1979) 216
Andrew Bigelow, United States v. (2009) 284
Bilzerian, United States v., 926 F.2d 1285 (2d Cir. 1991) 66
Richard T. Bistrong, United States v. (2010) 293
Biswell, United States v., 406 U.S. 311 (1972) 49
BJ Services, *In re* (2004) 252
Blackmon, United States v., 839 F.2d 900 (2d Cir. 1988) 33
Block Drug Co., Inc. v. Sedona Labs., Inc., 2007 WL 1183828 (D. Del. 2007) . . 59
Blondek, United States v., 741 F. Supp. 116 (N.D. Tex. 1990), *aff'd sub nom.*, United States v. Castle, 925 F.2d 831 (5th Cir. 1991) 119, 240
Bodmer, United States v. (S.D.N.Y. 2003). 250
Bok, United States v., 156 F.3d 157 (2d Cir. 1998) 98
Bourjaily v. United States, 483 U.S. 171 (1987) 27n13, 71
Brady v. Maryland, 373 U.S. 83 (1963) 200
Branzburg v. Hayes, 408 U.S. 665 (1972) 165
Braswell v. United States, 487 U.S. 99 (1988). 15, 47
Bridgestone Corporation, United States v. (2011) 314
Bristow Group, Inc., *In re,* SEC Release No. 34-56533
(Sep. 26, 2007) 120n17, 263
Brown, United States v., 06-CR-316 (S.D. Tex. 2006). 257, 321
Brown, United States v., 459 F.3d 509, *cert. denied,* 127 S. Ct.
2249 (2007). 32–33
Brown v. United States, 524 F.2d 693 (Cl. Ct. 1975), *as amended,* (1976) . . . 90n64
Bruton v. United States, 391 U.S. 123 (1968). 28, 28n17
Bryant, United States v., 766 F.2d 370 (8th Cir. 1985) 31
Bryan v. United States, 524 U.S. 184 (1998). 25
Caceres, United States v., 440 U.S. 741 (1979). 50
Manuel Caceres, United States v. (2010) 308
Patrick Caldwell, United States v. (2009) 284
Camara v. Municipal Court, 387 U.S. 523 (1967) 49
Cantor, United States v. (2001) 243
Caremark Int'l Inc. Derivative Litig., *In re,* 698 A.2d 959 (Del. Ch. 1996) 217
Carpenter, United States v. (1983). 238
Carpenter, United States v. (1985). 238
Hong (Rose) Carson, United States v. (2009) 279
Stuart Carson, United States v. (2009) 279

Carver, United States v. (S.D. Fla. 1979) 236
Castle, United States v., 925 F.2d 831 (5th Cir. 1991) 119, 240
Catfish Antitrust Litigation, *In re,* 908 F. Supp. 400 (N.D. Miss. 1995) 69
Cavin, United States v., 39 F.3d 1299 (5th Cir. 1994) 66
C.E. Miller Corp., United States v. (1982) 237
Centracchio, United States v., 265 F.3d 518 (7th Cir. 2001) 28
Cheek, United States v., 3 F.3d 1057 (7th Cir. 1993) 213
Cheek v. United States, 498 U.S. 192 (1991) 25
Chen, United States v., 99 F.3d 1495 (9th Cir. 1996) 56
Chernin, United States v., 149 F.3d 805 (8th Cir. 1998) 97, 97n16
Chevron Corp., United States v., 1996 WL 264769 (N.D. Cal. 1996) 56
ChevronTexaco Corp., United States v., 241 F. Supp. 2d 1065
(N.D. Cal. 2002) 56
Chiarella v. United States, 445 U.S. 222 (1980) 38, 39
Chiquita Brands International, Inc., In the Matter of (2002) 247
Wojciech Chodan, United States v. (2009) 279
Cincotta, United States v., 689 F.2d 238 (1st Cir. 1982) 204
Darrold Richard Cities, United States v. (1998) 242
City of Vernon v. S. Cal. Edison, 955 F.2d 1361 (9th Cir. 1992) 70
CNH France S.A., United States v. (2008) 276
CNH Italia S.p.A., United States v. (2008) 277
Yochanan R. Cohen, United States v. (2009) 285
Collins v. Commodity Futures Trading Comm'n, 737 F. Supp. 1467
(N.D. Ill. 1990) 53
Colonnade Catering Corp. v. United States, 397 U.S. 72 (1970) 49
Commodity Futures Trading Comm'n v. Weintraub, 471 U.S. 343 (1985) 57
Comm'r v. Heininger, 320 U.S. 467 (1943) 94
Continental Group, Inc., United States v., 603 F.2d 444 (3d Cir.),
cert. denied, 444 U.S. 1032 (1979) 68
Continental Management, Inc. v. United States, 527 F.2d 613
(Cl. Ct. 1975) 90n64
Control Components Inc., United States v. (2009) 281
Control Systems Specialist Inc., United States v. (1998) 242
Copperweld Corp. v. Independence Tube Corp., 467 U.S. 752 (1984) 29n18
Paul Cosgrove, United States v. (2009) 280
Couch v. United States, 409 U.S. 322 (1973) 48
County of Erie, *In re,* 2008 U.S. App. LEXIS 21496 (2d Cir. Oct. 14, 2008) 66
Mario Covino, United States v. (2008) 274
Crawford Enterprise, Inc., United States v. (1982) 237
Crites, United States v., 98-CR-073 (S.D. Ohio 1998) 323
Cuellar v. United States, 553 U.S. 550 (2008) 37
Cuthbertson, United States v., 630 F.2d 139 (3d Cir. 1980) 71
DaimlerChrysler Automotive Russia SAO, United States v. (2010) 294
DaimlerChrysler China Ltd, United States v. (2010) 295

Daimler Export and Trade Finance GmbH, United States v. (2010) 295
Diagnostic Products, In the Matter of (2005) 254
Diaz, United States v., 09-CR-20346 (S.D. Fla. 2009) 321
Juan Diaz, United States v. (2009) 281
Dirks v. United States, 463 U.S. 646 (1983) 38, 39
Doe, United States v., 465 U.S. 605 (1984) 47
DOJ v. Siemens Venezuela (2008) 273
Donovan v. Dewey, 452 U.S. 594 (1981) 49–50
Dornier GmbH, United States v. (D. Minn. 1990) 239
Dose, United States v., 2005 WL 106493 (N.D. Iowa 2005) 59
DPC (Tianjin), United States v. (2005) 254
Eagle Bus., United States v. (1991) 240
David Edmonds, United States v. (2009) 280
Electronic Data Systems, *In re* (2007) 263
Environmental Tectonics Corp. Int'l v. W.W. Kirkpatrick & Co. Inc. (1983) . . 238
Joel Esquenazi, United States v. (2009) 282
Exxon Corp., United States v., 94 F.R.D. 246 (D.D.C. 1981) 65–66
Thomas Farrell, United States v. (S.D.N.Y. 2003) 251
Federal Trade Comm'n v. Am. Tobacco Co., 264 U.S. 298 (1924) 50
A.F. Feitz, United States v. (2001) 244
Feng Juan Lu, United States v., 248 Fed. Appx. 806 (9th Cir. 2007) 15
F.G. Mason Eng'g Inc. and Grancis G. Mason, United States v. (1990) 239
Fisher, United States v., 425 U.S. 391 (1976) 15
Fisher v. United States, 425 U.S. 391 (1976) 47, 57
Fisher v. United States, 529 U.S. 667 (2000) 36
Fitapelli, United States v., 786 F.2d 1461 (11th Cir. 1986) 48
Flowserve Corp.,United States v. (2008) 269
Follin, United States v., 979 F.2d 369 (5th Cir. 1992) 55
Jean Fourcand, United States v. (2010) 293
GAF Corp., United States v., 928 F.2d 1253 (2dCir. 1991) 70
Galaxy Computer Servs., Inc. v. Baker, 325 B.R. 544 (E.D. Va. 2005) 16
Gallego, United States v., 191 F.3d 156 (2d Cir. 1999) 28
Gall v. United States, 552 U.S. 38 (2007) 8
Haim Geri, United States v. (2009) 285
Giffen & Williams, United States v. (S.D.N.Y. 2003) 249
Giglio v. United States, 405 U.S. 150 (1972) 86n42, 200
Gilmore, United States v., 372 U.S. 39 (1963) 94n4
Stephen Gerard Giordanella, United States v. (2009) 285
Go-Bart Importing Co. v. United States, 282 U.S. 344 (1931) 50
John Gregory Godsey, United States v. (2009) 283
Amaro Goncalves, United States v. (2009) 288
Goodyear Int'l, United States v. (1989) 238
Jorge Granados, United States v. (2010) 308
Marguerite Grandison, United States v. (2009) 282

Grand Jury Proceedings, *In re,* 219 F.3d 175 (2d Cir. 2000) 66
Grand Jury Subpoena, Matter of, 406 F. Supp. 381 (S.D.N.Y. 1975). 59
Grand Jury Subpoena No. 06-1, *In re,* 274 Fed. Appx. 306 (4th Cir. 2008) 57
Grand Jury Subpoenas, *In re,* 902 F.2d 244 (4th Cir. 1990) 58
Grand Jury Subpoena: Under Seal, *In re,* 415 F.3d 333 (4th Cir. 2005) 58
Green, *et al.,* United States v., 08-CR-059 (C.D. Cal. 2008). 320
Green, United States v. (2007-2008) 268
Gurule, United States v., 437 F.2d 239 (10th Cir. 1970) 52
Gypsum Co., United States v., 438 U.S. 422 (1978). 67
Haas v. Henkel, 216 U.S. 462 (1910) 50
Hale v. Henkel, 201 U.S. 43 (1906) 45, 52
Halford, United States v., 01-CR-221 (W.D. Mo. 2001) 323
R.K. Halford, United States v. (2001) 244
Halliburton Co. v. Dow Chem. Co., 514 F.2d 377 (10th Cir. 1975) 13
Halper, United States v., 490 U.S. 435 (1980). 53
Hammerschmidt v. United States, 265 U.S. 182 (1924) 27, 30
Harris Corp., United States v. (1990) 239
Harrison, United States *ex rel.* v. Westinghouse Savannah River Co.,
352 F.3d 908 (4th Cir. 2003). 14–15
Harrison v. United States, 7 F.2d 259 (2d Cir. 1925). 26
Harry G. Carpenter and W.S. Kirkpatrick, Inc., United States v. (1985) 238
Hartley, United States v., 678 F.2d 961 (11th Cir. 1982). 29
Hartsell, United States v., 127 F.3d 343 (4th Cir. 1997) 54
Head, United States v., 06-CR-1380 (S.D. Cal. 2006) 257, 322
Hearn v. Ray, 68 F.R.D. 574 (E.D. Wash. 1975) 66
Helmsley, United States v., 726 F. Supp. 929 (S.D.N.Y. 1989) 18
Helmsley, United States v., 941 F.2d 71 (2d Cir. 1991), *cert. denied,*
502 U.S. 1091 (1992) 98
Henke, United States v., 222 F.3d 633 (9th Cir. 2000). 59, 60
P.B. Hernandez, United States v. (2001) 244
Herzberg, United States v. (1994) 240
Hickman v. Taylor, 329 U.S. 495 (1947) 60
Hilton Hotels Corp., United States v., 467 F.2d 1000
(9th Cir. 1972), *cert. denied* (1973) 13, 69–70, 216
Hioki, United States v., 08-CR-795 (S.D. Tex. 2008). 321
Misao Hioki, United States v. (2008) 272
Holloway v. Arkansas, 435 U.S. 475 (1978) 59
Howes v. Atkins (1987). 238
Hubbell, United States v., 530 U.S. 27 (2000). 48
Huff v. Comm'r, 80 T.C. 804 (1983). 96
Hughes, United States v., 191 F.3d 1317 (10th Cir. 1999) 67–68
Hughes Aircraft Co., United States v., 20 F.3d 974 (9th Cir. 1994). 29–30
Hunton & Williams, LLP v. U.S. Dep't of Justice,
2008 WL 906783 (E.D. Va. 2008) 58

In re/In the Matter of __ *(see name of party)*
Int'l Harvester Co., United States v. (S.D. Tex. 1982) 237
Int'l Material Solutions Corp. and Donald K. Qualey,
United States v. (1999) 242
Int'l Trading Co. v. CIR, 484 F.2d 707 (7th Cir. 1973) 97, 98
InVision Technologies, United States v. (2004). 252
Ionia Management, S.A., United States v., 526 F. Supp. 2d 319
(D. Conn. 2007). 42–43
Iveco S.p.A., United States v. (2008) 277
Jefferson, United States v., 07-CR-209 (E.D. Va. 2007). 262, 320
JGC Corporation, United States v. (2011) 310
Jimenez, United States v., 513 F.3d 62 (3d Cir. 2008) 33
Jimenez Recio, United States v., 537 U.S. 270 (2003) 26
Johns, United States v., 742 F. Supp. 196 (E.D. Pa. 1990), *aff'd,*
972 F.2d 1333 (3d Cir. 1991) 16
Jumet, United States v., 09-CR-397 (E.D. Va. 2009) 321
Charles Paul Edward Jumet, United States v. (2009) 281
Kanne v. Am. Factors, Ltd., 190 F.2d 155 (9th Cir. 1951) 94
Kastigar v. United States, 406 U.S. 441 (1972). 18, 18n3
Kay, *et al.,* United States v., 01-CR 914 (S.D. Tex. 2002) 320
Kay, United States v., 513 F.3d 432 (5th Cir. 2007), *aff'd on reh'g,*
513 F.3d 461 (2008) 120
Kay, United States v., 539 F.3d 738 (5th Cir. 2004) 116n9, 120
David Kay, United States v. (2001-2002) 245
Kenny Int'l Corp., United States v. (1979) 236
Kilpatrick, United States v., 594 F.Supp. 1324 (D. Colo. 1984),
rev'd, 821 F.2d 1456 (10th Cir. 1987), *aff'd sub nom.* Bank of
Nova Scotia v. United States, 487 U.S. 250 (1988). 53
Han Yong Kim, United States v. (2009) 280
Kimbrough v. United States, 552 U.S. 85 (2007) 8
Kim Nguyen, United States v. (2008) 271
King, *et al.,* United States v., 01-CR-190 (W.D. Mo. 2001). 320
King, United States v. (2001) 264
King, United States v., 134 F.3d 1173 (2d Cir. 1998). 55
Marquis King, United States v. (1983) 237
Kovel, United States v., 296 F.2d 918 (2d Cir. 1961) 56
Kozeny *et al.,* United States v., 05-CR-518 (S.D.N.Y. 2005). 256, 320
Kraft v. United States, 991 F.2d 292 (6th Cir. 1993) 97, 97n16, 98
Lake Shore & Mich. S. Ry. Co. v. Prentice, 147 U.S. 101 (1893) 12
Latin Node, Inc., United States v. (2009) 279
Clayton Lewis, United States v. (S.D.N.Y. 2003) 250
Liebo, United States v., 89-CR-076 (D. Minn. 1989) 320
Liebo, United States v., 923 F.2d 1308 (8th Cir. 1991) 120, 239
Liparota v. United States, 471 U.S. 419 (1985). 24, 25

Lockheed Corp, United States v. (1994) . . . 241
Love, United States v. (1994) . . . 241
Lucent, *In re* (2007) . . . 266
Joseph Lukas, United States v. (2008) . . . 271
Maine v. Moulton, 474 U.S. 159 (1985) . . . 53n4
Marshall v. Barlow, 436 U.S. 307 (1978) . . . 49
Martin Linen Supply Co., United States v., 430 U.S. 564 (1977) . . . 55
Massiah v. United States, 377 U.S. 201 (1966) . . . 52
McLean, United States v. (1985) . . . 237
McLean v. Int'l Harvester Co. (1987) . . . 237
McNally v. United States, 483 U.S. 350 (1987) . . . 16, 16n2, 31
Mead, *et al.,* United States v., 98-CR-240 (D.N.J. 1998) . . . 320
David H. Mead, United States v. (1998) . . . 241
Metcalf & Eddy, United States v. (D. Ma. 1999) . . . 242
Miano v. AC & R Advertising, Inc., 148 F.R.D. 68 (S.D.N.Y.),
adopted, 834 F. Supp. 632 (S.D.N.Y. 1993) . . . 53
Michigan v. Jackson, 475 US. 625 (1986) . . . 53n4
Micrus, United States v. (2005) . . . 255
Middle Atl. Distribs., Inc. v. Comm'r, 48 T.C. 15 (1967) . . . 94n2, 97n14
Minneman, United States v., 143 F.3d 274 (7th Cir. 1998),
cert. denied sub nom., Punke v. United States, 526 U.S. 1006 (1999) . . . 98
Saul Mishkin, United States v. (2009) . . . 285
Monsanto, United States v. (2005) . . . 255
Montedison, S.P.A., United States v. (1996) . . . 241
Mark Fredrick Morales, United States v. (2009) . . . 283
Richard Morlok, United States v. (2009) . . . 277
Morrison v. National Bank Ltd., 130 S. Ct. 2869 (2010) . . . 40
Morton, United States v. (1990) . . . 240
Morton Salt, United States v., 338 U.S. 632 (1950) . . . 49, 51
Motz, United States v., 652 F. Supp. 284 (E.D.N.Y. 2009) . . . 41
Munsey Trust Co., United States v., 332 U.S. 234 (1947) . . . 90n63
Muntain, United States v., 610 F.2d 964 (D.C. Cir. 1979) . . . 35
Jenna Mushriqui, United States v. (2009) . . . 287
John M. Mushriqui, United States v. (2009) . . . 287
Nader v. Saxbe, 497 F.2d 676 (D.C. Cir, 1974) . . . 164
Nam Nguyen, United States v. (2008) . . . 271
Napco Int'l Inc. and Venturian Corp., United States v. (1989) . . . 239
Nasca v. Town of Brookhaven, 2008 WL 4426906 (E.D.N.Y. 2008) . . . 49
Nassar, United States v. (1994) . . . 241
Neder v. United States, 527 U.S. 1 (1999) . . . 31
Newman v. United States, 382 F.2d 479 (D.C.Cir. 1967) . . . 164
New York Central & Hudson River Railroad Co. v. United States,
212 U.S. 481 (1909) . . . 13
New York v. Berger, 482 U.S. 691 (1987) . . . 50

New York v. Microsoft, 2002 WL 649951 (D.D.C. 2002) 5n9
Nexus Technologies, United States v. (2008) 272
Nguyen, *et al.*, United States v., 08-CR-522 (E.D. Pa. 2008) 321
Nippon Paper Industries Co., Ltd., United States v., 17 F. Supp. 2d 38 (D. Mass. 1998) 54
Nippon Paper Industries Co., Ltd., United States v., 62 F. Supp. 2d 173 (D. Mass. 1999) 68
Nixon, United States v., 418 U.S. 683 (1974), *superceded by,* Bourjaily v. United States, 483 U.S. 171 (1987) 51, 71
Nobles, United States v., 422 U.S. 225 (1975) 60
Novak, United States v. (E.D. Wash. 2006). 258
Paul G. Novak, United States v. (2008) 269
Novaton, United States v., 271 F.3d 968 (11th Cir. 2001). 28n15
O'Hagan, United States v., 521 U.S. 642 (1997). 39
Oil States International, In the Matter of (2006). 259
Oklahoma Press Publishing Co. v. Walling, 327 U.S. 186 (1946) 50
Old Monastery v. United States, 147 F.2d 905 (4th Cir. 1945). 204
Omega Advisors, United States v. (S.D.N.Y. 2003) 250
John Joseph O'Shea, United States v. (2009) 282
Ott, United States v., 07-CR-608 (D.N.J. 2007) 260, 322
Oyler v. Boles, 368 U.S. 448 (1962) 164
David R. Painter, United States v. (2009) 287
Panalpina World Transport, *In re* (2007) 261
Paradigm BV, United States v. (2007) 263
Pankesh Patel, United States v. (2009) 287
Ofer Paz, United States v. (2009) 286
Antonio Perez, United States v. (2009) 280
Peterson v. Weinberger, 508 F.2d 45 (5th Cir .1975). 90n64
Philip Morris USA, Inc., United States v., 449 F. Supp. 2d 1 (D.D.C. 2006) 14, 68
Pinkerton v. United States, 328 U.S. 640 (1946) 27–28, 67
Pitchford, United States v., 02-CR-365 (D.D.C. 2002) 246, 322
Pitt v. Dist. of Columbia, 491 F.3d 494 (D.C. Cir. 2007). 213
Frerik Pluimers, United States v. (1998) 241
Poindexter, United States v., 698 F. Supp. 300 (D.D.C. 1998) 19
Potashnick v. Port City Constr. Co., 609 F.2d 1101 (5th Cir.), *cert. denied,* 449 U.S. 820 (1980) 53
Potter, United States v., 463 F.3d 9 (1st Cir. 2006). 13, 204, 216
Joaquin Pou, Alfred G. Duran and Jose Guarsch, United States v. (1989) 239
Powell v. Ratzenbach, 359 F.2d 234 (D.C. Cir. 1965), *cert. denied,* 384 U.S. 906 (1966) 164
Pride Forasol S.A.S., United States v. (2010) 305
Pride International, *In re* (2007) 262
Punke v. United States, 526 U.S. 1006 (1999) 98

Qualey, United States v., 99-CR-008 (S.D. Ohio 1999). 323
Quan-Sheng, United States v., 08-CR-194 (E.D. Va. 2008) 321
Rackley, United States v., 986 F.2d 1357 (10th Cir.), *cert. denied,* 510 U.S. 860 (1993) 33
Rad-O-Lite of Philadelphia, Inc., United States v., 612 F.2d 740 (3d Cir. 1979) 52, 53n4
Randock, *et al.,* United States v., 05-CR-180 (E.D. Wash. 2005). 322
Ratzlaf v. United States, 510 U.S. 135 (1994) 25
Rayburn House Office Building, United States v., 497 F.3d 654 (2d Cir.), *cert. denied,* 128 S. Ct. 1738 (2008) 35
Regent Office Supply Co., United States v., 421 F.2d 1174 (2d Cir. 1970) . . . 30–31
Reich, United States v., 479 F.3d 179 (2d Cir. 2007) 44
Reitz, United States v., 01-CR-222 (W.D. Mo. 2001). 323
Renault Trucks SAS, United States v. (2008) 270
R. Enters., Inc., United States v., 498 U.S. 292 (1991). 51
Resolution Trust Corp. v. Dabney, 73 F.3d 262 (10th Cir. 1995). 61
Rhonda, United States v., 455 F.3d 1273 (11th Cir. 2006) 43
Flavio Ricotti, United States v. (2009). 280
Rivera, United States v., 912 F. Supp. 634 (D.P.R. 1996). 54
Rodriguez, United States v. (D.P.R. 1983) 238
Carlos Rodriguez, United States v. (2009) 282
Rothrock, United States v., 01-CR-343 (W.D. Tex. 2001). 323
Daniel Ray Rothrock, United States v. (2001) 244
Rowe, United States v., 96 F.3d 1294 (9th Cir. 1996) 55n12
Ruston Gas Turbines, Inc., United States v. (1982). 236
RW Professional Leasing Services Corp., United States v., 452 F. Supp. 2d 159 (E.D.N.Y. 2006) 33
Michael Sacks, United States v. (2009) 286
Saks, United States v., 964 F.2d 1514 (5th Cir. 1992) 33
Salam, United States v., 06-CR-157 (D.D.C. 2006) 258, 322
Manuel Salvoch, United States v. (2010) 308
Sam P. Wallace Co., United States v. (1983). 238
Santa Rita Shore Co., United States v., 16 N.M. 3, 113 P.620 (N.M. 1911) 29
Santobello v. New York, 404 U.S. 257 (1971). 196
Santos, United States v., 553 U.S. 507 (2008). 37
Sapsizian & Acosta, United States v., 06-CR-20797 (S.D. Fla. 2006) 258, 322
Saybolt, Inc., United States v. (1998). 241
Saybolt North America Inc., United States v. (1998) 241
Schaltenbrand, United States v., 930 F.2d 1554 (11th Cir.), *cert. denied,* 502 U.S. 1005 (1991) 56
Schnitzer Steel Industries, In the Matter of (2006). 257
Science Applications International Corp., United States v., 555 F. Supp. 2d 40 (D.D.C. 2008). 14
SEC v. ABB, Ltd. (2004) 253

SEC v. ABB, Ltd. (2010) 303
SEC v. AB Volvo (2008) 270
SEC v. AGCO Corporation (2009) 291
SEC v. Alcatel-Lucent, S.A. (2010) 309
SEC v. Alliance One International, Inc. (2010) 302
SEC v. American Bank Note Holographics, Inc. (2001) 243
SEC v. Amersham plc (2010) 300
SEC v. Amoako (2005) 255
SEC v. Yaw Osei Amoako (2008) 274
SEC v. Armor Holdings, Inc. (2011) 313
SEC v. Ashland Oil, Inc. (1986) 238
SEC v. Avery Dennison Corporation (2009) 290
SEC v. Baker Hughes (2007) 259
SEC v. Baker Hughes, Inc. (2008) 275
SEC v. Ball Corporation (2011) 311
SEC v. Bellsouth Corp. (N.D. Ga. 2002) 248
SEC v. Bobby Benton (2009) 292
SEC v. Brown (2006) 257
SEC v. Campbell (D.D.C. 2006) 258
SEC v. Chevron (2007) 265
SEC v. Chiquita Brands International, Inc. (D.D.C. 2002) 247
SEC v. CNH Global N.V. (2008) 276
SEC v. Converse Technology Inc. (2011) 312
SEC v. Con-Way, Inc. (2008) 275
SEC v. Daimler AG (2010) 294
SEC v. Gioacchino De Chirico, Civil Action File No. 1:07-CV-2367 (N.D. Ga 2007) 264
SEC v. Delta Pine (D.D.C. 2007) 263
SEC v. Delta & Pine Land Co. and Turk Deltapine, Inc., SEC Release No. 34-56138 (July 25, 2007) 131n55
SEC v. Diageo plc (2011) 314
SEC v. Dow Chemical (2007) 262
SEC v. Bobby J. Elkin, Jr. (2010) 295
SEC v. El Paso Corp. (S.D.N.Y. 2007) 262
SEC v. ENI, S.p.A. (2010) 298
SEC v. Faro Technologies (2008) 274
SEC v. Fiat S.p.A. (2008) 276
SEC v. Monty Fu (D.D.C. 2007) 262
SEC v. General Electric Company (2010) 299
SEC v. GlobalSantaFe Corp. 306
SEC v. Halliburton Company (2009) 278
SEC v. Helmerich & Payne, Inc. 290
SEC v. Ingersoll-Rand (2007) 265
SEC v. Innospec Inc. (2010) 294

SEC v. International Business Machine Corp. (2000) 242
SEC v. International Business Machine Corp. (2011) 311
SEC v. International Systems & Controls (D.D.C. 1979) 236
SEC v. InVision, Inc. (2005) 252
SEC v. Ionics Inc. (2010) 300
SEC v. ITT Corporation (2009) 288
SEC v. Paul W. Jennings (2011) 309
SEC v. Johnson & Johnson (2011) 312
SEC v. Kay Industries (N.D. Ill. 1978) 235
SEC v. KBR, Inc. (2009) 278
SEC v. KPMG-SSH (2001) 245
SEC v. Charles Martin (2005) 255
SEC v. Eric L. Mattson and James W. Harris (2001) 245
SEC v. Maxwell Technologies, Inc. (2011) 310
SEC v. Oscar Meza (2009) 291
SEC v. Monsanto (2005) 255
SEC v. Munro (D.D.C. 2006) 258
SEC v. Douglas A.Murphy (S.D. Texas 2002) 246
SEC v. Baxter J. Myers (2010) 296
SEC v. Ousarna M. Naarnan (2010) 301
SEC v. NATCO Group, Inc. (2010) 293
SEC v. Noble Corporation (2010) 305
SEC v. Novo Nordisk A/S 289
SEC v. Ott (2007) 260
SEC v. Page Airways (D.D.C. 1978) 235
SEC v. Panalpina, Inc. (2010) 305
SEC v. Pillor (N.D. Cal. 2006) 258
SEC v. Pride International Inc., (2010) 304
SEC v. RAE Systems Inc. (2010) 308
SEC v. Thomas G. Reynolds (2010) 296
SEC v. Rockwell Automation (2011) 313
SEC v. Royal Dutch Shell plc (2010) 306
SEC v. Samson (D.D.C. 2006) 258
SEC v. Schering Plough (2004) 253
SEC v. Shell International Exploration and Production Inc. (2010) 307
SEC v. Siemens Aktiengesellschaft (2008) 273
SEC v. Snamprogetti Netherlands B.V. (2010) 299
SEC v. Srinivasan (D.D.C. 2007) 263
SEC v. Albert Jackson Stanley (2008) 275
SEC v. Joe Summers (2010) 300
SEC v. Syncor (2002) 246
SEC v. Technip (2010) 297
SEC v. Tesoro Petroleum Corp. (1980) 236
SEC v. Texas Gulf Sulphur Co., 401 F.2d 833 (2d Cir. 1968) 38–39

SEC v. Textron (2007) 260
SEC v. Tidewater Inc. (2010) 307
SEC v. Titan Corp. (2005) 254
SEC v. Transocean Inc. (2010) 304
SEC v. Triton Energy Litig., Release No. 15266 (Feb. 27, 1997) 122n22, 241
SEC v. David P. Turner (2010) 301
SEC v. Tyco (S.D.N.Y. 2006) 259
SEC v. Tyson Foods, Inc. (2011) 310
SEC v. United Industrial Corporation (2009) 289
SEC v. Universal Corporation (2010) 302
SEC v. UTStarcom, Inc. (2009) 292
SEC v. VerazNetworks, Inc. (2010) 298
SEC v. Westinghouse (2008) 268
SEC v. Whelan (D.D.C. 2006) 258
SEC v. Tommy Lynn Williams (2010) 297
SEC v. Wooh (2007) 260
SEC v. Thomas Wurzel (2009) 289
SEC v. Young (2007) 260
SEC v. Zandford, 535 U.S. 813 (2002) 39
See v. City of Seattle, 387 U.S. 541 (1967) 49
Self, United States v., 08-CR-110 (C.D. Cal. 2008) 321
Martin Eric Self, United States v. (2008) 270
Sells Engineering, Inc., United States v., 463 U.S. 418 (1983) 173
Sengupta, United States v., 02-CR-040 (D.D.C. 2002) 247, 322
Shapiro v. United States, 335 U.S. 1 (1948) 48
Shortt Accountancy Corp., United States v., 785 F.2d 1448 (9th Cir. 1986) 42
Shu Quan-Sheng, United States v. (2008) 272
Siemens Bangladesh Limited, United States v. (2008) 273
Siemens Investigation, *In re* (2007) 266
Siemens S.A. Argentina, United States v. (2008) 273
Silicon Contractors, Inc., United States v. (1985) 238
Silverthorne Lumber Co. v. United States, 251 U.S. 385 (1920) 50
Singh, United States v., 518 F.3d 236 (4th Cir. 2008) 13
Jittisopa Siriwan, United States v. (2009) 277
Juthamas Siriwan, United States v. (2009) 277
Skilling v. United States, 130 S. Ct. 1568 (2010) 31–32
Smith, United States v. (C.D. Cal. 2007) 262
S. Pac. Transp. Co. v. Comm'r, 75 T.C. 497 (1980) 96
Jonathan M. Spiller, United States v. (2009) 283
SSI International Far East, United States v. (D. Or. 2006) 257
Stanley, United States v., 08-CR-597 (S.D. Tex. 2008) 323
Staples v. United States, 511 U.S. 600 (1994) 24–25
Starrett, United States v., 55 F.3d 1525 (11th Cir. 1995) 67
Statoil, In the Matter of (2006) 256

Statoil, United States v. (S.D.N.Y. 2006) 256
Steindler et al, United States v. (1994) 240
Steph, United States v., 07-CR-307 (S.D. Texas 2007) 261, 321
Stephens v. Comm'r, 905 F.2d 667 (2d Cir. 1990), *rev'g,*
93 T.C. 108 (1989) 96, 97
Stevens, United States v., 771 F. Supp. 2d 556 (D. Md. 2011) 26n12
Stevens, United States v., 909 F.2d 431 (11th Cir. 1990). 29
Sun-Diamond Growers of Cal., United States v., 138 F.3d 961
(D.C. Cir. 1998), *aff'd,* 526 U.S. 398 (1999) 13, 32, 34, 69
Swiss Family Farms Co., United States v., 912 F. Supp. 401
(C.D. Ill. 1995) 67
Syncor, *In re* (2002) 249
Syncor, United States v. (C.D. Cal. 2002) 246
Herbert Tannebaum, United States v. (1998). 242
Tannenbaum, United States v., 98-CR-784 (S.D.N.Y. 1998) 323
Teleglobe Commc'ns Corp., *In re,* 493 F.3d 345 (3d Cir. 2007). 57, 58
Tellier v. Comm'r, 383 U.S. 687 (1966) 94
Jeffrey Tesler, United States v. (2009) 279
Textron, United States v. (2007). 260
Thevis, United States v., 665 F.2d 616 (5th Cir.), *cert. denied,*
459 U.S. 825 (1982) 52
Thompson *et al,* United States v. (N.D. Al. 2005) 256
James K. Tillery, United States v. (2008). 269
Titan Corp., United States v. (S.D. Cal. 2005) 254
Lee Allen Tolleson, United States v. (2009) 284
Totten, United States *ex rel.* v. Bombardier Corp., 380 F.3d 488
(D.C. Cir. 2004) 154
Treacy, United States v., 2009 WL 812033 (2009). 62n20
Triumph Capital Group, Inc., United States v., 260 F. Supp. 2d 432
(D.C. Conn. 2002). 28n15
Trustees of Dartmouth College v. Woodward, 17 U.S. 518 (1918). 12
Twentieth Century Fox Film Corp., United States v., 882 F.2d 656
(2d Cir. 1989). 55
Unimex, Inc., United States v., 991 F.2d 546 (9th Cir. 1993). 52, 53n4, 54
United Mine Workers v. Bagwell, 114 S. Ct. 2552 (1994) 55
United States v. __ *(see name of party)*
Universal Leaf Tobaccos Ltd., United States v. (2010) 302
Unruh, United States v., 855 F.2d 1363 (9th Cir.), *cert. denied,*
488 U.S. 974 (1989) 34
Upjohn v. United States, 449 U.S. 383 (1981) 55–56, 210
Useni, United States v., 516 F.3d 634 (7th Cir. 2008) 70
Valdes, United States v., 437 F.3d 1276 (D.C. Cir. 2006) 35
Juan Pablo Vasquez, United States v. (2010) 309
Vetco, United States v. (S.D. Tex. 2007) 261

Vitusa Corp., United States v. (1993) 240
Vought, United States v., 2006 WL 1662882 (D. Conn. 2006). 41
Wade v. United States, 112 S. Ct. 1840 (1992) 196
Waldman v. Comm'r, 88 T.C. 1384 (1987), *aff'd,* 850 F.2d 611
(9th Cir. 1988) 96
Waldroop, United States v., 431 F.3d 736 (10th Cir. 2005). 33
Wallace, United States v. (D.P.R. 1983). 238
Lee M. Wares, United States v. (2009) 288
Warwick, United States v., 09-CF-449 (E.D. Va. 2009). 321
John W. Warwick, United States v. (2009) 288
John Benson Weir III, United States v. (2009). 286
Israel Weisler, United States v. (2009). 286
Wenger, United States v., 427 F.3d 840 (10th Cir. 2005). 213
Wheat v. United States, 486 U.S. 153 (1988) 60
White, United States v., 322 U.S. 694 (1944) 46
Whitmore, United States v., 35 Fed. Appx., 307 (9th Cir.),
cert. denied, 123 U.S. 659 (2002) 34
Williams v. Hall (1988) 238
Williams v. United States Dep't of Transp., 781 F.2d 1573
(11th Cir. 1986) 53
Wolf, United States v., 90 F.3d 191 (7th Cir. 1996) 97n16, 98
Wooh, United States v. (2007) 260
Yellow Freight Sys., Inc., United States v., 637 F.2d 1248
(9th Cir.), *cert. denied,* 454 U.S. 815 (1981) 48
York International, United States v. (2007) 259
Young, United States v., 07-CR-609 (D.N.J. 2007) 260, 322
Young & Rubicam, Inc., United States v. (1990) 240
Zolin, United States v., 491 U.S. 554 (1989). 58, 213

INDEX

accounting manipulation
  cookie jar reserves as, 107
  corporate crimes based on, 103–112, 143–145
  creative acquisition accounting as, 106–107
  criminal prosecution of, 111–112
  large-charge restructuring as, 105–106
  materiality as, 107–109, 145
  overview of, 103–104
  revenue recognition as, 109, 110, 111–112
  statutory reforms related to, 143–145
  warning signs of, 109–110
Act of Production doctrine, 47
actus reus, 24–26
Adelphia, 4
affirmative defenses
  defense of no successor liability as, 69
  defense of qualified immunity, 66
  defense of withdrawal as, 67–68
  defense theory instructions on, 70–71
  good faith as, 65–66
  pretrial issuance of subpoenas for, 71
  unauthorized acts of agents as, 69–70
agents. executives
  corporate criminal liability for acts of, 12–13, 15–17, 204
  fiduciary duty of, 16–17, 18
  privilege assertions by, 15–16
  unauthorized acts of agents defense, 69–70
agreements
  charge, 179–180, 186–187
  cooperation, 76
  deferred prosecution, 75, 76, 85–89, 104, 111–112, 130, 136, 203, 226–233
  joint defense, 58–59, 60, 214
  multi-district (global), 199–200, 224
  nonprosecution, 75, 76, 85–89, 104, 128, 130, 136, 191–199, 200, 203, 226–233
  plea and settlement (plea and settlement agreements)
  sentence, 179, 180–181, 186
AIG, 7
American Bar Association Task Force on Implementation of Section 307 of the Sarbanes Oxley Act of 2002, 147
antitrust violations, 207, 215, 216
Arthur Andersen
  defense theory instructions in case against, 70–71
  document shredding by, 42, 43, 74n3
  Enron collaboration with, 5, 6
  postprosecution demise of, 7, 74, 104
  Sunbeam collaboration with, 108
Ashcroft, John, 88
attorney-client privilege
  affirmative defense impliedly waiving, 66
  bankruptcy trustee waiver of, 57
  conflict of interest in representation and, 59–60
  crime-fraud exception to, 58, 213
  joint defense agreements on, 58–59, 60
  limitations on waiver of, 62–63
  materiality standards on waiver of, 149–150

attorney-client privilege, *continued*
plea and settlement agreement waiver of, 80–81
prosecution policy on, 209–210, 211–213, 215, 222, 223
scope of, 55–57
Attorney-Client Privilege Protection Act (2007), 81

bank fraud, 33–34
banking and financial institutions
bank fraud against, 33–34
corporate crime collusion or collaboration of, 4, 5–6, 104
Department of Justice prosecution of, 6, 22–23, 104
subprime mortgage investment by, 5, 7
bankruptcy trustee waiver of privilege, 57
Bear Stearns, 5, 7
Bernanke, Ben, 3, 151
bribery and illegal gratuities
antibribery provisions on, 116, 118–122
DOJ opinion procedure releases on, 132–135
enforcement of legislation prohibiting, 117–118, 123–130, 135–136, 235–314, 315–333
Foreign Corrupt Practices Act on, 75n7, 88, 114–137, 235–314, 315–333
global marketplace use of, 113–114
grease payments as, 117, 136–137
OECD on, 116–117, 121, 123–125, 127–128, 130, 315
recordkeeping provisions on, 116–117, 122–123
red flags for, 131–132
settlement agreements on, 75n7, 88, 128, 130, 136
statutory tools to prosecute, 34–35, 75n7, 88, 113–137, 155–156, 235–314, 315–333
tax deductibility of payments, 117, 136–137
voluntary disclosure of, 115, 122, 131, 135–136
Bristol-Myers Squibb, 111–112
Brock, William, 123nn24–25
business judgment rule, 17–18

channel stuffing, 109, 111
charge agreements, 179–180, 186–187
charges, prosecution selection of, 174–178, 187–190, 221
Chinese Walls, 18–20
Cisco Systems, Inc., 105
civil proceedings
bribery prosecutions via, 116, 129, 318–319, 331
collective knowledge doctrine in, 13, 14
evidence in, 91
fraud prosecution in, 38, 40, 116, 129, 153, 318–319, 331
parallel criminal and, 89–91
plea agreements not resolving, 85
prosecution policy consideration of, 172–173, 203, 220
right to counsel in, 53
tax deductibility of costs associated with, 94
Clayton Act, 69
Coca-Cola, 109
codes of ethics, 9. corporate compliance programs
collateral consequences, 219–220
collective entity doctrine, 15–16
collective knowledge doctrine, 13–15
Commodity Exchange Act, 161
confidentiality. privilege
conflicts of interest
attorney-client privilege issues due to, 59–60
duty of loyalty addressing, 17

executive compensation tied to performance creating, 4, 7
fees paid to service providers creating, 5, 104
confrontation, right to, 54–55
conspiracy
acquittal of individual coconspirators, 29–30
affirmative defenses against, 67–69
elements required for, 27
intercorporate, 29
intracorporate, 29
statutory tools to prosecute, 26–30
Constitutional amendments.
cookie jar reserves, 107
cooperation
cooperation agreements, 76
obstruction 5, 27, 40, 42–44, 70–71, 156, 213–214
prosecution policy consideration of defendant's cooperation, 169–170, 184, 191–198, 208–209, 210–215, 222
corporate compliance programs, 9, 79, 83–85, 87, 205, 215–217, 218, 222
corporate crime
accounting manipulation in, 103–112, 143–145
agreements related to (agreements)
bribery and illegal gratuities as, 34–35, 75n7, 88, 113–137, 155–156, 235–314, 315–333
codes of ethics and, 9 (corporate compliance programs)
conspiracy as, 26–30, 67–69
Constitutional protections for, 15–16, 28, 45–63
corporate culture influencing, 4, 6, 9–10, 83
corporate self-regulation and (self-regulation, corporate)
credible oversight absence as incentive for, 139–142
defenses in (defenses)
elements required for, 24–26, 27, 30–31, 37–38, 39
evidence related to (evidence)
fraud as, 21–44, 58, 67–69, 75n7, 88, 99–100, 103–112, 113–137, 143–145, 153–154, 155–156, 160–162, 235–314, 315–333
immunity from (immunity)
internal corporate investigations of, 61, 211–212, 223
laws regulating (legislation; statutory tools)
money laundering as, 36–38, 114
privilege issues related to (privilege)
process crimes as, 40, 42–44
prosecution policy on (prosecution policy)
punishment for (punishment)
rational-choice theory on criminal behavior in, 6–8
reasons for, 1–10
reputational cost of, 7
tax issues related to (tax consequences and planning)
theories of corporate criminal liability, 11–20, 29, 32, 54, 70, 203–204, 207, 216
corporate culture, 4, 6, 9–10, 83. corporate compliance programs
corporate monitors, 88–89, 222, 226–233
corporate privilege. privilege
corporate tax fraud, 25, 41–42
corruption. bribery and illegal gratuities
counsel
attorney-client privilege for, 55–60, 62–63, 66, 80–81, 149–150, 209–210, 211–213, 215, 222, 223
in-house and outside, 56, 145–150
legal fees and costs of, 94–95
materiality standard for, 146–150
right to, Sixth Amendment protection of, 52–54, 59
creative acquisition accounting, 106–107

credible oversight, failure of, 139–142
Criminal Justice Act, 54

defenses
affirmative, 65–71
defense theory instructions on, 70–71
good faith, 65–66
joint, 58–59, 60, 214
no successor liability, 69
pretrial issuance of subpoenas for, 71
qualified immunity, 66
unauthorized acts of agents, 69–70
withdrawal, 67–68
deferred prosecution agreements (DPAs)
corporate monitors mandated in, 88–89, 226–233
definition of, 76, 85, 226n2
prosecution policy on, 203
use of, 75, 85–89, 104, 111–112, 130, 136
Department of Justice (DOJ)
Antitrust Division of, 207, 215
banking and financial institution prosecution by, 6, 22–23, 104
bribery investigation and prosecution by, 114, 116, 120–121, 124–130, 131–136, 235–314, 315–333
corporate crime investigation and prosecution by (corporate crime)
Filip Memo of, 41n28, 59, 61, 74n2, 77, 80–81
former DOJ employees as corporate monitors, 88–89
fraud investigation and prosecution by, 22–23, 41–42, 114, 116, 120–121, 124–130, 131–136, 153, 235–314, 315–333
Holder Memo of, 41n28, 74n2, 79n22
joint defense agreement policy of, 59
McNulty Memo of, 41n28, 74n2, 77, 80, 81, 95n6
Morford Memo of, 86n41, 88–89, 226–233
opinion procedure releases of, 132–135
parallel proceedings policy of, 89–91
plea and settlement agreement guidelines by, 75, 77–85, 89–91, 163–200
prosecution policy of (prosecution policy)
right to counsel policy of, 52–53
Tax Division of, 41–42, 207
Thompson Memo of, 41n28, 74n2, 77, 79–80nn18–19, 21–22, 24–27, 80–81, 95
U.S. Attorneys' Manual of, 41, 59n14, 70, 74n2, 75n8, 77, 78, 79nn17, 20, 81, 82–83, 85–87, 88n55, 90, 153n26, 163–200, 201–224
Department of Treasury, 94, 96, 101
directors and managers. executives
Dodd-Frank Reform Act. Wall Street Reform and Consumer Protection Act (2010)
Double Jeopardy, 48, 55
Douglas, William O., 2, 140
Drug Enforcement Agency, 24
duty of care, 16–17, 18
duty of loyalty, 17

earnings and profit performance
cookie jar reserves impacting, 107
corporate crime incentive based on, 4, 6–7, 103–112, 143–145
creative acquisition accounting impacting, 106–107
criminal prosecution for earnings manipulation, 111–112
earnings management, 103–112, 143–145
executive compensation tied to, 4, 7
large-charge restructuring of, 105–106
materiality impacting, 107–109, 145
revenue recognition impacting, 109, 110, 111–112
warning signs of earnings manipulation, 109–110

economic downturns, 4, 7
economic sanctions. fines and penalties
e-mail, evidentiary use of, 5
Enron
  bankruptcy of, 75n5
  corporate crime involving, 4, 5, 6, 8, 31–33, 34, 42, 104, 118, 141–142, 148–149
  credible oversight of, 141–142
  FCPA regulation avoidance by, 118
  fraud charges against employees of, 31–33, 34
  legal fees and costs of, 95n7
  post-Enron reforms, 30, 42, 139–157, 159–162
evidence
  conspiracy trial inclusion of, 28
  e-mail as, 5
  hearsay, 28, 55, 67
  parallel proceeding usage of, 91
  selecting charges based on sufficient, 175
  statutes prohibiting destruction or alteration of, 42–43, 71
  subpoenas to collect, 15, 46–48, 50–52, 71
executives. agents
  business judgment rule applied to, 17–18
  compensation of, 4, 7
  fiduciary duty of, 16–17, 18
  insider trading by, 38–40, 161
  plea agreement signature by, 83
  right to counsel for, 52–54, 59

False Claims Act (FCA), 14, 153–154
Family Support Act (1988), 95n9
Fannie Mae, 7
Federal Bureau of Investigation (FBI), 22–23, 24, 35
Federal Labor Standards Act, 50–51
fiduciary duty, 16–17, 18
Fifth Amendment
  coconspirator assertion of, 28
  corporate agent inability to assert, 15–16
  corporation inability to assert, 45–48
  defining "organization" for privilege assertion under, 46
  Foregone Conclusion doctrine under, 47–48
  "John Doe" Act of Production immunity under, 47
Filip, Mark/Filip Memo, 41n28, 59, 61, 74n2, 77, 80–81
financial institutions. banking and financial institutions
Financial Stability Oversight Committee (FSOC), 3, 151
fines and penalties. restitution
  bribery prosecution including, 127, 128, 129, 130, 324–329, 332–333
  earnings management prosecution including, 111–112
  federal sentencing guidelines on, 8–9
  fraud-related, 30, 41, 127, 128, 129, 130, 153, 324–329, 332–333
  plea and settlement agreements on, 73–75, 79, 87, 222
  tax deductibility of, 82, 96–97
Fisher, George, 156–157
Foregone Conclusion doctrine, 47–48
Foreign Corrupt Practices Act
  antibribery provisions of, 116, 118–122
  bribery regulation under, 75n7, 88, 114–137, 235–314, 315–333
  DOJ opinion procedure releases on, 132–135
  enactment of, 114–115
  enforcement of, 117–118, 123–130, 135–136, 235–314, 315–333
  recordkeeping provisions of, 116–117, 122–123
  red flags for prosecution under, 131–132

Foreign Corrupt Practices Act, *continued*
settlement agreements under, 75n7, 88, 128, 130, 136
summary of, 114
tax deductibility of grease payments under, 117, 136–137
voluntary disclosure under, 115, 122, 131, 135–136
Fourth Amendment, 45–46, 48–52
fraud
accounting, 103–112, 143–145
bank, 33–34
bribery and illegal gratuities as, 34–35, 75n7, 88, 113–137, 155–156, 235–314, 315–333
conspiracy as, 26–30, 67–69
elements required for, 24–26, 27, 30–31, 37–38, 39
mail, 30–33, 114, 155, 162
money laundering as, 36–38, 114
overview of, 21–24
privilege exception in furtherance of, 58, 213
process crimes as, 40, 42–44
program, 35–36
prosecutions and enforcement of, 22–24
securities, 38–41, 161
statutory tools to prosecute, 21–44, 75n7, 88, 113–137, 153–154, 155–156, 160–162, 235–314, 315–333
tax, 25, 41–42
tax consequences of fraud losses, 99–100
wire, 30–33, 114, 155
Fraud Enforcement and Recovery Act (FERA/2009), 37, 40, 153–154
Freddie Mac, 7
Freedom of Information Act, 152n24, 182

good faith defense, 65–66
grand jury subpoenas, 15, 47, 49, 51–52, 71
grease payments, 117, 136–137. bribery and illegal gratuities
Greenspan, Alan, 3
Gulf Oil, 114–115

Halliburton, 131–132, 133
Hand, Learned, 26
HealthSouth, 4
hearsay evidence, 28, 55, 67
Hobbs Act, 34
Holder, Eric/Holder Memo, 41n28, 74n2, 79n22

immunity
Chinese Wall doctrine on, 18n3, 19
defense of qualified immunity, 66
"John Doe" Act of Production immunity, 47
plea and settlement agreements use of, 76, 80, 197–198
prosecution policy on, 192–193, 197–198, 214–215
insider trading, 38–40, 161
intent, 24–26, 27, 30–31, 38, 39
internal corporate investigations, 61, 211–212, 223
Internal Revenue Service (IRS), 22, 23–24, 41, 99–100, 101
Iran-Contra affair, 124

Jenks Act, 71
"John Doe" Act of Production immunity, 47
joint defense agreements, 58–59, 60, 214
jurisdiction, prosecutory, 171–172
Justice Department. Department of Justice

knowledge, 13–15, 24–26, 27, 39. intent

large-charge restructuring, 105–106
laws. legislation; statutory tools
lawyers. counsel

legal fees and costs, 94–95
legislation
  Attorney-Client Privilege Protection Act (2007), 81
  Clayton Act, 69
  Commodity Exchange Act, 161
  Criminal Justice Act, 54
  False Claims Act (FCA), 14, 153–154
  Family Support Act (1988), 95n9
  Federal Labor Standards Act, 50–51
  Foreign Corrupt Practices Act, 75n7, 88, 114–137, 235–314, 315–333
  Fraud Enforcement and Recovery Act (FERA/2009), 37, 40, 153–154
  Freedom of Information Act, 152n24, 182
  Hobbs Act, 34
  Jenks Act, 71
  post-Enron reforms to, 30, 42, 139–157, 159–162
  Public Corruption Prosecution Improvements Act (2011), 35, 155–156
  Sarbanes-Oxley Act (2002), 2–3, 5, 9, 17, 19, 30, 40–41, 42–43, 71, 108, 109, 123, 142, 143–150, 151–152
  Securities Act (1933), 38
  Securities Exchange Act (1934), 2n1, 19, 38, 40, 115, 141n1, 152–153nn23–24, 161
  Sentencing Reform Act, 181
  Sherman Antitrust Act, 29n18
  Tax Reform Act (1969), 96n11
  Travel Act, 34, 114
  Victim Witness Protection Act, 98
  Wall Street Reform and Consumer Protection Act (2010), 3, 39, 40, 84, 150–152, 159–162
Lehman Brothers, 7
Levitt, Arthur, 103–104, 105, 106, 107

mail fraud, 30–33, 114, 155, 162
managers. executives
materiality
  as earnings management manipulation, 107–109, 145
  as element of fraud, 31
  of violation, counsel's standard for, 146–150
McDonough, William, 4, 142
McNulty, Paul/McNulty Memo, 41n28, 74n2, 77, 80, 81, 95n6
24–26, 37, 65–66
Merrill Lynch, 7
monetary penalties. fines and penalties
money laundering, 36–38, 114
Morford, Craig/Morford Memo, 86n41, 88–89, 226–233
multi-district (global) agreements, 199–200, 224

New York Stock Exchange, 2n1, 9
Nixon, Richard, 114
nonprosecution agreements (NPAs)
  approvals needed for, 198–199
  considerations to be weighed in, 195–197
  corporate monitors mandated in, 88–89, 226–233
  definition of, 76, 85–86, 226n2
  limiting scope of, 197–198
  prosecution policy on, 191–199, 200, 203
  records of, 200
  use of, 75, 85–89, 104, 128, 130, 136, 191–199, 200
no successor liability defense, 69

obstruction of justice, 5, 27, 40, 42–44, 70–71, 156, 213–214
Organization for Economic Co-operation and Development (OECD), 116–117, 121, 123–125, 127–128, 130, 315

parallel proceedings, 89–91
penalties. fines and penalties

plea and settlement agreements
approvals needed for, 198–199
binding nature of, 85
bribery-related, 75n7, 88, 128, 130, 136
charge agreements as, 179–180, 186–187
considerations to be weighed in, 183–187, 195–197
cooperation agreements as, 76
corporate compliance programs under, 79, 83–85, 87, 222
corporate monitors mandated in, 88–89, 222, 226–233
deferred prosecution agreements as, 75, 76, 85–89, 104, 111–112, 130, 136, 203, 226–233
Department of Justice guidelines on, 75, 77–85, 89–91, 163–200
desirability of entering into, from government perspective, 78, 86, 163–200
limitations on, 78–81, 197–198
multi-district (global), 199–200, 224
negotiating opportunities with, 81–83
nonprosecution agreements as, 75, 76, 85–89, 104, 128, 130, 136, 191–199, 200, 203, 226–233
parallel proceedings policy for, 89–91
pretrial choices regarding, 73–75
prompt disposition via, 185–186, 187
prosecution policy on use of, 6, 7, 75, 77–78, 87, 104, 176, 178–200, 203, 221–224
records of, 190–191, 200, 222
selecting charges for, 187–190
sentence agreements as, 179, 180–181, 186
tax considerations while negotiating, 82, 93–101
types of, 75–77
Postal Inspection Service, 22, 24
pretrial issuance
of plea and settlement agreements, 73–91
of subpoenas, 71
privilege
affirmative defense impliedly waiving, 66
attorney-client, 55–60, 62–63, 66, 80–81, 149–150, 209–210, 211–213, 215, 222, 223
bankruptcy trustee waiver of, 57
coconspirator assertion of, 28
collective entity doctrine on, 15–16
crime-fraud exception to, 58, 213
Fifth Amendment assertion of, 15–16, 28, 45–48
internal corporate investigations and, 61, 211–212, 223
joint defense, 58–59, 60
limitations on waiver of, 62–63
plea and settlement agreement waiver of, 80–81
prosecution policy on, 61, 209–210, 211–213, 215, 222, 223
work product, 60–61, 62–63, 80, 210, 211–213, 215, 222, 223
probable cause, 165–166
process crimes, 40, 42–44
profit. earnings and profit performance
program fraud, 35–36
prosecution policy
additional charges under, 177–178
bribery-related, 135–136
business organization prosecution under, 201–224
collateral consequences considered in, 219–220
corporate compliance program considered in, 215–217, 218, 222
corporate liability considerations under, 203–204, 207, 216
defendant's attitude considered in, 185, 205

defendant's cooperation considered in, 169–170, 184, 191–198, 208–209, 210–215, 222
defendant's criminal history considered in, 169, 184, 197, 205, 208
defendant's culpability considered in, 169, 196–197, 205, 207
defendant's obstruction of investigation considered in, 213–214
defendant's personal circumstances considered in, 170
deterrent effect of prosecution considered in, 169, 203
federal law enforcement priorities considered in, 168
Filip Memo on, 41n28, 59, 61, 74n2, 77, 80–81
grounds for commencing or declining prosecution, 166–167
Holder Memo on, 41n28, 74n2, 79n22
immunity under, 192–193, 197–198, 214–215
impermissible considerations in, 173–174
initiating or declining prosecution under, 165–174
jurisdictional issues impacting, 171–172
McNulty Memo on, 41n28, 74n2, 77, 80, 81, 95n6
Morford Memo on, 86n41, 88–89, 226–233
multi-district (global) agreements under, 199–200, 224
nature and seriousness of offense considered in, 168–169, 184–185, 205
non-criminal alternatives to prosecution, 172–173, 203, 220 (civil proceedings)
nonprosecution agreements under, 191–199, 200, 203
pervasiveness of wrongdoing considered in, 207
plea agreement considerations under, 183–187, 195–197
plea and settlement agreement use as, 6, 7, 75, 77–78, 87, 104, 176, 178–200, 203, 221–224
pre-charge plea agreements under, 178
privilege protection under, 61, 209–210, 211–213, 215, 222, 223
probable cause requirements for, 165–166
probable sentence considered in, 170–171, 172, 186–187
prosecutors' and corporate leaders' duties under, 202–203
purpose of, 164–165
records of, 174, 190–191, 200, 222
restitution and remediation considered in, 218
selecting charges under, 174–178, 187–190, 221
special policy concerns under, 206–207
substantial federal interest served by, 167–171, 203
Thompson Memo on, 41n28, 74n2, 77, 79–80nn18–19, 21–22, 24–27, 80–81, 95
Public Company Accounting Oversight Board (PCAOB), 4, 108–109, 142, 143–145
Public Corruption Prosecution Improvements Act (2011), 35, 155–156
punishment, 8–10. fines and penalties; plea and settlement agreements; prosecution policy; restitution; sentencing

rational-choice theory, 6–8
Reagan administration, 123nn24–25, 124

recessions, 4, 7
Refco, 4, 104
regulation. legislation; self-regulation, corporate; statutory tools
reputational cost, 7
respondeat superior, 12–16, 29, 32, 54, 70, 204, 207, 216
restitution, 97–99, 111–112, 218. fines and penalties
revenue recognition, 109, 110, 111–112
rights
  Constitutional, 15–16, 28, 45–63
  right to a jury trial, 55
  right to confrontation, 54–55
  right to counsel, 52–54, 59

sanctions. fines and penalties
Sarbanes-Oxley Act (2002)
  accounting standards under, 108, 109, 143–145
  evidence destruction or alteration under, 71
  in-house and outside counsel under, 145–150
  passage of, 2–3, 5, 142
  post-Enron reforms under, 30, 143–150
  process crimes under, 42–43
  punishment enhancement via, 9, 30
  recordkeeping and certification provisions of, 123
  securities fraud under, 40–41
  theories of corporate criminal liability under, 17, 19
  whistleblower protections under, 151–152
"Seaboard Report," 76–77, 141
Securities Act (1933), 38
Securities and Exchange Commission (SEC)
  accounting regulations by, 106, 108–109, 109–110, 143–145
  bribery investigations and prosecutions by, 114–115, 116, 122, 123, 124, 126, 127, 129
  Chinese Walls applied by, 19
  counsel ethics under rules of, 145–150
  creation of, 1, 140
  credible oversight under, 140–142
  "Seaboard Report" of, 76–77, 141
  settlement agreements used by, 76–77
Securities Exchange Act (1934), 2n1, 19, 38, 40, 115, 141n1, 152–153nn23–24, 161
securities fraud, 38–41, 161
self-regulation, corporate
  corporate compliance programs as, 9, 79, 83–85, 87, 205, 215–217, 218, 222
  corporate crimes due to, 1–4, 141–142
  credible oversight and, 140–142
  Fisher Principle of Leadership on, 156–157
sentencing. fines and penalties
  bribery-related, 320–323
  federal sentencing guidelines, 8–10, 84–85
  fraud-related, 30, 41, 320–323
  probable sentencing as prosecution policy factor, 170–171, 172, 186–187
  selecting charges consideration of, 174–176, 177–178, 190, 221
  sentence agreements, 179, 180–181, 186
Sentencing Reform Act, 181
settlement agreements. plea and settlement agreements
Sherman Antitrust Act, 29n18
Sixth Amendment
  Double Jeopardy protection under, 55
  right to a jury trial under, 55
  right to confrontation under, 54–55
  right to counsel under, 52–54, 59
sole proprietors, 15–16, 46, 47–48, 223

statutory tools. legislation
bribery and illegal gratuities
prosecution under, 34–35, 75n7, 88, 113–137, 155–156, 235–314, 315–333
failure of credible oversight leading to, 139–142
fraud prosecution under, 21–44, 75n7, 88, 113–137, 153–154, 155–156, 160–162, 235–314, 315–333
post-Enron reforms to, 30, 42, 139–157, 159–162
Stewart, Martha, 38, 40
stock exchanges, 2n1, 9
subpoenas
Fourth Amendment on overly broad, 50–52
grand jury, 15, 47, 49, 51–52, 71
pretrial issuance of, 71
privilege assertions in response to, 15, 46–48
trial, 51, 71
Sunbeam, Inc., 108
Sutherland, Edwin, 11

tax consequences and planning
fines and penalties deductibility, 82, 96–97
fraud loss deductibility, 99–100
grease payment deductibility, 117, 136–137
legal fees and costs deductibility, 94–95
overview of, 93–94
plea and settlement agreement negotiations including, 82, 93–101
restitution deductibility, 97–99
Treasury Department regulations on practice before IRS, 101
tax fraud, 25, 41–42
Tax Reform Act (1969), 96n11
theories of corporate criminal liability
business judgment rule, 17–18
Chinese Walls, 18–20
collective entity doctrine, 15–16
collective knowledge doctrine, 13–15
corporate fiduciary, 16–17, 18
evolution of, 11–12
prosecution policy on, 203–204, 207, 216
respondeat superior, 12–16, 29, 32, 54, 70, 204, 207, 216
Thompson, Larry/Thompson Memo, 41n28, 74n2, 77, 79–80nn18–19, 21–22, 24–27, 80–81, 95
TRACE International, 133–134
Transactional Records Access Clearinghouse (TRAC), 22–23
transparency, 3–4, 101, 106, 140, 148
Travel Act, 34, 114
Treasury Department, 94, 96, 101
trial subpoenas, 51, 71

U.N. Oil for Food Program, 126, 127, 129
U.S. Attorneys' Manual, 41, 59n14, 70, 74n2, 75n8, 77, 78, 79nn17, 20, 81, 82–83, 85–87, 88n55, 90, 153n26, 163–200, 201–224
U.S. Justice Department. Department of Justice
U.S. Treasury Department, 94, 96, 101

Victim Witness Protection Act, 98
Vinson & Elkins, 149, 150
Volcker, Paul, 126

Wall Street Reform and Consumer Protection Act (2010)
corporate compliance programs under, 84
criminal offense conduct under, 151, 159–162
enactment of, 3, 150–151
insider trading under, 39, 40
whistleblower protections under, 151–152
Washington Mutual, 5, 7

Watergate, 114–115
whistleblowers, 40, 135–136, 151–152, 153
white collar crime, 11–12. corporate crime
Wilde, Claude C., Jr., 114–115
willfulness, 24–26, 27, 39. intent
wire fraud, 30–33, 114, 155
withdrawal defense, 67–68
witness protection programs, 198
work product privilege
  limitations on waiver of, 62–63
  plea and settlement agreement waiver of, 80
  prosecution policy on, 210, 211–213, 215, 222, 223
  scope of, 60–61
WorldCom, 4, 7, 34, 75n5, 104, 106–107